Gonna See All My Friends

A PEOPLE'S HISTORY OF FAIRPORT CONVENTION

Richard Houghton

Spenwood Books
Manchester, UK

SUFFOLK LIBRARIES	
30127 08944428 0	
Askews & Holts	30-Mar-2023

First published in Great Britain 2022
by Spenwood Books Ltd
2 College Street, Higham Ferrers, NN10 8DZ.

Copyright © Richard Houghton 2022

The right of Richard Houghton to be identified as author of this work has been asserted in accordance with Section 77 of the Copyright, Design and Patents Act 1988.

A CIP record for this book is available from the British Library.

ISBN 978 1 9168896 7 5

Printed and bound by by Sound Performance Ltd, 3 Greenwich Quay, Clarence Road, Greenwich, London, SE8 3EY.

Design by Bruce Graham, The Night Owl.

Front cover image: Danielle Croft
Front cover design: Bruce Graham
Rear cover images: Carol Law, Niklas Nilsson, Oliver Ilgner
All other image copyrights: As captioned.

spenwoodbooks.com

GONNA SEE ALL MY FRIENDS:
A PEOPLE'S HISTORY OF FAIRPORT CONVENTION

BY THE SAME AUTHOR

The Beatles - I Was There

The Who - I Was There

Pink Floyd - I Was There

Jimi Hendrix - The Day I Was There

Led Zeppelin - The Day I Was There

The Smiths - The Day I Was There

The Jam - The Day I Was There (with Neil Cossar)

Black Sabbath - The Day I Was There

Rush - The Day I Was There

The Wedding Present - Sometimes These Words Just Don't Have To Be Said (with David Gedge)

Orchestral Manoeuvres in the Dark - Pretending To See The Future

Simple Minds - Heart of the Crowd

Shaun Ryder's Book of Mumbo Jumbo

Cream - A People's History

Queen – A People's History

Jethro Tull – Lend Me Your Ears

Thin Lizzy – A People's History

The Stranglers (Live) - Excerpts

The Rolling Stones in the Sixties - A People's History

All Down the Line - A People's History of the Rolling Stones 1972 North American Tour

GONNA SEE ALL MY FRIENDS:
A PEOPLE'S HISTORY OF FAIRPORT CONVENTION

ACKNOWLEDGEMENTS

This book would not have been possible without the support and help of a considerable number of people. I am particularly indebted to everyone who took the time to send me their memories or agreed to be interviewed by me.

I'd like to thank: Ian Burgess; Dr Oliver Ilgner; Kevin Smith; Gareth Williams; Dominic Walsh, for permission to reproduce his review of Fairport's 2017 *Cropredy* appearance, originally published by louderthanwar.com (see also atthebarrier.com for more great Fairport stuff); Kerry Croft and Danielle Croft for permission to use the cover image; Kingsley Abbott for permission to quote from his 1997 publication, *Fairportfolio*; Richard Thompson for permission to use the lyric 'gonna see all my friends' from the Fairport anthem 'Meet on the Ledge' as the book's title; Nigel Schofield for suggesting the book's title and for writing the introduction and general fact checking; Gabriel Smith for proofreading and editorial assistance; design wizard Bruce Graham; and tech wizard Bruce Koziarski.

And a huge thanks to Simon Nicol and to Peggy for agreeing to do the book in the first place, and for putting me in touch with so many members of the Fairport family.

And finally, a very special thank you to my new bride, Kate Sullivan, for her love, support and tolerance. I am lucky to have met her, as she often reminds me.

Richard Houghton
Manchester, September 2022

GONNA SEE ALL MY FRIENDS: A PEOPLE'S HISTORY OF FAIRPORT CONVENTION

FOREWORD BY SIMON NICOL

It's frequently mentioned that Fairport Convention made our first appearance using that name in May 1967 – at the time of writing almost fifty-five and a half years ago – and despite many tweaks of personnel (particularly in the earlier decades) we have managed to maintain performing and creative momentum ever since. Despite even declaring the shop closed for business (for a variety of disparate reasons) in 1979.

All that history, all those albums, tours and gigs, the uncountable miles, have been achieved without ever once really troubling the mainstream music industry or exciting more than innocently niche interest.

Yet we're still a vital and committed group of musicians without an obvious centre of focus – a real band of brothers in search of the lost chord – and the diary continues to fill, with gigs through the forthcoming couple of years and studio time earmarked for the next, still-to-be-written CD.

How is this irritatingly non-standard misfit band still merrily toiling away, ploughing our lonely furrow, while remaining insulated from the furious questing for the 'next thing' which has always been the Holy Grail of popular music – the thing that sells concert tickets, streaming and downloads?

You'll find the answers (for there is no single, perfect one) between these endpapers: but it boils down to the completely serendipitous fact that Fairport has at some time, in some unique way, reached out over the footlights and touched the hearts of their individual audience members.

I know this because at our annual shindig, *Fairport's Cropredy Convention* (held every August in the North Oxfordshire village of that name), I am the one currently given the massive honour of singing the final song of the weekend, Richard Thompson's 'Meet on the Ledge', the lyric of which gives this book its title. And when I do, and the stage lights illuminate the audience singing the chorus back to us on that mighty stage, my second home, I can almost see those connections like thousands of strings connecting them all back to us.

Each one is different – not even parallel: every one is special and personal but is held in common: creating a community of souls who share nothing else in background, age, upbringing, socio-economic grouping, nationality, even other musical tastes. We are the vector of their commonwealth.

I understand that one of the reasons for this is that the band members have always eschewed the idea of showbiz mystique and have naturally rubbed shoulders with the ticket buyers at the bar, answering even the most bizarre questions over a signing table, and making time to respond to written requests for dedications or for help in deciphering an indistinct lyric (or on one occasion even being the band at a private birthday party). We relish our approachability and our inclusivity – a good gig should always feel like a conversation rather than a recital, whether you're an actor, a comic or a musician.

And reading the proofs of this odd book that Richard Houghton has worked so hard to referee and edit down to a reasonable size, this is shown over and over. Some observations are fleeting but deeply embedded, while in more than a few cases it seems a song or a shared experience at a gig has cemented (or even created) a lasting bond inside a family. It is empowering, heartening and humbling to learn this in others' words.

Also, I have learned quite a lot I didn't know about my bandmates through their personal interactions with this widespread tribe of Fairporters – and it's made me love and appreciate them all the more. Truly, I have been blessed.

Simon Nicol
Canterbury, 2022

GONNA SEE ALL MY FRIENDS:
A PEOPLE'S HISTORY OF FAIRPORT CONVENTION

INTRODUCTION

In modern culture, there are certain big bang 'you-should-have-been-there moments' – The Beatles on *Sunday Night at the London Palladium*, the first moon landing, *Live Aid* – to which even those who were not around at the time can relate. And there are timeline indicators by which eras and indeed ages can be dated. Most people in the UK will recall 'their' *Blue Peter* presenter, Dr Who or Radio 1 *Breakfast Show* host, or maybe their favourite soap storyline, pop music genre or USS Enterprise crew. Most Fairport Convention fans have 'their' Fairport. So which is your Fairport?

When invited to submit entries for this book about 'the first time I saw Fairport Convention', fans were being asked the same question. With a notoriously metamorphic personnel, at least until the Eighties, the line-up you saw first, and which perhaps shaped your impression and expectations of the band, is a stratum-line in folk-rock geology. Because of the way the band came into public awareness in the late Sixties, many class Fairport as a folk band, something they have never really been. They are an English folk-rock band, a term coined to describe them and which they have earned the right continually to redefine.

Very often, fans will define specific line-ups not by date or band members, but by the album that line-up created. This effect has been consolidated by the reconvening at the *Cropredy Festival* from 1982 onwards of classic line-ups with as many original members as viable. (The festivals before that recreated the *Full House* line-up, though no one thought of it in those terms at the time.)

So, one has the first album Fairport, the *What We Did on Our Holidays* and *Heydays* Fairport, the *Liege & Lief* Fairport and the *Full House, Angel Delight, Nine, Rising for the Moon, Bonny Bunch of Roses* and *Jewel in the Crown* Fairport, selected by common consent from the handful of albums made by the Nicol/Pegg/Alcock/Sanders/Mattacks configuration. (For different reasons, no one refers to the *"Babbacombe" Lee, Rosie, Gottle O'Geer* or *Gladys' Leap* versions of Fairport.)

The long-term fans who provide the accounts of the early days of the band might be surprised to learn that newer fans are often unaware of its back story; several follow up their account of first seeing Fairport with how they then set about acquiring and discovering the band's earlier output. This is no fault of their own; often it depends on them reaching an age when, putting aside childish things, they were receptive to the kind of music Fairport make. Some were introduced to the band by accompanying their parents to concerts (the so-called 'Cropredy Effect') and it is just one of the reasons why the annual global pilgrimage to a tiny Oxfordshire village that few had heard of until the 1980s is such a family friendly event (and perhaps explains why the risqué 'The Bonny Black Hare' so rarely gets an airing).

Those older fans would be surprised to discover that for some 'solid' Fairport fans, the names Ashley Hutchings, Trevor Lucas or Bruce Rowland mean nothing in the context of Fairport Convention. Conversely, as we awaited their arrival at a 2003 festival in Altamont, New York, I was asked whether Sandy Denny was still with them!

What emerges is an understanding of the way in which Fairport have retained their appeal to successive generations; many were not even a twinkle in their father's eye when Fairport played their first gig.

Your Fairport may just as easily be the band that played a gig at a far-flung town in an area that was a rock music desert as the young pioneers in London clubs merging West Coast rock with traditional English folk. You may have encountered them in your local college hall, on one of the world's great auditorium stages or in an Oxfordshire field at Britain's friendliest festival.

Reading through these memories, you'll find first Fairport encounters that were the result of pure happenstance and others that were the fulfilment of a long-held ambition. For many it was 'a life-changing moment'; the phrase crops up more than once. There's the story of how 'Rosemary's Sister' found its way into the Fairport setlist, told by the man who wrote it. You'll even discover how Fairport saw in the new millennium (despite the champagne haze). You'll encounter people whose first experience of Fairport was via the series of classic samplers issued by Island Records in the late Sixties and early Seventies (*You Can All Join In*, *Nice Enough to Eat*, *Bumpers* and *El Pea*) and how this led to a decision to investigate their albums before seizing the opportunity to see them live.

Significant recollections from familiar and even famous names sit side-by-side with fascinating nuggets of nostalgia from otherwise anonymous

GONNA SEE ALL MY FRIENDS:
A PEOPLE'S HISTORY OF FAIRPORT CONVENTION

Fairport fans. Closer to the present day, memories of first encounters are fewer because the long-term significance of that first encounter has not yet sunk in.

You'll be transported to the Golders Green Church Hall for their first ever public performance, to America, Australia, Scandinavia, Southern Europe, a boat on the Rhine and beyond the old Iron Curtain where 'it was much more difficult to be a Fairport fan'.

From 1980, Fairport and Cropredy became inextricably linked: there are many recollections centred on that special place, whether it is conversations with music legends, time travel to the English Civil War, the best festival food, the kids' entertainment area, linseed memories of Sunday cricket or annual family reunions. Often the recordings from these festivals have become a permanent souvenir of the gig they recall (one chap is still trying to track down a copy of the *25th Anniversary* concert). In this people's history of Fairport Convention, you'll regularly be stopped short by a well-chosen phrase that makes you say, 'Yes, that's exactly right.'

One person sums up Cropredy as being like a 'midsummer Christmas'. Another donned a full Santa suit to help Roy Wood convince us it was just that. A memory from Hawaii ends, '(I could) fill this missive with an abundance of exclamation points, but I realise I am preaching to the choir.' Here we have scores of Fairporters recalling their Fairport, via their first Fairport.

Not every memory is 100 per cent accurate – these are eye-witness accounts and no two people see the same event in exactly the same way; these are emotions recollected in tranquillity, often many years after they occurred. Memories can be seriously affected by the passage of beer and the consumption of time; objects in the rearview mirror may appear closer than they are.

Where recollections have been vague about precise dates, years, venues and band members, extensive research has (where possible) fleshed out the details.

You'll discover friends and fans who attended the same gigs as you. The first time I saw Fairport, future crime writer Peter Robinson was also in the audience, as I discovered when I got in touch to thank him for including a reference to my *Fairport UnConventional* boxset in one of his

GONNA SEE ALL MY FRIENDS:
A PEOPLE'S HISTORY OF FAIRPORT CONVENTION

DCI Banks stories.

At the time of writing, Fairport Convention are planning the fifty-sixth year of the band – although no one has been in the band for all that time (even when it seems it must have been longer). Along the way, they've lost count of the number of gigs they've played, how many band members they've had, how many meetings on the ledge have taken place, how many miles have been travelled (whether by road, riverboat, plane or indeed steam) and how many Matty murders have taken place.

The story stretches from the first time Fairport publicly convened to the most recent gig at the time of writing. Who knows where the time went? How many roads must a band walk awhile? How many deaths will it take till we know that too many Mattys have died? The answer is probably blowing herein.

Nigel Schofield
August 2022

Photo: Ian Burgess

GONNA SEE ALL MY FRIENDS:
A PEOPLE'S HISTORY OF FAIRPORT CONVENTION

WILLIAM ELLIS SCHOOL
1966-67, HIGHGATE, LONDON, UK

MARTIN FOSTER

I was at school with Richard Thompson. We went to William Ellis School in Highgate, and were in the same year. I have a recollection of firing a quantity of milk over RT in one of the William Ellis quadrangles during the usual morning milk break. It didn't go down too well! My abiding memory is of a very early gig in the hall at William Ellis and in particular a rendition of 'Red House', at that time a highlight of Jimi Hendrix gigs. I remember both Richard and Simon Nicol with long guitar leads wandering about in the audience while they played. I've seen them regularly ever since.

Martin Foster was at school with RT

ST MICHAEL'S CHURCH HALL
27 MAY 1967, GOLDERS GREEN, LONDON, UK

KINGSLEY ABBOTT

Fairport Convention's first official gig took place at Saint Michael's Church Hall, about half a mile down the Golders Green Road from Golders Green bus and tube station.

I was a school friend of Martin Lamble and a self-taught drummer who had dabbled in various school bands. Martin and I teamed up and spent quite a lot of social time together. We shared a broadly similar taste in music, listening to the emerging Love, The Byrds and other West Coast bands like The Sunshine Company who were to bridge the gap between the 'Sunshine Pop' of the mid-Sixties and what was to become psychedelia. Against this background we were both interested to hear of these supposedly talented lads who were to be playing a gig at Golders Green. So it was that Martin and I, along with our friends Barbie and

GONNA SEE ALL MY FRIENDS:
A PEOPLE'S HISTORY OF FAIRPORT CONVENTION

Pam, set off to 'A Mass Conversion to the Fairport Convention' and paid our six shillings on the door, to be given a large buff card ticket with what turned out to be a drawn-around hand of Richard Thompson. I don't believe we had heard of the gig through publicity. The probable news route was a banjo player called Mark Sullivan that Pam vaguely knew, and another friend called Jules Burns.

We went along with upwards of 35 to 40 others to a pretty sparsely populated hall. I can't remember what the band played that night other than Love's 'Seven and Seven Is' and 'My Back Pages' by The Byrds. They may also have played a Chuck Berry tune, possibly 'Johnny B Goode', and an early Byrds B-side Ashley 'Tyger' Hutchings was keen on. Even at that stage Richard was obviously very talented and I remember watching his fingers on the fretboard. Simon and Tyger, as he was known at the time to virtually everyone, looked cool and well in control, very much enjoying what they were doing. Only Shaun Frater, who was on the drums, seemed a little ill at ease. He seemed to be out of place and Martin and I reckoned he really ought to be a soul drummer.

At the end, when the lights came on Martin announced that he 'wanted to play drums for that band'. We were all keen to show our appreciation to them for a great night, so we went up and talked to Tyger initially, who seemed surprised to get such enthusiasm from us. After about ten minutes, addresses and phone numbers had been swapped and enough coded discussion had taken place over drum skills and suitability for Martin to have arranged a meeting for the following week.

JOHN PENHALLOW

Simon Nicol and I were teenage friends from 11 or 12 years old. We went to different schools, but we had a mutual friend in Nick Davey, who went to school with Simon. Nick was in my patrol in the 7th Muswell Hill Boy Scouts Troop and would get us together at his house during the school holidays. We also went along to the Methodist Church's Friday night youth club at North Bank House. It was a large house with big gardens in Muswell Hill. On the left hand side of the hallway was a smaller room where Ashley sometimes met up with his musical mates for a public rehearsal with his various bands. On the right was a big reception room where the rest of us were 'Twistin' the

GONNA SEE ALL MY FRIENDS:
A PEOPLE'S HISTORY OF FAIRPORT CONVENTION

John Penhallow at the Friends of Fairport reunion in 2017. Right: John Penhallow with Kingsley Abbott in 2017

Night Away' to the record player. It was in that room where, at the tender age of 14, I organised a special night featuring that other group from Muswell Hill – The Ravens. I can't remember how I linked up to Ray and Dave Davies and Pete Quaife, but I volunteered to run the dance. I got the tickets printed and sold every last one. Ashley and Simon were there, of course. The room was full, and everyone was thrilled at the energy on stage. So started my short career at organising gigs. I booked them for a second gig at a bigger church hall in November 1963. By the time that came around a few months later, they were The Kinks, and the hall was packed with 'Norf London Yoofs'. A couple of years later Ashley, Simon and Richard were rehearsing in Fairport. A friend of us all, Richard Lewis, had come up with the name Fairport Convention. I said I would help organise the first gig at St Michael's Church Hall with Keith Roberts, my girlfriend's brother-in-law. Keith was a bit older than us. He was a silkscreen printer and owned a car. Judy, Richard and Nick produced the artwork for the dayglo orange and black poster (that later became a t-shirt at Cropredy in 2017). Keith printed the posters, and he and I stuck them up on trees and telegraph poles around the neighbourhoods from Muswell Hill to Golders Green. I dispute the stories that say only 20 turned up. To my memory it was more like 60 or more. I remember it was a ten-pound profit that paid for the Chinese dinner afterwards. That came from 40 people paying five shillings each. So, another 20 people had to be there to generate the hall rental of five pounds, even if we didn't pay Keith back for printing the posters.

ELECTRIC GARDEN
14 JULY 1967, LONDON, UK

KINGSLEY ABBOTT

I began driving them to gigs early on. I wasn't quite a 'roadie', as it is known nowadays, because we all carried equipment in and set it up, but certainly I was the regular driver. Many of the early dates were sparsely attended. The Electric Garden, which was to become Middle Earth, did not usually attract more than 50 to 75 people in the very early days. However, they did provide Fairport with a valuable platform for them to hone their skills and provide testing grounds for new material. They usually played two sets and the intervening periods were spent chatting to audience and other band members. We would often encounter the same batch of bands on the London circuit: Eclection, Blossom Toes, The Action and Alan Bown are all names that frequently occurred.

All of the local gigs were round about North London or the West End, but inevitably as the name got known we started to venture further afield. The college and university circuit began to cotton on to the group, so before too long we found ourselves going to places like Brighton, Warwick, Liverpool and Leeds. These trips were not too much fun in an old Commer van. We would allow extra time for breakdown possibilities. One Saturday, I had to work the morning at the bank and so Simon drove the van to Friern Barnet where the band waited patiently outside until we had finished and I was released, whereupon we drove straight up to Leeds, or somewhere. The Fairport humour was ever-present on these drives, especially whenever we had to cross the Thames enroute to the south. Cries of 'Aaaagh, transpontine!' would ring out with typical North Londoners' derision of any parts of south London.

Before Iain Matthews joined, the band had been performing regularly around the West End of London, mainly at the Electric Garden, Happening 44 and at The Speakeasy. These are probably my fondest memories of the whole era. Here was a group that I was involved with, who were playing very much the American folk-rock music that I loved, and at the same time were adding their own distinctive stamp to it all through their talent.

It was easy to see that Richard's playing was attracting a lot of interest even then. I loved his inventiveness and especially the way that he would interweave other themes into various songs. My favourite of these often happened during 'East West', the Paul Butterfield Blues Band number, when Richard used to insert a piece of 'Coronation Scot' towards the end. This tune, loved by all steam train fans, harked back to the Fifties when it would often be featured on the radio programme, *Children's Favourites*. It was then, and is now, a great tune. All these gigs were initially sparsely attended, but the people who were seeing them were people of influence in the business. Consequently, the Fairport name became mentioned with increasing regularity in the pop/rock music weeklies of the time.

UFO CLUB
28 JULY 1967, LONDON, UK

JOE BOYD

I don't remember exactly how I first became aware of Fairport Convention, but I know it was when 'Hoppy' (John Hopkins) and I were running the UFO club. By the summer of 1967, UFO was becoming so successful that everybody wanted to play there. But once they played, a band's price went up or they got busier, and it was harder for us to book them again, so we were constantly on the lookout for new bands, because we needed two bands and four sets every Friday night.

I got a tip off about this band playing on a Tuesday night in a former strip club in a basement on Gerrard Street. I went down and it was basically just me and a couple of others, friends of the group really, not much of an audience. They played a set and I really liked them. It sort of felt like home; they were so American. I was a bit ambivalent in those days about the whole singer-songwriter thing. I really loved traditional Blues and British traditional songs. Middle-class white kids strumming a guitar and singing about their angst didn't really interest me. But they had pretty good taste so I booked them to open for the Floyd at the end of July or early August.

I was pretty impressed. But then they did 'East-West (instrumental)' by the Butterfield Blues Band, and I remember thinking, 'Oh, this was a mistake, a big mistake.' Yet, to my amazement, Richard then played this blinding solo that, in that moment, put Mike Bloomfield into the shade. So I went into the dressing room after they finished playing and said, 'Let's make a record.'

SPEAKEASY
27 AUGUST 1967, LONDON, UK

KINGSLEY ABBOTT

Much has been written of the famous occasions at the Speakeasy when Jimi Hendrix jammed with them – twice that I can recall. My own memories of these two nights are quite strong, and I have more than once cursed that I did not have my camera with me on those nights. Jimi was often there late at night, and he was very friendly to everyone, and on one night he came and sat at our table and chatted extensively. It was obvious that he was impressed with the band, and that he enjoyed the sense of humour. Fairport usually played two sets at the Speak: one at about 10.30pm and another later, somewhile after midnight. The time would depend on who, and how many, were in the club.

When Jimi played it was well after the second set each time, about half three or four in the morning, when there were perhaps only between twelve to 20 people left in the club. Each time they played for about 40 minutes or so, and the song that really sticks in my mind is an extended version of 'Like a Rolling Stone', during which Richard and Jimi took turns at exploratory solos with both obviously enjoying each other's talents. It's been said that Jimi often sat in with bands here, but I'm sure that he really dug playing with Fairport.

Fairport in Brighton

Middle Earth

After one of these occasions, Martin and I were outside in Margaret Street about to go home in my car when Jimi walked up with a broad grin on his face and suggested that we go with him to a friend's flat. He was looking for a ride, and he proceeded to plead with me as the driver in a mock childlike tone, going down on his knees grinning all the time. We did go to his friend's flat and chilled with Jimi.

JOHN PENHALLOW

After that initial performance at St Michael's Church Hall, we were all encouraged to keep going, so I took the next step and 'sold' the band to Bryan Morrison of the Bryan Morrison Booking Agency. His other bands included Pink Floyd and the Pretty Things. This led to bookings at Happening 44, the Speakeasy and the legendary UFO Club, run by Joe Boyd. In July '67, Joe Boyd took the band and I to dinner at a nice restaurant in Hampstead. The band now included Martin Lamble on drums and Judy Dyble on vocals. Iain Matthews was soon to join. During dinner, Joe passed around the Witchseason contract to produce their records and become their manager. Joe also took me on to look after the group's diary. I made sure they got to the gigs, the BBC radio session recordings, the photoshoots, etc. I did that until we came back from the Rome Pop Festival the following May. Judy left the band, and I followed just before Sandy joined. Years later, I thanked Joe for letting me go, as there's no doubt, I could have also been in the van on the way back from Mothers.

There's also no doubt that my subsequent 50-year career selling hifi systems on London's Tottenham Court Road and then running a commercial audio equipment company in Sydney is due to my twelve months spent with Fairport in '67 and '68. I learnt a lot, attending gigs and sessions at Sound Techniques and BBC radio recordings, listening hard to what was going down.

RICHARD PEARL

I knew Richard Thompson from school. He told us he was in a band and that they were playing at a party at Highgate tennis club in North London. As I recall it was Richard, Simon Nicol, Ashley (then known as Tyger) Hutchings, Judy Dyble and a drummer called Shaun. Ashley lived next door to Richard's friend Brian Wyville, and we would listen to stuff by The Who and other bands.

When I next saw them, at a school in Friern Barnet, Martin Lamble had replaced Shaun. They played West Coast stuff and jug band music. My friends and I went on to see them at clubs like UFO and Middle Earth. They would support bands like Doc Kay's Blues Band and The Pretty Things. Later, when Iain Matthews joined Fairport, Richard, Iain and our mutual friend Paul Ghosh (recently deceased) shared a flat in Brent Cross. Sandy Denny was often there when we visited and we would hear albums by Neil Young, The Band and other modern classics. I loved the choice of songs in their set, especially The Butterfield Blues Band's 'East-West', Leonard Cohen's 'Suzanne' and Richard Farina's 'Reno Nevada' (which Iain sang at *Cropredy* in 2022).

Richard Pearl knew RT from school

I was invited to a John Peel session at the BBC studio in Abbey Road. Fairport played 'Sir Patrick Spens' and a couple of other folk numbers, and then mucked about on 'The Lady is a Tramp', swapping instruments and Richard singing, 'She's broke – that's okaaaay, California.'

I went to Warwick Uni and was delighted to find that Fairport were the band at Freshers' weekend. After the tragic crash, I lost touch with the band, but contacted Richard again and I try to touch base with him when he is in the UK. I have been to several Cropredy festivals and love the vibe. I was honoured to be asked to provide a voice over for Richard's partner Zara Phillips' one woman show, which she performed in Camden in 2022.

UNIVERSITY OF BRADFORD
21 OCTOBER 1967, BRADFORD, UK

DAVID FARRAR OBE

As a member of the University Students' Union Entertainments Committee, I was involved in booking the bands for the regular Saturday night concerts. Blues bands were the normal order of the day – Ten Years After, Long John Baldry, Chicken Shack and the like were regulars. But it was 1967 and the music was changing.

My principal route to bands was via the Ian Hamilton Organisation, a promoter based in Manchester. My contact was Chris Wright, subsequently of Chrysalis fame. I think that it was he who suggested that we should book Fairport Convention. Goodness knows what we agreed to pay – most probably not more that £50. After all, around that time, we only paid £25 for Joe Cocker to come over from Sheffield and £150 for the Pink Floyd in the early Syd Barrett days.

As I recall, the first Fairport gig did not go to plan. Transportation problems led to a late arrival, a short set, and an invitation for the band to join us at the after-gig party in the local teacher training college dorms. I have a memory of a young Richard Thompson sitting on a bed, strumming his guitar. But they were a hit with our 'patrons' and came back to Bradford several times during my tenure and beyond.

My liking for Fairport Convention and their music was cemented at that time. As my personal life priorities changed significantly and having to concentrate on other commitments, opportunities to go to live gigs were limited. But (just ask my eldest daughter, Michelle) Fairport's music pervaded the family household. *A History of…* and *Fairport Live Convention* made it to the turntable most weekends, if not more frequently.

MIDDLE EARTH
11 MAY 1968, LONDON, UK

KINGSLEY ABBOTT

Another memorable Middle Earth night was one of the very best things that I would have a privilege to witness. This time I was with Tyger and Harvey, who had taken over as the group's regular driver, and we were heading down there to try to get in to see The Byrds, who were supposedly playing there. I say 'supposedly' because word had reached us that their tour was apparently not the best organised in the world.

When we arrived and parked the van behind the club in our normal spot, we found it was absolutely packed out with many more people than we had ever seen before. They agreed to let Tyger be squeezed in, but try as I might I could not wheedle myself in. Disconsolately I wandered back round to the van (Tyger said he'd get himself home), and I came upon The Byrds' van and their roadie, Jim Seiter. He was panicked as their PA was malfunctioning. Harvey suggested that they use Fairport's, so we hurriedly took it into the club and set it up, and I of course had then to stay. I then saw an amazing set lasting over two and a half hours during which The Byrds, with the lanky Doug Dillard sitting in on electric banjo, played their older stuff first and then introduced their newest member. Gram Parsons ambled around, looking resplendent in a white Nudie suit, and they launched into the country rock material which no one had heard at that point. For a good 40 minutes or so, Gram took control and led them through what was to be the *Sweetheart of the Rodeo* material. Much has been written about the Gram Parsons magic, and it was certainly there that night. I was sitting on the side of the stage with an enthralled Roy Harper, next to what passed for the dressing room, and I could see Tyger in the middle of the mass of people in front of the stage. I knew that he had always loved The Byrds, and I've often wondered if that evening's exposure to that band discovering some of their traditional roots helped at all when Fairport eventually followed a similar route. Either way, that night was a magical gig which I'm sure would be remembered by anyone who was there, with the probable exception of The Byrds, who were somewhat out of their heads.

FAIRPORT CONVENTION
RELEASED JUNE 1968

UNIVERSITY OF EAST ANGLIA
22 JUNE 1968, NORWICH, UK

OLIVER GRAY

The soul groovers who wanted to dance had had their day, because the social secretary – a burly, determined Welshman called John Morgan – had an agenda of 'progressive rock'. He pulled off quite a coup by arranging for Pink Floyd to visit UEA, in a surprising but clever double bill with Fairport Convention, both of whom were represented by the Bryan Morrison Agency. Being UEA's official rock bod, I was keen, if not confident, to try and do some interviews. But, apart from the friendly-looking Sandy Denny, the Fairports looked scary. Tyger Hutchings in particular seemed aloof and unsmiling, so I decided to go for the brilliant guitar player with the Bolan-style corkscrew hair. 'Excuse me, have you got a few minutes to spare?' 'Only if you ask extremely intelligent questions,' he replied. Despite the total change of appearance since those days, Richard Thompson was as affable then as he is now.

This version of Fairport still contained Iain Matthews as well as Sandy Denny, who was cheerful and relaxed. On drums was Martin Lamble and later that night I met a girl who knew him from home in Golders Green. She went on to become his girlfriend and they were still going out together a few months later when Martin was tragically killed in a crash in the band's van.

The interview revealed exciting things such as the fact that they would describe their music as 'electric folk' (goodness), that they never had trouble winning over audiences and that, if they had to compare themselves to any other bands, they would say Big Brother and the Holding Company. At the time, I was astonished. There didn't seem to be any similarity between Sandy Denny and Janis Joplin. History was to prove, however, that there were, indeed, a number of similarities, not least in their volatility and their embracing of the darker side of the rock lifestyle.

The Fairports gave a revelatory performance. Sandy broke the audience's hearts with her versions of 'Who Knows Where the Time Goes?' and Leonard Cohen's 'Suzanne', and we sat cross-legged on the floor, enraptured.

Fairport's return visit to UEA was not a success, because Sandy had a bad throat and was also in a black mood. At first, she refused to go on, but the Social Secretary waved the contract in her face and insisted. She coughed her way through the first song, but during the second, her voice gave out completely. The band left the stage and I had to rush back to my post to put on a record. Sitting backstage on a flight of steps was Sandy Denny, just in the process of lighting up a king size Benson and Hedges.

'Do you think that's a good idea?' I enquired, remembering what a warm, friendly person she had been on the band's last visit. 'What do you mean?' 'Maybe smoking a cigarette isn't a very good idea if you've got a bad throat.' 'Well,' replied Sandy, 'You are just a pathetic little creep and you can fuck right off.'

JOE BOYD

When we first started in the studio, the idea was that we would record something for Track Records, and Track wanted a single. There was nothing that I heard in their shows that immediately grabbed me as a single, so they came over to my place and we spent a couple of hours playing records and talking through ideas. At one point I put on a compilation of folk songs by Maxine Sullivan, who sang with John Kirby and his Orchestra, an African American jazz band. One of the songs was 'If I Had a Ribbon Bow', and they were really charmed by it. We agreed we'd go into the studio and cut that as our single. It's a cool record. It most certainly was not a hit, but it did get some play.

GONNA SEE ALL MY FRIENDS:
A PEOPLE'S HISTORY OF FAIRPORT CONVENTION

But the deal with Track fell apart and we migrated over to Polydor, where we got the go-ahead to make an LP. Suddenly it wasn't about trying to think of clever ideas for new and startling material; it was about making a record that represented what the band was like on stage.

From the beginning I was totally enamoured of Richard as a guitar player. I thought he was fantastic. I saw that as Fairport's appeal. But the more I heard them, the more I felt Judy was a weak link. But I couldn't really say anything, she was Richard's girlfriend, and she was nice. I felt bad. Yet the band had real potential, and she was a little soft. And so, I can't remember to whom exactly, but I broached the idea of adding a vocalist. I think the band sensed the issue. Only - where do you go and find a vocalist?

I was friendly with producer Denny Cordell and he suggested that we go see a group that was in the middle of breaking up but would be doing a final gig at the Cromwellian Club. So – me, Richard, Simon, Ashley and maybe Judy – we went down there and saw Pyramid. Iain Matthews was the lead singer, and he was pretty good. We had a drink with him afterwards and then the group met with him to try some things out. They called me later and said, 'Yeah, he's going to join.'

When I first heard them, they were young, inexperienced kids. But they would turn out to be absolutely fantastic musicians. The four core guys were monsters. I didn't realise what a great rhythm guitarist Simon was at first, but I did pretty soon. And I also didn't realise what a great bass player Ashley was, or what a great drummer Martin was – but I had grasped all this by the time we finished the record. I knew that they were really good.

There was this problem of Judy, who wasn't that strong. So we brought in Iain, and Iain's presence was stronger. He overshadowed Judy and led to her leaving. And then Sandy came in and overshadowed Iain and led to him leaving. Not until Richard and Sandy started to sing did you have a vocal department the equal of the instrumental department.

Sandy was a whole different beast. They were all 'wee, tim'rous beasties'; you could never imagine any of those guys getting into a bar fight. But you could with Sandy. She was older and had been around a lot more. She did not take prisoners and had a sharp, four-letter-word-filled tongue. I was worried about her dominating the group.

But when I went to the first rehearsal with her, she was purring, she was so happy to be with them. She understood immediately how good they were, so she was very well behaved, and didn't make any trouble for a long time. It worked brilliantly.

I think she knew what a good singer she was, what a good musician she was, and she absolutely recognised Richard as a peer. She may have lacked confidence in terms of her looks, and her sense of herself as a woman – it was hard to be a girl in a man's world – but I don't think she had any doubts about her talent, particularly after 'Who Knows Where the Time Goes?'

She was sometimes tortured by guys, but she wasn't tortured by music.

WHAT WE DID ON OUR HOLIDAYS RELEASED JANUARY 1969

JOHN MCGETTIGAN
The late Sixties was a great time to be young, with so much new and interesting music as pop and rock started to get serious. In most youth clubs there was the clever kid, the one who resented *Top of the Pops* and most of the radio. He (it tended to be 'he' in those days) was an expert in what was new and interesting. I entered my local youth club on one occasion, where the local smart arse played me an album called *What We Did on Our Holidays*. I liked it so much I went out and bought a copy the next day. I've been hooked ever since.

GREG STURDY
I was back home and doing very little, an 18-year-old getting under my parents' feet and not progressing job-wise or educationally. There was a geological course just commencing at the technical college. That would suit me in my pursuit of an agricultural career: rocks are interesting. That September 1971 Monday morning, I grabbed the bus into town to recommence my fractured education. I took a vacant seat in the lecture room next to a studious-looking individual called Glyn. As the first lesson about sedimentary limestones commenced, I warmed to Glyn's cheerful and friendly disposition. 'Fancy a coffee back at my place?' he offered. His delight in my acceptance was rather extraordinary. He wore trendy

GONNA SEE ALL MY FRIENDS:
A PEOPLE'S HISTORY OF FAIRPORT CONVENTION

Chelsea boots extending above his bell bottom jeans. The heel of these boots extenuated his stature and cool appearance.

Glyn lived on the edge of town in a modern suburb of Swansea in a small semi where his mother greeted me with delight. She made us a couple of mugs of instant coffee, accompanied by some gypsy cream biscuits, which we took upstairs to Glyn's room. There, he proudly showed off his prized possession, an expensive stereo system. 'What music do you like?' he asked. I rattled off some of my favourites of the time – Cat Stevens, Simon and Garfunkel, and Crosby, Stills and Nash. 'Have you heard any Fairport Convention LPs?' I had to confess I hadn't. He lovingly produced a vinyl disc in a glossy black sleeve with white scribbling on it. 'This is my favourite Fairport album, *What We Did on Our Holidays*.' Glyn cautiously drew the disc from the sleeve and gently laid it on the turntable. He carefully lowered the stylus on to the edge of the disc and immediately clicked a small counter by the side which registered how long the stylus had been used, as it had to be replaced frequently in order to minimise damage to the grooves on the disc and maximise musical quality.

It was a mesmerising album. The windows of Glyn's room were wide open, letting the warmth and late summer sunshine filter in as he gave me an enthusiastic running commentary on each track of the album. 'Fotheringay', about the castle in which Mary Queen of Scots was imprisoned, a heavy bass track about an inventor followed by a beautiful ballad about a book or reading a book. 'Listen to this track,' Glyn enthused. 'It's recorded in a church and you can hear someone drop their four pennies' church collection at the end. It's only a minute and a half long and it's brilliant.' It was. These were magical musical heights that I was being introduced to and at maximum volume.

Glyn sunk back in his chair, delighted to share his passion of music with someone who he knew genuinely was enjoying the experience. He talked me through the other tracks, a cover of a Joni Mitchell song, a Dylan song and a couple of traditionally arranged folk songs. Then a track, 'Meet on the Ledge', which sounded familiar, finishing with an acoustic guitar melody entitled 'End of a Holiday'.

'Have you got a girlfriend?' he enquired. 'Well, yes I have actually.' He was very intense, which rather unsettled me. 'What's she like? I bet she's pretty.' 'Well, she is actually,' I offered, 'she has long dark hair down to her waist and huge brown eyes, but she's only five foot two and a half inches tall. She tells me that the extra half inch is important.' 'I've got a girlfriend too. She sounds just like yours. Perhaps the four of us can meet up for a drink in the Vivian Arms next Saturday.' It was time for me to leave. Pleasantries were exchanged with Glyn's mum as I retreated through the front door with a promise to meet up next Saturday.

Next week at college, Glyn told me that he was unable to make the Saturday rendezvous but was okay for the week after. After a couple more cancellations, Glyn phoned me to say that he and his girlfriend had finished and that he hoped that I was getting on well with mine. I could have said, 'Yes, we are fine and are going to get married,' (which did happen, although it didn't last) but I didn't. If his short-lived romance existed, like my longer one, it was just tattered history as we lost contact. I failed to finish the geology course and took a job on a dairy farm in Sussex.

I returned to Swansea and saw Fairport Convention perform at the Brangwyn Hall a couple of years later. An obviously altered line-up from that of the album, *What We Did on Our Holidays*, but new lead member Trevor Lucas introduced a special unexpected guest – Sandy Denny, who had left the group. You can just imagine the enthusiastic roar from the crowd at that appearance of the iconic earlier member of the band. In hindsight, it shouldn't have been a great surprise as Sandy was his wife.

I never saw my friend Glyn again after that autumn of 1971, but often reflect on that time he introduced me to Fairport Convention. *What We Did on Our Holidays* is still my favourite album of all time. I would take it on a desert island if Radio 4 asked me. I listen to the CD I have of it, but sadly the sound of the pennies dropping to the floor in the church is absent. I hope Glyn still has his stereo, and that the grooves of that vinyl album still echo the sound of those pennies. Have you heard them?

JIM MCINTYRE

I first heard them on John Peel's *Top Gear* radio programme and liked them instannntly. I went straight out and bought *Holidays*. The song that struck me from the radio was 'Close the Door Lightly'. I was disappointed it wasn't on the album but that vanished after playing the album.

GONNA SEE ALL MY FRIENDS:
A PEOPLE'S HISTORY OF FAIRPORT CONVENTION

COUNTRY CLUB
2 FEBRUARY 1969, HAVERSTOCK HILL, BELSIZE PARK, LONDON, UK

MICK DONOVAN

The Country Club in Haverstock Hill, Belsize Park, north London was such an intimate venue there was no room for a stage. I was sitting in one row of about half-a-dozen facing a Fairport Convention stretched out in a line against the wall in front of us, as if in a police suspects line-up.

Far right was Sandy Denny, in a full-length floral dress, and almost directly in front of me, a handful of feet from touching distance. From memory, as the eyes of the 100 or so crowd members moved to the left, there was Simon Nicol, tucked behind Sandy's right shoulder, Richard Thompson, Iain Matthews and Ashley Hutchings, before our gaze lowered to drummer Martin Lamble sat on his drum stool who tragically lost his life a few weeks later.

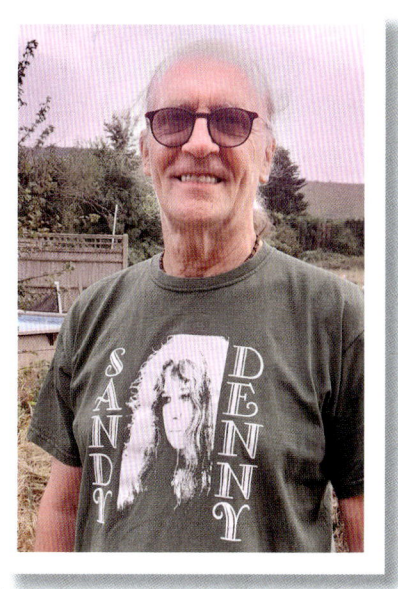

Mick Donovan had fallen in love with Sandy's voice

I'd been attracted by the presence of Sandy Denny, having fallen permanently in love with her voice at first hearing on *What We Did on Our Holidays*, the first of three defining Fairport albums that year. By its end, Sandy and fellow vocalist Iain were no longer in the band. It was my privilege to have heard the voice of an angel live for the first time and a band which provided the perfect accompaniment.

Nicol was the last surviving current Fairport member at Cropredy in 2022, where Thompson and Matthews also performed. When I asked him during the festival to sum Sandy up, he described her as 'unforgettable'. The same word also fits that night in the capital all those years ago. I'll be eternally grateful to Fairport for it.

GONNA SEE ALL MY FRIENDS:
A PEOPLE'S HISTORY OF FAIRPORT CONVENTION

UNIVERSITY OF BRADFORD
6 FEBRUARY 1969, BRADFORD, UK

NIGEL SCHOFIELD

At the start of 1969, I was just 18 and in a kind of limbo. I'd finished school. University was nine months away. With a limited income and a teetotal upbringing, my social musical options were limited. The big package tours that always came to the Gaumont were a thing of the past. I'd 'got into folk music' (as we said back then) via a reference to Martin Carthy in the notes to *The Freewheelin' Bob Dylan* and had attended The Topic, the world's oldest folk club, regularly.

Then I saw a poster, 'John Peel presents Fairport Convention with Principal Edward's Magic Theatre and Bridget St John at Bradford University, Thursday February 6, 1969.' The thought of seeing Peel in person appealed; I knew Fairport's music through hearing it on his programme; I confess initially I confused my Bridget St Johns with my Buffy Sainte-Maries. During my A-level years at school, I'd learned the trick of getting into university gigs without being a student: it involved buying a ticket in advance (or getting someone to buy one for you), entering the venue early (before security were checking tickets and Students' Union cards), then staying discretely within the building – maybe the canteen or coffee bar (the Students' Union Bar tended to ask to see your Union card); on this occasion, however, I somehow ended up entering the concert hall balcony where, hidden in unlit darkness, I heard Fairport live for the first time as they played a couple of songs to set up.

It was my first chance to see Fairport, the first time they had ventured into Yorkshire. Years later, I was informed, I could have seen them a week earlier, as a diary mix up saw them arrive on the wrong day: they didn't play but headed back to Fortis Green with Sandy observing, 'Well, at least we know where it is for next week.'

I joined the queue for the main auditorium filled with anticipation. Fairport's set included 'Meet on the Ledge' (still years from being the inevitable encore), Leonard Cohen's 'Suzanne', 'Nottamun Town' and their version of 'A Sailor's Life', which I knew having heard it as the last track on side two of Martin Carthy's second album. This electrified atmospheric version was very different from Martin's – a slow, building, pulsing accompaniment which, at the end of the song burst into a guitar improvisation (I noted in my diary, 'Variations, à la Cream/great drumming.'). I was hearing British folk-rock for the first time. One song, introduced by Ashley Hutchings, really grabbed me: he explained it was written by 'Our girl singer Sandy Denny' and, though it wasn't on the new album, it would be on their next LP.

I was converted that night. It was a life-changing moment. I made a note to buy their next LP when it came out. In the meantime, Friday saw me looking under F in the rock section of Vallance's record shop. (Fairport were not regarded as folk at this stage and the British version of folk-rock was yet to be named.) There were two LPs – on different labels, with different line ups (yes, we soon got used to that). The rear photo of *What We Did on Our Holidays* looked as if it could have been taken at the previous night's gig; the front cartoon – clearly depicting a band who played the university circuit – had the word 'Bradford'. I took it as some kind of weird omen – finding out many years later that it was the name of their dog.

When I left home for my first term at university, *Holidays* had been joined by the first album (an end-of-an-era mono copy) and the sublime *Unhalfbricking*. They kept me good company and have been constant reliable companions ever since.

By the time I next saw Fairport (Oxford Town Hall, November 1970), I owned two more Fairport albums; the line-up had changed; the songs had all come into the repertoire since our first encounter. Before the gig I interviewed them for the first time – to be precise, Simon and Richard had disappeared to the nearby guitar emporium, DM was doing things with his drumkit, Swarb declared himself busy and I ended up talking to new boy, Dave Pegg. Neither of us said, 'I think this is the beginning of a beautiful friendship,' but it was.

CORN EXCHANGE
25 FEBRUARY 1969, CAMBRIDGE, UK

TIM EDMONDS

It was the incomparable John Peel radio programme *Top Gear* that introduced me to Fairport in 1968. In the same year I bought the Island sampler album, *You Can All Join In*, which included my first Fairport recording, 'Meet on the Ledge'. I was still at school and short of cash but Terry, a classmate, shared many musical interests and had more disposable income so could afford *What We Did on Our Holidays* soon after its release early in 1969. He lent it to me in exchange for a loan of my copy of Simon and Garfunkel's *Bookends* album. In February 1969, Terry and I went to the Cambridge Corn Exchange for our first Fairport concert, with Eclection (including Trevor Lucas and Gerry Conway) as the support band. This was where I learned how much better it could be to hear the music live. The first Fairport album I owned was *Unhalfbricking* in the summer of 1969, and it is also my favourite, with the outstanding track being 'A Sailor's Life' – in my view the greatest folk-rock track ever, surpassing what soon followed on *Liege & Lief* (my next album).

Tim Edmonds was introduced to Fairport by John Peel

I followed Fairport less closely after Sandy and Ashley left, and my next concert was not until February 1973, at Hull University. The line-up had changed completely from Cambridge four years earlier, but I learned the lesson that Fairport's music is always more than the band – it was still a great sound. I bought *Rosie* on the back of that concert and have since got every album as it has been released, as well as filling in my collection with the albums I had missed.

After a move to London in 1974 I got to six Fairport concerts over three years at five different venues, including a memorable Royal Albert Hall performance with Sandy in June 1975. By then my parents were living in a village a few miles from Banbury, which provided the perfect base for a day in a field at *Cropredy* in August 1979. I was able to use the same base (by then accompanied by my wife) to get to Broughton Castle in August 1981 and *Cropredy* in August 1982, before my parents moved out of the area. Apart from a period of absence from the mid-1980s to the mid-1990s, I have continued to go to concerts on a further

21 occasions at nine different venues, usually on the Winter tour. My son Matt came to a few of the concerts and at the Wycombe Swan in February 2002, I embarrassed him by requesting a dedication for his 15th birthday (two days later). Simon obliged, although unfortunately Matt's favourite song 'Dangerous' wasn't in the set that night.

Thanks, Fairport, for being part of my life for over 50 years – long may you keep it live and always play it well.

REDCAR JAZZ CLUB
2 MARCH 1969, REDCAR, UK

BRIAN SMITH

I had Fairport booked six times at the Redcar Jazz Club beginning in March 1969. On two occasions they played to sell out audiences of around 1,000 people. I have vivid recollections of the highly presentable performances, particularly with Sandy Denny fronting the group with her vocals. By the third appearance at the club in February 1970, they were going through many personnel changes before pulling in full houses again around August 1970, with Dave Swarbrick being the on-stage inspiration. Their album production was drying up and this then affected their later appearances in 1971-72. But in their prime they were a very big audience attraction.

Brian Smith booked Fairport to play at Redcar Jazz Club on several occasions

GONNA SEE ALL MY FRIENDS:
A PEOPLE'S HISTORY OF FAIRPORT CONVENTION

VAN DIKE CLUB
11 APRIL 1969, PLYMOUTH, UK

BRENDA RAWLINGS

I first met my husband Mike at a Fairport gig at the Van Dike Club. He was sitting on a ledge at the side of the stage. I expect you can guess what our favourite Fairport song is. We're still together and celebrated our 50th wedding anniversary last year. We go to Fairport gigs whenever we can and are so looking forward to Cropredy this year and can't wait to sing our song again.

Brenda Rawlings met husband Mike at a Fairport show and they've now been married 50 years

ROYAL LONDON HOSPITAL
12 MAY 1969, LONDON, UK

KINGSLEY ABBOTT

1969 did not start well when one of our close friends died most unexpectedly during what should have been a routine operation. Martin and I sadly helped her flatmate sort out her effects to make things easier for her mother, who lived a long way away. I was now working in the West End near Baker Street at the poster company offices, and it was here a few months later that I had a mid-morning phone call from a mutual friend to tell me of the news of Fairport's crash. Numbed, I went out to buy a first edition of the evening paper, where the stark confirming news was in black and white. The details were sketchy, but Martin's and Jeannie's deaths were clearly reported. A phone call to Witchseason gave further details, and that evening I was on my way to the hospital up the end of the Edgware Road with Iain.

The scene at the hospital was quiet, subdued and very sad. Everyone was in the same small ward, with Richard and Tyger near the door on the right, and Harvey over in the far-left hand corner. Tyger's face was bad, but he was making the best of things to some degree. Richard was very quiet. Harvey spoke a little but appeared mentally detached. We did not stay long, as the staff did not want them overtired. Simon was around and was managing to rise above events to a certain extent as he kept himself busy with press enquiries and people like Anthea Joseph from Witchseason. Over the next few days, we went up again, but I can't recall how many times. I recall that John Walters, who was the BBC producer for John Peel's *Top Gear* show, came up one night on his bike. The two Johns have been very good friends to the band over the past 18 months or so by championing their cause frequently on the show. Peel had earlier donated an electric autoharp to replace the old black one that Judy used to play.

My main link with Fairport had gone with Martin's passing, and things would never be the same for me again. I had nothing to do with Fairport's eventual decision to carry on, but at some point, I did go with Simon and Sandy to the BBC one evening to John Peel's studio where he interviewed them about the future. Simon went off afterwards leaving Sandy and I standing rather listlessly outside the Beeb. We walked slowly down towards Oxford Circus, passing Margaret Street where they had so often played so beautifully, and she gave me a kiss and a grin before she too left. I stood for a little while, realising that a special part of my life was over.

Fairport, of course, continued on to greater heights and eventually to further sad losses. I made a point of going to what was the official farewell concert at Cropredy in 1979, so that I could have been to the first and last ever gigs, and I remember feeling slightly cheated when I heard that they were performing the following week somewhere in Europe. However, the spirit was not to die, and remains to this day. It takes its place as a part of modern British culture, and all the musicians that have been a part of it can feel proud. Fairport has become the launching pad for a variety of musical directions, yet it remains a viable force in its own right. It was a long way from Fortis Green, but mostly a good journey.

UNHALFBRICKING
RELEASED 3 JULY 1969

JOE BOYD

I didn't see every show, I didn't go out of town much. But I saw them when they played in London, and they just got better and better. Every time I saw them, they had taken a few more leaps in terms of confidence, complexity of arrangements, tightness of the band, everything. It was very impressive to watch. They appealed to students, so the audience grew more slowly than some other groups around at that time. But the audiences grew.

The most important thing I did material-wise at this time concerned Joni Mitchell. I had a tape she had given me before she had a record deal, which had 'Eastern Rain' and 'Chelsea Morning' on it. Fairport listened and they were knocked out by it. But they had their ears to the ground, so they already knew who she was. But otherwise, I don't think I really contributed much. They knew where they were going. They're nerds, they're collectors, they're scholars. They were all students of what was going on. I met my match in them, they were middle-class music nerds like me.

When Fairport wanted to record 'A Sailor's Life' and 'Si Tu Doir Partir', they thought about getting a fiddler for some extra colour. I had known Swarb for some years and had made a record with him and Martin Carthy. Fairport were just at the beginning of their discovery of traditional British folk music, so when I said I'd call Swarb, they were impressed. I booked him for a session, and looking at the electric instruments, he realised that he wasn't going to compete; it became the first time he'd ever played through an amp. They went through 'A Sailor's Life' very quickly and then we did a full-length take. And that's it, that's the one on the record.

After the accident, at first, I think there the sentiment was, 'We are just going to break up.' They couldn't picture being Fairport Convention without Martin. But after a couple of weeks, they started to think, 'Well maybe we should stick at it?' But they were never going to play those songs again, so they had to do a whole new repertoire.

They were so excited, about 'A Sailor's Life', and about playing with Swarb on *Unhalfbricking*. So the first idea was, 'Let's get Swarb and Martin Carthy.' At one moment that was a done deal, and then Martin decided against it. But Swarb said, 'I'll stick with the idea,' so Swarb and Dave Mattacks became core members of the band.

I knew Swarb and I liked Swarb. But I was aware that he wasn't an easy guy. And he was already, in 1969, having problems with his ears that stemmed from teeth issues. Just after he joined, the band all came to me with a problem – Swarb needed all this dental work done, and it was expensive. I got him to sign a letter saying that the money would be recouped out of royalties, a royalty advance. Then of course after *Liege & Lief* there was a royalty pay-out. Everybody got about £600 but Swarb got £100. He was beside himself; he was furious. He never forgave me. I said, 'Listen Swarb, it's here in writing, you agreed to it, you're wearing the teeth that we bought for you, you've already had the money!' But he didn't see it like that.

It got even crazier after I was no longer involved. In my time, the tragedy, and then the departure of Sandy and Ashley, that was all very dramatic and difficult.

But the change of direction in *Liege & Lief* from American-style folk-rock to British folk is one of the great transformations in music. They reinvented themselves. If you listen to *Liege & Lief* and the live records, and do nothing but listen to Mattacks, it's fascinating. It is not like any other folk-rock band. When you hear other bands' up-tempo jigs and reels, it is a different thing entirely. It is one of the great personnel changes in the history of rock music: hiring somebody who isn't a rock drummer, to make folk-rock.

Mattacks was a dance band drummer, a strict-time drummer.

He played for people who actually danced – not idiot dancing, but formatted, strict-tempo dancing. Bringing that into this music as they were exploring these jigs and reels and the traditional dance melodies of Celtic and English music gave a propulsion that just worked out brilliantly. It set the course of Fairport for the next 50 years.

JOHN GEORGE

I bought *Unhalfbricking* when it came out. I showed it to a friend who said, 'I didn't know Mr and Mrs Denny had made a record.' Apparently, they were neighbours with the Dennys when Sandy was young.

VINCE STRAWSON

I've been a fan of Richard Thompson for quite some time now but never really listened to Fairport Convention properly before. I only heard of their reputation when I got into Free, Led Zep and Yes as a teenager back in the mid-1980s. When I received Richard Thompson's biography from my wife for my birthday, I listened to 'Who Knows Where the Time Goes?' and was gobsmacked. I'm struggling to express how I felt hearing this song for the first time. I've listened to it five times today in complete silence and awe. It's just so beautiful.

Vince Strawson was gobsmacked on hearing 'Who Knows Where the Time Goes?'

KAILUA BEACH
4 JULY 1969, O'AHU, HAWAII

STEPHEN STRAWN

The day we heard of the death of Brian Jones I played hooky from work. I took psilocybin and wandered the beach in Kailua on O'ahu. I was at home when my brother, who worked for the record distributor on O'ahu, showed up with three new releases – Canned Heat's third LP, called

Vintage; Jeff Beck's *Beck-ola*; and *What We Did on Our Holidays*. The Heat was on first and they were a known quantity, for sure. Next was the fantastic Jeff Beck sophomore recording, and it was out of this world. Then came the first track I ever heard of Fairport, 'Fotheringay'. Talk about being enfolded in a sound. Just the first cut and I was entranced. Everything about each tune was superlative to the nth degree. I could ramble on endlessly about that record and fill this missive with an abundance of exclamation points, but I realise I am preaching to the choir.

PRIMROSE HILL
29 AUGUST 1969, LONDON, UK

DAVID GOLDING, AGE 7

I remember going to one of (my uncle) Simon Nicol's parties in August 1969. He lived on the third story of a flat in Primrose Hill, at the corner of Fitzroy and Chalcot Roads. He and I had been spitting olive pips out onto the passers-by below. It was obviously a period of time when it was of no surprise to me that men had long hair – after all, Simon had long hair. There was however one man that I clearly recall as his hair was very curly. Something I had not seen before. It was not until I saw the cover of *Liege & Lief* that I recognised him and learnt that his name was Richard Thompson.

ROSEMARY BRECKENRIDGE GOLDING (NÉE NICOL)

I emigrated from England in April 1970 along with my husband and three young children, aged seven and under, as £10 Poms. It was a big change in life, and there were many things to do, including finding doctors and dentists to register with. We moved to Brisbane and the only dentist that I could get an appointment with was fucking miles away from where we lived. So be it. I took the kids and booked myself

David Golding's mum is Simon's sister

and the kids in. The dentist was a nice guy but seemed really weird. He knew I was married, and he still had the three kids to see in the waiting room.

During the cleaning of my teeth, I got fed up and asked him what the matter was. I could see that something was wrong. He insisted that everything was fine, however I persisted. I finally made him cough up that I reminded him of someone. He was insisted that it was stupid, but I would not let it go. Eventually I forced it out of him, and he asked, 'Have you ever heard of a band called Fairport Convention?' 'Why yes indeed I have,' I replied. It's just that you look like one of the members,' he said. Well fuck, didn't he drop his drill when I explained who I was?

FESTIVAL HALL
24 SEPTEMBER 1969, LONDON, UK

FRANK PARRY, AGE 15

I first saw Fairport Convention at the Festival Hall. I had to get special permission from my parents to travel to London from my home in Maidenhead. I knew nothing at all about the band, but the show set me off on a lifetime of musical adventure. How did all this happen? My sister and I used to share childminding duties for a neighbour who worked for the Robert Stigwood music management group, and he happened to say, 'I've got a ticket for this really rather good group at the Festival Hall. Interested?' Yes, I was. Isn't it strange how lifetime passions start?

The concert was terrific. I'd never in my young life heard music this fascinating, new and different. Shortly after, I raced to Our Price and found that they only had the first Fairport album in stock. I bought it and was amazed at how different it was to the music I had heard at the concert. It was only much later that I came to realise just how

Frank Parry got tickets from a neighbour

radical the shift in musical direction would turn out to be. I have been a fan ever since.

A short while ago, I went to a Fairport concert at Norden Farm in Maidenhead with my 93-year-old mother, who was seeing the band for the first time. I mentioned this and Ric kindly gave her a name check and joked, 'What took you so long?' My mother likes the music, particularly 'Who Knows Where the Time Goes?'

UNIVERSITY OF MANCHESTER
8 OCTOBER 1969, MANCHESTER, UK

JOHN WHITING

Music was an important part of growing up in the Sixties. Not many groups made it to my hometown of Hull but radio – especially pirate radio – introduced me to a wide range of sounds. I wasn't much of a 'pop-picker' but discovering West Coast music was exciting (once I'd worked out that it was from California and not Lancashire) and I'd also become a 'folkie' thanks to Folk Union One, the Watersons' old club.

LPs were discussed and analysed at parties. Mine were deemed interesting but not friends' favourites, a position seemingly reserved for the god Clapton and others whose eclectic – and electric – playing even reached Hull. There was a disc played at a few parties that seemed to pick up that West Coast sound but in an English way. The cover of the album, with the group round a table, in the dark with just a bit of illumination from a lamp, stuck in my mind.

My musical journey was about to take a major leap. I left school, went to work in a hotel for four months and then, at the end of September 1969, Manchester University. Freshers' Week passed in a blur and then in the first few days of October, a friend asked if I had spotted that Fairport Convention were playing that Wednesday, and was I doing anything? She wanted to go but didn't want to go on her own. 'No' and 'yes' were my answers.

Off we went to an evening that legendarily broke the attendance record for a concert in the Union building. Maybe it was crushingly full, but the evening passed in a revelatory blur, my mind desperately trying to remember every song they played and their instrumental medley. There was no doubt: this was it. This was 'my' music. But what was it? How to categorise it? How to describe it to my new friends? That was something I tried to do with all the fervour of a born-again preacher who has suddenly seen the light.

I had been fortunate enough to be at one of the limited number of concerts that autumn at which Fairport revealed the results of their summer's work at Farley Chamberlayne. Yes, this was the birth of folk-rock and what I had heard was of course *Liege & Lief*. The course of my musical life had been set and 50-plus years later I'm still a Fairport fan, follower and aficionado. Thanks to Fairport, I'd combined my folk music strand with that West coast guitar, added harmony singing and flying fiddle strings.

I managed to buy *Liege & Lief* when it came out and started to follow the comings and goings of the group. Sandy and Tyger leaving – oh dear. Who is this guy Pegg? Ah, hearing 'Dirty Linen' convinced me that Fairport had acquired a new star. Then Richard left and how could FC manage without hi… oh, Simon steps up to the plate, obviously. I could go on but… I bought *Full House* as soon as it hit the streets and, as funds permitted, started to work back through the old Fairport albums: *Unhalfbricking* – 'A Sailor's Life', 'Percy's Song', fantastic. *What We Did on Our Holidays* – 'Meet on the Ledge' – that's where it came from. And then I managed to track down their first album (I had to order it). Just a minute – I recognise this… that picture. Yes, it was that long-ago (actually only about three years) album and 'Chelsea Morning' was as good as it ever was, and what I now knew to be Richard's guitar work showed the potential magic I'd then sensed.

Since then, I've been a faithful Fairport groupie, accumulating about 50 CDs, innumerable concerts, about 20 *Cropredy*s and so many memories (including a fantastic Rhine cruise – lucky me). My daughters at one stage wondered if there were any groups other than Fairport. But where it all began was that epic concert which led me back to the disc that really did start it, proving that it all comes round again.

GONNA SEE ALL MY FRIENDS:
A PEOPLE'S HISTORY OF FAIRPORT CONVENTION

FAIRFIELD HALLS
10 OCTOBER 1969, CROYDON, UK

DAVID ALLAWAY

I became a fan of Fairport Convention about a year before I first saw them live. A friend of mine, Mike, heard the single 'Meet on the Ledge' on the radio and went out and bought *What We Did on Our Holidays*. He played it to me, and I was hooked straight away, particularly enjoying Sandy's wonderful song 'Fotheringay'.

Unhalfbricking then came along, and I bought both albums, looking into *Melody Maker* every week, hoping to see that Fairport were touring. Alas, the motorway accident happened, and I thought I'd probably never get the chance to see the band live, doubting they'd ever get over the loss of Martin Lamble and of Richard's girlfriend.

Thankfully I was wrong, and eventually the album *Liege & Lief* was issued. I went out and bought a copy straight away and was not disappointed, even though the sound and style of the band was quite different from the previous albums.

David Allaway was at the Fairfield Halls in '69

Having always been interested in drums, though never having played, I was particularly struck by the precision and inventiveness of their new drummer, Dave Mattacks. When I heard, in late 1969, that they were playing at the Fairfield Halls in Croydon (I lived in Sutton), Mike and I grabbed a pair of tickets as soon as we could.

By sheer good fortune, we happened to get tickets for front row seats in the choir stalls, a few rows of seats set behind the stage in a crescent. And I couldn't believe it when we sat down and saw that the drum kit was set up just a few feet in front of where we were sitting.

I think 'mesmerised' would be the only word to describe my state that evening. The whole band were fantastic, with Sandy sounding angelic and telling silly jokes between songs, Dave Swarbrick and Richard Thompson swapping amazing licks and solos all evening, and Ashley Hutchings and Simon Nicol steadily holding everything together, as they always did. But it was what DM was doing right in front of me that stayed with me. That was the moment I decided I really had to get a kit and start playing, which is what I did a few months later.

Initially, after I bought a second-hand Premier kit, I just wanted them for my own amusement and had no intention of trying to join a group, so I decided not to take drum lessons or to learn drum sheet music, something I later regretted. I just listened to and played along to records, trying to copy what I was hearing the drummer doing.

The first snare and bass drum pattern I mastered was the beat laid down by DM on the original version of 'Matty Groves'. After I managed that, quite a few other patterns came to me quite quickly. A couple of years later, after Dave had left Fairport, I plucked up the courage to write to him, c/o Island Records, asking for a bit of advice as to how he tuned his snare drums, the sound of which had always knocked me out. To my amazement, he wrote back to me and, in great detail and with several hand-drawn illustrations, described his tuning methods, which was so kind of him.

We continued to correspond, and he eventually mentioned that he was soon playing at Southampton Gaumont, backing Joan Armatrading, and how it would be good to meet me there after the show if I could get along to it. Needless to say, I got there. It was a great gig, soon after Joan's album *Love and Affection* had been released. After we'd met and chatted about music and drums for about ten or 15 minutes, I drove home in a bit of a trance – I think I may have even gone through a set of red lights on the way out of Southampton.

Dave continued to tell me about upcoming gigs he was doing around where I lived (quite often leaving tickets on the door for me), and recommend albums he'd been a session player on, many of which I still have on vinyl. Also, after he'd got an endorsement deal with Yamaha Drums, he sold off several of his old kits, one of which I had admired for several years, and he asked if I'd like to buy it off him. I didn't hesitate, and I still have that small red Eddy Ryan four-piece custom-built kit to this day, my most prized possession (if only I could play them half as well as the original owner).

I have continued to follow Fairport through all their various incarnations, seeing them live whenever I can, and now my wife, Jane, also loves to see the band on stage.

On their 50th anniversary tour a few years ago, we went to see them at the Tivoli, a lovely little old theatre in Wimborne, Dorset, close to where we live. I handed them a 'Happy Anniversary' card during the interval, which I think they appreciated. Inside the card, I wrote, 'Thank you all so much for a life time of great music and wonderful performances,' a sentiment which still holds true today. Long may you continue to give musical joy and pleasure to all of your fans, Fairport Convention, and thank you again.

TOWN HALL
23 OCTOBER 1969, LEEDS, UK

TIM SULLIVAN

A crowd of us at school used to meet up at people's houses. We would listen to albums and drink Newcastle Brown Ale. We were into Fairport Convention, and one night we got together and played the first four albums right through – *Fairport Convention*, *What We Did on Our Holidays*, *Unhalfbricking* and *Liege & Lief*. It was a long evening and lots of Newcastle Brown was drunk.

Although I've seen them numerous times over the years, Leeds Town

Hall in October 1969 was the only time I saw them with Sandy Denny. I don't remember anything about what they played but I do recall that, instead of a support act, they had a beauty contest from Leeds University students. Leeds United's manager Don Revie was one of the judges, and when they introduced him, he was greeted by a big round of booing.

Tim Sullivan saw Fairport with Sandy but particularly remembers Don Revie

I saw them again in October 1970. Sandy had left by then. She was a fabulous singer.

MOTHERS
2 NOVEMBER 1969, BIRMINGHAM, UK

DAVE PEGG

The first time I saw Fairport was in November 1969 at Mothers Club in Birmingham. It was the occasion of my 22nd birthday and my wife Christine and I had gone along with Harvey Andrews and his lady to check the band out. I hadn't heard them live before, but had purchased the *Liege & Lief* album and enjoyed listening to it. I had heard Dave Swarbrick playing with Martin Carthy on many occasions and was a huge fan of Swarb. He knew of me through the Ian Campbell Folk Group, who I had played double bass with, including on an album on which Swarb had guested. But Swarb knew that, really, I was an electric bass guitarist with a rock background rather than a 'folkie'.

The band blew me away that night. The interplay between Richard and Swarb was incredible, and the rhythm section of DM, Simon, and Ashley worked wonderfully together. All this was topped with Sandy's amazing vocals.

I said to Christine after the gig that I would love to join Fairport. Imagine my surprise when the next day I got a call from Swarb, asking if I wanted to audition as Ashley was leaving. Luckily, I passed the test, and to this day I am still in the band and enjoying making Fairport music. Long may it continue. Though I sometimes think that if I hadn't gone to that gig on my 22nd birthday, the band might not have been here in 2022.

CHRISTINE PEGG

I remember the gig at Mothers Club in Erdington, Birmingham really well. We were with several folk music performers and experts from the Jug O' Punch Folk Club in Digbeth. Fairport were fantastic, but a heated discussion came after the show about both the rock re-arrangements and the interpretations of traditional songs and tunes, especially the Scottish lament 'Flowers of the Forest'. The traditional folk music fans were not happy. However, folk rock music had arrived and would introduce these great songs to the masses. This rebirth was originated mostly by Fairport Convention, and we should be eternally grateful for the joy their music has given us over the years.

DECEMBER 1969, LONDON, UK

JOE BOYD

In some ways, you could say that the year and a half from when Sandy and Ashley left in November or December of '69, until Richard left in the spring of '71, was, in terms of Fairport as a live band, probably their golden age. Without Sandy, there were no brakes on touring, it was 'get us more gigs'. They just played. They loved playing, they loved being on the road, they loved the camaraderie, they loved the beers, they loved the shows, they loved the rehearsal, they loved how much everybody adored them, they loved America. You can hear it on *Live at the LA Troubadour*. It was a great 18 months.

UMIST
17 APRIL 1970, MANCHESTER, UK

JOHN WHITING

I dragged friends to a concert at UMIST. It was the *Full House* ensemble, mirrored by the full house they had attracted. So full, in fact, that the cry went up from the back to those at the front of the room to 'move forward'. This was picked up by Swarb, who immediately launched into 'Music to Move Forward to'. Simon and Peggy joined in, and it was a great impromptu tune.

Partway through the concert, Simon asked if anyone in the audience could remember discs that were a bit smaller than today's but went round faster. Apparently, Fairport's contract required them to make one. He built it up well and many in the audience (me included) were wondering, 'Why 78s?'. The punchline was a reference to Fairport's latest single, 'Now Be Thankful'. I couldn't find it in local record shops, which perhaps explains why it didn't trouble the charts.

I drifted away from Fairport in the mid-Seventies, after *Rising for the Moon*. My new wife preferred the Albions and indeed they did seem to be doing so much more. My wife also led me towards opera, and then children arrived in the mid-Eighties. A business trip took me to New York where I found myself bored and rather low, so went wandering round a shopping mall in search of something to cheer myself up. Passing a record shop, I went leafing through the racks and found something amazing – a new Fairport album! Where did that come from? I bought it and still have my prized US version of *Gladys' Leap*.

Back in the UK, I tried to research Fairport (there was no internet then) and found out about Cropredy – sadly family commitments meant there was no chance of going for many years. But a couple of years later I discovered that they did a regular winter tour, and I saw them at nearby St Albans. And I've since logged 20 or more Cropredys, even persuading my wife to join me a couple of times.

FILLMORE WEST
30 APRIL & 1 MAY 1970, SAN FRANCISCO, CALIFORNIA

IAN ANDERSON, JETHRO TULL

I have only brief memories of early days with the Fairports, at Birmingham Town Hall in (I think) 1968 or '69, although I can find no evidence of this today, and at the Fillmore West in 1970. I remember that Iain Matthews was singing then. The Fairports have always struck me as more American folk-influenced rather than by traditional English folk at that time. Their music fitted with the Fillmore West audience much better than Tull. We did well at the Fillmore East in NYC. But the Fillmore West was not a good gig for me. Too many stoned hippies who paid no attention to our music.

Over the years, of course, we toured with Fairport a few times and some of the band performed with us on record, and a couple were even official Jethro Tull band members for a while. I felt I got to know their music well in the '80s and '90s and had a growing love of their balance of trad-folk with their contemporary singer-songwriter style, especially with Simon Nicol taking the helm at times. Swarbrick was a strong musical personality although I knew him less than the others. I played on a benefit concert for him when he was very ill and unable to work and pay the bills. A gentle man with much to look back on.

UCLA
12 MAY 1970, LOS ANGELES, CALIFORNIA

JIM BICKHART

I first became aware of the band when their first album came out. I didn't buy it then, but I was curious and kept looking at it in record shops. It wasn't getting any FM radio airplay in Los Angeles, and I was a college student just scraping by, so I wasn't taking too many chances in the record shops. I also was just becoming an album and concert reviewer for the *UCLA Daily Bruin* but hadn't begun getting review copies of albums yet.

I was, however, the campus

Jim Bickhart has had a long association with Fairport

promotion representative for A&M Records, which had the rights to *What We Did on Our Holidays* through a deal with Island Records. My supervisor, the late, beloved Bob Garcia, sat me down one evening and played me a test pressing of the album and asked me to guess who it was. 'Tale in Hard Time' was about half-way through when I correctly guessed that it was Fairport. To me it sounded like they looked on the cover of their first album, weird as that may seem. It was the beginning of my now half-century-plus appreciation for the band, its people and music.

After the deadly motorway accident, Sandy Denny, Richard Thompson and Simon Nicol paid a 'recuperation visit' to Los Angeles with Anthea Joseph of Witchseason management, hung out with Mr Garcia a bit and, I was later told, dropped by the famed Troubadour Monday night 'hoot' (the venue in which the Byrds and other later-to-be-famous denizens of the LA scene first alit) to play a song or two. Unfortunately, I was not around when Garcia called to invite me to meet the trio (pre-message machine, voicemail, email, text, etc.), so that opportunity was lost.

Subsequently, despite the accident, the band produced a total of three 1969 albums, culminating in *Liege & Lief*.

Because A&M got a late start, the pipeline was clogged and… *Holidays* (as 'Fairport Convention') and *Unhalfbricking* were out in the US by the time the *Full House* line-up of the band was booked to tour the US in May 1970, with *Liege & Lief* just being released. The band were booked for a memorable week at the Troubadour, and I arranged for them to play a lunchtime free concert at UCLA after they finished at the Troubadour.

An A&M executive hosted a little reception for the band and company staff at his posh Coldwater Canyon home. That's when I first got to meet them. Mr Garcia then invited them to dinner at his favourite Italian restaurant in Hollywood and I had the privilege of driving Richard T over to the dinner. That's where I was first introduced to their proclivity for bottles of Foster's Lager ('tubes', they called them). They drank the restaurant clean out of Foster's, then went to a local radio station for an interview which was cut short when an inebriated Swarb swore on mic.

Things then got complicated, at least for me. The shooting of four students at Kent State University in Ohio took place and the situation on many American college campuses – including UCLA – went bonkers. There were riots, demonstrations, you-name-it. The Friday Fairport were supposed to play, the campus was locked down, so we improvised a re-scheduling to the following Tuesday. I was on thin ice because (don't tell anyone) I had, without college administration authorisation, signed the band's booking contract on behalf of UCLA because the UCLA student activities people typically wouldn't do that for visiting performers. So, one way or the other, that re-scheduled gig had to take place or I'd be on the hook for paying the band whether they played or not.

Pink Floyd were in town at the same time (*Umma Gumma* tour) and somebody who knew them got them to come over to UCLA on the Sunday afternoon to play for free. They set up their big quadraphonic sound system outdoors in the same general location where Fairport were set to play on the Tuesday. That was all fine, except it wasn't publicised so only a few hundred students and hippies showed up for the treat. Joe Boyd also showed up, sauntered over to me and said, 'This is great. I'll call the lads back at the Tropicana Motor Lodge and maybe they can bring their instruments over and complete their obligation.' All I could do is groan and pray that they wouldn't. Thankfully, they didn't.

Tuesday rolled around and Fairport played a fine set that had students doing circle dances and having a good old time listening to this exotic group with whom most were unfamiliar. From the stage, Simon acknowledged the political upheavals of the moment by congratulating the crowd on finally getting their dog licenses. A classical musician friend of one of my colleagues at the *Daily Bruin* said Peggy was the most arresting musician on the stage (and this with Swarb, Richard, Mattacks and Simon all playing at the stratospheric levels that line-up were capable of).

At the same time, as the A&M rep, I'd set up a two-for-one sale on …*Holidays*, *Unhalfbricking* and *Liege & Lief* in the campus record store staffed by none other than Ron and Russell Mael of Sparks. We moved more than 75 copies of each, which was a pretty good result for Fairport in one store over the course of just a few days.

GONNA SEE ALL MY FRIENDS:
A PEOPLE'S HISTORY OF FAIRPORT CONVENTION

FILLMORE EAST
10 JUNE 1970, NEW YORK, NEW YORK

JOHN SCHWETJE

I first saw Fairport in June 1970 at the Fillmore East on a bill with Traffic headlining and Mott the Hoople opening. It was the *Full House* line-up. I went with my older brother, who took me as a gift for my fourteenth birthday which was about a week prior to the show. I remember them playing an incredible set. I was a young bassist, and I was floored hearing Peggy. Hearing him right along with Swarb and RT on 'Dirty Linen' had an incredible impact on me. I really loved seeing Swarb onstage too. He danced while playing, and that made me get the reference in 'Angel Delight' to 'and on the ground his feet are never'.

John Schwetje with his wife Jeanne at Cropredy

I next saw them at Avery Fisher Hall in New York after *"Babbacombe" Lee* had come out. Only Swarb and Peggy were left from the Fillmore line-up – they had Tom Farnell and Roger Hill – but I was generally pleased with what I heard, and Swarb seemed to defy gravity throughout. After the show, my brother turned around to exhort us to move faster and, when he turned back, walked right into a street sign.

Through the Seventies, *Gottle O'Geer* largely left me cold but I did like *Farewell, Farewell*. I didn't see Fairport again that decade but was delighted to see Peggy with Tull at Madison Square Garden – I was working there for the *Stormwatch* tour – and his playing didn't disappoint, although the ship stage set and pirate outfits were corny.

I was unaware of Fairport's doings in the '80s until I bought a used copy of *In Real Time*. I finally saw them again at the Bottom Line in New York in 2002 after *XXXV* came out. Both Gerry and Chris Leslie were in the band. I brought my wife, who loved them. When I told Simon afterwards that I'd seen the *Full House* band at the Fillmore, he didn't believe I looked old enough. Peggy was gracious as I told him of my own bass playing and how I valued his playing as much as that of fusion players like Jaco Pastorius. Ric, of course, was a great guy to talk about jazz and fusion, and he was happy to hear I knew his playing going back to Soft Machine.

After that, we kept seeing them in New York and Long Island. One particular memory is of Joe's Pub one June. We brought a few quarts of our fresh strawberries along with a bottle of a local white Viognier, which Simon drank most of during the band's set. Everyone liked the berries too.

We got to *Cropredy* twice. In 2006, we were delighted to see Swarb with Lazarus in 2006, and in 2009 to see RT, which reacquainted me with the *Full House* line-up because DM was there with Feast of Fiddles and guested with Fairport on a few tracks. We've not been back to *Cropredy* since 2009, and they no longer come here to the USA, so who knows when the live connection might be re-established, but it's been great whenever it's happened.

FRIENDS (SAMPLER ALBUM) RELEASED 19 JUNE 1970

PETER HOLSAPPLE

When I was a 14-year-old dyed-in-the-wool rock music fan in Winston-Salem, North Carolina, I sent off to A&M Records for a free artist sampler called *Friends*. There was an ad in one of the magazines I had bought, and surely there was nothing better than a free LP. When it arrived, one had to get past the unappealing black-and-white photo of John Ned Mendelsohn, noted rock writer and malcontent, dressed in a chicken suit on the cover. I'm not sure whose brilliant

Peter Holsapple discovered Fairport via an A&M sampler

marketing strategy that was, but it's probably good that the record didn't cost anything.

A&M had already proven itself an open-minded record company who were willing to take chances on artists like those on *Friends*, in the hope that something would be hugely successful, but they were undoubtedly pragmatic enough to know that that was still a crapshoot at best. Herb Alpert and Jerry Moss had had plenty of success with the Tijuana Brass, Sergio Mendes and Brasil '66, the Baja Marimba Band and the We Five, but it was the beginning of a new decade so A&M was looking to expand their horizons in a rock-dominated world.

Track one, side-A was 'Walk Awhile' from *Full House*, and I'd frankly never heard anything like it. The very, very British singing (no ersatz American blues accents here), the searing fiddling from Swarb, Peggy's mobile bass, DM powering the band effortlessly through the song's changes – I needed to hear more. Then at the end of side-A was 'Peace in the End' from Fotheringay. The other part of the puzzle, with Sandy, was thus exposed to me.

Granted there were many tracks on *Friends* that held massive appeal – you can't beat Free or Humble Pie, I was already in love with Blodwyn Pig and Spooky Tooth (who'd become even cooler with the Grease Band infusion), and The Move were just about my favourite band on Earth – but the eye- and ear-opening sounds of Fairport and Fotheringay made a trackway to my heart. I got *Full House* and absorbed every second of it. I even got my nasty little pre-punk high school rock and roll band, Little Diesel, to work up a two-guitar-bass-and-drums version of 'Poll Ha'penny', the final tune in the 'Dirty Linen' medley (with mixed results, of course, but it went right over the Allman Brothers-craving audiences' heads every time).

I bought every Fairport record I could get my hands on – not always easy in North Carolina, to be honest. Although I'll bet that I was among the first folks in the US to get *AKA Henry the Human Fly* when it was released, and it steered me toward Steeleye Span, the Watersons, Nic Jones and Shirley Collins as well. I sank into a mild depression that I'd missed the band opening for Traffic at Cameron Indoor Stadium at Duke University in Durham in October 1971, and eventually steered a subsequent band (Continental Drifters) into the Fairport world with a performance at The Arts at St. Ann's (Brooklyn NY) in November 1998, backing up a surfeit of singers like Robyn Hitchcock, Mike Mills (R.E.M.) and Darius Rucker (Hootie and the Blowfish). Continental Drifters also recorded their own EP of Fairport/Richard/Sandy songs called *Listen Listen*. I've also become friends with Iain Matthews, with whom I've shared a number of stages.

And my love of all things Fairport has never abated. The mystery of the music is never lost on me, and it still takes me to that extraordinary place and time whenever I hear it, many miles and many years away from suburban 1970s North Carolina.

BATH FESTIVAL
27 JUNE 1970, BATH, UK

PETER EMERY
Sandy had left and the guys had just released *Full House*. I'd only seen them on *Top of the Pops* doing their crazy version of 'Si Tu Dois Partir', and thought back then that they were just odd. At Bath they woke the place up, got people up dancing and the quality of the playing was superb. 'Sloth' blew me away. I was so impressed that, when I finally got home, I bought *Full House* plus every other album released before, and so my love affair with the Fairport family commenced. I still love them now, so many offshoots, so much great music. My only regret is I never got to see them with Sandy.

MAIDSTONE FIESTA, OAKWOOD PARK
5 JULY 1970, MAIDSTONE, UK

TRISH COULSON
The *Maidstone Fiesta*, held in the summer of 1970, at Oakwood Park in Maidstone, Kent, was my introduction to the wonderful world of live music and set me on the road to many happy times going to gigs, concerts and festivals over the past 50 years. I and a group of friends were students at the college on the campus at Oakwood and loved

going to the many events promoted by the attached art school.

The highlights at the *Fiesta* were Fairport Convention, who performed a collection of songs and jigs. I fell in love with the amazing Richard Thompson, Dave Swarbrick, Dave Pegg, Dave Mattacks and Simon Nicol, and have been a fan ever since. I did not know the concert was being filmed by Tony Palmer until I discovered the DVD. I recently bought a copy which I played with my husband Richard and daughters Lisa and Johanna. They loved watching me enjoying the music with my pals all those years ago, and nowadays Richard and I enjoy going to see Fairport Convention perform at various venues in Kent.

In the words of Sandy Denny's beautiful song, 'Who Knows Where the Time Goes?' Happy times – and thanks guys for the great music, fun and laughter.

Trish Coulson (centre) remembers Fairport being a highlight at Maidstone Fiesta

YORKSHIRE FOLK, BLUES & JAZZ FESTIVAL
14 – 16 AUGUST 1970, KRUMLIN, BARKISLAND, UK

ED WALLAGE

I saw Fairport at the now infamous *Yorkshire Folk, Blues, and Jazz* or Krumlin Festival. Music festivals were in their infancy and the influence of Woodstock in '69 was high, but trying to recreate Woodstock in the Pennines was, with hindsight, optimism over reality. I had just finished my 'O' levels, and rather worrying in retrospect, I was allowed to go along to this festival by myself. I had

GONNA SEE ALL MY FRIENDS:
A PEOPLE'S HISTORY OF FAIRPORT CONVENTION

Ed Wallage was at the infamous Krumlin Festival

no tent, no proper sleeping bag, just an old quilt sewn up, carried in my school haversack. (Times were different, and I don't know whether to be pleased or disappointed with my parents!)

The line-up for the festival was a who's who of the time. Pink Floyd and The Who were amongst those scheduled to play. For me, however, the big draws were Fairport and Fotheringay.

All went roughly to plan on Friday. Elton John was a particular highlight, just sitting and playing piano along with bass and drums. That night I was offered the use of a tent (without groundsheet) by some lads from Liverpool, who also provided beans for breakfast. Saturday started, but the promised acts were not all forthcoming. Rumours began to circulate that the organisers were running out of money and/or bands were not turning up. There were still some excellent performances by some top acts. As the day wore on the weather started to deteriorate and by early evening it started to rain. With no shelter I took the big decision to spend 5 shillings on a survival bag. The festival ticket was two pounds and ten shillings, so a big expenditure, but it lived up to its name. The rest of the evening was spent in my orange cocoon.

Fotheringay lived up to expectations, and I am still proud to be able to say I saw this too short-lived band. Chaos seemed to be growing, and the rumour that bands were not willing to play until they had been paid continued. I began to be fearful that the main reason I was there would be fruitless. Eventually, though, those Fender amps arrived on stage and hopes were raised. Then Fairport arrived. Simon announced that they would be, 'Doing the usual mechanical stuff starting with the usual mechanical 'Walk Awhile',' and off they went. It was not the most accomplished Fairport vocally, but instrumentally they were on fire and furious. The tunes especially were fast, with RT and Swarb sparring to see who could keep up, while the sides of the stage were filled with more onlookers than for any other act. For me it was the highlight of the festival. I still tell anyone who will listen that, whenever 'Walk Awhile' is played, it was the first song I ever saw Fairport play, as it brings back that moment.

The rest of the festival is a bit of a blur, probably because I retreated into my survival bag. I remained there until the following morning, when around five o'clock the police were walking around the field gently kicking survival bags to see if there was anyone in them. There was an announcement from the stage via a megaphone that the festival was called off (the PA could not be used given the danger of water versus electricity). Rather meekly and without any fuss, people started to shuffle off site. I think I caught a bus back to Halifax, but my memory has either blocked out details, or I was suffering from lack of food, as the only thing I can remember eating all weekend was those beans for breakfast the previous day.

The festival programme said, 'We know that there will be many fans who have travelled many hundreds of miles to see and hear the lads – I don't think they will let you down.'

It was true, and that first time seeing Fairport remains locked in my memory, but not necessarily for all the right reasons.

TOM NOBLE

A cold, wet weekend in Halifax, 1970. In Krumlin, actually. A festival that promised much but delivered mainly extremely inclement weather. Weeks earlier, as a naïve 18-year-old I had written to the organisers pretending to be a music journalist. Much to my shock and delight, two press passes were duly delivered. Having decided to brave the backstage bar hoping that my credentials wouldn't be questioned, I was confronted by two bands sampling the delights that were on offer. Seriously sampling you might say. Pentangle and Fairport appeared to be engaged in a battle of the bands – a battle to see who could drink the most.

GONNA SEE ALL MY FRIENDS:
A PEOPLE'S HISTORY OF FAIRPORT CONVENTION

When Fairport were on stage the crowd were wrapped in polythene as the heavens opened again and the trusty faux journalist stepped over bodies to get close to the stage. Despite facing a curtain of rain, Fairport soldiered on and converted at least one person to be a *Cropredy*-attending, lifelong 'fan'. Stories abound about what Fairport actually got up to on stage that day, and perhaps don't bear repeating for a family audience. Later, that fan would actually become a music writer, penning reviews for *NME* and even getting his mug on a Groundhog's album cover (*Split*), standing at the back of the stage at that very festival.

Tom Noble blagged his way into the Krumlin Festival... poor lad

I have every Fairport and Richard Thompson album and a proud record of having seen Fairport 15 times and Richard Thompson 32 times, in such diverse places as Brussels and Ashington.

GRAHAM NEWTON

My first-time seeing Fairport Convention was at the doomed *Krumlin Festival* near the top of the M62 in West Yorkshire. At the time, I didn't realise that Peggy had shat himself after the previous night's curry. I also didn't realise that Swarb pissed on the press corps through a hole in the stage wall. Talking to Simon many years later, he said they never got paid. Having said that, from a punter point of view it was great, with Fotheringay

Graham Newton was at the unmitigated disaster that was Krumlin and remembers it as 'brilliant'

and many more amongst the acts on the bill. Friday and Saturday were actually brilliant – it was just the disastrous weather on Saturday night that led to a major incident.

LITTLE HADHAM FETE
22 AUGUST 1970, LITTLE HADHAM, UK

DAVE MONK

Ever since my older brother brought the first Fairport Convention album into the house in 1968, a lifelong love of the band took a firm hold, though I wasn't able to see them perform at the time. But that would change almost by accident a couple of years later. In fact, the first encounter with Fairport wasn't at a gig at all. It was in the George Hotel bar in Bishop's Stortford when a bunch of young men with long hair came in and asked me and my mates where the Boar's Head pub was. They were looking for a folk club, they said. Well, definitely not in the George Hotel but the Boar's Head was just up the road in Windhill and off they went, with me and my mates a few minutes behind as the penny dropped. This was Fairport Convention, who apparently lived somewhere locally. Needless to say, when we got to the Boar's Head there was no sign of a folk club nor the Fairports. Perhaps someone had put them right about the location of the folk club, at the Railway Hotel across the town, also the venue for Rambling Jack's Blues Club and a bit later replaced by The Angel Underground – a name chosen by pure coincidence with no known Fairport connection to the former Angel pub in Little Hadham where they were living at the time.

Dave Monk saw two Fairport shows in Little Hadham

GONNA SEE ALL MY FRIENDS: A PEOPLE'S HISTORY OF FAIRPORT CONVENTION

This chance encounter must have been about the same time they were persuaded to perform in a field between Little Hadham and Much Hadham. And that was my first experience of actually seeing Fairport Convention perform live. I went with my brother, Mick, and his friend, Tom, from university who drove us there in his by then ancient Austin A40. According to my copy of Patrick Humphries's *A History of Fairport Convention* it was a benefit show held in early July 1970 for Little Hadham's St Cecilia's church organ fund. They raised the princely sum of £450 for the fund so I can proudly say that my small contribution was my entry fee.

This was only the third live show I had ever been to, the first being at Rambling Jack's Blues Club in Bishop's Storford to see Eire Apparent which was loud and then the even louder Who performance at Sheffield Uni where my brother's Uni band, Superslug, were the support act. Clearly Fairport Convention playing outdoors was a far more comfortable listening experience to my young ears. Sadly, not much sticks in my mind about the performance overall apart from the introductory story before they played 'Matty Groves', whose tale of deceitful liaison and death has been a staple in the set list ever since. I already knew the song, of course, because my brother had added *Liege & Lief* to the Fairport collection by then. So that was the first time I saw Fairport play. It was the *Full House* line-up, but did I imagine that Ashley Hutchings dropped by and played a bit too? My brother confirms that he did.

There wasn't a big audience, though the weather was warm, as we stood and watched the band run through their *Full House* repertoire, with a couple of rock'n'roll numbers thrown in. The stage was a tractor trailer. According to my brother the pub across the road, The Nag's Head, ran out of beer.

Far more memorable for me was the second Little Hadham concert later that summer, another benefit, this time for the local police, which Dave Pegg notes in his *Off the Pegg* memoir, was odd given 'the more nefarious and less salubrious habits of certain members of the band.' They played in the same field but this time it was a much larger venture with a far bigger audience of about 4,000, who, according to RT's recollection in *Beeswing*, clogged up the single-track roads in the area.

The stage was erected at the foot of the field, this time overlooked by a slight hill where I sat midway up and just to the left of the stage. It was a warm evening with support act Trees playing a very good opening set of songs from their now collectable two albums released on CBS. But what stands out for me sitting up on that low rise overlooking the stage was the staggering interplay of guitar and violin on 'Sloth', the twin talents of Thompson and Swarbrick at their swashbuckling best. It was one of those shivers down the spine experiences, the final seal of a lifelong devotion to Fairport Convention along with the solo career of Richard Thompson.

I remember blistering renditions of 'Walk Awhile' and 'Now Be Thankful', along with another old favourite 'Sir Patrick Spens', but the real standout was 'Sloth' which has led me, like a Pied Piper, to numerous Richard Thompson concerts ever since, starting in 1975 at Harlow Playhouse when he was part of the double act with wife Linda. Simon made an appearance, too, at that show.

I was fortunate enough to catch a Sandy Fairport concert in Harlow Town Park in June 1974. Sadly, I don't remember it with the same fondness of those first two gigs in the field in the Hadhams, precursors perhaps to the marvellous *Cropredy Festivals* of later years.

The last show I went to before lockdown was delightfully local again. It was the Fairports at Saffron Hall, safely within walking distance of home and also the venue where I last saw Richard Thompson, by now the complete maestro of all things guitar, performing solo and recalling for me those memorable Hadham concerts.

THE ANGEL
22 AUGUST 1970, LITTLE HADHAM, UK

DAVE TWEEDIE

I listened to the first album but not too sure I liked it. I was, like many, introduced properly to the band with the Island sampler, full of many classics but 'Meet on the Ledge' stood out. We played it often in the sixth form at school. *Liege & Lief* gave us all something different. But my real devotion started with *Full House*. Every track is remarkable.

But it got odd. My dad, a builder, came home from work one day and said he was doing some work on an old ex-pub in Little Hadham called

GONNA SEE ALL MY FRIENDS: A PEOPLE'S HISTORY OF FAIRPORT CONVENTION

The Angel that had a band living there called Fairport Convention. We lived fairly close so I wandered over one day. I was welcomed into the house and had long chats with Simon and Richard, while Swarb turned up later. Other visits witnessed jam sessions in the garden with rock classics belted out.

It would be boring to try to list all gigs I have been to in the 50 years since; it probably reaches near to 100. There were some really fun times, including Swarb being the worst for drink, Ric's comedy sessions, Simon's use of words, etc.

Fairport have changed and so many different line-ups give a different sound – Judy to Sandy changed vocals, Peggy's pounding bass, the loss of Richard's guitar mastery – but through all the earlier versions the unique sound was Swarb. He was a character and a master of his instruments. The next sound was when Ric and Maart joined. We all love Ric, but he even says he cannot match Swarb. Maart gave me one of my favourite Fairports, a guitar-based sound with a heavier touch. The current sound with Chris is far folkier, but shows how versatile Fairport are, and I love that sound.

I did not get to *Cropredy* until 1983, but then made nearly every year. I would meet friends by turning up and knowing where we sat each year. We've had all weathers. The sunny days were fantastic, but we had some very, very wet ones. One day that stands out was when, during heavy rain, we had a fishing tent that zipped up and we sat in that with about a twelve-inch gap at the top, watching the whole of a Saturday. It was our own exclusive dry box with a perfect view. Each year Fairport would play a perfect set. But the guests really were also amazing. I remember Fairport doing a Zeppelin set with Robert Plant, and Roy Wood doing 'I Wish it Could be Christmas Every Day' in the August sun. I have to admit that seeing Swarb getting on stage with Fairport at *Cropredy* was always special. His last appearance doing a rather disjointed 'Sir Patrick Spens' is special to me.

I have seen many concerts at various venues and hope to do many more. I attended a number of *Cropredy* days with a close friend. Along with many others he did not survive Covid. His funeral, which we could attend by video link, started with 'Meet on the Ledge'. Tears flowed, but it showed how important Fairport are to so many of us.

GONNA SEE ALL MY FRIENDS:
A PEOPLE'S HISTORY OF FAIRPORT CONVENTION

PHILADELPHIA FOLK FESTIVAL
30 AUGUST 1970, PHILADELPHIA, PENNSYLVANIA

CHRISTOPHER DOLMETSCH

I went to the *Philadelphia Folk Festival* in 1970 to see what I thought was Fairport Convention. This rag-tag crew came out onto the stage and started in on a song I can't recall, but I remember distinctly yelling out, 'Where's the chick (singer)?' And someone standing nearby replied: 'Oh her? She's split. Don't you know?'

TROUBADOUR
2 – 6 SEPTEMBER 1970, LOS ANGELES, CALIFORNIA

JOE BOYD

The opening night at the LA Troubadour was pretty special. We agreed with A&M Records that we would record them. Ricky Nelson was the headliner and Fairport the opener. They played their first set, then Ricky went on. But after his first set he came into their dressing room to tell them that he was unwell and wouldn't be going back out. It wasn't a full house, it was a Tuesday night, but A&M had got a lot of press and people down for Fairport, so Nelson, understanding that there were people there to see them, told them they had the whole night.

They did this great set and everybody loved them. But they didn't have a huge repertoire. They did the stuff from *Liege & Lief* and the stuff from *Full House*, but everyone was still clapping. Simon went up to the microphone and said, 'We don't have any more songs,' and the audience weren't too happy. Then he looked out, 'Well we could do some more songs if Linda would come up and sing with us,' and he pointed at Linda Ronstadt in the audience. This was before she was a big star, but she was well-known, she'd headlined at the Troubadour. She giggled and said, 'But I don't know any English folk songs.' 'That's okay, we know all your songs.' And people at her table pushed her up.

She didn't realise that these guys could play everything. They knew every country record, they knew every rock record, they knew everything. Richard could just sit down and play Duke Ellington or Davey Stewart or The Byrds, and the rest of them were also like that. She was looking very nervous, 'Well what are we going to do?' And Simon suggested 'Silver Threads and Golden Needles'. She thought about it for a minute and then I think she realised; she was absolutely petrified because on her record it starts with her voice, there's no instrumental intro, and I think she was hoping to get a feel of what the band was like before singing. But she knew she had to go a cappella before the band would come in on the downbeat.

She looked as though she was thinking, 'What the fuck have I got myself into?' But she began, she hit it and then they crashed in at the right moment, absolutely the arrangement on her record, note for note. And then it came to the break and Richard took a solo. The original solo on the record was by James Burton, and Richard just stepped forward and started quoting him but also going James Burton one better. And Linda was astonished. They kept playing then for another hour, covering her songs, and doing country favourites.

Everyone was in ecstasy. The next morning all the A&M executives were talking about Fairport, and what a great night it was. That was a pretty great memory.

JIM BICKHART

I saw the band when they returned for another US tour and played at the Troubadour again. After their May visit to the Troubadour, during which they drank enough beer to use up their entire booking fee, Garcia and I prepared opening night invitations for the media to check them out both in LA and at the Bitter End in New York, which in part read, 'You better bring plenty aspirin, because Fairport's gonna drink you under the table.' Before it got to that point, Mattacks asked me to drive him to the San Fernando Valley to get new drumheads from the Remo factory store, which I was honoured to do.

Needless to say, a good time was once again had by all. This visit was the one which produced the *House Full* live album. It also was the one during which Led Zeppelin came to see FC and jammed a bit with them.

GONNA SEE ALL MY FRIENDS:
A PEOPLE'S HISTORY OF FAIRPORT CONVENTION

ROYAL ALBERT HALL
7 OCTOBER 1970, LONDON, UK

SUE TOPHAM

Three days since I'd arrived at university – a wide-eyed 19-year-old would-be hippie lass from Nottingham, rocking up to the well-known bastion of maleness that was Imperial College to study chemistry, knowing not a soul and wondering what would happen next in my life. A poster outside the Royal Albert Hall announced that Fairport Convention were on that night, so I bought a ticket and took up my standing space high in the gods. It was the only time I've ever been to a gig on my own, but I promptly found myself amongst a gaggle of like-minded souls.

Sue Topham was a 'would-be hippie'

The first memorable moment of the concert was the sight of support act Roger Ruskin-Spear sitting astride a large transparent inflated plastic tube, 'playing' it with his knees. Well, it was 1970!

That night's incarnation of Fairport was the line-up that made *Full House* (appropriately reprised beautifully at this year's *Cropredy* with Chris Leslie as a very capable substitute Swarb). At the 1970 concert I think they started with 'Walk Awhile' and finished with 'Sir Patrick Spens', with my favourite 'Sloth' coming somewhere in the middle. It was wonderful to have heard the band that made the record do it live. A memorable third evening in London for me.

The study of chemistry served me well in life, and Fairport has been a constant for me since the 1960s, waxing and waning and waxing as stuff happened in all our lives.

GONNA SEE ALL MY FRIENDS: A PEOPLE'S HISTORY OF FAIRPORT CONVENTION

CITY HALL
16 OCTOBER 1970, SHEFFIELD, UK

RICHARD GASCOYNE

I first saw Fairport on the *Full House* tour at Sheffield City Hall. My best concert memory is being at *Cropredy* and watching The Incredible String Band whilst standing in the field with Peggy and Robert Plant. We discussed the merits of the band and all agreed that it was great to see them again.

My favourite song has to be 'Golden Glove' as Julia and I fell in love to it. However, I have a real feeling for the live version of 'Wat Tyler' from the *Cropredy Box*.

I remember playing skittles after winning the *Cropredy* raffle. I think it was the last time we were able to do this. Peggy and I got smashed afterwards and ended up singing hymns.

BRIGHTON DOME
21 OCTOBER 1970, BRIGHTON, UK

STEPHEN ROYSTON

This was my first Fairport concert. Simon came on stage alone, and explained that the rest of the band had all gone for a wee! He did his best to entertain the audience with his repartee until they trooped on stage and went into 'Walk Awhile' followed by 'Dirty Linen'. 'Right, that's two-thirds of side one,' he commented, before they started their next number. They were joined later by Brighton singer Allan Taylor, one of their support acts, to accompany him on his song, 'I'm A Senile Delinquent'.

FREE TRADE HALL
6 NOVEMBER 1970, MANCHESTER, UK

ROY TURNER, AGE 16

I was at Cropredy in 2022. Hearing Peggy recount how Swarb taught him to play mandolin brought to mind the time I first saw Fairport live. I went to see them at the Free Trade Hall when they performed their *Full*

House set. I remember distinctly that Simon and Swarb seemed to enjoy winding Peggy and Richard up, who both looked a bit uncomfortable with the banter – Richard was very serious and Peggy a bit nervous. When they got round to playing 'Dirty Linen', Swarb seemed to be baiting Peggy, who played the other mandolin, by telling everyone that this was a memory test in order to put him on the spot. Peggy got through it fine, much to his relief.

Roy Turner recalls onstage banter back in 1970

TOWN HALL
9 NOVEMBER 1970, OXFORD, UK

NIGEL BANKS

I was in my first term at college and keen to soak up as many new experiences as possible, having led a very sheltered life previously. I'd heard the name 'Fairport Convention', but knew nothing about the band's history, or what kind of music they played. I found myself sitting on the very back row of the town hall, unsure what to expect. The support acts were Allan Taylor, the folk singer and Roger Ruskin Spear's Giant Kinetic Wardrobe, a suitably bizarre act from the ex-Bonzo Dog member. There was an air

Nigel Banks was pinned to his seat by the volume

of anticipation as we waited for FC to take the stage. A diminutive figure dressed in a fringed, suede jacket with a gypsy earring, carrying a violin said, 'Side one, track one' and immediately launched into 'Walk Awhile'. I was pinned to the back of my seat by not only the sheer volume of the sound that issued forth but also the capering antics of said fiddler. Little did I realise at the time that this would be the start of a 50-year connection with the band and its various offshoots, which would take me to venues all over the country and cost me many shekels in terms of tickets, records, CDs and books – money willingly spent, I hasten to add.

As the performance continued through tracks from the *Full House* album, which would subsequently become ingrained in my consciousness, my eyes were drawn more towards the tall figure of the lead guitarist, who stood stock still but through whose magical fingers amazing sounds flowed, the like of which I'd never heard before. This was also the beginning of my Richard Thompson idolatry, which also continues to this day.

The thought of being able to attend 2022's *Fairport Cropredy Convention* (after two years Covid hiatus) and see the *Full House* line-up (minus Swarb, of course, RIP) recreate the whole of that iconic album, represented a suitably poignant bookend to those halcyon student days and my initiation into the cult of Fairport Convention.

Nigel Schofield, Fairport's long-time archivist and collaborator, was at that same gig in Oxford in 1970. He had interviewed a couple of the band earlier in the day for a student magazine. We both remembered that the Town Hall management turned all the house lights on to stop the band playing as they'd overrun their allotted time. When we filed out, there were firemen in the foyer who'd been attending to a nearby incident and had somehow come into the Town Hall.

TWENTSE SCHOUWBURG
29 JANUARY 1971, ENSCHEDE, THE NETHERLANDS

FRITS WIELENS

The first time I came across the name Fairport Convention was on a sampler LP, *The Best of Island*, which was released in the UK as *You Can All Join In* and which included Fairport's 'Meet on the Ledge'. The front cover of the LP showed a bunch of Island artists in a park, of which only the Traffic guys were familiar to me. On the back of the sleeve, a few covers of released Island albums were reproduced, one being Fairport's *What We Did on Our Holidays*, showing a confusing but intriguing drawing.

When Fairport embarked on a short Dutch tour in January 1971 and Enschede was on their itinerary, I was unaware that, not only had the line-up changed from the *Holidays* album, but the entire repertoire as well. Little did I know that Richard Thompson had also recently left the band, and this was one of the first gigs without him.

So, having heard just the one song and as a visual, having only seen a small drawing of the band, I was surprised to see a four-piece Fairport appearing on stage that evening. I got a dodgy recording of the gig sometime later, and pieced together the band (Simon Nicol, Dave Pegg, Dave Mattacks and Dave Swarbrick) and the set list, with the aid of Fairport's back catalogue that I acquired quickly after seeing them. They opened with 'Walk Awhile' and it sounded sensational. I'd never heard anything like it. 'Dirty Linen' and 'Sloth' followed, and there was even a rare performance of 'Sir William Gower' on the tape.

I kept the review, which appeared the following day in the local paper, and it mentions, 'What Fairport showed in front of a packed house last night stood out and one can assume and hope that they will be around for years to come.'

When I became aware of past members pursuing their own careers, I followed them all. I was lucky to see The Albion Country Band in The Netherlands in 1972 and 1973, and at a Steve Ashley (ex-Albion Country Band) solo folk club gig in the early 1970s, I met another Fairport fan with whom I forged a long-lasting friendship. I went to see the Albion Country Band at the 1973 *Cambridge Folk Festival* and bought the first Planxty album as they were also appearing at Cambridge. After seeing them I delved into Irish music, culminating in an Irish holiday and finding (and marrying) the love of my life, leading to a permanent move to Ireland in 1978.

Over the years I've been to 18 or 19 more Fairport shows, including every Dublin show since 1978, the last one in January 2022. They were all very enjoyable but that very first one in 1971 was special and is probably the reason why *Angel Delight* is one of my most played Fairport albums. 51 years later and the memory of that first Fairport gig still resonates.

GONNA SEE ALL MY FRIENDS:
A PEOPLE'S HISTORY OF FAIRPORT CONVENTION

BRT
JANUARY 1971, SCHAAEBEEK, BELGIUM

MARIUS ROETING, FREELANCE MUSIC JOURNALIST AND RADIO PROGRAMMER, THE ROOTTHING AGENCY

It was the beginning of the 1970s when my father bought a reel-to-reel tape machine. It was a simple one, but it had two microphones. I figured out how it worked and bought some tapes. One evening, I was watching television and zapped to the Belgium BRT TV channel. Four or five English musicians had just started a show. Their music inspired me immediately. I was in my teens and had just discovered British folk music. But who were these guys?

They had a long-haired guitar player (Simon), a lanky bass player (Peggy), a drummer wearing glasses (Mattacks) and a non-stop smoking and fiddling fiddler (Swarb), who also sang a couple of songs (I can't remember if he had a cigarette between his lips or not). There was possibly a curly-haired guitarist too (RT). The titles of the tracks were on screen, but there was no band name, or if there was, I had missed it because I was too busy handling the microphones as I recorded their set on the reel-to-reel. There was no stereo, of course, as it was just a black-and-white television with a mono speaker, and definitely not high fidelity. But it didn't matter to me. The music was great.

I remember they performed 'Sloth', 'The Journeyman's Grace', 'Walk Awhile' and probably 'Sir Patrick Spens', so it was around the time they released the album *Angel Delight*. But I couldn't catch their name.

The next day at school, I talked about it with my schoolmates. Two brothers, who always had 'the newest of the newest' releases, did some research and told me they were sure the band was called Fairport Convention. So, at the weekend,

Marius Roeting taped Fairport from a Belgian TV broadcast

I went to the record store where I found some albums by that band. I took home copies of *Full House* and *Liege & Lief*. The spell was broken. I bought the then-back catalogue and have complemented it with almost every release since. The healthy Fairport Convention disease had grabbed me and continues. I have been privileged to see Fairport play festivals, clubs and theatres over the years and have even organised gigs at the Arsenaaltheatre in Vlissingen (a double bill with the Dylan Project in December 1998) and at the Acoustic Convention in December 2000, as well as interviewing past and present members. All thanks to a reel-to-reel tape machine.

AINSDALE BEACH
30 JUNE 1971, SOUTHPORT, UK

TERRY NIGHTINGALE, AGE 15

My history of following the band goes all the way back to June 1971. I had spent the day earning some pocket money down on my friend's farm. In the late afternoon, his older sister and her boyfriend pulled up and said, 'Get in, we are going to a concert on the beach at Ainsdale,' about eight miles away. I'd never been to a live gig but had a liking for *Top of the Pops*. This was my first experience of folky stuff. The location was the Sandhills, and it was ideal; the stage was in the centre with the crowd banked up around it and I remember everyone having good views of the performance. The concert was filmed for Granada TV, and featured Fairport and Steeleye Span. I remember some mayhem at the end when the electric was turned off because we wanted more.

This experience set me off on a love of folk. A couple of weeks later I went out and bought *Angel Delight* and played it to death. I've since spoken to Peggy at The Atkinson in Southport about the gig, and he told me he remembers it well – he got his car stuck in the soft sand. Maddy Prior told me she has fond memories of the night too. It was well and truly a watershed moment for me.

PAUL TURNER

I'd been vaguely aware of a band named Fairport Convention but hadn't really taken much notice. Then in 1971, a friend suggested we hop on the train from Crosby to Ainsdale sand dunes as Granada TV were recording a free show featuring FC and Steeleye Span. Well, I enjoyed Steeleye's set, but was just bowled over by Fairport. Thus began my lifelong following of the band.

Later that summer, I bought *Angel Delight* and was playing the LP at home when my grandmother happened to call in. She was always interested in my (and my sister's) musical tastes and asked me what was playing. I showed her the LP sleeve, and to my amazement she recognised Swarb – and proceeded to tell me she'd seen him and Martin Carthy when my aunt took her to a folk concert in Solihull back in the mid-Sixties.

When the *"Babbacombe" Lee* album was released, I bought it (naturally) and it transpired there was another link – my Nana had seen the silent movie made of Lee's story at a cinema in Bootle way back in the 1920s – and she remembered that John Lee himself (or possibly the actor who played him in the film?) made a personal appearance and talked about his life. Later, when chatting to my then-wife's maternal grandmother – whose late husband had been the manager of that very same cinema – she also remembered the film and the talk – which she had always believed was given by Mr Lee.

In 1979, after seeing FC live a number of times and buying all the LPs, I was gutted to hear of the band's decision to jack it in. I wrote off and procured two tickets for the *Farewell* gig at Cropredy, never ever thinking that I'd be a regular camper in that very field many years later. My pal couldn't make it, so my sister accompanied me, and developed a taste for Theakston's Best Bitter – 'just a half' was uttered numerous times that day. (We slept in my car, in a layby that turned out to be the entrance to a sewage treatment works.)

There's a generation missing from this tale so far – but that was rectified in the 1980s when my sister and I decided to take our mother along to see FC at the Southport Arts Centre; at the interval, we left Mum standing by the stairs while we queued at the bar. Drinks eventually procured, we returned to find Mum holding a half-consumed pint of beer. Peggy's beer – he'd come out to chat to fans, someone asked him for his autograph, and so he asked the nearest person – Mum – to kindly hold his glass for a minute. We were gob smacked, she was a little starstruck, and Peggy was of course the perfect gentleman, thanking Mum profusely with a huge smile.

Actually, four generations of my family have a Fairport Connection, as I took my two sons to Cropredy in the mid-'90s, and they too had the pleasure of seeing Swarb playing 'in the flesh'.

LINCOLN FESTIVAL, TUPHOLME MANOR PARK
24 JUNE 1971, LINCOLN, UK

LES JEARY
I'd heard them on the radio on *Top Gear* and bought the first album as soon as I could. It was so musical and different from anything else. I never saw them live, just missing them at Glastonbury in 1971, but I saw the boys (minus Swarb) backing Sandy at *Lincoln Festival* the same year. Geniuses. They were never as good without Thompson.

WINTERLAND BALLROOM
28 & 29 OCTOBER 1971, SAN FRANCISCO, CALIFORNIA

JIM BICKHART
After Richard T departed and Simon and the Daves recorded *Angel Delight*, they came back on a US tour opening for Traffic, playing a series of large venues and sounding like a streamlined version of the *Full House* band. Simon did yeoman work as a lead guitarist. As A&M was preparing *Angel Delight* for release just prior to the tour, my ambitious self somehow managed to convince the label to let me replace road manager Robin Gee's oblique liner notes from the British release with a little essay I called 'By way of explanation…'. That was nice of the suits. When the Traffic tour hit Winterland in San Francisco, several of us went up and hung out with Fairport at a Japanese restaurant before the show. Simon generously complimented me on the liner notes, and everybody got a buzz on drinking sake at a

Japanese restaurant before heading over to the show.

1971 was an interesting time. In sequence, Richard Thompson visited LA as an accompanist for Iain Matthews and then Sandy Denny. Both played at the Troubadour. Iain's record label threw a release party for *If You Saw Thro' My Eyes* during which I met him for the first time. When Sandy was touring for *The North Star Grassman and The Ravens* I got to meet her for the first time as well.

VAN DIKE CLUB
25 NOVEMBER 1971, PLYMOUTH, UK

MARTIN SATTERTHWAITE

I was working at Island Records and Island was the first record company in the country to have their own field promotion team – people looking after radio, press and things like that. This was mainly because, at that time, Island had a lot of artists out on the road, and Fairport were one of them.

One of the first gigs I was at, doing local promotion, was down in Plymouth. They were promoting the *"Babbacombe" Lee* album. It's an infamous gig because it was at the Van Dike Club, and it got raided by Devon and Cornwall's finest, plus the Royal Navy military police. They raided the club and I believe that they found, or

Martin Satterthwaite (right) with Dave Pegg

something was put in, Mr Swarbrick's violin case.

He had to go to court. I was on the front door with the owner, Peter Van Dike. He was arrested for supposedly assaulting a police officer, which he didn't, and I had to go to court and testify on his behalf. I don't think Swarb was convicted of anything, although he may have got a small fine. That was the very first time I met the band.

In the mid-Seventies, they were on tour in Aberdeen, and I said to the hotel manager, 'Can you just arrange a couple of sandwiches and a couple of beers for the band when they come back from the gig?' We got back from the gig, and it was absolutely ridiculous.

He showed us into this room which was one of the banqueting suites at the hotel and there was a massive banquet laid out for the band, with the centrepiece being a pig's head with an apple in its mouth. There must have been catering for 50 to 100 people. I got into a lot of trouble with the record label because somebody had to pay for that. I found out subsequently that Paul McCartney had been there the week before and so this hotel manager thought that all bands want that sort of thing after the gig. That was fairly costly.

The first *Cropredy Festival* was held in the garden of Richard Crossman, the Labour MP, who had moved to the village. He had a lovely big house. I've been to every one since then.

In the mid-Eighties, my two kids were born. My son is 35 now and he loves going. It's the same for so many people. The parents went and the kids are going now. It's really expanded in the 40-plus years since that first one. It's got a reputation as Britain's friendliest festival. People go there with their families. There's never any trouble. It's not like a big rock 'n' roll festival. There's a place for the kids where they have entertainers and conjurors and suchlike. There's something for everybody. And there are offshoots in the village as well.

One year, Brian 'Goldbelt' Maxine – the wrestler, and friend of the band who had put out a couple of albums – appeared at Cropredy. We formed a little group called the Fairpets to back him vocally. And I remember at the time Peggy said, 'I don't know what this band's coming to.' There were three of us, including Alec Leslie, who was their promoter at the time.

GONNA SEE ALL MY FRIENDS:
A PEOPLE'S HISTORY OF FAIRPORT CONVENTION

RAINBOW THEATRE
27 NOVEMBER 1971, LONDON, UK

ROB JEFFRIES, AGE 17

Watching Edward II at *Cropredy 2022* perform a Caribbean medley which included 'Day-O (The Banana Boat Song)' and 'Yellow Bird' sparked a Fairport memory for me going back to 1971.

My first experience of the band was as a 17-year-old schoolboy growing up in Hackney, East London. I was persuaded by some mates to go with them to watch Fairport play at what used to be the Finsbury Park Astoria. All I knew about Fairport was that they were a popular 'electric folk' group but I was eager for my first experience of live music.

Rob Jeffries was transported back to 1971

The warm up act was a young singer, song-writer named Jonathan Kelly. I was fascinated by his vivid tales including stories of disappearing woodland nymphs, social injustice and unrequited love. Fairport took the stage and immediately launched into 'Walk Awhile' and... I was hooked.

Their set was divided into two parts. In the first part they played their popular (although new to me) standards. During part two, they played their latest album release, *"Babbacombe" Lee*, in its entirety. I was held spellbound as the story unfolded and the music changed from sea shanties, jigs and reels to laments and narrations. Eventually, we were told how John Lee's conviction and resultant death sentence for murdering his landlady was ultimately commuted to life imprisonment after the gallows apparatus failed to end his life on three separate occasions.

Modern concert venues have time schedules, and everything must run strictly to the clock. Things were rather different in 1971. John Lee had survived the gallows for yet another performance, but it seems Fairport

Convention were not ready to call it a night and asked the audience for their requests.

We were in the cheap seats, very much towards the back of the stalls, and since we didn't really know the band, we couldn't offer any suggestions but others nearer the stage certainly did, and the band launched into several extra songs which were all received with enthusiastic applause.

As soon as they finished each request, the band would shout out, 'Any more?' and I can remember there was one particular member of the audience (possibly under the influence of alcohol) who kept on shouting out, very loudly, 'Play 'Yellow Bird'.' The band took it all in good humour but ignored his pleas. Nevertheless, at every opportunity, he continued to shout out, 'Play 'Yellow Bird'!' Dave Swarbrick was becoming increasingly irritated with this bloke going on about his 'bloody 'Yellow Bird'!'

And so, we didn't hear 'Yellow Bird' that night, or indeed at any other Fairport Convention concert over the years… until August 2022, when Edward II at last put the record straight. In the cab back to our hotel, I did wonder if perhaps the man who had made those impassioned requests all those years ago at the Rainbow had been at *Cropredy* in 2022 and, if he was, whether he was smiling at the memory as much as I was.

YOUNGER HALL, UNIVERSITY OF ST ANDREWS
NOVEMBER 1971, ST ANDREWS, UK

FRASER NIMMO

I first encountered Fairport convention in 1971 when I was a student at St Andrews University. They were The Beatles of folk music. That's the only way you could describe them. It was Swarb, Simon Nicol, Dave Mattacks and Dave Pegg. They came to play in the Younger Hall, a daunting, dark and rather forbidding building. It was rather like being in church, a hallowed hall where you behaved yourself and where you failed exams – and, if you were lucky, you graduated.

We sat in reverential silence waiting to be entertained. I was quite prepared to hate them because I was an acoustic guitar player and a great Corries fan. Fairport walked out and knocked all of that into an eagerly awaiting waste bin in one minute flat. Simon looked up at this Gothic-vaulted ceiling and said, 'Some of you are going to hear this twice,' which was the wittiest thing I'd heard in a long time. They just blasted into 'Dirty Linen' and all of my preconceived ideas about these upstarts mixing electricity and folk music were blown away. It was a road to Damascus experience. I was a committed fan within two minutes.

BELFRY HOTEL
29 APRIL 1972, SUTTON COLDFIELD, UK

JOHN TWIGGER

I used to meet Dave Pegg at The Boot Inn, in Sutton Coldfield. Over the years I would bump into him at various clubs – the Carlton Ballroom, Mothers and the Belfry, with my friend Andy Everett. I went to the Belfry in April 1972 to see Fairport, and it turned out to be a momentous day in my life as I met my wife there.

On my wife's 25th birthday we were on a canal trip with my parents in Oxfordshire, and we decided to spend the night at Cropredy. We booked a meal at the Rose and Crown in the afternoon and walked through this lovely Oxfordshire village when suddenly we heard music playing. I knew nothing of the *Cropredy Festival* at the time but recognised Fairport music playing,

We started going to *Cropredy*

John Twigger met wife Bernadette for the first time at a Fairport gig

regularly. We have made some wonderful friends there and had some lovely times. We will be celebrating our 50th anniversary at *Cropredy Festival*, as it always coincides with the date of our wedding. We always get a mention on stage for our anniversary, and raise a glass to the many people who we have lost along this road.

LISEBERG AMUSEMENT PARK
18 MAY 1972, STOCKHOLM, SWEDEN

KURT THULIN

I first heard of Fairport Convention in 1969. The local newspaper enthusiastically reviewed *What We Did on Our Holidays*, calling the band England's answer to one of my favourites, Jefferson Airplane. Next day I went to the record store to have a listen. Stunned by the beautiful acoustic guitar arrangement and Sandy Denny's voice on the opener, 'Fotheringay', I immediately bought the record.

Gothenburg has an amusement park, Liseberg, where they also arrange concerts. How thrilled were my six years younger brother and I when we heard that Fairport Convention were booked for a show in 1971? Sandy Denny, Ashley Hutchings and Richard Thompson had left and most bands would have called it a day, but not Fairport who were continuing as a four piece, with Simon Nicol on lead guitar. Their main songwriters having left, the group concentrated on fine arrangements of traditional songs. The four man concert was a big success, the band being in great form. During 'Dirty Linen', my friends and I joined hands and started a long line of jolly people dancing to their wonderful tunes.

The organisers must have taken note of the good vibes, as they booked the band for another gig the following year. This was a bigger show with

Kurt Thulin saw Fairport in Stockholm in 1972

Photos: Kurt Thulin

GONNA SEE ALL MY FRIENDS: A PEOPLE'S HISTORY OF FAIRPORT CONVENTION

the boys headlining. The support acts were Steve Tilson, who years later would write songs for Fairport, and Mott the Hoople in full glam rock outfits. Bass player Pete Overend Watts had silver boots up to his thighs and had dyed his hair silver. Very cool!

Fairport had been through further line-up changes since 1971. Simon and drummer Dave Mattacks had left and the band consisted of Daves Swarbrick and Pegg, who were joined by Peggy's old Brummy friend Roger Hill on guitar and Tom Farnell on drums.

The show was introduced with, 'Ladies and gentlemen, Fairport Convention!', which brought a big cheer from the audience. Many of the audience had clearly turned up the previous year. The atmosphere was electric, and people promptly joined hands in a long row reaching behind the park seats, around the big fountain and back around in front of the stage.

I will never forget that evening, and even though this short-lived Fairport line-up never recorded an album, they were wonderful live, doing great versions of songs from their recent album, *"Babbacombe" Lee*. Little did I know then that Dave Pegg would later become a dear friend. Who knows if that would've happened if it wasn't for that magical concert at an amusement park in Gothenburg.

GONNA SEE ALL MY FRIENDS: A PEOPLE'S HISTORY OF FAIRPORT CONVENTION

EMMANUEL COLLEGE
JUNE 1972, CAMBRIDGE, UK

CHRIS SAUNDERS

My first encounter with Fairport was at the Emmanuel College May Ball in June 1972. A few hours before it started, my tutor had come round to my digs and told me – unofficially – the result of my degree exam. It was good news, so there was plenty to celebrate. Fairport Convention shared the billing with Steeleye Span and an unknown group who – I must admit – made little impression on me as the lead singer seemed rather bored and wishing he wasn't there. They soon became better known, however: the lead singer's name was Brian Ferry and the group Roxy Music.

Fairport were last in the line-up. They didn't make it onto the stage until almost four in the morning, by which time the champagne had run out and it was daylight again. Simon was on his break at the time, but the big attraction of their gig was the return of Sandy Denny, who appeared with the three Daves. I can't claim to remember any of the playlist – I was probably a bit worse for wear, especially as I had been to another May Ball the night before.

RAINBOW PAVILION
6 AUGUST 1972, TORQUAY, UK

KATHERINE MILTON

My dad, Kevin Bennett, was the manager of Flox Records in Torquay during the 1970s. My dad's fond stories of his time at Flox have created some of my lasting memories, notably thanks to Fairport Convention. Fairport Convention passed through Dad's record shop along with thousands of other artists whilst he was there, but it is Fairport who – for me – characterise my dad as a record collector. After living in London for a spell, Mum and Dad returned to Newton Abbot in 1991. Dad has seen Fairport a number of times spanning the last five decades, including at Torquay Pavilions (in August 1972 and July 1976), Exeter (25th June 1971), and again in May 2015 he and Mum saw them at The Watermark, Ivybridge where Dad had a chat with Dave Pegg.

GONNA SEE ALL MY FRIENDS:
A PEOPLE'S HISTORY OF FAIRPORT CONVENTION

He has a number of autographs (on napkins) from the band from the '70s, as well as a number of their records in his collection. The stand out album for me, as it is for dad, is *"Babbacombe" Lee*. We're fascinated by the epic recount of John Babbacombe Lee, which I've only learned from Fairport, and Dad also loves it for 'I Was Sixteen', being 'the song where they sing about Newton Abbot': 'So it's off I went to Newton Abbot to get myself the deeds to sign,' the only song he's ever known to reference our home town. When I think of my dad, I think of Fairport Convention; when I think of Fairport Convention, I think of my dad!

Katherine Milton's dad Kevin always cheers the mention of Newton Abbott in the song 'I Was Sixteen'

STEVE WHITEFIELD

I discovered Fairport when *Angel Delight* came out. At that time, *Top of the Pops* weirdly had an album spot where each week someone would play two tracks from their new album. They played 'Lord Marlborough' and the intro immediately grabbed my attention. It was a musical epiphany for me. Then they played the title track. I bought the album as soon as I could and fairly soon after that I saw them live at Torquay Pavilion with the line-up of Swarb, Peggy, Simon and Dave M. Another revelation and the beginning of a lifelong affection for them.

Steve Whitefield discovered Fairport via *Top of the Pops*

DAVID PEARCE

In the summer of 1972, my mate Clive and I were 16 years old and serious young long-haired folk rock geeks. Sat cross-legged on the floor, we listened endlessly to *"Babbacombe" Lee*, having serious discussions on the evidence of the case, the verdict and, obviously, the playing of Messrs Nicol, Pegg, Mattacks and Swarbrick. I can't sit cross-legged on the floor anymore… I get cramp.

THE HISTORY OF FAIRPORT CONVENTION RELEASED 10 NOVEMBER 1972

RICHARD GASCOYNE

The weekend following the release of the *History* double album, a favourite uncle of mine visited us. He was a very clever man, an incredible music teacher and musician. I was playing the album and my uncle commented, 'It's too early for a 'History' album, and bands like Fairport Convention won't last long anyway.' He went on to say that Fairport would be finished in 18 months' time. He lived long enough for me to tell him about the 25th anniversary, which he gracefully acknowledged was a great achievement.

TOP RANK
10 NOVEMBER 1972, SUNDERLAND, UK

PETER SMITH

I have always recognised the importance of Fairport Convention in the history of rock and pop music, and particularly folk-rock. I've seen them several times in concert, in many different venues, spanning a 50-year period. I first discovered them when at school. I used to play 'Meet on the Ledge' a lot when I was younger; it featured on the album *You Can All Join In*, which was a popular low price sampler album of the late-1960s. Everyone at school had the album and 'Meet on the Ledge' was a favourite track. I also had a Polydor three LP record box set, which was called *Pop Party*, and had a couple of very early Fairport tracks on it, including 'If I Had a Ribbon Bow', which I thought was great fun. I also love 'Who Knows Where the Time Goes?'.

My first exposure to Fairport Convention live in concert was in 1972 when the line-up was (probably) Dave Swarbrick – fiddle, mandolin, vocal; Dave Pegg – bass guitar, mandolin, backing vocals; Jerry Donahue – guitar; Trevor Lucas – guitar, vocal; Dave Mattacks – drums, keyboards, bass guitar.

Jerry Donahue had just joined the band, from the USA, and gave them a much rockier and louder edge. I remember being surprised just how loud the band were, particularly for a folk-rock group. Their set list at the time included favourites such as 'Matty Groves' and – surprisingly – covers of rock 'n' roll songs by Jerry Lee Lewis and Chuck Berry (presumably the influence of Jerry Donahue). I also remember being disappointed that they did not play 'Meet on the Ledge'.

RUTHERFORD COLLEGE, KENT UNIVERSITY
NOVEMBER 1972, CANTERBURY, UK

ALAN PROSSER

I saw them at Rutherford College at Kent University around the time of *Nine*. I was blown away. Swarb had a row of joints on his amp and proceeded to chain smoke. I'd been at the cookies, and it made for a most fun gig. Donahue and Swarb made the sparks fly!

GREAT NGARUAWAHIA MUSIC FESTIVAL
7 JANUARY 1973, NGARUAWAHIA, NEW ZEALAND

DES COLLINS

It was a blazing hot day in the hills of the Waikato, New Zealand. I was sitting on a camp seat in front of a stage. It was New Zealand's first rock festival – the *Great Ngaruawahia Music Festival*. In the distance there was nude swimming in the river, but I was waiting for the *NME*'s most promoted bands of the time. Top billing for the festival was shared by the extremes of English music, Black Sabbath and Fairport Convention.

Fairport ambled on to the stage, tuned their instruments in the heat, broke a string, and then went into Dylan's 'Country Pie'. Dave Swarbrick was supreme on the mandolin, playing at breakneck speed. Dave Mattacks and Jerry Donahue played with taste, the clear Fender notes ringing out, while Dave Pegg rolled along with his booming base. When Trevor Lucas sang, we all realised he was an Aussie – shame. But the highlight was when the bubbly, capricious Sandy Denny was introduced. Her clear rendition of 'Who Knows Where the Time Goes?' stilled the field.

I have seen Fairport since, when I lived in England in the Seventies, and finally got to *Cropredy* in 2009. I have every CD and DVD, lots of vinyl and the t-shirts but is that enough? I wonder why the band rattle around in a van over the English winter when they could be in the sun at one of the many festivals in this country. Come on lads, we are all getting older.

ROSIE RELEASED FEBRUARY 1973

DAVE RUSSELL

We were fresh-faced sixth formers at Quarry Bank High School in Liverpool, alma mater of one John Winston Lennon. The sixth form had a very free and easy common room – an adventurous idea in those far off days, and an album called *Rosie* suddenly started appearing tucked under the arm of some of the cognoscenti; a badge of honour that one was into this new-fangled folk rock. It was the run-up to our A-levels and a few of us were collaborating on revision, often helped along by listening to some new music. We thought we'd look into the back catalogue of the band who recorded *Rosie* and thus I chanced upon a

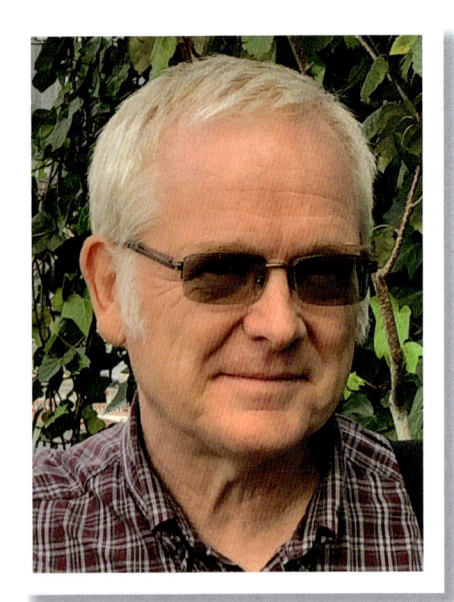

Fairport are woven into Dave Russell's life

record called *Full House*. It's impossible to overstate the sudden excitement of hearing 'Walk Awhile' for the first time; akin to the first time I heard 'She Loves You' by The Beatles. Here was a way of taking folk-influenced music, which I already loved, and doing something new and even more vibrant with it.

Since then, Fairport have woven their thread through my life as they have for so many others. I have so many memories: Sandy and Trevor; 'Farewell, Farewell' at Cropredy in 1979; Swarbrick, Nicol and Pegg acoustic at Liverpool University in 1980; Simon staying with us during his brief foray into solo folk club touring; the gradual return to annual tours; our numerous returns to North Oxfordshire; bumping into the band in Malmo, Sweden in 2003 and sharing a drink in the green room; Peggy joining my folk band on stage at Middlewich Folk Festival in June 2006; Peggy and then Maart depping on bass for the Family Mahone when we trod the Cropredy boards in 2008; and second son Greg, BBC Young Folk Award winner, strutting his stuff on that very same stage in 2013.

And most recently, in 2022, nearly 50 years on from that first hearing and Simon's final dulcimer chord of 'Flowers of the Forest' rang out in the Oxfordshire night and the circle was complete. I shed a small tear…

JON HERD

In 1973, when I was aged eleven, my older sister was going out with a local DJ in our hometown of Ayr. He was very cool and trendy, with the biggest flares and hairiest sideburns, and would only play the coolest, trendiest music of the day – everything from Slade to Bowie, with various points of crassness in between. One day, while walking past my sister's room, I heard the most extraordinary music. She was playing a couple of promotional records that he had given her. He didn't like them and wouldn't play them in the discotheque as they didn't fit the definition of 'cool'; he had given them to her to dispose of. She didn't like them either, but I was transfixed. The records were the newly released *Rosie*, and *The History of Fairport Convention*. I had never heard anything like it, and my sister happily gave them to me.

Music without words, vocals that weren't American, songs which told a story – a world away from the pop charts. I still have those two records, and everything else produced by the band. 49 years on I am still a devoted fan. The music has helped me through my late childhood and entire adult life, and inspired me to take up guitar, mandolin and fiddle. I've been lucky enough to get to *Cropredy* a couple of times too. It has also introduced me to the wider Fairport family: Richard Thompson, Iain Matthews, the Albions, Maart, and off on tangents to John Martyn, Al Stewart, Home Service, Ralph McTell and many others. Thank you, Fairport Convention.

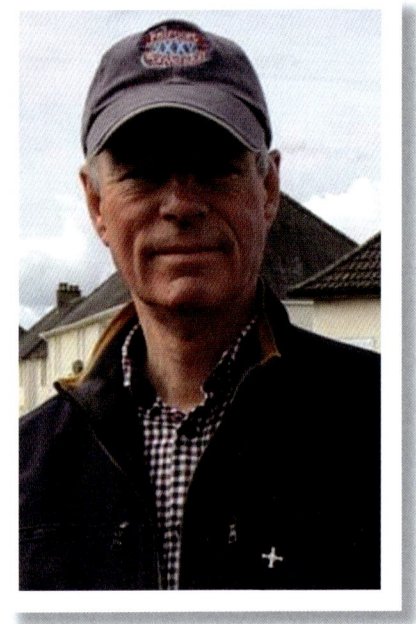

Jon Herd discovered Fairport because someone else decided they weren't cool

UNIVERSITY OF BRADFORD
9 FEBRUARY 1973, BRADFORD, UK

TIM MOON
El Pea. That's where I first encountered Fairport. Probably. I was working night shifts in a computer room. The Island sampler had 'Lord Marlborough' and it intrigued me enough to look further. I saw a solo Richard Thompson playing at *Great Western Festival* in Lincoln and, pre-internet delving, linked it together. I saw them live at Bradford University with the *Rosie* line-up of Peggy and Swarb, DM, Jerry Donahue and Trevor Lucas. They played songs from the album, 'Country Pie' and jigs. I was won over. Subsequently I went to every gig I could, back at Bradford with Sandy back in the band, the same line-up at Salford where a rough crowd chanted that they wanted Fairport not Fotheringay (can you imagine?) and cans flew. DM stormed off stage after telling the audience he wasn't there for their target practice and Trevor threatened to jump into the crowd and smack a few faces. After the band played

a few drummer-less numbers, DM returned. Soon it was the return of Simon to join Swarb and Peggy and Bruce Rowland for such friendly warm shows that I still love that line-up, and seeing that farewell tour left a lump in my throat. But then they were back with my acquaintance

Tim Moon has been on the Fairport journey for nearly 50 years

from Yorkshire, Maart Allcock, and around that time I steadily became friends with the band, drinking Guinness backstage with Peggy in Leeds and seeing every tour, the early *Cropredy Festivals*, the playing with Peggy and Chris in sessions. Such a band, such a history, such a journey.

YOUNGER HALL, UNIVERSITY OF ST ANDREWS
26 FEBRUARY 1973, ST ANDREWS, UK

FRASER NIMMO

In 1973 they came back to the Younger Hall but with a different line-up. It was Swarb, Trevor Lucas, Jerry Donahue, Peggy and Tom Farnell. I was already an established folksinger, and I was asked by the university to open for them with my little group, the Nimmo Children and Craig Gilbert. Craig was a banjo player, and my brother Gibby played the bass. It was a full house, and we did quite well – we didn't get booed off – and everybody was anticipating a repeat of the previous visit by Fairport. But it was sadly disjointed, and it didn't have the same feel to it.

The music was good, but the content was somewhat questionable. It culminated in the late great Trevor Lucas singing a song, the chorus of which went, 'If it was raining virgins, I would be locked up in the dunny with a poof.' I was sitting right at the front, and a lot of female students from the women's liberation group were there and they started chanting and throwing empty beer cans and stuff at the stage. It was quite polarising. I polarised myself up to the back of the hall in order to survive.

Despite the questionable material, Trevor Lucas was a truly great singer and had the first acoustic guitar I ever saw that plugged in. It's commonplace now, but at the time it was a revelation.

Fraser Nimmo played the St Andrews show with Fairport

STATE THEATRE
20 MAY 1973, SYDNEY, AUSTRALIA

IAN JONES

It was as an avid reader of *Melody Maker* from the late 1960s that I discovered Fairport Convention. I first purchased the local version of the *Unhalfbricking* LP and was hooked. I still remember walking into Phantom Records in Sydney and finding an import copy of *Full House*. I then gradually continued to purchase all the Fairport vinyl. Fairport finally started to tour to Australia as did Steeleye Span and Pentangle. I first saw Fairport at Sydney's ornate State Theatre in May 1973. They were supported by local country rock group Country Radio. The band was touring the *Rosie* album and their special guest was Trevor's wife, Sandy Denny.

The next gig was the magical concert at Sydney Opera House concert hall in January 1974. Sandy was in the band and her performance was breath-taking. The concert was subsequently released as *Fairport Live Convention*.

GONNA SEE ALL MY FRIENDS:
A PEOPLE'S HISTORY OF FAIRPORT CONVENTION

In August 1975 Fairport returned to the Hordern Pavilion, located at the Sydney Showground. Once again Sandy was in the band. The support act was Greg Quill, who'd had his band, Country Radio, support in Fairport in 1973.

After a Ralph McTell concert at Sydney's City Recital Hall in March 2019, I met up with old Fairporter John Penhallow. John introduced me to Trevor and Sandy's daughter, Georgia, and it was so delightful to be able to tell Georgia how much I'd enjoyed her parents' music and the wonderful 1974 concert at the Sydney Opera House.

ROSKILDE FESTIVAL
1 JULY 1973, DARUPVEJ, ROSKILDE, DENMARK

RICHARD MAJER
I travelled to Roskilde and the third day of the festival just to see Fairport. It was a jaw dropping experience.

Photos: Richard Majer

Richard Majer was at Roskilde in 1973

GONNA SEE ALL MY FRIENDS:
A PEOPLE'S HISTORY OF FAIRPORT CONVENTION

EMPIRE THEATRE
28 AUGUST 1973, EDINBURGH, UK

GRAHAM SPENCER

I was introduced to Fairport by my best mate Pete who came round to my house one evening late in 1972 clutching an album which he told me I had to listen to. The album in question was *Angel Delight* – I did play it and I was hooked, so much so that I went to our local record store in search of more music by this band.

Graham Spencer first saw Fairport in the summer of 1973

As luck would have it the shop had just taken delivery of stock of a newly released album – *The History of Fairport Convention*. I purchased a copy and the two discs went on heavy rotation, being played virtually non-stop while I eagerly read the excellent sleeve notes and Pete Frame's family tree on the front of the sleeve, giving some excellent background info for fans old and newbies like me, wondering how on earth this great music had passed me by.

I quickly went about rectifying that omission and my record collection expanded as I tracked down all of the albums from *Fairport Convention* to *Rosie*. All that was missing was an opportunity to see the band live and in the summer of 1973 that opportunity was to arise.

Bruce's Record Shop – an excellent independent institution in Edinburgh – were putting on a series of late-night concerts during the *Edinburgh Festival Fringe* in the Empire Theatre which, at the time, was a bit of a shabby relic, its glory days behind it, largely used for Bingo, thus the need for the concerts to be scheduled for very late in the evening after the last numbers had been called.

I happened to be in Bruce's one day in early summer and they had a notice up announcing a change to the programme. The Albion Country Band had been scheduled to appear but they had just split up and Bruce's were pleased to announce that they had booked Fairport Convention to take their place. Tickets were purchased on the spot.

So it was that, along with a couple of mates, we headed to the Empire Theatre to see Fairport, supported by Michael Chapman. It must have been close to midnight when Fairport took the stage but what a great show it was. *Nine* was a month away from being released so some of the set was unfamiliar but Messrs Swarbrick, Pegg, Mattacks, Lucas and Donahue played a stormer.

I went on to see Fairport live many times during the 1970s – with Sandy Denny back in the ranks, the 'Three Desperate Mortgages' (Swarb, Peggy and Simon) playing some wonderful music as well as providing backing for a (mercifully) short set by wrestler Brian Maxine, the short lived two fiddle line up with Roger Burridge and the great Dan Ar Bras on guitar and then the joy of seeing Simon back in the band full time in the *Bonny Bunch/Tipplers Tales* line up.

One gig that I remember vividly was their appearance at the short-lived *July Wakes Folk Festival* in Lancashire in 1977. The festival's main arena was usually used at that time for show jumping and the water jump was a little to the side of the stage and for some reason, the water hadn't been emptied out. Swarb announced to the crowd that the first person to jump in would win Simon's t-shirt. Someone duly jumped in and claimed his prize, which Simon reluctantly handed over, and then got his own back by setting a similar task but this time the prize was to be Swarb's trousers. Swarb's jeans were duly claimed by an audience member and the set was finished with a topless Simon and with Swarb in his underpants. Peggy had retreated well out of this and was almost hiding behind Bruce Rowland.

Then it was 1979 and as I was preparing for my final exams at university it was announced that Fairport were calling it a day and that their final, farewell appearance would be at a place called Cropredy. Well, I couldn't miss that so there I was in August 1979 to say a fond farewell to a band which had come to mean so much to me. It felt like the end of an era for me – I had just graduated and I was about to start a new job and at the same time my favourite band had split up.

News came of annual reunions but for one reason or another I never managed to get to any of them. Then in 1985 browsing in a record shop I came across an album with a blue sleeve and the name Fairport Convention. Was this some compilation? No, it was *Gladys' Leap* – a brand new album by a new three-man line up. No Swarb but with Dave Mattacks back in the fold along with Peggy and Simon and a batch of great songs. I was hooked all over again and delighted to see they were going to tour again, joined by Ric Sanders and Maartin Allcock.

The live shows in the late Eighties and early Nineties were an intriguing mix of old and new with the new boys making their mark on the music and Ric also making an impression with his peripatetic movement around the stage – his step count must have been massive during concerts in those days.

In due course Maart and DM left and along came Chris Leslie and Gerry Conway and I continued to look out for their new recordings and their visits to Scotland, playing venues large and small from the Royal Concert Hall and Old Fruitmarket in Glasgow and the Queens Hall in Edinburgh to the Bein Inn in Glenfarg in Perthshire where the capacity was 40 and only because the show was moved out of their regular basement venue into the Inn's dining room). The 40 of us were lucky to witness an excellent performance by the Acoustic version (at that time without Peggy) of the band really up close & personal.

Here we are now in 2022 and I'm delighted to say I'm still enjoying new Fairport experiences. I was lucky enough to be on the Rhine River cruise with the band in June when I fulfilled a lifelong ambition to sing with the band during their Beatles night – an unforgettable experience. I've also attended my first *Cropredy* since 1979 and had a magical time in the scorching heat – the cherry on the cake being for me to see Richard Thompson playing with the band for the first time in the *Full House* set.

Fairport and their music have been my companion since I first encountered them back in 1972 and that will, I'm sure, continue as long as I'm still upright and they're still going.

NINE RELEASED 5 OCTOBER 1973

JOHN GREY

In Brisbane, Australia, the year is 1973. I'm out of school and working in the city. Amongst my favourite reading material is *Nation Review*, a leftist weekly newspaper edited by co-founder of the notorious *OZ* magazine,

GONNA SEE ALL MY FRIENDS:
A PEOPLE'S HISTORY OF FAIRPORT CONVENTION

Richard Walsh. The regular music columnist raves about the A-side of the latest album by the English band, Fairport Convention. That record is *Nine* and I rush to the store to purchase the same. So, my first introduction to the group is the one-two punch of 'Hexhamshire Lass' and 'Polly on the Shore'. I'm hooked. So hooked that I quickly acquire the previous eight Fairport albums.

Boringly, my favourite album remains *Liege & Lief*. It's not my fault that it still sounds perfect to these ears, all these years later. (If I'm to have a least favourite it would be that '70s album where the 'Convention' half of the band was deleted.) My second favourite however varies from one year, one month, one day, to the next. Currently, it's *50:50@50* though I can't understand why the guy that sings 'Jesus on the Mainline' hasn't been offered a permanent position in the band. And I do have a soft spot for those two late '70s orphans, *Tipplers Tales* and *The Bonny Bunch of Roses*.

John Grey was hooked by *Nine*

The songs on my best of Fairport mix-tape would vary by the hour but here's ten random choice cuts: 1/ Simon's gallop through 'The Naked Highwayman', 2/ Chris Leslie's 'John Gaudie' tour-de-force, 3/ the 'Wat Tyler' history lesson, 4/ Sandy's 'Reynardine', the song I want played at my funeral or 100th birthday, whichever comes sooner, 5/ 'If I Had a Ribbon Bow', Judy Dyble and co at their quirkiest, 6/ Iain Matthew's wistful 'Book Song', 7/ 'Polly On The Shore' with its dour Trevor Lucas vocal beautifully counterpointed by the band's the evocative rendering of a naval battle, 8/ Peggy's 'Hungarian Rhapsody' travelogue, 9/ the oddest of covers – XTC's 'Love on a Farmboy's Wages', 10/ 'She Moves Through the Fair' – with such a redolent haunting title it doesn't even need to be a song – but it is and the combination of Sandy, Richard and the rest sounds as fresh to me now at it did back then.

Unfortunately, I've never been to *Cropredy* and have only seen the band twice in concert, both times in a small club in south-eastern Massachusetts. First was back in the '90s with Maart and DM still in the band. The second was in the 2000s with the current line-up. Talk about your intimate setting. During that last show, the bald-headed bass player rested his beer on my table. That didn't happen when I saw the Rolling Stones.

Lastly, I've always thought that Fairport Convention deserved a place in the Guinness Book of Records. And I don't mean for volume of alcohol consumed. I refer to the fact that Dave Swarbrick, Sandy Denny, Richard Thompson, Dave Pegg and Ashley Hutchings all have the honour of being represented by box sets, in some cases more than one. I don't believe there's any band, current or past, with five different members considered worthy of such an honour.

As a footnote, many years ago, when I first started dating the woman I would later marry, I did my best to convert her to Fairport. She did actually purchase her own copy of *Liege & Lief* but, somehow or other, that conversion didn't happen. Yet, at the time, she was a huge fan of Joan Armatrading. My cursory glance at the credits on Joan's self-titled third studio album revealed the names, Dave Mattacks on drums and Jerry Donahue on guitar. So, she was a Fairport fan. She just didn't know it.

PETER BROWN, AGE 14

In 1973, I was at the musically influential age of 14. In the spring of that year my sister-in-law got a job at the pressing and packing plant of Island Records in West Drayton, Middlesex. Each week, she was allowed to take a choice of an LP and hence often came home with a brand-new release – some popular, some obscure. As a result, my music experiences skyrocketed.

In the autumn she arrived

Peter Brown (left) tempted his friends with 'Big William'

home with Fairport Convention's *Nine*. To that date I had heard nothing of Fairport's output other than 'Si Tu Dois Partir'. *Nine* blew me away and set me up on a wider exploration of Fairport connections and folk rock generally. It remains my favourite album of theirs, as it has a real band feel and a range of music within the folk-rock genre from the 'Cherokee Shuffle' through to AOR folk rock ('Polly on the Shore'), country rock ('Possibly Parsons Green') and progressive folk ('Tokyo'). At the time, I would take *Nine* round to my friends and, amongst the other platters featuring The Sweet, Mud, Roxy Music, Alice Cooper, etc., I would venture to play what I felt was a potential folk pop classic, 'Big William', and my friends loved it too. Singing, 'You can put it where the monkey sticks his nuts' had great adolescent appeal.

FAIRFIELD HALLS
16 DECEMBER 1973, CROYDON, UK

NEIL WELLS

My first memory of Fairport is of 'Si Tu Dois Partir' on *Top of the Pops* in 1969. I was eleven years old and an avid *TotP*-watcher. Let's face it, that's all there was on TV except the late-night forerunner to *The Old Grey Whistle Test*, called *Disco 2*. On vinyl it came via the wonderful and cheaply-priced samplers that Island Records put out. My elder brother bought *Bumpers* in 1970 which featured 'Walk Awhile', and I acquired *Nice Enough to Eat* (with 'Cajun Woman' as the opening track) and *You Can All Join In* (with 'Meet on the Ledge'). So many of the essential, distinctive Fairport ingredients are – with hindsight – already there. I think it gets rather overlooked today that lots of people got to hear so many great artists thanks to these samplers.

Top of the Pops went through a phase of featuring album tracks so -

Neil Wells, who saw the Fairport Live line-up, and friend Robbie

along with appearances by the Strawbs ('The Hangman and the Papist', would you believe), Yes, and the Groundhogs – I recall seeing Fairport showcasing 'Angel Delight' on the show in 1971. There was life after Richard Thompson, and their infectious bonhomie – a golden thread that runs through all their iterations – shone through. By then I was also an avid reader of *Melody Maker* and the *NME*. If I hadn't heard all the music, at least I'd read about it.

My real turn towards Fairport as a big fan came in 1973 after the *Old Grey Whistle Test* clip of 'Polly on the Shore' by the Fairport *Nine* line-up, filmed in the gardens of the Brasenose pub in Cropredy. Our TV was still black and white. Unlike today, albums were expensive, while the gigs were cheap, and in my group of friends we each bought different artists' LPs. I was Steely Dan, Zappa and Zeppelin, and my school friend Robbie from just down the road (who had Beatles, Who and Stones records) bought *Nine* on the back of that clip. I still recall him bringing it round to my house one Saturday morning, together with *Clear Spot* by Captain Beefheart, possibly borrowed from one of his sisters. We both had elder siblings who were so useful like that. I therefore heard two of my all-time favourite albums in just one morning.

Robbie and I went to see Fairport after that, a couple of times at the Fairfield Halls and the Greyhound, in Croydon. Sandy Denny was back in the band by then, the *Fairport Live* line-up. Aged 15, gigs now became a regular feature of life. I've seen Fairport and Thompson countless times since. I was at the Cropredy 'Farewell' in 1979 and at Thompson's 70th bash at the Royal Albert Hall 40 years later. Nowadays, *Full House* is another strong favourite of mine.

Before I left the UK in 2007, I lived near Nettlebed in Oxfordshire. The folk club there is an absolute treasure, and a quiet secret. I saw Fairport doing an acoustic set (i.e., without Pegg on the bass) and my eleven-year-old son collected the band's autographs at half time. It was like a torch being passed to my younger generation – I certainly didn't do gigs with my father. I recall chatting with Dave Swarbrick, who played there with Martin Carthy around the same time, which was another lovely gig.

I'm not sure that those people who have left Fairport ever got to really leave. It is like a society they join and are forever a member of. Similarly, regardless of the actual line-up that convenes in the name of Fairport, there is a spirit they all share. Perhaps King Crimson is the only other band that has managed to ever get anywhere near that continuity, regardless of band members.

As a postscript, my old pal sent me the *Nine* CD with the bonus tracks a few years back. I hadn't realised how Country and Western that Fairport line-up were. Perhaps more 'flat cap' than 'big hat', but the American influence is there. By now, Robbie McIntosh has enjoyed an illustrious musical career of his own (on guitar with the Pretenders, Paul McCartney, and John Mayer to mention just a handful of artists). However, whenever I listen to *Nine*, I can become that 15-year-old music fan hearing it for the first time, and I rather suspect that the same goes for Robbie too.

JIM BICKHART

Nine was released in 1973 as the band's final A&M album and was considered a resurrection of sorts. When they came to LA as part of what they called a 'round the world tour', A&M hosted them in one of its recording studios for a private concert with both Sandy Denny and Joni Mitchell in the audience. Joni then took Sandy and a few others of us over to another studio, sat down at a piano and played instrumental versions of a couple of songs that would end up on *Court and Spark* the next year. I then was able to get Fairport back to UCLA for another lunchtime gig, with Sandy and all the members of Steeleye Span (who were playing in town) in attendance. That was another great afternoon.

They then went on to Australia, by which time Sandy had more or less rejoined. They recorded *Fairport Live Convention* (their first American Island release, as *A Movable Feast*), then eventually found their way back to the Troubadour in LA, where they played to a good reception. Between sets, in the small dressing room, I hyped Peggy on the idea of them recording RT's 'When I Get to the Border' (they already had Trevor Lucas singing 'Down Where the Drunkards Roll'), again to no avail.

During these visits I got to know Jerry Donahue, himself an LA native and great guy. After he left FC post-*Rising for the Moon*, he came back to LA, got married and we became acquaintances. He went to the same health club I did, so I'd see him there, and he played on some demo sessions

GONNA SEE ALL MY FRIENDS:
A PEOPLE'S HISTORY OF FAIRPORT CONVENTION

I produced later in the '70s. After his marriage ended, he went back to England, and I don't recall having seen him again until I ran into him at two FC gigs in LA in 2006. His subsequent debilitating stroke is a tragedy.

By sometime in 1974, Iain Matthews relocated to LA and recorded *Some Days You Eat the Bear*. After he toured to support that album, a friend from the local Island Records office invited several rock writers and musicians to play Sunday morning basketball at Hollywood High School. One of them was Steve Diamond, who'd played guitar for Iain on the tour. Somehow Diamond pulled Iain into those basketball games. A skilled footballer, Iain will never be mistaken for an accomplished point guard, but he seemed to have fun and kept showing up for the several months these games went on.

That led to Diamond (who's now an accomplished songwriter and producer in Nashville) and I working up a songwriter demo of Richard T's 'I Want to See the Bright Lights Tonight' for Island Music. We recorded the same evening as the LAPD shoot-out with the Symbionese Liberation Army took place, using a little independent studio called Dubbington Downs, where famed drummer Hal Blaine's drum kit was set up. We used it for the demo, which was an attempt to 'Linda Ronstadt-ise' what eventually became Richard's greatest hit with the help of Julie Covington. The music publisher fellow who hired us liked what we did, but I was told Richard wasn't taken with it.

For the rest of the '70s and into the '80s, the only Fairporters I came in contact with were Richard, Jerry, Simon and Peggy. Peggy was playing with Jethro Tull in 1979 and held court in his hotel after a Tull concert. He played his advance cassette of *Sunnyvista* and complained that Richard wouldn't hire him to play in the back up band at his gigs. But he still loved Richard and liked being on the album.

Around this same time, Richard finally began touring the US primarily as a solo acoustic act and would play McCabe's in Santa Monica when he periodically came to LA. Jerry had a little bar band he played with between session work called the Roommates, and a couple of times I gave Richard a ride to their gigs so he could sit in with them. This also was the period during which he was getting to know Nancy Covey who did bookings for McCabe's before his marriage with Linda ended. I tried to stay out of all that. At some point when he was visiting Ms Covey, he and I got together for a vegetarian breakfast in Santa Monica.

In what turned out to be the last show Linda did on the infamous Richard and Linda 'US tour from hell', to support *Shoot Out the Lights* in 1982, I snuck backstage at the Roxy in West Hollywood to say hello to Richard, Simon and Mattacks. Jerry was also there after having gotten on stage to play 'Hanks for the Memories' with Richard and Simon. Linda, who had performed admirably on stage, appeared to be in an agitated state but I did get a chance to say hello before Linda Ronstadt spirited her away. As I understand it, she never returned to finish out the tour (which had one or two more stops on the itinerary).

In 1984, Simon and Swarb came to the US to play some rollicking sets of vocal and instrumental folk as only they could do. Their set at McCabe's was a treat and it was nice to see and say hello to them both.

More recently, my main contact has been with FC when they've periodically visited LA, either as a full band or as Fairport Acoustic Convention, and with Richard at his various gigs in Southern California. There was a fine Fairport show at CalTech in Pasadena where I sat next to Jerry in the audience and then we went down to the stage to do a post-gig celebratory ritual. Then I went backstage with Ric Sanders and Chris Leslie where we pilfered various food goodies from the table the college had laid out for the band. FC's most recent US tours (none in the last decade or so) were definitely budget-conscious affairs, so no one could blame them for bagging up some fruit and snacks for the road.

I don't know if I'll ever make it to *Cropredy* or if I'll ever again see any of these folks, except possibly Richard, who still gets around the States periodically. Between pandemics and perilous politics, one never knows.

As many probably have seen, at some FC gigs Simon has taken to wearing shorts. I've recently joked with him via email that he must be doing it so he won't get carried away and go to extremes to show off his knees on stage as he did back in 1970. Once a career is probably enough for that. We also chatted once after a gig about the fact that neither of us have lost our hair. Small favours.

Neither has Simon lost his appreciation for the fact that he's been blessed with an opportunity to make a career of playing music in what probably seemed like an unlikely prospect when he first began. And I've been fortunate to have been able to spend a little, but long-lived, part of my life appreciating what he and all his partners have done over the years. Pegg once dedicated 'Meet on the Ledge' to me at a gig, and thankfully I haven't been blown off this mountain in the wind quite yet.

SYDNEY OPERA HOUSE
26 JANUARY 1974, SYDNEY, AUSTRALIA

ANDREW BROCKIS

In 1974 my wife Trish and I drove a minivan 4,000 kilometres across Australia from Perth to Sydney, 700 of them over unsealed, potholed gravel roads at only 40 kilometres per hour. It was a long trip. To entertain us on the way, friends gave us a cassette of music by a folk-rock band called Steeleye Span. We had never heard of them; they had yet to penetrate the antipodean consciousness, but on the journey, we fell in love with their style of music. Arriving in Sydney as wide-eyed tourists, we naturally went to see the Sydney Opera House and were given the option of a tour or attending a show. The show choices were Tommy Hanlon (a mediocre Australian variety act), or a band called Fairport Convention. We had never heard of the band, but anything had to be better than a dated music hall act.

And it sure was. This turned out to be what I think is the all-time best Fairport line-up: Sandy Denny, Jerry Donahue, Dave Pegg, Dave

Sandy was back in the band for the 1974 tour of Australia

Andrew Brockis and wife Trish chose Fairport over a variety act

Mattacks and Trevor Lucas. They were awesome, the crowd were dancing in the aisles. It got even better when the show was later released on record. If you don't have it, do yourself a favour and get a copy.

Since that day we have remained loyal Fairport fans. Long may they rule. Thanks for all the music.

TROUBADOUR
31 JANUARY 1974, LOS ANGELES, CALIFORNIA

CHUCK MOODY

On a rainy night in Los Angeles in late January 1974, I received a phone call that would have a tremendous impact on the course of my life. I was taking time off from school and living with my parents for a few months. My college roommate from the previous year, Chuck Mandel, called me to ask if I would like to go with him to the Troubadour to see a band he had seen play a free concert at Janss Steps on the campus of UCLA a few years earlier. He then said a name I had never heard before, Fairport Convention. When he described the style of music they played, I was intrigued and said, 'OK, I'm game.'

Chuck Moody met his wife Barbara as a result of being a Fairport fan

Chuck picked me up and we drove up to the Troubadour in West Hollywood. This legendary 500 seat club has witnessed so much astounding music over the years. We got there early and took seats down front on the right side of the stage near a piano. I had no idea what to expect. Being three months shy of my 21st birthday, I ordered a Coke and waited for the show to begin.

When the room lights dimmed, five guys took the stage: an Australian named Trevor, an American named Jerry and three Brits, all named Dave. When they started playing, I was immediately impressed with the talent being displayed: Trevor Lucas's rich baritone, Jerry Donahue's impossibly fast fingers on the fretboard, the rock solid rhythm section of DM and Peggy and the incredible presence of Swarb.

Swarb was on the right side of the stage, a blur of motion, dancing a jig while simultaneously playing his fiddle, smoking a cigarette and pulling draws from a bottle of beer. I had never seen anything like it. The five of them played three or four songs, including jigs and reels. I didn't know any of the material, but immediately felt that I was witnessing the best music being played in the world that night. And then it got even better.

After the first few songs, one of them said, 'We'd like to bring out a friend of ours,' and with that, out strode Sandy Denny. She took a seat at the piano we were sitting by. She sang with a voice so pure and clear that I was enthralled by the sheer beauty of it. I cannot give you any indication of what was played because, once again, I had never heard of them before, but it was all great. (Many years later, this gig was released as a bonus disc on the rerelease of *Rising for the Moon*. And I was there!)

At one point during the show, Sandy asked if anyone in the audience had a straw she could use. I was sitting down front, so I eagerly held up my straw. She asked me, 'What are you drinking?' I said, 'A Coke.' She looked at it and said, 'I guess that'll do.'

After this amazing show, I convinced Chuck to drive up to Tower Records on the Sunset Strip to look for an album of theirs. After much discussion, he convinced me to buy *Liege & Lief*. This became the first entry in what has become an extensive collection.

Over the next twelve years, I collected albums from Fairport and other bands in the folk rock movement. Fairport didn't appear on these shores during that period but I did get to see Richard Thompson a few times. On a visit to McCabe's Guitar Shop in Santa Monica in 1986, I noticed a flyer advertising a three week tour of the British Isles centred around the Cropredy Festival and run by Nancy Covey, Richard Thompson's wife at the time. So I went to Cropredy. It was an amazing time seeing the band that I had seen in a small club twelve years before in a cow pasture with 12,000 other people.

The tour was so much fun I immediately signed up for the tour in 1987. This included tickets for Fairport's warm up gigs at the Half Moon pub in Putney. Waiting for the show to begin, I noticed a woman in the front row with short blonde hair. This turned out to be Barbara Bannon, another person from the tour. We got to know each other and fell in love. I was living in Denver by then and she was living in Boston. After a year of travelling between the two cities, she joined me in Denver and we were married in 1989. We've had two children who directly owe their lives to a rainy night in Los Angeles in January 1974.

We have seen Fairport many times in the ensuing years and gotten to know many members of this extraordinary band. In 2017, Barb and I returned to Cropredy for Fairport's 50th anniversary and the 30th anniversary of our meeting. We stood on that hallowed field singing 'Meet on the Ledge' with tears streaming down our faces.

There is no better place in the world to be than in an Oxfordshire cow field in August. It all comes round again.

SANDERS THEATRE
10 MAY 1974, CAMBRIDGE, MASSACHUSETTS

KEN ROSEMAN

Although I owned all of the Fairport albums through to the 1974 'live' album, I did not actually see the band in concert until May 1974, in Cambridge, Massachusetts. I can't remember anything about the actual performance, but I did meet Sandy Denny and I got her autograph.

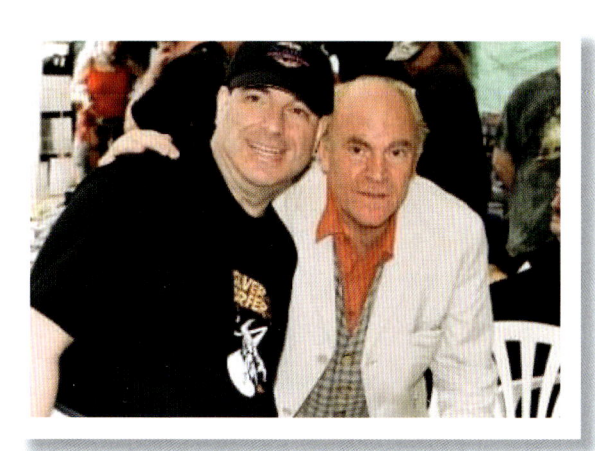

Ken Roseman with Ashley Hutchings

I did not see Fairport in person again until my first trip to England in 1983. I met Dave Pegg at the *Goodwood Festival*. He told me about Fairport's festival ('A Weekend in the Country') and gave me a ticket. One night I slept in someone's truck. The music was great, of course, but the most special thing for me was meeting the Guv'nor himself, Ashley

Hutchings. We had been corresponding for several years and I really enjoyed (and still do) those early Albion Dance Band, Albion Band and Albion Country Band albums.

Fairport regularly toured the United States throughout the 1980s and '90s. I saw them at the Birchmere in Alexandria, Virginia and Adams and the Bayou in Washington, DC. In 1985, a four member line-up of Fairport (Dave Swarbrick, Simon Nicol, Dave Pegg and Bruce Rowland) played a fantastic set opening for Steeleye Span at Lisner Auditorium, a venerable concert hall in Washington, DC. The after party was a late night dinner with all of the members of both bands at a restaurant in Dupont Circle. I could not have asked for better dinner companions.

I still follow Fairport Convention and the entire English folk rock scene. I have made many friends in that community. I look forward to the day when I can return to that sacred field in Oxfordshire, home of what is now called *Fairport's Cropredy Convention*. I am a Jewish guy who grew up in Maryland and Massachusetts. I do not know where my affinity for things English comes from, but I'm happy with it.

UNIVERSITY OF BIRMINGHAM
22 JUNE 1974, BIRMINGHAM, UK

JERRY FORD

The 1974 line-up was the *Nine* line-up, and my recollection is that the album provided the spine of the set list, but it also welcomed back Sandy Denny. This gig was filmed by some students at the Uni and I'm sure I've seen some very grainy footage on YouTube, but my story relates to the green room after the gig. A friend was involved in the filming, and he took us into the backstage area where the band were watching the film play back.

I was on my way to Arran from Exeter for a geology mapping exercise and had brought with me victuals for the journey, including a loaf of Polish rye bread. Happily, the loaf avoided the cascade of a pint of beer which had somehow sloshed over my trousers earlier in the evening. Feeling peckish while standing in company with Sandy et al, I broke off a piece of the loaf and gobbled it.

Sandy looked at my bread and I offered her some. Sadly, she really wasn't interested, although she may have wondered why my hitherto very smart two-piece denim safari outfit smelt quite so beery and looked so damp. Meanwhile, Trevor had taken out a packet of fags and lit one for himself. Sandy nudged him for a fag and Trevor passed the packet to Sandy, who stared at an empty box and glowered at Trevor.

Ever the gentleman, I proffered my packet of ten Park Drive (student grants evidently weren't all they were cracked up to be). Sandy gratefully accepted the offer, and passed the ciggies round the room. When it came back to me, it too was empty. Back to the Polish rye bread then.

LISEBERG AMUSEMENT PARK
24 AUGUST 1974, GOTHENBURG, SWEDEN

STAFFAN WENNERLUND

On a cold and snowy afternoon, a couple of days before Christmas 1969, I walked down the Avenue in Gothenburg. As always, I popped into the record shop on my way home to browse through the LPs in the 'just in' section. When I came to an album with a grey, rather inconspicuous cover, I turned the sleeve around to read the small print on the back. I noticed the bass guitar and drums were played – so something on the rockier side – but also violin and viola. I had fronted a local sixties pop group in my home town a couple of years before, but also played the violin for several years, so I found the combination of instruments promising. 'The music on this record could really be something up my street,' I thought, and bought the album. When I came home to my student digs and put it on my record player, I was overwhelmed; the sound, the electric guitar, the bass and drums, the violin and – on top – this angelic voice. I was blown away and immediately hooked. From that day Fairport Convention became my favourite group.

I have followed them ever since, more and more closely as the years have gone by and as technology has made information ever more accessible. It would take almost five years, until August 1974, before I saw the band live for the first time: on an outdoor stage in Gothenburg's amusements park, Liseberg. I have 36 black and white photos, rather shaky, from excitement probably. But it was truly great, and I remember the far-from-capacity crowd dancing intensely in front of the stage to the instrumentals. They returned to Gothenburg a year later. I was in a hurry to get to Konserthuset and thought I wouldn't make it in time.

'Should I take the detour home and fetch my camera?' I decided against it, thinking, 'I can bring the camera the next time they come.' Sandy would not return for concerts in Sweden, either with Fairport or solo.

Staffan Wennerlund took a few snaps at the Liseberg show

GONNA SEE ALL MY FRIENDS: A PEOPLE'S HISTORY OF FAIRPORT CONVENTION

FAIRPORT LIVE CONVENTION RELEASED JULY 1974

MAXWELL HALL, UNIVERSITY OF SALFORD
NOVEMBER 1974, SALFORD, UK

JOHN BARLASS

My first Fairport Convention gig was at Salford University's vast Maxwell Hall in November 1974. With Sandy Denny back within the band's ranks, Fairport were riding high, and the gig was a sell-out. They were coming up with excellent material and their forthcoming album, *Rising for the Moon*, promised to be a stonker. Unfortunately, even before they'd finished recording it, the Fairport curse had struck and drummer Dave Mattacks had left the band, apparently over disagreements over the working methods employed by the album's producer, Glyn Johns.

In true Fairport fashion, the band appointed a replacement drummer, Bruce Rowland, dusted itself down and got on with the job of finishing the album and going out on tour to promote it. But all was not well and in December 1975, after a year of gruelling tours and fraught relationships, the band was split apart when first Jerry Donahue and then the husband/wife pairing of Trevor Lucas and Sandy Denny decided that they'd had enough. And from my own point of view, this all kicked off just when I was daring to harbour optimistic thoughts that Fairport was on the cusp of achieving the major breakthrough they'd always deserved.

TURFSCHIP
23 JANUARY 1975, BREDA, THE NETHERLANDS

PETER VAN DORST

Bart (van Poppel, friend of Peggy) and I brought Peggy and Simon – who was just back in the band – back to their hotel near Breda one night, after a Fairport gig. We took them to Bart's place to have a drink, or several. Poor men, they had to listen to an EP we had just released with our version of 'Sloth' on it. I remember that Simon was very interested in Bart's girlfriend but that didn't work out.

We all lived in Breda at that time, and I remember seeing Fairport in January 1975 at the Turfschip in Breda, with Sandy and Trevor. It was 1976 when Peggy and Simon visited Bart's place. After drinking a lot of beer, I asked Simon why he left the band and later decided to join again. He simply said it that in both cases it seemed a good idea. We had a great night and the four of us had to sit in a very small old red Fiat 500 when I drove them to their hotel.

UMIST
11 OCTOBER 1975, MANCHESTER, UK

STEPHEN ROYSTON

I had been to see the *Rising for the Moon* line-up in Croydon in 1974, after Sandy rejoined. That was a great show. But sadly, by the time I saw them the following year at UMIST, with Bruce Rowland on drums, they seemed to have run out of energy and enthusiasm. It turned out to be the worst Fairport show I can remember. I wrote in my diary the following day:

The band weren't on stage until nearly 11.00pm! Appalling conditions, with far too many people crammed into the hall, all standing up and with sweat dripping all over the place. The band were very disappointing; humourless and tired. All rather depressing for me. I don't really want to see Fairport again.

UNIVERSITY OF LEICESTER
1 NOVEMBER 1975, LEICESTER, UK

PETER ROBINSON

I first saw Fairport completely by accident in November 1975. I was 16. Someone had told me about the support act, Bryn Haworth, so I'd gone to see him. He was great. But I stayed, because I loved live music (still do!) and I'd heard the name Fairport Convention. The gig was fantastic – I'd never heard anything like it. Dave Swarbrick was amazing – and that voice! Sandy Denny was something else. She stopped the gig at one point. Some prat had climbed a ladder to get a better view, and then fell off, and she stopped to check that he was okay. What a brilliant night, and the only time I saw Sandy.

I've seen Fairport many times since, but that's the most memorable. I went to UEA a couple of years later, and went to the Norwich Folk Festival. I remember Alex Campbell playing 'Who Knows Where the Time Goes?' in memory of Sandy.

TOWN HALL
1 JUNE 1976, CHELTENHAM, UK

DAVID GEORGE

It all began as a 16-year-old – I mean 18-year-old – who loved to sing whatever folk music I could learn in my local. My sister loaned me a copy of *The History of Fairport Convention* and suggested the older members of the village might like to hear about the exploits of 'The Bonny Black Hare'. This led to my first live gig experience at Cheltenham Town Hall, with Swarbs on the *Gottle O'Geer* tour, and

David George's granddaughter Millie baked a cake for Fairport's 50th

many a wonderful opening night since at Tewkesbury's Roses Theatre.

As a mature senior aircraftman (SAC) in the Royal Auxiliary Air Force (Med Assist), I was approached one day by a fledgling SAC by the name of Kris Spurling, who, out of the blue, asked my what sort of music I liked. Strange question, I thought. 'I doubt if you would have even heard of the group that I follow. You're far too young,' I replied. After he stopped laughing, he explained that he had more than a passing liking for the group and was indeed a friend and musical associate of one of its' members. And so my *Cropredy* experience began, with fantastic music and an annual meet up with wonderful friends, Kris, Wendy and the kids.

Around the mid-2000s, my five-year-old granddaughter Millie, was bought a ukelele to encourage her into the world of music from an early age. I thought it would be funny to take her picture as if she were a young Mr Dave Pegg. Picture taken, it was off to the Roses to have it autographed by Mr P. His reply? 'Only if I can have a copy!'

The following year, I was working in Guernsey when the Tewkesbury date came around. Try as I might, I could find no electronic way to get the photo to Peggy. I persuaded my middle daughter (not an FC fan) to go to Tewkesbury with Millie and her mum so that Millie could hand Peggy's copy to him in person. The girls, Millie especially, were treated like royalty. Aunty Roxy was utterly amazed at the way that the band not only interacted with them but also with the rest of the audience, and Fairport Convention had a new convert.

50 years of Fairport Convention and Millie, now that bit older and into baking, suggested making an anniversary cake to give to the lads. With a little help from me, the Roses stage was recreated in flour, eggs and Jelly Babies. I think the cake went down okay, as there were no reports of food poisoning.

Now that Millie is older her musical likes have changed, not necessarily for the better. That said, there is no way on God's earth that she would miss out on her annual visits to Tewkesbury or *Cropredy*. My eldest granddaughter Phoebe has also become something of a convert and enjoys the *Cropredy* experience. 50 years plus and still performing? Thank you and bless you all, both past and present, for allowing me and my family to be part of the Fairport Convention experience.

GONNA SEE ALL MY FRIENDS:
A PEOPLE'S HISTORY OF FAIRPORT CONVENTION

REGENT'S PARK OPEN AIR THEATRE
11 JULY 1976, LONDON, UK

COLIN GUTHRIE

Capital Radio broadcast a series of concerts from the Regent's Park Open Air Theatre and I tagged along with my older brother, Andy. It was a combination of a beautifully warm summer's evening, the light fading and the Regent's Park stage lights beautifully illuminating the stage and the surrounding trees and the incredible music. It was around the time of *The Bonny Bunch of Roses* – I remember Swarb singing the title track, a theatre being the perfect setting for the dramatic build of the song. 'Royal Selección No 13' has always been one of my favourite medleys – the fun and the energy and the sheer joy of the tunes. But for me, the real highlight was 'Flowers of the Forest'. Those harmonies, the perfect setting and the bitter sadness of the lyric made it a performance I will not forget. In retrospect, the mid-Seventies was obviously a difficult time for the band, but all I remember is four incredible musicians giving us a magical experience. A perfect setting where the band and the audience enjoyed each other's company and shared a remarkable evening. As an introduction to the band, it could not be bettered.

Colin Guthrie (left) tagged along with his brother Andy

HEYDAY
RELEASED FEBRUARY 1977

LEEDS POLYTECHNIC
5 NOVEMBER 1976, LEEDS, UK

DAVID POLLARD

It was the four-man Fairport – Swarb, Peggy, Simon and Bruce. The band played their last number and left the stage but the shouts for an encore intensified. To the right of the stage and one floor above was a large curtained window. The curtain was pulled back to reveal four arses (eight arse cheeks) pressed against the window). F and A was written on two arse cheeks, I and R on the next, followed by P and O and then R and T. Spelling, of course, 'F-A-I-R-P-O-R-T'. Would that I had had my camera.

STEPHEN ROYSTON

I saw the *Heyday* cassette advertised in the *NME* in 1977, sent off for it (and actually bought my first ever cassette player so that I could play it) and glued the advert to my copy of the cassette. As the cassette had no track listing, I wrote to Ashley Hutchings, who that time was living with Shirley Collins in Etchingham, not far from my home in Bexhill-on-Sea. I had hoped that he might know something about the tracks; much later, I was to learn that he had actually assembled *Heyday* himself from his own archive.

As you can see from Ashley's helpful and friendly reply, I had also asked him if he knew anything about Richard Thompson's whereabouts, as there had been no news of Richard since 1975's *Pour Down Like Silver* album with Linda. Ashley was able to answer both my queries, although I did need to dig a bit further to find out about the remaining tracks on the cassette.

Stephen Royston bought *Heyday* after seeing an *NME* ad

Stephen Royston got a letter from Ashley Hutchings

THE BONNY BUNCH OF ROSES
RELEASED JULY 1977

GONNA SEE ALL MY FRIENDS:
A PEOPLE'S HISTORY OF FAIRPORT CONVENTION

CHORLEY WAKES FESTIVAL, PARK HALL
15 – 17 JULY 1977, CHARNOCK RICHARD, UK

STEPHEN ROYSTON

After seeing them at UMIST, I vowed I would never see Fairport again. But, of course, I did! Having seen Three Desperate Mortgages perform in Manchester in 1976, full of energy and good humour, we went to see the Nicol/Swarbrick/Pegg/Rowlands line-up in Eastbourne later that same year, and realised that Fairport had come alive again. So it was that we travelled up from Sussex to Chorley in Lancashire in the summer of 1977 and saw Fairport at the July Wakes Festival. One particular event made this performance especially memorable, and all because there was a pond between the stage and the audience. I wrote this in my diary:

It was really great to see our old friends Fairport. Simon Nicol was really on form… after Swarbrick offered Nicol's t-shirt to the first person to jump in the pond, Nicol offered Swarb's trousers to the next person to do so! Amazing to see a trouserless Swarb fiddling away!

SIMON JONES (OF THE LATE *FROOTS* MAGAZINE)

It was the summer of 1977, and being young, foolish and generally obsessed with all things folk rock, notice of that year's *Chorley Wakes Festival* was like a gift from God. For some price (which now seems like peanuts – it was £5.50 as I recall) you got a bill which neatly presented virtually the whole genre in one place just an hour away from where I lived. Tent packed and tickets in hand, my mate Roger Dykins and I arrived and parked ourselves all weekend smack in line with the centre of the stage. A great view.

Simon Jones remembers being young and foolish

One of the undoubted reasons for attendance was the promise of a Saturday afternoon set by Fairport Convention; this was the four man, back-to-basic line up of Swarbrick, Nicol, Pegg and Rowlands who'd duly signed to Vertigo and released the decidedly folk-centric *Bonny Bunch of Roses*. Bounding on, they began with a will and a way fulfilling all predictions that this was going to be memorable.

There was at the side of the stage a small pond. The afternoon was hot and some of the crowd were dipping their feet or paddling in the water to cool down. Mr Swarbrick noticed this and promptly announced from the stage that he'd donate Simon Nicol's t-shirt to the first person to jump in. Splash! The guitarist duly handed over his shirt and continued strumming away, doubtless plotting the revenge which came a couple of songs later.

Mr Nicol announced that he would donate Swarb's jeans to the next person to jump into the pond. Splash! Dave was now minus his trousers and played the rest of the set in his underpants. Two members of the audience went home with trophy clothing. Nor do I think either of the Fairporters put on replacement garments until they left the stage. Mr Rowlands and Mr Pegg were obviously gentlemen of high renown and too sensible to join in the game.

Many years later, on a winter tour around 2014, my wife Helen and I were at the Buxton Opera House enjoying a lively night with Fairport, where they always get a great reception, and this February evening was no exception. 'We're all enjoying ourselves, aren't we?' said Peggy from the stage, to a roared, positive response. 'They say it's going to snow tonight but don't take any notice of that. I know it won't, it'll be fine. We'll play on and then we'll all go home, no trouble.' More roared positive response from the gathered faithful.

Five minutes out of Buxton over the tops on the way home to Cheshire, we were hit by a blizzard that whirled, swirled and blew a gale around the car. That meant we had to inch forward through the snowy maelstrom so a normally 30-minute journey took close on three hours. It has to be said that maybe Dave Pegg's weather forecasting abilities are not the most accurate after all. I still think Fairport are splendid!

CROPREDY VILLAGE FETE PRESCOTE MANOR
23 JULY 1977, CROPREDY, UK

MARTYN GROVE

My introduction to Fairport Convention and *Cropredy* was a stroke of luck for me. By 1977, I'd only heard a couple of their songs from my older

GONNA SEE ALL MY FRIENDS:
A PEOPLE'S HISTORY OF FAIRPORT CONVENTION

brother's record collection. Then, while I was out with friends for my 17th birthday, one of my mates announced he had tickets for a village fete that he couldn't go to, and his girlfriend asked if I'd like to go with her. Just over a week later, four of us – my friend's girlfriend, myself, her brother (driving), and his mate – travelled to a place I'd never heard of, Cropredy.

Martyn Grove with wife Alison in 2022

We arrived in the village and followed the crowd to the large garden of Prescote Manor, where the concert was to be. We headed straight to a stall selling wine and settled in. The first of several acts came on shortly afterwards. I can't remember any of the support acts who appeared that day, but I do remember there was trouble with the power, as at some point a call was put out from the stage asking if anyone knew anything about diesel-powered generators. A guy sat on a hay bale near me wobbled to his feet, saying, 'I'll have a look'. He was then taken through a hole in the hedge to return 15 minutes later to much applause. Power restored.

Sometime later I noticed a small chap in a large hairy coat moving amongst the crowd, greeting people and leaving everyone with big smiles on their faces. 'That's Dave Swarbrick, the fiddle player.' My first brush with folk royalty!

Before Fairport came on, I thought I'd better relieve myself of some of the ale I'd been drinking so, spotting a line of portaloos, off I trotted. As they were all occupied, I made my way behind them to a brook where, looking up- and down-stream, I noticed many others had had the same idea. It was like a fishing contest. There were loads of us, facing the stream, tackle in hand.

Shortly after, Fairport took to the stage. They were incredible and I was converted on the spot and I've been a fan ever since. Their new album at the time was *The Bonny Bunch of Roses* and the highlight for me was the majestic title track, a fantastic vocal performance by the little fiddler

GONNA SEE ALL MY FRIENDS:
A PEOPLE'S HISTORY OF FAIRPORT CONVENTION

I'd seen earlier. (Although the real highlight came on the journey home when, while her brother drove and he and his mate tried valiantly to ignore us, my mate's girlfriend and myself got very friendly in the back of the car, but that's another story. It was the '70s.).

After that, I was an infrequent visitor to *Cropredy* until the year 2000 when I returned with my wife, brother and sister-in-law. I first recounted this tale for the booklet *Cropredy Chronicles* in 2002, since when my brother has sadly passed. He loved the festival and my sister-in-law is making plans for a memorial to be included at Jonah's Oak. Since 2000, I've only missed one festival and our group has expanded to include the next two generations. There were 12 of us this year and we'll be regulars for as long as it lasts. Britain's friendliest festival and largest village fete.

GREM DEVLIN

My first opportunity to see Fairport came in 1977. I was a Merchant Navy engineer cadet staying in Cosham, in digs with another cadet called Brian Davies – we were both Fairport fans and were also in a band called Agaric. Brian's girlfriend had a birthday that fell the same weekend as mine, and this weekend was also Fairport's gig at Cropredy, at Prescote Manor. Brian bought tickets for us all to go – the tickets for me and his girlfriend were birthday presents – and drove us up to Cropredy in his old Wolseley Hornet.

We arrived in plenty of time to explore the village and attend the country fayre in the afternoon at the Manor.

Grem Devlin was at the 'first' Cropredy Festival

GONNA SEE ALL MY FRIENDS:
A PEOPLE'S HISTORY OF FAIRPORT CONVENTION

At tea time, we all had to leave to allow the soundchecks and those of us with tickets were allowed back in for the gig later. I remember that Karl Dallas was the compere and I definitely saw Bob Davenport perform. I've also been told that Ralph McTell played along with Chris Leslie and his brother, although I don't have a clear recollection of them. Fairport played a blinding show and the amp stack toppled over in the wind during 'Bonny Bunch of Roses', which was quite spooky. Eventually we left during the encores in order to catch last orders at the Red Lion and make a visit to the loos before heading south again. Leaving the Gents I heard Fairport play Dylan's 'Country Pie', so God alone knows how many encores they played but it was a lot. A smashing way to celebrate becoming 19.

STAFFAN WENNERLUND

It was not easy to follow my favourite band from Sweden, but I was an eager reader of British music mags. One day in 1977, I saw a notice that the band was going to do a charity gig in Cropredy – for the church hall, if I recall correctly – so I travelled to London and made my way to this little village in Oxfordshire. I arrived very early and was almost hanging on the gate in order to get my ticket. Once inside I came to hang out with two Daves, studying in Oxford, and we basked in the sun, drank a few pints, walked around and took photos. When the band had half an hour until stage time, I stumbled down to the portaloos. Then I saw a green Rover park nearby and out climbed Trevor Lucas and Sandy, who was in a long, beautiful, white summer dress and my thoughts went directly to the 'Rising

Staffan Wennerland met Peggy at Cropredy in 2017 and Simon in Lübeck, Germany in 2014

for the Moon' song. In spite of the afternoon's pints, I was too shy to address her and tell her how much I loved her music. They walked up the path to the stage area and when I returned, excited, to the two Daves, I told them that the couple had arrived, and I was certain that Sandy would join the band for a song or two. It didn't happen, but I thought the four-piece line-up gave us a tremendous evening, with several highlights. An exciting day ended with the last train to Oxford and me kipping on an Oxford living room floor.

After the band called it a day, I started writing to Peggy, first about the *Farewell, Farewell* album, but, later on, about everything Fairport, and I kept myself informed. That is how we came to Broughton Castle 1981 and to several *Cropredys* during the 80s. When the reformed Fairport came to Gothenburg in 1985 and 1987, a new era began and from then on, I have seen them in Sweden, Denmark and Germany several times, and even at *Cropredy* in jubilee years like 2007 and 2017. They are my band, whatever happens, and it has been great fun to, over the years, become a member of the great 'Fairport Family'.

DALYMOUNT PARK
21 AUGUST 1977, DUBLIN, IRELAND

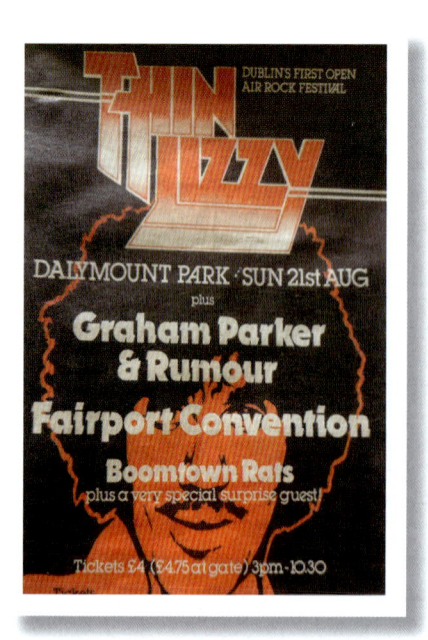

SUSANNE BLEY

I was at Dalymount Park, and I wrote this poem about Fairport...

Susanne Bley was at Dalymount Park

How to explain what happened there. One of those things that in life are rare

While you had been playing all those years I was missing such feast for my ears

Seeing your music and hearing that song was striking a chord inside me so strong

Some harmony, lost long ago in the past – like coming home now having found at last.

Thank you, my lovely Fairport past & present!

Keep going strong!

GONNA SEE ALL MY FRIENDS:
A PEOPLE'S HISTORY OF FAIRPORT CONVENTION

PHONOGRAM RECORDS
1978, LONDON, UK

KEN MALIPHANT

In 1978 I was faced with a terrible dilemma. I had been a Fairport fan since they began and grew up immersed in the Scottish folk scene – Hamish Imlach, The Humblebums, Dick Gaughan, etc. I was also the Managing Director of Phonogram Ltd, the record company co-owned by Philips of Eindhoven and Siemens of Hamburg. The company owned and operated a range of labels including Philips, Fontana and Vertigo, mainly a home for guitar bands and rock groups.

Ken Maliphant has a special place in Fairport's hearts

Fairport were on Vertigo and had delivered two out of a four album deal, *The Bonny Bunch of Roses* (1977) and *Tipplers Tales* (1978). Unfortunately, they didn't sell, and I was in the middle of a clear-out of the artist roster. I had discovered and signed Dire Straits and was having success with 10cc and Status Quo, but needs must when the Dutch and Germans pay the piper. Despite my personal preferences, I couldn't justify excluding the band from the strict viability criteria demanded by the shareholders and so I had to let them go. How could I salve my conscience? Despite any contractual nuances, I decided to pay them in full for the remaining two albums which were as yet undelivered. It is claimed by members of the band that this was the only recording money they had seen up to that point.

Our paths didn't cross until 20 years later, when I was retired and curating the Arts Festival at St George's Church in Beckenham. I had booked the band and was nervous about entering the green room given the history. I needn't have worried as the first to greet me was Peggy with a hug and a big thank you for paying off his mortgage. Simon Nicol was also vocal in his gratitude.

Sometime later I was in the audience at a Fairport concert in the Fairfield's Hall, Croydon, enjoying the gig when Peggy announced to a slightly bewildered crowd that the man who paid off their mortgages and paid them the only money they ever received from recordings in those days was in the audience and would I please stand up. I still love these guys and have booked them five times for my festival. They always deliver. Thanks to them I have an artist's pass at *Cropredy* and can use the posh loos.

WOOLWICH ODEON
17 & 18 JUNE 1978, LONDON, UK

STEVE CARSON

I was a really big fan. I got to see them only one time with Sandy Denny in the early '70s, but I was a fan from the beginning of the band. When my first wife and I were in London in 1978, we saw that Fairport were playing at the Woolwich Odeon. We went

Steve Carson was at Woolwich Odeon

out to Woolwich, not knowing what to expect, and Peggy was the first person I ran into from the band. He was hanging around before the show and we talked for a few minutes and he said, 'Oh, come backstage after the gig.'

It was a really great show, and at the end of the night, we came to the edge of the stage while they were packing up. I had a bit of American marijuana with me, and I asked if anybody wanted a toke. Swarbrick, who always had terrible hearing, seemed to hear me from across the stage and came over, and we had a few tokes. As we were getting ready to leave, Peggy asked us what we were doing. We were just drifting around Europe at the time, and they said they'd be playing in Amsterdam, Vienna, Salzburg and other places. They gave us a schedule and t-shirts and told us to show up at the soundcheck if we were there in the city at the same time.

A few weeks later we were in Amsterdam, and we were anxious to see them. We got to the venue, and it had been cancelled. We thought well, in a week or two we'll be in Salzburg, so we'll see them there.

In Salzburg it was a great show, and afterwards we went out with them. It was fairly late and a reporter from the newspaper took us to a very nice tavern. It was closed for the night, but they opened it for the band, the reporter, and my wife and me. That was quite a night, quite a piss-up. It was outrageous debauchery. And for some reason or other, the guys didn't have the same feeling towards the Salzburg journalist, who had a hell of a camera with him. At one point, the guy got up to take a piss. Without a word, Simon picked up the camera and Peggy – who was on the other side of the table – stood up, dropped his trousers and mooned Simon, who took a photograph of Peggy's arse and set the camera back on the table. When the guy came back nobody said anything or raised a smile. I thought that that was a bit outrageous.

What won them over to us was that, not only did I have some American weed, but my wife was quite a wine drinker. She didn't quite outdrink them, but she stayed with Peggy and Simon and Swarb and Bruce. To hang in there with those professionals was the thing that did it. By the time the evening was over, everybody was absolutely wrecked, and it was about two hours before they had to catch a train to Vienna. They said, 'Why don't you come with us?' So we did of course. I just thought they were great; they were so nice to us. A couple of them shared a room so my wife and I could have a room to ourselves. The next morning when we all split up they all, to a man, made the fatal mistake of giving Sue and I their addresses and telephone numbers, and invited us to come and stay whenever we wanted. A terrible mistake on their part. We took advantage of that, and for many, many years we've been good friends.

GONNA SEE ALL MY FRIENDS:
A PEOPLE'S HISTORY OF FAIRPORT CONVENTION

LA PRAIRIE DE COLOVRAY
22 JULY 1978, NYON, SWITZERLAND

RAFFAELE GALLI

I knew Fairport Convention through a record shop in London at the beginning of the Seventies. Being touched by the cover of *Liege & Lief* exhibited in the window, I asked to hear the album and, wow, I was caught by its music. I was a big fan of the Byrds and I was in England to spend the New Year's holidays with some friends, taking advantage of the closure of university lessons (I was studying law). I got the opportunity to see the show of Crosby, Stills, Nash & Young at the Royal Albert Hall. Back home, I bought the previous three LPs recorded by Fairport before *Liege & Lief*, which I had lost. I particularly loved *Unhalfbricking* because of the Bob Dylan songs they covered in it, 'Percy's Song', with Iain Matthews being my favourite, while I found Sandy Denny's voice so great, especially on 'A Sailor's Life'.

I heard the group live for the first time in Nyon, Switzerland: a beautiful town on the banks of Geneva's Lake, where they played at a big festival in July '78, after The Red Clay Ramblers and Try Yann's sets. At the time I was

Raffaele Galli captured Fairport in action in 1978 in Nyon

Photos: This page and opposite Raffaele Galli

a contributor to a new rock magazine written in Italian, titled *Il Mucchio Selvaggio*, run by a few friends really fond of American and English music; we were so young, full of enthusiasm and love, happy to hear some of our new heroes.

The foursome Fairport of the time – Simon, Peggy, Swarb and Bruce Rowland – were wonderful. I remember Simon with a Rickenbacker (he was a follower of Roger McGuinn) and a wild Swarbrick was the star of the event. Many of us rock fans were there and at the end of the performance we socialised with Simon and Pegg. They answered all our questions, spoke about the past, present and future of the band, and seemed really glad to know foreign fans of their music, even if they had some problems in perfectly understanding their language. It was a fantastic evening - they even put me on their shoulders.

CROPREDY VILLAGE CHARITY FETE
13 JULY 1978, CROPREDY, UK

WES MASON

I first met Dave Pegg in the spring of 1978. I was stationed at RAF Upper Heyford while in the US Air Force and was at a folk festival at Broughton Castle. While sitting in a luthier booth playing banjo on some old-time southern mountain music, Dave stopped to listen. I guess he liked my playing as he searched me out to play music with him and several other Banbury area players for a charity folk gig. That started a 44-year friendship with Dave Pegg, Chris Leslie and Simon Nicol. I was in an opening band at *Cropredy* '78 and '79. It was a great treat to be befriended and mentored by such incredible players and members of my long-time favourite band. I rotated back to the States in 1980 and thankfully have seen them a few times in Massachusetts and Virginia when they were able to tour America. It's a bucket list trip to come back to *Cropredy* and listen to them live again.

HEXAGON THEATRE
17 OCTOBER 1978, READING, UK

RICHARD HAMILTON

I was born in Rome, to British parents who were working there for a British airline. We lived in the suburb of EUR (Esposizione Universale Roma). From our fourth-floor apartment, we could see the Palazzo Dello Sport. In 2018, an erstwhile Italian childhood friend found me on Facebook. Although my schoolboy Italian is now very rusty, and his English not much better, we have since kept in touch. He noticed that I had likes and posts relating to Fairport Convention. And in 2021, he sent me a poster of a festival that took place in EUR in May 1968.

Although I was taken to several sporting events at this venue, my parents wouldn't have heard of most of the acts advertised here and wouldn't have thought that it was something for them – or me. Mum was into Ray Conniff and Frank Sinatra. Dad wasn't musical at all: not appreciative of any genre.

Richard Hamilton could have seen the band in Rome in 1968

But, as we'll see shortly, it was probably best that I didn't get to go...

GONNA SEE ALL MY FRIENDS:
A PEOPLE'S HISTORY OF FAIRPORT CONVENTION

I forwarded this poster to Simon Nicol and asked whether it brought back any memories. Simon responded:

Hi Richard. I remember it very well. The Palazzo was rapidly erected for the 1960 Olympics and was showing signs of – hem, hem – jerrybuilding. Also, and characteristically, the schedule had gone to hell, and we played between The Association and The Move.

The Carabinieri were very edgy about all these long-haired hippies (I mean, Rome was VERY buttoned-up then and the whole 'alternative' thing was dangerously subversive to the establishment). They formed a cordon facing the crowd in front of the stage, which I found diverting and very foreign. Although dandruff on dirty uniforms is a universal part of paramilitary life at all times. Anyway, not a sell-out by any means. We played about 6 or 7 o'clock and things got edgier during the changeover.

Something triggered them with The Move, maybe the smoke machines, or Roy and Carl's outrageous personas, and the plug was pulled along with a great deal of hoohah, with everyone being rushed outside with alarming force. No tear gas, and I didn't see anyone getting clubbed, but it was the worst overreaction I've ever seen to this day.

Nice meal afterwards though...

I had Simon's recollection translated (properly) into Italian and sent it back to my Italian Facebook contact. I added: *Fairport Convention esistono ancora* – explaining that the band is still going strong, and that I have since become friends with its members and associates. And I sent him some YouTube links of the current line-up at *Cropredy* (also explaining what *Cropredy* is, and that it's a stone's throw from where I live now). His reaction to the footage was, 'Eccezionale!' A new fan – he mentioned that he particularly enjoyed the two violins.

But it wasn't until two years after Fairport's visit to EUR that I heard Fairport Convention for the first time, when another friend (Italian, four years older than me) played *Liege & Lief* to me. His father was a passionate fan of British music: returning from one business trip to London, he had brought back *Abbey Road, Let It Bleed, Trespass,* and *Liege & Lief*. The latter had been playing in a Slough record shop, an enquiry was made, and its purchase duly completed. A few days later the phone rang: '*Riccardo, Riccardo, you must come here… we have some fantastic(o) music to play for you.*'

GONNA SEE ALL MY FRIENDS:
A PEOPLE'S HISTORY OF FAIRPORT CONVENTION

Which is how 'Come All Ye' started my 50-plus year Fairport journey, while being fed pizza by Massimo's grandmother (my love of Fairport and artichoke hearts began on the very same day). We played *Liege & Lief* three times. The Beatles, Stones and Genesis weren't touched – at least, not on that afternoon. Shortly afterwards, on a fortnight's family return to the UK, I wouldn't shut up until my constant demands to be taken to a record shop were met.

I didn't return to England until September 1978. Within a few weeks, I saw Fairport Convention (Nicol; Pegg; Swarbrick; Rowland) at Reading's Hexagon Theatre in October 1978, ten years after I could have done. (And, while writing this, I have just noticed that the poster was prophetic: Fairport are listed underneath Ten Years After!)

UNIVERSITY OF LEICESTER
2 DECEMBER 1978, LEICESTER, UK

TIM GOOSEY, AGE 17

I had a ticket for the Leicester University Ball. There was cheap booze, a disco and Fairport Convention live. Prior to this, I had never heard of Fairport Convention, but I found myself at the front of the stage, right in front of Dave Swarbrick. Dave Pegg still had a good head of hair and Simon Nicol was clean-shaven. At the back on drums was Bruce Rowland, who I later found out was the only member of Fairport to have played *Woodstock*, and who can be seen behind Joe Cocker in the movie of the festival.

Tim Goosey hadn't heard of Fairport and was there for the cheap booze

The gig was part of the *Tipplers Tales / The Bonny Bunch of Roses* tour, which despite poor record sales, remain my favourite Fairport albums and line-up. The albums were heavily influenced by Swarbrick's contributions of traditional folk songs and instrumentals. The band seemed to be really enjoying themselves, and despite having only one guitarist to play rhythm and lead, which Simon did admirably, they managed to play a number of tracks from the two recent albums and many others from their extensive history. I became a fan that day.

Sadly, Dave Swarbrick and Bruce Rowland are no longer with us. I have since been to many Fairport gigs with various different line-ups and *Cropredy Festivals* over the years and even wrote a song ('Maiden Voyage') that was recorded by Simon Nicol on his second solo album, *Consonant Please Carol*. So in a small way I feel part of the Fairport story.

THE VENUE
7 DECEMBER 1978, LONDON, UK

PAUL HARRISON

My love of the music of Fairport Convention began in the autumn of 1970. I was aware of them before then, but I had not seriously listened to their music and, for some reason, I kept mixing them up with Fairfield Parlour. My older brother, Geoff, returned from a trip to London with several LPs and amongst them were *Liege & Lief* and *Full House*. It was the start of a love of the music of Fairport Convention for both Geoff and myself. The wonderful world of traditional folk music, electric folk and folk rock had been opened up to us.

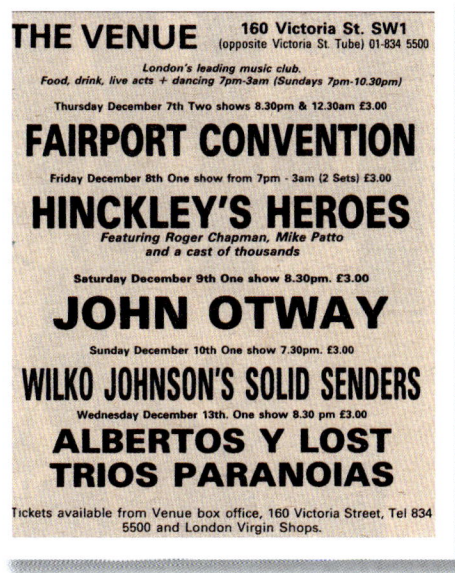

Paul Harrison recalls a very short set at The Venue in 1978

Mine and Geoff's paths separated when we went to university, but we were reunited in late 1977 when we both got jobs in London and we resumed our shared interests in music and football. Over the next 35 years, we attended many Fairport

Convention concerts together. As Geoff's other commitments increased, the frequency of our shared attendance at concerts decreased, but in February 2012 we found ourselves at the same Fairport concert at the Alban Arena in St Albans. We hadn't told each other that we were going to the concert and bumped into each other in the foyer. It was the last time I saw Geoff; he died suddenly and unexpectedly a month later.

I was not sure if my interest in Fairport would continue. I had tickets for a gig by the Ric Sanders Trio at the Green Note in Camden Town shortly after Geoff died, but I couldn't face it. I returned my tickets, as I did not want to deny others the opportunity of seeing and hearing Ric, and explained the reasons to the organiser of the gig. I was later told that Ric kindly played Warren Zevon's 'Keep Me in Your Heart', in commemoration of Geoff.

I did resume my interest in the music of Fairport, and whenever I listen to them I think of Geoff; without him, I may never have developed my love of their music – the quiet joys of brotherhood.

We never discussed our favourite Fairport concert but we remembered one gig in particular. It was at the Venue in Victoria, London in 1978 and the first of two scheduled sets that night. It was memorable for the wrong reasons. The gig lasted no more than about 30 minutes; I don't know if the second scheduled set ever took place. Sometime later, we realised that Dave Swarbrick was probably having difficulty with his hearing that day. The experience obviously didn't put us off Fairport.

LOCH LOMOND ROCK FESTIVAL, CAMERON BEAR PARK
27 MAY 1979, ALEXANDRIA, UK

BOB MULLEN

I had purchased tickets for the *Lomond Folk Festival*, which was being held in a small town called Balloch. After calling every hotel in the area without joy, the lady at one hotel said her sister ran a small bed and breakfast in the area, and she might be able to help. I called her and got the last room. It was a Saturday evening and Fairport were the last act. I arrived early evening, booked in and went to the festival. The next morning, we were going downstairs to the breakfast room, and I stopped to look at the brochures as my wife carried on. After about 30 seconds, I heard my wife Wilma saying, 'Oh you are staying here as well.' I then went down to the room to find my wife at the table with a gentleman from Europe, Chris Leslie, Ric Sanders and Vo Fletcher from Ric Sanders Trio. He was deputising for Peggy as he was ill at that time. It was a pleasant surprise and we enjoyed our breakfast.

FAIRFIELD HALLS
3 JUNE 1979, CROYDON, UK

ANDY LEONARD

How did I fall under the spell that is Fairport Convention? Back in 1979 I used to work nights every four weeks, and when I did, I used to chat to a fellow worker who loved his music and had it playing from various cassettes he owned. One was *Nine*, which he played a lot. So much so that I ended up buying my own copy and that was the beginning of it all. I started buying their LPs and soon owned them all apart from *Fairport Live at the LA Troubadour*, which had been deleted and was no longer available.

Then I found out that Fairport were splitting and going on a final farewell tour. I now loved the band and their music but had never seen them. As a result, I got tickets for the Fairfield Halls in June 1979. It was a truly amazing show, and at the very end Simon Nicol said there were a few tickets available for the following night

Andy Leonard discovered Fairport just as they were splitting up

at the Dome in Brighton. I was free so, knowing I'd never see the band again, I drove there and saw them one final time. I also put my name onto a mailing list as they intended to record and release a live LP of that farewell tour.

That should have been the end of it; it wasn't, it was the start. They had a one-day festival reuniting the band in a small village called Cropredy the following summer. I was informed of this by the mailing list. There were no emails or internet in those days. I had to go because the band might never play together again, and that has been how I have seen the band from that date to this. Literally hundreds of gigs, every *Cropredy Festival* since 1980 (apart from Covid postponements) and almost 43 years later, I still love them and their music as much as ever, and long may that continue. So, all of this can be traced back to a single cassette I heard at about two in the morning when I should no doubt have been working. I did eventually get that vinyl copy of *Fairport Live at the LA Troubadour*, at a stall at the *Cropredy Festival* in the mid-1980s. Where else?

OPEN AIR THEATRE
24 JUNE 1979, APELDOORN, THE NETHERLANDS

ARJAN DEN BOER
As a huge Fairport fan in Holland since 1970, I was delighted when they played a gig in 1979 at the open air theatre in my hometown of Apeldoorn.

Arjan den Boer saw Fairport in '79

THORESBY HALL
21 JULY 1979, OLLERTON, UK

HOWARD JOHNSON

As a student in Brighton during the early Seventies, I saw Fairport on several occasions. I was playing with various folk groups and bands and their original music was just a revelation. After getting a job as a teacher in Yorkshire, I saw many gigs 'up t'north' before getting the dreadful news that the 1979 tour was to be their farewell. I immediately booked to see them one last time at Thoresby Hall in Nottinghamshire.

Howard Johnson set up a video company that filmed rock gigs

Thankfully, the farewell was not to be and within a year I saw a flyer for a reunion gig in a field at Cropredy. So my musical prospects for 1980 were getting better, as were my job prospects. I had previously worked on a university television unit and when my new bosses got to hear of this, I was drafted in to work on developing teaching methods using the latest portable video cameras and recorders. Suddenly my ambitions as a physics teacher faded. Within six months, I met a like-minded colleague by the name of George Fretwell and (while still working in schools) we borrowed money from our families, rented premises and set up our company, Videotech. After spending loads of money on equipment, we started making videos for schools and businesses in our spare time. One day I had a burst of inspiration – we could record concerts on video and maybe sell them to fans or even the telly!

I wrote to Peggy and asked him if we could record the 1980 show at Cropredy. The results are on YouTube and, whilst they leave a lot to be desired, it was a great learning curve and the band were incredibly helpful to us.

We returned to the 'Folk Rock Belt' for several years after that first foray, each time with more gear and crew. We hired in an ever-increasing amount of kit, always trying to find innovative ways to record live events on no budget. Thankfully, we did sell quite a few VHS tapes of the 1982 and 1983 Fairport reunion shows and that helped with the costs. As did our crew, who were friends and former students of mine who all, like myself and George, worked tirelessly for free.

By 1984 we had graduated to working on concerts with lots of bands, from Steeleye Span to Magna Carta and Lindisfarne. But eventually the labour of love had to come to an end as we were spending far more on recording the shows than we were earning from selling tapes. We had left our secure teaching jobs in 1983 and the need to keep the bank happy eventually took over our lives. So we went back to business and educational television, and that has kept us in work for almost 40 years.

Our Fairport experience was in many ways the foundation of our business and one that we all treasure greatly. Myself and George saw the company go through many names and transformations, and in doing so we have worked around the world for clients across the UK, Europe, the Far East, South America and the USA, producing documentaries and promotional films for broadcast, education and industry. Today, we are almost retired but still have over six thousand films and tapes in our archive. At present we are researching our collection of music tapes and finding some real gems that have never been seen. Only last week I came across a tape from an evening with Bert Jansch and Michael Chapman. It was shot in a studio store room one night in the 1980s. Who knows what else we may discover? The guys on the crew still talk about Cropredy as a defining moment in their lives and many have gone on to have very successful careers in business and the media.

Like everyone in the FC family I have lots of stories, photos and memorabilia. The 1982 Cropredy was (I think) the first festival to feature a large video screen on stage. This was a massive 50 inch rear projection unit we had bought from a car showroom. The screen successfully relayed the band's performance to a very appreciative crowd, but it felt like it weighed half a ton and it was invisible if the sun shone on it. However, it was great at night!

In 1984 we succeeded in getting Fairport into the video juke box charts (at number 57) with the 1982 recording of 'Sloth'. I well remember Peggy telling me they had gone into a pub and he was amazed to hear

'Sloth' booming out of the speakers of several TVs. We had many more video hits before the network closed down… If only I could find the paperwork to remind me what they were.

In 1983 we received a thank you letter from a lady who really enjoyed watching the Cropredy tape, having missed out through illness. However, she had encouraged her husband to go on his own and she was delighted to see him in one of the crowd shots. Sadly, she also saw he had his arm around her best friend and he is now her ex-husband.

I have not attended as many Cropredy festivals as I would have liked but the band and its spiritual home remain in my DNA. It has been a pleasure and a privilege to have known the guys for so long, and I am proud that our somewhat quirky and iffy recordings from those early festivals have survived and contributed to our collective memory of those happy days. Thanks to all the members of Fairport and all the family that surrounds them to this day.

VELODROMO VIGORELLI
25 JULY 1979, MILAN, ITALY

RAFFAELE GALLI

Having first seen them in Switzerland the previous year, I saw Fairport for the first time in my home country at Vigorelli, a velodrome made famous by pistards such as Antonio Maspes and Sante Gaiardoni in the late Fifties and early Sixties. They were so kind to me again and even dedicated a song, 'Journeyman's Grace', to me. I got a good quality bootleg of that event years ago and it's possible to hear their words.

Raffaele Galli caught the Fairport soundcheck at the Velodrome in Milan

But that wasn't the first time Fairport Convention had played in Italy. In May 1968, they played at Palazzo dello Sport in Rome at a big international pop festival, a kind of European *Woodstock*. The event was scheduled to last a week but was shut down by the authorities on the third day after a performance by The Move that set fire to the stage. The Fairport line-up consisted of Ashley, Richard, Simon, Martin Lamble and Judy Dyble. Judy was on stage with the band for the last time, having been asked to leave by Ashley a few days before. I didn't go to the festival since I didn't know about it. Italy didn't have musical magazines such as *Melody Maker* or *New Musical Express* and so news of the event reached me a few days after it was over.

MASSIMO FRANCINI
My first meeting with the band took place back in 1973. I was following a musical program on Swiss TV, entitled *Match Box*, which showcased new singers and groups of various genres. I heard the Fairport Convention *Nine* line-up and it was like an electric shock. Already a fan of The Beatles, I found myself blown away. This band had something different and magical for me. The first song was 'Polly on the Shore' and it left a mark on me as if it were Zorro's sword. In the following weeks, two more songs were broadcast, 'The Hexamshire Lass' and 'The Brillancy Medley'.

I started my spasmodic search for all of the discography produced by the band. It was very difficult to find the various LPs in Italy then, but

Massimo Francini discovered Fairport in 1973

I had many friends and working acquaintances in England and thanks to them I succeeded and my perseverance and determination were rewarded. However, I had to wait until July 1979, during the *Farewell* tour, to be able to attend one of their concerts. There were 10,000 people there. I have the recording of that concert and it's two hours with another of the Fairport line-ups that I love the most. I loved the last two LPs, *The Bonny Bunch* and *Tipplers Tales*).

In 1981, I decided to go and see them at Broughton Castle in Banbury. I met Peggy there and began a correspondence and telephone contact with him. The following year, I returned and it was like I was amongst old friends.

I have many memories with both Swarb and Maart, to whom I lent my Martin guitar in 1994 because his guitar broke on the plane. Thank you, Simon, for asking me to introduce them on the 2007 tour. Thank you, Peggy, for always replying to me and sending me material. I have so many things to tell but I want to reiterate just one: without Fairport my life would certainly have been different. They have always kept me company making me feel among friends. Ciao from Italy.

STADIO DEI PINI CERVIA-MILANO MARITTIMA
29 JULY 1979, RAVENNA, ITALY

MARCO DANESI, AGE 17

I can't remember how, but I learned of a *Farewell Tour* date in Italy and, moreover, a few miles from Ravenna where I was born and where I lived. I got my first vinyl just two years before and immediately an unbridled passion for folk rock and the Fairport was born – just to realize with dismay that the *Farewell Tour* would have put an end to a thrilling adventure.

Marco Danesi saw Fairport on a 'Farewell' tour in Italy

So, I went to a local radio station to buy tickets for me, my friends and even our parents, as we didn't have a driving license yet. The outdoor show took place in July at the Stadio dei Pini in Cervia-Milano Marittima on the Romagna coast. It was, of course, a wonderful evening with the only issue being a swarm of mosquitoes happily feasting on the concertgoers.

At the end of the show, we went backstage looking for information on the release of the tour's live album. A kind and helpful Dave Pegg wrote in my notebook how to buy and get the vinyl by mail. We stupidly didn't even ask for an autograph, distracted by Swarb walking down the stage, unsteady on his legs, waving and offering us a bottle of Vecchia Romagna, a brand of quite famous brandy in Italy. We politely refused, being underage.

I still have the show recorded on a cheap tape recorder and a C90 MAXELL, too short for the complete set: running out of tape on 'Sir B McKenzie'. The quality is not the best, but it is a precious memory. I've never digitally transferred the tape, fearing too much an irreparable damage.

FAREWELL FAIRPORT
4 AUGUST 1979, CROPREDY, UK

ADRIAN COWLEY, AGE 19

My friend Andie and I attended Fairport's gig at Derby Assembly Rooms in 1979 as part of their farewell tour. Placed on the seats were small flyers advertising a final 'hurrah' at somewhere called Cropredy. We thought this would be a good idea and give us a last chance to see them forever, so we sent off a postal order and waited for the tickets.

We were both 19 and neither of us could drive so we decided we'd hitch there. Andie's dad kindly offered us a lift to the M1 from where we planned to hitch a lift. On the Friday evening, we went to our local pub and told all our mates we'd be away camping at this small place in Oxfordshire the following night and bidding farewell to Fairport.

We were up early on Saturday and Andie's dad dropped us at junction 24 of the M1 for 7am. We had a tent and some bits and pieces to make a brew and warm up some beans. The weather proved fair and we made our way to the top of the southbound slip road, thumbs at the ready. There wasn't a great deal of traffic initially, so we had plenty of time to earmark anyone going by.

Time passed – eight o'clock, nine o'clock – and not a hint of anyone slowing down as they drove past. By ten o'clock, we'd been there three hours. It was at the time when long hair still had some connotations of delinquency and we wondered if maybe that was hindering us, not that there was nothing we could do about it.

Adrian Cowley hitched to Cropredy in 1979

Time continued to pass and there was still no sign of anyone stopping. We'd spent so long the previous night describing where we were off to and saying that we'd be unavailable on Saturday night that we agreed we couldn't just go back home. We started to plan camping on the M1 Junction 24 island. There were trees and a nice grassy area, and we thought it would be fine for one night.

That was until eleven o'clock came and, miracle of miracles, there was a car going down the slip road with its brake lights on. We simultaneously couldn't believe it and ran like the clappers – before they changed their minds. We got in and set off and spent the first ten minutes thanking the young couple, who had picked us up and who were perhaps a few years older than us, describing how we'd been there since the crack of dawn.

We had made a list of places we planned to hitch to in order to get to Cropredy, but here we were on our way. Fairport were on at the end of the evening, and if we only saw them then so be it. They asked us where we were heading and almost apologetically, we tried to explain that we weren't exactly sure but that we were aiming for a small folk festival in Oxfordshire. They said, 'That's interesting, because we're also going to a music festival in Oxfordshire.' 'Great,' we thought, 'we may be able to break the back of the journey with this first lift.' 'So where exactly are you going?' they asked. 'Well, it's a village called Cropredy,' we replied. 'What a coincidence,' they said, 'that's exactly where we're going!' So, after waiting four hours for a lift, we had managed to get a lift with one of the few thousand people from all over the country who were attending that first festival.

We camped adjacent to them, and they kindly brought us back the next morning. A *Cropredy* miracle. I wonder if they still go to the festival.

I've subsequently attended *Cropredy* many times with brothers and friends. In 2006, my kid brother's band, Shameless Quo, managed to get a slot.

KATHRYN AINSWORTH

My mum and dad, Des and Chris Ainsworth, were at the farewell concert. As was I, because Mum was five months pregnant! Fairport's power to guide us through difficult times and create so much infectious positive energy is precious beyond words. It brings us constantly closer. I can't thank my parents enough for all they do, including the joyful Fairport experiences year after year. I have countless happy memories to thank Fairport for, and a tattoo that says 'Meet on the Ledge'. It's my home, and where my heart is. I can't, nor ever want to, imagine life without the inspiration of the Fairport friends and family.

Kathryn Ainsworth was at Cropredy in 1979 with mum Chris and dad Des

JOHN BARLASS

The late 1970s were a difficult period for Fairport Convention. Punk had arrived in 1976, along with a sea-change in attitude within the music press, and bands such as Fairport, whose musicality had, for many years, had the likes of *Melody Maker* and *NME* fighting their

GONNA SEE ALL MY FRIENDS:
A PEOPLE'S HISTORY OF FAIRPORT CONVENTION

corner, suddenly found themselves persona non grata. On *Tipplers Tales*, Fairport took a bit of a critical mauling and their record label, Vertigo, eventually took the decision to terminate Fairport's recording contract. If that wasn't enough, Swarb had been told by his doctor that he risked going deaf if he continued to play loud amplified music. So, in late 1978, Fairport took the reluctant and inevitable (as it seemed at the time) decision to call it a day.

John Barlass remembers Fairport's farewell

Fairport has always had a following that has compensated for its lack of overwhelming numbers with immense loyalty, and the band decided that the best way to say a fond farewell to their fans would be to undertake a lengthy national tour before rounding off the band's career at an open-air concert in their home village of Cropredy in Oxfordshire.

And so to Cropredy. Arrangements and preparations for the show were, by the standards of today's *Fairport's Cropredy Convention* events, primitive and miniscule. Admission to the site was by programme, obtainable in advance for the princely sum of £2.50, or at the festival gate for £3.00. Security was virtually non-existent and facilities were modest. One arrangement that did prove to be adequate was the supply of beer – Fairport had arranged for the team at The White Bear in Masham, North Yorkshire to bring their mobile bar, along with several thousand gallons of Theakston's Best Bitter and Old Peculier, to ensure that proceedings were kept well-lubricated.

To someone arriving from the part of the country that the newly elected government was about to re-designate as post-industrial Lancashire, the village of Cropredy and its rural environs were nothing short of a revelation. We were stunned, and when we ambled down into Cropredy and were confronted by the very pub that I'd studied and pondered over for years on the cover of the *Nine* album, I truly believed that I'd arrived in heaven.

Nowadays, festivalgoers start to gather in Cropredy from around a week before the festival but in 1979, the only unusual (at least, I'm assuming it was unusual) presence was a group of Cavalier soldiers from the Sealed Knot Society, all in full uniform, who were mustering in the wake of their recent re-enactment of The Battle of Cropredy Bridge.

The sun shone all afternoon, and the evening was cool, but dry. The first time I'd ever experienced clement weather at an open-air concert. Truly, the gods were on our side. This first festival set the standard that Cropredy has maintained ever since – brilliant music, a wonderful, friendly, considerate crowd, good beer, edible food and a wonderfully tolerant, peaceful vibe. Memories of the music on that momentous day are fairly sketchy, partly owing to the passage of time and partly to the consumption of the aforementioned Theakston's products, but we all had a wonderful time.

Peggy was, unsurprisingly, hanging around outside the beer tent with his young son, Matthew, who had decided to spend the day in the guise of a punk, and had, to his mother's clear disapproval, found some means of colouring his hair a rusty orange hue. My mate passed Swarb meandering slowly up School Lane wearing the cheesecloth top that he'd worn onstage at Knebworth and would also wear for Fairport's performance that night, and my mate was incredulous that he'd seen the star of the day's top attraction mingling so obliviously, and expressed his doubts that Jimmy Page would be behaving in a similar manner at Knebworth.

There was a lengthy wait whilst the stage was prepared for the main act of the day, the year, the decade. We really, honestly, all believed that this would be the band's swansong. As we took our seats on the ground in front of the stage the atmosphere was a potent combination of the expectation of Christmas and an impending sense of loss. During the *Farewell* tour, the band had dug back into their extensive archive to revive a selection of songs that had fallen from their repertoire, and their set at the Farewell show followed along similar lines.

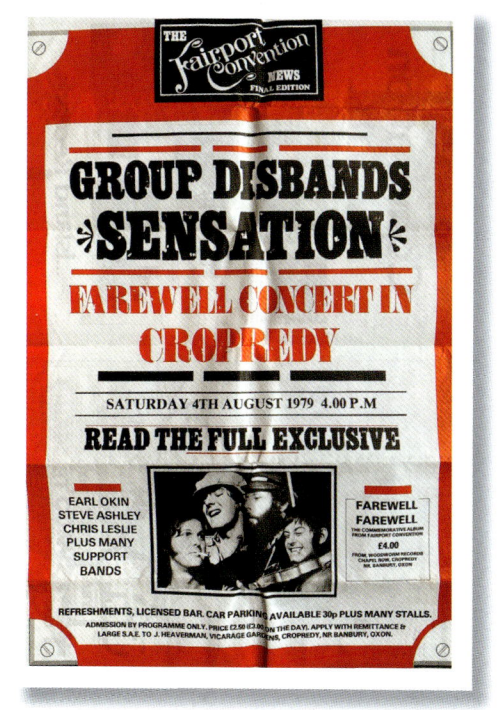

Fairport hit the stage at some time around 11pm and, as usual for that era, opened their set with 'Royal Selecction No 13'. The band then burst into 'Walk Awhile', the crowd now on its feet packed tightly together and swaying. 'Dirty Linen', 'The Journeyman's Grace' and 'Adieu Adieu' all followed before Simon stepped up to the mic for 'John Barleycorn', the only song from their recent *Tipplers Tales* album that they featured on that momentous night. After 'Me with You', a Swarb piece-de-resistance from the *Rosie* album, we were treated to the first guest appearance of the evening. It was no secret that Ralph McTell was around. He'd spent most of the afternoon in close proximity to the Theakston's pumps, and his state of refreshment was pretty evident as he stumbled onto the stage to join the band for 'White Dress' and, appropriately, 'Stagger Lee'.

After Ralph's appearance, Fairport continued with 'The Hen's

March…', 'The Eynsham Poacher' and 'Flatback Caper'. At some point along the way, Maddy Prior appeared, to a rousing reception, and enchanted us all with a cappella version of the lovely 'Mother And Child' before Fairport headed into the home straight with 'Matty Groves' (not then the showpiece set-closer that it later became, but indispensable nonetheless), 'Bridge Over the River Ash' (renamed 'Bridge Over the Oxford Canal' for the occasion) and a version of Loudon Wainwright's 'Red Guitar' before the finale of 'The Lark in the Morning' and, inevitably, appropriately and devastatingly, 'Meet on the Ledge'. We bayed for more but, as compere/organiser Johnny Jones reminded us when he arrived onstage to close down proceedings that, 'We never follow 'Meet on the Ledge'.'

The next day, we called in at the Brasenose for a last drink before heading back north and were pleasantly surprised to see the Fairport guys, still wearing the clothes they'd worn on stage the night before, all gathered and quaffing Draught Bass as though nothing special had happened.

Thank you, Fairport, for saying 'Farewell', and then deciding that you didn't mean it after all.

BOB BRADBURY

My first experience of Fairport was at the Jug O' Punch Folk Club at Digbeth Civic Hall in Birmingham. The club was run by the Ian Campbell Folk Group, who would gather around a single mic to sing their traditional and contemporary folk songs. The entry fee was two shillings (10p) for members and I was just 17, underage for the pints of brown and mild I was drinking.

Daves Swarbrick and Pegg had each been members of the Ian Campbell Group and the band used the club to warm up for their tours. They were always unannounced, as far as I recall, and the entry stayed at two shillings. The big clue to their appearances was the swathe of equipment and loudspeakers where we expected none. These were truly surprising, exciting and memorable experiences.

I went on to see them many times at Birmingham Town Hall and other venues, including a church in Kent and at least 30 *Cropredy Festivals*, starting with the 'Farewell' performance in 1979, which I thought was the complete end of an era.

GONNA SEE ALL MY FRIENDS:
A PEOPLE'S HISTORY OF FAIRPORT CONVENTION

CROPREDY FESTIVAL
30 AUGUST 1980, CROPREDY, UK

RACHEL LEONARD

I have a love/hate relationship with Fairport Convention. Yes, I like the music, though they come some way behind Mozart and Beethoven in my affections. They seem to be a decent bunch of people, generally friendly and approachable. I like hearing them on tour every year, as long as I have a comfortable seat and an ice cream at half time. I love their version of 'The Hiring Fair' and I sing along enthusiastically to 'Meet on the Ledge'. I even used their versions of 'Sir Patrick Spens' and 'Matty Groves' while teaching English ballads to an A-level English group, to highlight the way the ballads evolve into different versions over time: certainly, Simon rarely sings exactly the same words twice.

Rachel Leonard is not a Cropredy fan but husband Andy is

But, and this is a big but, *Cropredy* and I do not get on. I was persuaded by my husband Andy to go along in 1980. He started the day by locking the keys to his car, along with all our proper waterproof gear, in his boot. As a result, we had to travel in my little car with a frankly inadequate mishmash of waterproofs, which had been discarded because they weren't waterproof. It rained the whole day. It wasn't possible to sit on the ground as it was soggy with mud. I was soaked through to the skin and frozen and, as it happens, I was five months pregnant. I vowed never to go to any open-air festival again.

Fast forward to 2008. After a period of 28 years memories had faded and I was persuaded to join my husband on the Saturday. Though the waterproofs were fairly efficient, I remember the rain driving so hard that it was getting between my face and my glasses. During the afternoon we had to retreat to the caravan to try to get our clothes dry in time for the Fairport set. I would have enjoyed that had I not been so damp and cold. I vowed 'never again'. Luckily my husband found a friend who was prepared to suffer all this misery with him every year. I have not been back.

RALPH MCTELL

I enjoy sport, especially team sport. However, as an individual I have never been any good at it. I never understood cricket as a kid and only ever played one game with a real cricket ball. I was clean bowled on the third ball. I played amateur football for the pub team known as 'The Blue Moon All Stars'. Some of the best Sunday mornings of my life were spent on rugged playing fields with broken glass, dog excrement and supermarket trolleys around south London, until by trickery and skulduggery we ended up in the Octopus League (so named because there were ten teams in it – I know, I know, an octopus has eight legs). I never scored a goal and, for that matter, even as a kid in the playground. I have never scored a goal. I cannot throw a ball very far and put this down to not having a dad to teach me. By the age of ten years all my sons could throw further than me. I throw like a male chimpanzee.

In 1980 the still fairly infant *Fairport's Cropredy Convention* had taken place and the ever-hospitable Peggs invited a fair percentage of the audience and players back to their tiny cottage in Cropredy. I am probably wrong about numbers (drink had been taken) but it seemed to me that there were at least a hundred people crammed into their tiny downstairs area. I had been to the cottage before, and Dave (Peggy) and I had recorded several demos there. On an early morning walk I had discovered the evidence in the local church of the battle at Cropredy Bridge that eventually became the song 'Red and Gold'.

Peggy and Christine had been made responsible for the takings at the festival which in those days was mainly cash. With all these guests coming to the house, the Peggs were slightly concerned for the money's safety. After a short while, I suggested hiding it in the bass drum of the kit upstairs in the little studio and that is where it was placed.

The cottage was swinging away to Peggy's favourite Ray Charles LP when Peggy suddenly came up with the idea of a game of darts. Their tiny triangular kitchen was about three metres at its longest and tapered to a point at which was hung a dartboard, under which their cat used to sleep on top of the boiler. The protestations from some guests that there wasn't enough room were quickly dismissed and two teams of approximately 30-people-a-side were drawn up on the blackboard. The game was changed from 301 to 1001 to accommodate all the players, and it went on so long that I almost forgot about it as I chatted away to some of the non-players and others, when suddenly my name was called.

'Ralph, it's your turn.'

I was standing in the little sitting area about another three metres away from the kitchen entrance and jokingly offered to throw from there. 'What do we need, Dave?' I shouted. 'Double five mate.' Someone handed me the three darts and I threw the first dart from behind the settee. It went straight into the double five. An audible gasp and a huge cheer went up. The first dart had travelled over the heads of the party goers, missed the cat, and won the game. It's estimated that the dart travelled at least six metres. No one could believe what they had witnessed, most of all me.

This was my finest hour and my greatest sporting achievement.

My reputation spread far and wide, and everyone was reluctant to take me on at 301. I basked it this moment of glory until my reputation was shattered at the first contest I undertook; it has remained an absolute fluke.

My achievement was largely overshadowed by the fact that no one could remember where they hid the money. Luckily it was found, and the festival went from strength to strength. Unlike my dart playing!

BROUGHTON CASTLE
15 AUGUST 1981, BANBURY, UK

STEVE CARSON

One of my favourite Fairport memories is the time, I was, Richard Thompson. This was in 1981, when they did *Live at Broughton Castle*. I was hanging out with the band a lot, and I was at the rehearsal they were doing just before. I was having a pleasant time just sitting at Woodworm studio, listening to them get ready. At the end of the rehearsal, Peggy announced to the guys, 'Tomorrow morning, bright and early, we have to

GONNA SEE ALL MY FRIENDS:
A PEOPLE'S HISTORY OF FAIRPORT CONVENTION

be at Broughton Castle, because the BBC people are going to be there tomorrow morning, really early.'

It was for a show called *Six Thirty-Five*. They would always show a quick clip of a British band on TV and were going to do a video of Fairport. When Peggy mentioned Richard said that he couldn't do it, he had to be in London. Peggy went, 'Oh shit'. He looked around at the guys, and then he looked at me and I remember him saying, 'Oh, Steve, you've always wanted to be Richard Thompson, you can be in the video with us tomorrow.' And so, why not?

Bright and early the next morning I was up at the top

Steve Carson pretended to be RT on VT

of the castle with Simon Nicols' electric 12 string Rickenbacker. I was wearing an old-fashioned, double-breasted, pin-striped coat, and the BBC people were enchanted. So when the video was put together, I got more time on the BBC than any member of the band, other than Swarb, which was quite hilarious. I pantomimed on the guitar, and it was great fun. It was shown all over Britain. That evening we watched it on the TV.

The next day, they were playing one of their warmup shows at the Half Moon in London. When we walked in, they were in the middle of a rehearsal. Dave Mattacks stopped the rehearsal with a drum roll, and said, 'Ladies and Gentlemen, the great Carsons have walked in, the stars, featuring the Fairport Convention band.'

I know Richard quite well, and many years later, I brought this story up, 'Do you remember that time I was you in a video.' He said, 'Yes, and I got hate mail from my audience.'

GONNA SEE ALL MY FRIENDS:
A PEOPLE'S HISTORY OF FAIRPORT CONVENTION

ALAN DELANEY

My first exposure to Fairport Convention was in 1973. I had only been out of school a short while and was in my first job. Every Friday, after I got paid, I was discovering the wonderful delights of the record store and thus starting my journey into what music there was to mould my interest. One week, the man behind the counter said, 'Try listening to this,' so I did. It was strange, like nothing I'd ever heard before, yet quite captivating. I bought it immediately and played it many times. It was *"Babbacombe" Lee*.

I was quite unaware of anything else by this strangely-named band, so my take-up was slow for a while. But one evening I was listening to a rock show on Radio London when the presenter played 'Rising for the Moon'. I absolutely loved

Alan Delaney saw a pub advertising the Broughton gig

the wonderful voice of Sandy Denny. Just hearing the tune gave me such a feeling of happiness, and to this day it is probably my favourite Fairport track.

A couple of other Fairport albums joined my rapidly-growing vinyl collection, but nothing else happened until 1981, when I was working away from home and staying in a B&B for the week. It was Thursday evening and I happened to enter the local pub for an evening meal when I noticed a poster behind the bar advertising a concert that Fairport Convention were putting on, and it was starting the next day. My plan to return home for the weekend was instantly cancelled. I left the pub with that poster in my hands, and it now lives tucked inside one of my Fairport albums.

The concert was at Broughton Castle. I slept in the van. The beer was Theakstons and that's where I got my second treasured piece of Fairport memorabilia, a commemorative glass beer tankard. The music was absolutely wonderful and quite other-worldly. Thank you, Fairport members past and present, for such an amazing music-filled journey.

CROPREDY FESTIVAL
13 & 14 AUGUST 1982, CROPREDY, UK

NICKY MANSFIELD

My brother Mic and I travelled by train to the *Cropredy* Festival in 1982, I was 19. Fairport were marvellous, of course, but it was wet. Very wet. At bedtime we were soaked but our Theakston's-addled brains could not find our tent on the small camping field. We trudged round looking, getting colder and a mild despair began to grow. Then we spied the mixing desk. Did we? Yes! Early next morning we were woken by voices and clanking of metal below and I shouted down to ask for a minute for us to climb off. The two crewmen found it funny, and we walked straight to the tent and collapsed there for a couple of hours of more comfortable kip.

Nicky Mansfield and her brother found somewhere dry to sleep at Cropredy

KEVIN WARD

As one of the first Theakston bar staff to work at the Fairport reunion concerts, and being a 22-year-old *Saturday Night Fever* music lover, I managed to get a half hour slot off from pulling pints so that I could go backstage to see what all this folk music fuss was about. Well, there was a small man of no resemblance to anyone I knew with a fiddle under his chin, playing what I later found out to be 'Sloth' – a certain David Swarbrick. I can honestly say that that moment changed my idea of what real music and its origins were about. As a Masham lad, 'Meet on the Ledge' will always be the ultimate song for me for 'white bear' reasons. Those that know, know!

Kevin Ward remembers seeing Swarb in action

MORON CAFÉ
20 MARCH 1983, KRISTIANSAND, NORWAY

SALLY AND JIM FARMER

Whilst working in Norway in the early '80s, we saw a poster advertising that Simon and Swarb were due to play at a hotel in Kristiansand in March 1983. It was in a cellar bar called the Moron Café. On admission, we had our hands stamped with 'Moron' which we thought was quite amusing. It was a very small audience. We chatted with Simon and Swarb afterwards and they signed a poster which was on the wall.

Sally and Jim Farmer found themselves labelled as morons

GONNA SEE ALL MY FRIENDS:
A PEOPLE'S HISTORY OF FAIRPORT CONVENTION

PARCO TROTTER
3 JULY 1983, MILAN, ITALY

RAFFAELE GALLI

My second Fairport concert in Italy was in a nice open location, green and warm, but really hot. Their show was perfect and the public appreciated it very much, I remember the guys were satisfied with their performance.

In 1981 our adventure with *Il Mucchio Selvaggio* ended and *L'Ultimo Buscadero* (later only *Buscadero* – still a monthly rock magazine), was born. Since then, I have reviewed almost all their records in its pages. I enjoyed particularly *Red & Gold*, that showed the new 'road life' of the band, and *The Five Seasons*, above all due to the fantastic arrangement of Archie Fishers' song, 'The Wounded Whale' realised by Maartin and his keyboards, and which captured the suffering of the creature.

Raffaele Galli saw Fairport stripped for action in 1983

During the Nineties and the first decade of the new millennium, Fairport visited Italy many times. I enjoyed each of their concerts, but I was very happy to hear them in Mezzago, a multicultural centre in Brianza, in 1994 when Fairport played unplugged due to the absence of drummer Dave Mattacks. They even sang songs written by the McGarrigle sisters like 'Foolish You' and Loudon Wainwright III's 'The Swimming Song' along with a strong version of their beautiful 'The Hiring Fair'. Maartin Allcock used a guitar that he found at the last minute, his having been damaged during the airplane transport.

July 1997 found the band in Sarnico on the beautiful Iseo Lake in the hills of Lombardia with Chris Leslie in the line-up. The show was good but not quite as rock heavy as I might have wished. I saw them again in Sarnico in the summer of 2003, where they played in a beautiful an old manor in front of the lake called Villa Fraccaroni, which the tour promoter, Gigi Bresciani, has described as the number one folk arena.

Fairport's concert in Zanica, near Bergamo, in July 2003 was in a square dedicated to Pope John Paul. The band celebrating its 40th anniversary but Dave Pegg was absent due to a minor operation and so Simon, Rick, Chris and Gerry had to play without him. They played a very interesting show, something more than a Fairport Acoustic Convention offer. I appreciated Ric Sanders's brilliance with his fiddle, Simon as the perfect spokesman and Chris' growth as a lead singer.

And two years later, they were in Trezzo d'Adda in the beautiful setting of the Castello Visconteo as guests of *Interceltic Festival*. They played new songs, including pieces taken from *Excalibur* composed by Alan Simon, and their interpretation of the Oxfordshire Morris dance, 'The Happy Man' was magnificent, while the encore murder ballad, 'Matty Groves', was strong as always.

But the best Fairport concert I attended wasn't in Italy. It was in England in '81 at Broughton Castle. At the end of the evening, the late Judy Dyble appeared on stage to sing Joni Mitchell's 'Both Sides Now' and 'When Will I Be Loved?' by the Everly Brothers.

CROPREDY FESTIVAL
12 & 13 AUGUST 1983, CROPREDY, UK

ARIE EUWIJK

I was at Cropredy in 1983 with a group of fans. Can you guess where from?

Arie Euwijk was part of a Dutch contingent at Cropredy in 1983

GONNA SEE ALL MY FRIENDS:
A PEOPLE'S HISTORY OF FAIRPORT CONVENTION

WIMBLEDON THEATRE
1 JANUARY 1984, LONDON, UK

ADAM PALMER

There seems to be a common belief that, except for *Cropredy*, Fairport split up in 1979 and re-formed in 1985. This is not quite correct. As a 17-year-old prog rock fan in 1983, myself and a bunch of friends started getting the train from Chelmsford into London to go to the Marquee Club on Wardour Street, and see bands from the 'New Wave of Progressive Rock' (a terrible name) spearheaded by Marillion, amongst other early Genesis sound-alikes. But a number of us, particularly my friend Pete and I, were much more into a folky prog band called Solstice (much later to play at *Cropredy*). With a female singer, and a violin player, they cited Fairport Convention as one of their influences.

Adam Palmer recalls seeing Fairport in January 1984

We'd never heard of Fairport, but the next week Pete went out and bought the double LP, *A History of Fairport Convention*. I'd frankly never heard anything like it, and it took me a few listens to get into it, but we were hooked, and they opened up a whole world of music to us. So, in early January 1984, we took the train into London and traversed the Underground across the capital, all the way to Wimbledon Theatre to see Simon Nicol, Dave Pegg, Dave Swarbrick and Bruce Rowland on their *Winter Tour*. I remember an epic version of 'Sloth' (with a lot of delay pedal used on guitar and violin) and, of course, 'Meet on the Ledge'. Friends thought we were crazy – 17-year-olds seeing a 'really old band' of guys in their mid-to-late-30s.

So that summer, myself and Pete were off to *Cropredy* for the first time of many – the 'Fifth Annual Reunion', and we were back to Wimbledon Theatre the next winter too.

After another *Cropredy*, the following year's winter tour was a bit of a shock. We were lining up outside the theatre to get in, and there was a poster of the band to advertise the gig. This was before social media's advance warning of everything, and to our surprise there were two new faces, along with Dave Mattacks replacing Bruce Rowland – and no Swarb! We had no idea. I must admit we grumpily watched the first half as Ric Sanders bounced around the stage (how dare he?), but we were ultimately won over by his sheer quality of playing, and the wonderful new songs, 'The Hiring Fair' being a personal favourite. They were now officially back as a touring/recording band.

From then on, I've lost count of the many times I've seen them. And, as a wonderful bonus, I joined BBC Pebble Mill as a sound engineer in 1987 and got to record them a few times for the *Folk Show* (based in Birmingham at the time) and go to the bar with them afterwards too.

ST DAVID'S HALL
2 JANUARY 1984, CARDIFF, UK

KEITH DHAN-WELLER
Fairport played the then newish St David's Hall in Cardiff. The band signed my double LP, *Fairport Chronicles*, which was an American import on A&M with a photo of Stonehenge on the cover, and Swarb said, 'I don't remember us doing this one.'

DIE ZECHE
19 FEBRUARY 1984, BOCHUM, GERMANY

UWE BROEMER
It all started when I got *Live at the LA Troubadour* in 1976. I had never heard such a powerful combination of folk and rock before. I played that record very loud over and over again. The band does not often play in Germany, so I didn't see them until the release of *Gladys' Leap*. It was great to finally see them live on stage after listening to so many of their albums. One of my favourite songs, 'The Hiring Fair', with great vocals from Simon, is on that album.

GONNA SEE ALL MY FRIENDS:
A PEOPLE'S HISTORY OF FAIRPORT CONVENTION

In 1992 I was planning a holiday in England when friends from a local folk club told me about Cropredy. I decided to include the festival in my holidays and went with a friend and my brother. It was the 25th anniversary and we enjoyed the music, the warm and friendly atmosphere and the wonderful food and beer. And then came Fairport's final performance – wow! It is a special moment when you have travelled so far to see a band and then the gig begins, and we were treated to hours of great music, with guest appearances by so many former Fairport members along with Robert Plant, with Fairport sounding like Led Zeppelin.

Uwe Broemer and wife Veronika visit Cropredy from Germany

I have since returned to Cropredy every five years (since 2000, with my wife Veronika). 2017 was the last time and it was great to see so many of the former members of the band, but also sad to realise how many have already passed away.

The last time we saw Fairport live was in 2018 at the Musiktheater Piano in Dortmund, Germany. The gig was fantastic, and somehow like a living-room gig. It was a bit strange to see all the band members sitting on their chairs but it made for a very intimate atmosphere. I realised that we all are getting older, myself included.

When the gig ended and the audience clapped for an encore, the band members stayed on their seats, turning to the back and trying to hide their faces, with one hiding partly behind the curtain. Then they turned to the audience again and played their encore. I don't know whether the stage exit was too small or they just didn't want to have an exhausting walk off the stage and back on stage again, but it showed once again how much humour these Fairport guys have got.

It is so difficult to choose a favourite song, but every time 'Meet on the

LONE STAR CAFÉ
30 JULY 1984, NEW YORK, NEW YORK

KEN WEXLER

I first discovered Fairport through an advert in a 1969 edition of *Rolling Stone*. It was a full-page ad for *Unhalfbricking*, with the track listing. I was amazed that it included three unreleased Bob Dylan songs, including one in French. Being a Dylan freak, I had to get the record. And I was hooked

Ken Wexler remembers Swarb's joke telling

on the group for life. I've been to nine *Cropredys* and have seen them every time they have played New York City, including a couple of memorable fits of temper at The Bottom Line. But my favourite shows were at the old Lone Star Café, a two-night stand in July 1984. They played two shows each night, and really switched up the setlists. A standout was the X-rated version of 'The Sailor's Alphabet' and the infamous 'She Is Woman'. Swarbrick told lots of great jokes. At one of the shows, I was sitting at the bar and who should sit next to me but Kate McGarrigle, another one of my favourites. I never had more fun than those two Fairport nights at The Lone Star.

GONNA SEE ALL MY FRIENDS:
A PEOPLE'S HISTORY OF FAIRPORT CONVENTION

CROPREDY FESTIVAL
11 AUGUST 1984, CROPREDY, UK

PETER ROE

My first Fairport album was *The History of Fairport Convention* which I bought on its release in 1972. I saw an advert in *Sounds* and a work colleague recommended it. I hadn't heard any Fairport before but took a punt as it was a very reasonable £2.49 for a double LP. I was immediately hooked, figuring that a band which could produce moving and beautiful songs such as 'Who Knows Where the Time Goes?', fun songs like 'Angel Delight' and 'Mr Lacey' and extended instrumental work-outs like 'Sloth' and 'A Sailors Life' were well worth exploring further.

Peter Roe saw an advert in music weekly Sounds

The family tree on the cover also looked intriguingly complicated, inspiring exploration of solo Sandy Denny, Richard Thompson, the Albion Band and Steeleye Span. It would take several such covers to reflect the many further changes and off-shoots since.

My first *Cropredy* was in 1984 when I was lucky enough to win two tickets in a competition in a local newspaper. Entrance security was provided by the local Cub Scout group who marked your hand with an ink stamp. So I have been on board since 1972. That was the best £2.49 I have ever spent.

GONNA SEE ALL MY FRIENDS:
A PEOPLE'S HISTORY OF FAIRPORT CONVENTION

STUDENTS' UNION UNIVERSITY OF BRISTOL
23 JANUARY 1985, BRISTOL, UK

ROB BRIGHTWELL

I had seen various bands as a student so when my mate suggested that we go to see some strange and ancient folk outfit, I was happy to join in. I didn't know any of the tunes, but the beer was cheap. Some way into the set they went into a number which I subsequently discovered was called 'Sloth'. It felt like it went on for about half an hour, with some hairy fella doing things with a fiddle which I never knew were possible. And that is when I discovered that live music is the art form that floats my boat above all others. I saw the band countless times over subsequent years, but 'Sloth' never seemed to be on the set list. The studio version of 'Sloth' is a shadow of the live experience. And then came August 2018 at *Cropredy*. The band were still ancient – but now I was too. And I finally got to demonstrate to my poor wife what I'd been going on about for so many years. At last – 'Sloth' live. And yes, she did notice the tears in my eyes.

MARTYN KENNEY

My first Fairport gig came soon after my first two ever gigs – T.Rex and King Crimson. My music tastes were eclectic from an early age. The Friends of Fairport was formed in 1982 following an advert where someone was seeking a copy of 'Meet on the Ledge' (or maybe 'Now Be Thankful') and someone else, living at the other end of the country, having said single. I thought, 'What if there was a fan-based group whereby people could contact and exchange and sell such items?' Little did I know what I'd created.

The Ledge fanzine followed on soon after, and when I called it a day, it saw an even longer run of success under the guidance of Ian Burgess. *The Ledge* also went on to spawn *Dirty Linen* in the US and *Fiddlestix* in Australia.

For some daft reason, I also chose to create an alternative scrapbook-type book of newspaper features, reviews, bit and bobs of promo stuff, *Cropredy* stuff and photos, etc. which was published as *Unscrapbooking* and limited to 100 copies. It rarely surfaces for sale anywhere today.

GONNA SEE ALL MY FRIENDS:
A PEOPLE'S HISTORY OF FAIRPORT CONVENTION

One particular gig springs to mind. I was part of the Yesterday's Folk Club in Bristol. In December 1985, we had Fairport booked but the snow was very bad, with traffic coming to a grinding – or sliding – halt. No buses were running. It was nearly 5pm and there was no sign of the band and no phone call. Moments before we were going to cancel the gig, the gear arrived, and by 7pm, so had the guys. The audience also arrived, having got there by any known (or possibly unknown) mode of travel, including one couple who had walked over five miles to be there.

Having soared through a sound check of sorts, Fairport were on stage at 8pm and giving it there all. What a memorable day and night, for so many reasons. Heroes all!

Martyn Kenney remembers a late arrival by the Fairports

GONNA SEE ALL MY FRIENDS:
A PEOPLE'S HISTORY OF FAIRPORT CONVENTION

BRASENOSE ARMS
JUNE 1985, CROPREDY, UK

GREG SWAIN

I'd been a Fairport fan since 1969 and saw them for the first time as a student at Sheffield University in 1972. I also visited *Cropredy* for one of the original festivals, in 1977. In 1985, my father had a heart attack and my brother Steve and I decided to do a charity bike ride to raise money for the British Heart Foundation. Armed with only a CAMRA *Good Beer Guide*, we plotted a course from Land's End and realised our route would take us through Cropredy. We sent a letter to the Fairport PO Box number (more in hope than expectation) to the effect that we'd be in the Brasenose Arms at lunchtime on the Wednesday of our marathon ride. Imagine our delight when we found Peggy and Ric Sanders in the pub. They bought us lunch and beers and treated us like long-lost friends. And as we left, a bank note was pressed into my palm for our charity. It was the first £50 note I'd ever seen. Thank you, Fairport – you made our week.

Greg and Pete Swain popped into the Brasenose on their charity bike ride

CROPREDY FESTIVAL
9 & 10 AUGUST 1985, CROPREDY, UK

STEPHEN ROYSTON

I remember hearing 'If I Had a Ribbon Bow' on the radio in 1967, but it was 'Genesis Hall', the B-side of their one and only hit single, 'Si Tu Dois Partir', in the summer of 1969, which started my lifelong devotion to Fairport Convention. I first saw the band with the *Full House* line-up in 1970.

I've kept a diary since I was 14 years old and Fairport have received innumerable mentions. Richard Thompson signed a page of my 1977 diary. Over the years I accumulated signatures of every past and present member of the band, including those who have since sadly left us, in my copy of Patrick Humphries' 1982 book *Meet on the Ledge: A History of Fairport Convention*.

My wife Frances and I first started going to the *Cropredy Festival* in 1980, as documented in the booklet which accompanied the *Cropredy Capers* box set. We have been almost every year since. In 1985, the *Full House* line-up dedicated 'Dirty Linen' to our one-year-old son James, making his first of many appearances at the festival. Ten years later, James had his photo taken with Jimmy Page at the festival bar. In 2002, James travelled overland from Hong Kong via the Trans-Siberian Railway to join us at the festival field, while for our daughter Emma, who has now been to over 30 festivals, it's one of the absolute highlights of her year.

Stephen Royston's son James was at his first Cropredy in 1985 and in 1994 met Jimmy Page and Simon

One year, the signposts were being replaced in the lane near the village. The old sign pointing to Cropredy a quarter of a mile away had been discarded. I picked it up, brought it home and restored it, and it has graced our kitchen wall ever since.

In 2001, after *The Daily Telegraph* had erroneously published Swarb's obituary, he had a stall at the *Cropredy Festival*, selling autographed copies of it. After he had gone, I picked up his hand-written sign which reads 'OBITS – I HAD TO DIE TO GET ONE'.

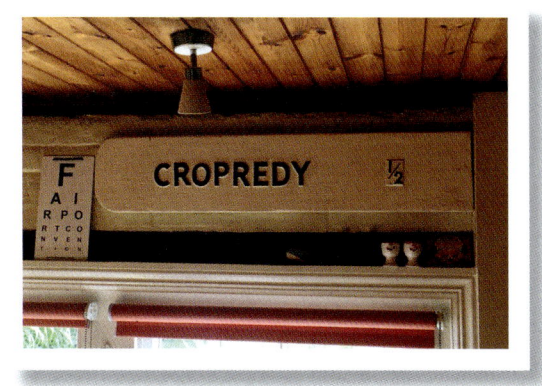

Stephen Royston's kitchen now houses the village sign

On the first day of the 2006 Cropredy, I noted in my diary that, 'I spoke earlier to Simon Nicol, suggesting they perform *Liege & Lief* in its entirety, à la Brian Wilson doing *Pet Sounds*. He seemed to have not thought of it and said 'it's doable' and they could do it on a Cropredy Friday night.'

And that is exactly what happened a year later, with Swarb back in the line-up and Chris While on vocals. I like to think that I helped to make that memorable performance happen.

EDDY MCCABE

My first hearing of Fairport Convention was seeing older guys at school around 1968 and '69 flaunting their street cred via carrying around the first couple of albums, along with their Zappa, Beefheart and Airplane records. My first Fairport purchase was *The History of Fairport Convention* and my first gig was at Caird Hall Dundee in late 1970, followed a few months later by one at the University Students' Union.

Years later, I persuaded Ray, a work colleague, to come along to my first ever festival, at Cropredy in 1985. Neither of us had camped

Eddy and Jane McCabe have a family gathering at Cropredy

before, so we borrowed a small ridge tent and set off from Middlesbrough for our weekend adventure. We arrived in Banbury just after all the shops closed on Friday afternoon, at which point I realised we hadn't brought any sleeping bags. My recollection is that the weather stayed reasonably dry, though it was very cold, especially at night. Ray slept in the car both nights, whereas I struggled to sleep in the tent, despite having an empty four-pint flagon for company.

Fairport closed both evenings, and were brilliant, as was the genius that is Billy Connolly. I'm not convinced that 'Meet on the Ledge' was embedded as the festival closer at that point. I do remember Jonah, when announcing the surprise guest The Big Yin, advising that some of the language might be a bit coarse for the delicate ears of young children, so parents should think about taking them up to the top of the field – where they could still hear every word!

I was hooked, and after another foray to North Oxon, my wife insisted on coming along to see what all the fuss was about. Since 1988, *Cropredy* has become the first thing to go into the diary each year.

When we had the first of our three children, fellow *Cropredy*-goers with older children assured us that when they hit teenage years, we would no longer be able to attend, as the festival and the music would be way too uncool. But our now 30-year-old son has only missed two *Cropredys*, one of our daughters skipped one to go to DisneyWorld and our youngest has been to every one since her birth in 1995. As the children grew, they quickly became very careful as to which friends they would invite along, as they realised that worrying about whether said friend was enjoying themselves would put a damper on their own enjoyment.

None of them would term themselves Fairport fans, and I very much doubt they would go out of their way to see the band in any other setting but the festival has become a cornerstone of the year at which we, plus my brother-in-law and his family, all meet up, rather like a midsummer Christmas.

JONI FRIEND

Dave Pegg moved to the village next to where I lived and he rode around on a little Kawasaki dirt bike. I had a Triumph Bonneville and worked at the garage he used, so we talked bikes. I also got to meet the very funny Billy Connolly when he came to compere the festival and stayed with the Peggs.

GONNA SEE ALL MY FRIENDS:
A PEOPLE'S HISTORY OF FAIRPORT CONVENTION

DOM POLSKI CENTRE
27 FEBRUARY 1986, ADELAIDE, AUSTRALIA

MICHAEL HUNTER

Sometime around mid-1977, the then-current line-up of Fairport Convention was touring Australia. Swarb, Simon and Peggy appeared on a late Saturday night radio programme called *Rocturnal* to talk about the tour and the accompanying *Bonny Bunch of Roses* LP. My interest was piqued. Their music was melodic and energetic, and a mix of past and present that was worth exploring. *Bonny Bunch of Roses* was the obvious first choice, followed by *History of*, which gave strong hints of the musical rabbit hole I was about to enter. Unfortunately, I missed their local gig at the time.

Michael Hunter (left, with Swarb in 1989) started the Fiddlestix fanzine

Now a fully-fledged Fairport tragic, in 1985 I was looking through some old *NMEs* when I saw a plug for the then-rare *Heyday* cassette and thought to write off for it. A reply came from Chris Pegg at Woodworm with details of the tape and a casual mention that there was a UK 'Friends of Fairport' with its fanzine, *The Ledge*.

After liaising with Martyn Kenney from that publication and TJ McGrath from the US equivalent *Fairport Fanatics* (which later became *Dirty Linen*), I started the Australian Fairport fanzine *Fiddlestix* to limited but growing interest. This lasted in physical form until 2001 and then as an email 'zine' until the late-2010s. One of the earliest subscribers was original band manager John Penhallow.

My first meeting with the band was at their Adelaide gig in 1986, and they seemed pleased with the whole fanzine idea. As things progressed, I got myself on a local folk radio show to talk about *Fiddlestix* and have now been doing the show myself for over 35 years. From that also came the invitation to write for a music magazine called *dB*, which led to interviewing multiple acts, folk and otherwise, for 25 years or so. All this from the idea to start a Fairport fanzine.

Before long, names on the Fairport album covers became real people and friends. I've had the pleasure of interviewing many members past, present and no longer with us, along with compering a couple of their local shows, and helping organise the band's South Australian gigs in 1999. How I had the chutzpah to jam with Swarb at Trevor Lucas' wake in 1989 with my limited ability astonishes me now, but thankfully there is only pictorial evidence of the event.

The whole idea of 'Fairport as a family' has proven itself correct so many times, and is something I'm sure everyone, band members included, is grateful for in their own ways. I'm just glad to have my own small part in that, and am still amazed at the natural way things progressed in my case.

BENDIGO TOWN HALL
5 MARCH 1986, BENDIGO, AUSTRALIA

JOHN PENHALLOW

This tour started in Perth and then headed east. They played gigs along the way, including one at the Ranch Restaurant in Murray Bridge where Maart famously said he bought the audience a drink – five men and a dog had turned up. This was the *Gladys' Leap* tour, with DM on drums, Maart on lead guitar and Ric on the fiddle with Simon and Peggy.

I caught up with them in Bendigo in March. Shane Howard from Goanna opened, followed by The Bushwackers (long known as Fairport's equivalent Australian band for the rocking up of Aussie Bush Music and for changing their line-up on a regular basis) and with Fairport topping the bill.

The next day I set off for Melbourne with Simon for company in my Mitsubishi L300 Express eight-seater van. The van overheated a couple of times in the hot summer temperatures, which tried my patience. However, we got there in good time for the soundcheck at Dallas Brooks Hall and the band went down well with the audience that night.

The next day was Friday, and the bands had a day off. Dobe Newton of the Bushies had invited us to his house for a barbeque. The lads piled into my van for the drive to Dobe's house in an inner northern suburb of Melbourne. We got there and the barbeque was in full swing. Peggy had contacted Danny Thompson, who was touring with Mara. Liz Hurtt Lucas also arrived with Georgia, aged 9, and Clancy Lucas, aged 6. We were introduced for the first time and have been good friends ever since. (Trevor Lucas was up in Mullumbimby recording songs for a movie.)

A good time was being had by all when, as the afternoon drew on, someone said, 'Hey, the McGarrigles are playing tonight at Dallas Brooks and left our names on the door.' So Fairport and Danny piled into my bus and into town we went. We managed to convince the officials backstage and went into the green room, where we met the McGarrigles and their band. Playing with the sisters were future Fairport drummer Gerry Conway and his bass-playing partner from Fotheringay, Pat Donaldson. Joel Zifkin, who later played in Richard Thompson's band, was the violin player and guitarist John Reissner was on guitar.

The McGarrigles played to a full house. They were wonderful singers, singing their beautiful songs. After the concert, there was a bit more socialising backstage for a while before we all went back to our hotels.

Fairport went off to do some country Victoria gigs over the next four days. I drove to Canberra and stayed with my brother until they arrived for the gig at the Canberra Workers Club. This gig was recorded off the desk by Barry the soundman, who gave me a copy. This led to me releasing the *Here, Live Tonight* bootleg cassette for the Aussie Friends of Fairport a few months later.

PADDINGTON TOWN HALL
14 MARCH 1986, SYDNEY, AUSTRALIA

IAN JONES

I had to wait until March 1986 to see Fairport again. They were originally scheduled to appear at the Hordern Pavilion with Australia's top bush band, The Bushwackers, but it was transferred to Paddington Town Hall for a rollicking night. Trevor Lucas had produced two Bushwhackers albums – the *Dance Album* and *Faces in the Street*. The

Fairport line-up was the three-piece version with Simon Nicol, Dave Pegg and Dave Mattacks. My friend Rowland Hilder remembers Dave wore really bright yellow overall-type trousers. The lead singer of the Bushwackers, Dobe Newton, was showing the effects a few beers and destroyed his 'lagerphone', a wooden stick covered in metal beer tops which was played with another wooden stick, on stage.

The band was a five piece. Ric and Maart played all the gigs on this tour.

PENNY DAVIES

Rog and I have been singing folk songs together since 1983 and have been fans of the band since we first heard their albums. In March 1986, when Fairport came through on a big Australian tour. Roger and I were producing a couple of radio programmes and we got most of the band into the studio for an interview before their Paddington Town Hall gig.

We went to the gig, which was fantastic, and then offered to drive some of the lads back to their hotel afterwards. We had Simon, Maart and Rick sitting in the back of our VW Kombi, and maybe Peggy too. When we got to the hotel, a lot of people were hanging out in the foyer where someone was playing the grand piano. We decided to stay and listen for a while and Ric got out his fiddle and started jamming with the piano player. It was first class music in every way. Then the pianist looked up and we saw that it was Peter Tork from The Monkees. He and Ric played together for quite a while and we just leaned on the piano, awestruck. It was an unforgettable end to an incredible night of music. Thanks, Fairport. We might never have begun singing folk songs if not for you.

CROPREDY FESTIVAL
8 & 9 AUGUST 1986, CROPREDY, UK

CLIVE WARNER

Picking out a single story from the multitude collected from working with the Fairies for many years is a big ask – but one story sticks out for me. It was at the *Cropredy Festival* in 1986 when I was working as a site crew member. We had enjoyed a week-long set up, catching up with great friends old and new and preparing for the weekend of music. It was something I looked forward to every year, an absolute highlight.

In the closing stages, after an amazing weekend of top music, drinking, great company and troubleshooting and fixing the site problems, I went into the Artists' Pod at the side of the stage. It was a space reserved for artists' friends, family and the crew, and finally I could relax and enjoy the last part of Fairport's set with Christine Pegg. The set was coming to an end and traditionally the band is joined by other performers on stage to belt out the final, famous number, 'Meet on the Ledge'. It's a great moment in the festival and everyone loves it.

At the appropriate moment in the number, Peggy looked over to the Pod where Christine and I were sitting and yelled out, 'Come on Christine and Clive!' I was really excited to be invited on stage and jumped at the chance. I made my way to the microphone to share it with Peggy and didn't notice the funny look he gave me. What I didn't realise was that he had been inviting Christine Collister and Clive Gregson, artists who had performed earlier in the day, to join him and not me or his then wife. Christine Pegg was aware of my mistake, but I had drunk enough wonderful beer to be totally oblivious. I knew all the lyrics and launched into the song, revelling in the huge audience and my five minutes of fame. Christine Collister and Clive Gregson did come on as well, but I stayed and loved every minute of it. Only after it was over did I realise my hilarious faux pas!

MEMORIAL HALL
25 SEPTEMBER 1986, CINCINNATI, OHIO

STAN GRAHAM

I was attending college at Miami University in Oxford, Ohio and, as an avid progressive rock fan, spent a lot of time in the local record shop browsing the G (Genesis) and E (Emerson, Lake and Palmer) sections. In the F section between them was an intriguing double album called *Fairport Chronicles*, intriguing because it was priced like a single album and because the cover had a picture of Stonehenge.

I had never heard of Fairport Convention. But when Jethro Tull released the album *A*, news articles mentioned that their new bass player, Dave Pegg, had come from Fairport. That lone copy of *Fairport Chronicles* at the record shop became ever more intriguing, even though the songs on it pre-dated Peggy joining the band. In 1982, I decided to take a chance and bought myself *Fairport Chronicles* as a graduation present. Life was forever changed.

I fell in love with Sandy's voice. I was just getting into female vocalists and her voice was pure beauty and magic, while the songs were amazing; well-crafted with wonderful stories, amazing vocals, and incredible musicianship. I embarked on a quest to find more Fairport albums and find out as much as I could about the band. As this was pre-internet, it was a difficult process.

The two most important pieces of information that I learned were devastating. First, I learned that Sandy had left this mortal plane long before I had even purchased that first *Fairport Chronicles* LP. And, secondly, I learned that Fairport had actually called it a day back in 1979. My favourite band no longer existed, and their beautiful vocalist was no more.

It didn't deter me from my quest to search out their extensive back catalogue. My next purchase was *Full House*, which I found in the cut out section of a department store. The vocals were 'interesting' without Sandy, but the musicianship was superb, and it was instrumental in developing my appreciation of the playing of Richard, Swarb, DM and Peggy.

In 1996 I was living in Cincinnati, Ohio, and one late summer day I noticed a small announcement in the local paper. Fairport Convention had reformed and would be playing Memorial Hall. I was stoked - I would finally get to see the band that I had fallen in love with.

Memorial Hall was located in a not-so-fine area of Cincinnati. The venue was crumbling and falling apart. Christine Collister and Clive Gregson might have opened for them, and I remember spotting Simon watching them from the back, clearly appreciating their performance.

Around 8.30pm, Fairport took the stage. There were probably only a couple of hundred people at the show, and I managed to get a centre stage seat just a few rows back from the stage. It was amazing. They opened with the medley from *Liege & Lief* and I was immediately transported.

Simon's vocals really impressed me, and I purchased both *Gladys' Leap* and *Expletive Delighted* at that show. And after listening to 'The Hiring Fair' and 'Wat Tyler', I felt that Simon's vocals really came into their own. It didn't matter to me that there was no Richard or Swarb. Simon and Maart carried the guitar work superbly and Ric Sanders was an amazing fiddler in his own right.

After the show, I was helping myself to a frosty adult beverage when Peggy walked up and ordered one for himself. I introduced myself and complimented him on the show. When I asked what was going on with Jethro Tull, he lit up! He began telling me about the new album (they were working on *Crest of a Knave* at that point) and how Ian Anderson would give him a ride to rehearsals. The promoter, Steve Carson, had to drag him away so that the lads could get to bed. But I thought, 'What a nice chap!' No ego. Someone that loved the music that he played and loved sharing it with others.

HOLSTEIN'S
SEPTEMBER 1986, CHICAGO, ILLINOIS

JOE SIPOCZ

I was 16 years old when I purchased a rock encyclopaedia circa 1976. The encyclopaedia was written by two guys from the UK, and the entries included many UK artists that didn't gain mainstream attention in America. I read the book cover to cover and was intrigued by the entry for Fairport that ended by saying something like, 'No band had done such great work and been rewarded with such wretched luck.' As I recall they had separate entries for Sandy Denny and Richard and Linda Thompson. At that point I had not heard any of these artists.

Joe Sipocz and son Vince are both fans

GONNA SEE ALL MY FRIENDS:
A PEOPLE'S HISTORY OF FAIRPORT CONVENTION

In the summer of 1982, I subscribed to *Stereo Review* and read an entry about Richard and Linda's 1982 American tour, listed as 'Anarchy in the 16th Century'. I was in the habit of recording Chicago's forward-thinking WXRT's Sunday evening concerts. The announcer said that evening's show was from Richard and Linda Thompson. I had started recording the show, remembered Fairport and Richard and Linda from the book and magazine, and decided to keep taping. When I listened to the show again, the following summer, I decided I really liked them.

At Christmas 1985 I visited Bugsy, a college roommate who lived in Park Ridge, Illinois with his parents and crashed in his basement after a party. The radio played 'Time to Ring Some Changes' by Richard Thompson, and I was bowled over. I vowed to find the song on my next visit to the record store. It turns out it was from *Small Town Romance*, all acoustic. I was used to the electric band on the Chicago 1982 tape, so I was left somewhat wanting. Over the next three years I purchased most of the Richard Thompson and then the Fairport discographies.

In September 1986 I heard that Fairport were coming to Chicago. I drove into the city with my new girlfriend Ellen and best friend Kevin in time to catch the show, which was pretty great and rocking, and we then hit every bar down Lincoln Avenue before driving safely home to South Bend.

I saw Fairport Convention again in 1989 at Biddie Mulligan's, just north of Chicago. I enjoyed the show, but not the drunkard that kept calling out for Sandy Denny for the first half of the show. I assume he stumbled out after the first set. I loved all the fast songs, especially 'The Noise Club'. I heard 'Meet on the Ledge' as we left – we had to miss the encore since my friend Tony had to be at work at 6am.

Fairport's early albums were frequently in the CD player of the family car, and mine and Ellen's two kids liked what they heard. Vince especially loved Fairport. In high school he had to write about the meaning of a song and he chose 'No Man's Land'. The teacher suggested writing to the artist, or looking up reviews. Vince wrote to Richard, who was on tour but responded via his manager with an email with a nice, personal reminiscence about the song. The teacher was impressed. I was touched. Thanks, Richard.

Vince remains a Fairport fan. We're both somewhat musical, so we play some of their songs together. He also owns a half a dozen Fairport albums in vinyl. When the kids were young, I couldn't justify the expense of seeing bands out of town. I can go now, so please come back!

THE ARK
27 SEPTEMBER 1986, ANN ARBOR, MICHIGAN

BRIAN O'MALLEY

When I was 12 in 1978, there were only two bands in my world, the Rolling Stones and Jethro Tull. I grew up in Chicago. My dad emigrated from Ireland in 1951 and was a traditional Irish accordion player. I loved traditional Irish music as a child. I think that's why I became a Jethro Tull fan; there was something about their music that kind of drew me in.

In 1980, my oldest sister MaryJane had a party and invited a guy that she'd had a few dates with. His name is Mike Mangan, he grew up in the UK in Leamington Spa. Today he is my brother-in-law. I hit it off with Mike that night and brought down my record collection, mostly Stones and Tull. Jethro Tull's album *A* was brand

Brian O'Malley and Peggy in 2018 and a little over refreshed

Peggy took part in a wheelbarrow race in the hotel corridor

GONNA SEE ALL MY FRIENDS:
A PEOPLE'S HISTORY OF FAIRPORT CONVENTION

Brian O'Malley with Peggy and Maartin counting the proceeds from the t-shirt sales

new at the time. He was studying the photograph on the back cover and said, 'Dave Pegg, I'm quite certain I saw him play with Fairport Convention.' To which I responded, 'Who's Fairport Convention?'

The next day I walked to Rainbow Records looking for this band Fairport Convention. There were a few albums available. I remember looking at the *Full House* album and thinking that this was the one I was going to buy. The only problem was, I had no money. I saved up the $6 for the album and bought it and I absolutely fell in love with what I was hearing.

Maartin tried to call his wife

GONNA SEE ALL MY FRIENDS:
A PEOPLE'S HISTORY OF FAIRPORT CONVENTION

It was exactly what I was looking for musically. I had more in common with Fairport Convention than I did with Jethro Tull because of the traditional Irish music that was being played in the house.

Fast-forward to December of 1985. My sister was with her husband at the Spa Centre in Leamington Spa for the *Gladys' Leap* tour. She purchased a programme for me. When she was exiting the theatre, she saw Dave Pegg and asked him for his autograph. He wrote, 'To Brian, all the best! Dave Pegg.'

I received that programme when they arrived back in Chicago. You can imagine how excited I was. I read it cover-to-cover until I knew it by heart. One of the things that I learned in reading it was that Dave lived just footsteps from Woodworm Studios. I remember thinking to myself, 'If I write him a letter at Woodworm Studios, I wonder if he'll get it?' I wrote him a one-page letter telling him how much I loved Fairport Convention and asking if he ever heard of a Chicago fiddle player and hero of mine named Liz Carroll.

A few months later, there was a postcard in the mail. It was a photograph. I couldn't really make it out. I looked at it, turned it over, read it twice and still didn't understand. It was from Dave Pegg, I couldn't believe it!

After a bit of time showing it off to all my friends, I responded with another letter thanking him for sending me the postcard. He responded with another letter of his and we became pen pals for a couple of years. In one of his letters, he told me that they would be in Chicago in early November 1986.

I'll never forget lining up in front of the venue to get a good seat. We were let in and took our seats in front of the stage. My friends and I were sitting in our seats when Dave walked in the room and stood by the wall, looking at the stage. I got the nerve to walk up and introduce myself. I was so nervous that I was shaking. I introduced myself and he said, 'Oh yes, Brian, did you meet the lads?' and he walked me into the bar to introduce me to them. It was there that I learned that all the lads called him Peggy.

They played that night for about two and a half hours. It was the most amazing concert I had ever been to. To be that close to such amazing musicians was just astonishing.

GONNA SEE ALL MY FRIENDS: A PEOPLE'S HISTORY OF FAIRPORT CONVENTION

After the show, Peggy invited us to dinner at a little Mexican place across the street. We had such a great time that night. We all got on like a house on fire. Part of that might have had something to do with the fact that I was drinking margaritas at 18 years old, but I digress.

We dropped the lads off at their hotel. I decided that I was going to show up tomorrow morning and wish them well. I was there the next morning with a notion that I might go to the next gig at the Ark in Ann Arbor, Michigan. Peggy and Maartin came down and we had a nice chat. I mentioned that I was thinking about going to the next gig and Peggy said, 'Bri, that'd be great, would you mind if myself and Maartin drove with you?' To which I naturally replied, 'Absolutely!'

We drove the four-and-a-half-hour journey from Chicago to Ann Arbor, Michigan listening to my cassettes of James Taylor, Liz Carroll, Tommy Maguire, Cat Stevens, De Dannan, Planxty and some Stones. We passed several signs that read, 'St Juliana wine tasting ahead' and 'Free wine tasting next exit.' I can hear Peggy's voice like it was yesterday saying, 'What do you reckon, should we stop?' There was never a dull moment the whole journey. Having said that, we had no idea what was about to happen!

We got off the expressway and Maartin was reading the map. I can remember him saying, 'Okay, go left up here.' I stopped at the intersection to turn left, when we heard this terrible screech of tires on hot pavement. I looked in the rear-view mirror. There was a 1973 red Dodge Charger screeching towards us at about 40 miles an hour. My car was a stick shift and I popped that clutch as fast as I could and started taking off, but I wasn't as quick as the Charger, and she barrelled right into our back end. I can honestly say that if I had not popped that clutch, and if we had been sitting still when the Charger hit us, there would not have been a gig at the Ark that night.

Myself and the driver of the Charger sorted things out, I tied up the bumper and we took off for the gig. On the way, Peggy asked me if I would sell t-shirts at the show. He said he would give me ten per cent of whatever I sold. I'll never forget the ambition that I had to sell those t-shirts. I went out and bought some poster boards and some markers and made a sign. I sold all the shirts for the entire tour at those two shows at the Ark.

After the gig, Peggy, Simon, Maartin, Ric and I hung on at the bar until the wee hours. We stretched Fairport scanty panties onto a ceiling fan. After closing the bar, Peggy asked Maartin if it would be okay if I stayed with him in his room. Maartin was more than obliging. The four of us arrived at the hotel and took the elevator up to the fourth floor.

We got off the elevator and Peggy shouted, 'Wheelbarrow race, now!', at which point Martin and Peggy immediately fell to the ground and Simon grabbed Maart's ankles and I grabbed Peggy's. Martin and Peggy push themselves up by their hands and we started running down the hall of the hotel. Wheelbarrow races; a first for me. We were laughing so hard that a door opened. It was Dave Mattacks, with his robe tucked around his neck saying, 'Stop this nonsense now or you're going to get us kicked out of this hotel.' Peggy and I were so drunk we couldn't stop laughing.

Maartin and I got to our room and there was only one bed. For as long as I live, I will never forget the feeling that I got when Maartin stripped down naked and got into the bed. I think I slept with my clothes on that night. I remember Maartin ordered us breakfast the night before and left it on the doorknob. The next morning the breakfast came in the room. I remember telling Maart how blown away I was that I was hanging out with Peggy, Simon, and Dave Mattacks. Maart said, 'I know how you feel, I've been pinching myself for the past year-and-a-half. This is the band that I've always wanted to play with, and now I'm touring America with them. I'm gobsmacked every day.'

That was 36 years ago. Peggy and all the lads and I have become the best of friends since then. A lot of water under the bridge.

CROPREDY FESTIVAL
15 AUGUST 1987, CROPREDY, UK

KEITH JORDAN

One night a mate of mine asked if I wanted to go to a folk festival. 'A what?' I replied.

'Well, it's great beer and I'm sure you'll like the music.' This was enough for me. Unfortunately, two days before we were to head off, I crashed my car and we had no transport. We decided to hitchhike and, to make it more fun, we made it a race, with the loser to get the beers in.

We set off from North Wales half a mile apart. A fellow with a sense of humour decided to drop me off at junction 6 on the M6 which is an exit only, in the middle of bloody Spaghetti Junction. A five mile walk later, I was back with my thumb out again. Suddenly, a white minibus full of students pulled up and the back door opened to a cheer of, 'We know where you're going.' They dropped me off at the pedestrian gate to the camping field, just as my mate jumped out of a car. We called it a draw.

Keith Jordan had trouble getting to Cropredy in 1987

After that, it's a bit of a blur, ending on Saturday night when, looking a little bemused by Fairport's set, I was grabbed by a very large biker on one side and a punk on the other and taught the words to 'Meet on the Ledge.'

I haven't missed a *Cropredy* since.

THE 40 THIEVES
SEPTEMBER 1987, HAMILTON, BERMUDA

BOB BRADBURY
In the mid-1980s, I was very involved with the running of a folk club in Bermuda, and we persuaded Fairport to play in exchange for air fares and a week's hospitality. The fares alone were by far the biggest expense the club had ever incurred for a single act. We persuaded Tony Brannon to let us use his nightclub, the 40 Thieves, for the concert and he in turn persuaded the house band to let us use their amplifiers. Dave Mattacks

was not impressed with the drum kit we borrowed for him.

There was a bar that ran in a semi-circle behind the stage, and we curtained this all off. I announced Fairport and walked off behind the curtain, which also hid the band. Poised to play their first note, Dave Pegg turned towards me and smiled. He had a black guitar pick pushed inside his upper lip giving the appearance of missing teeth. In an instant, I knew that they were having fun and that this would be a very special gig. It was. We sold enough tickets to just cover our costs.

I taught Dave Pegg to water ski during that trip, which he told me years later was the most expensive hobby he ever had. Beer and guitars must have come a close second though.

GRUGAHALLE
24 OCTOBER 1987, ESSEN, GERMANY

WOLFGANG HÖHL

My first great rock band love was Jethro Tull at the end of the Seventies, but I was also very interested in all kinds of traditional music so it was only a matter of time before I discovered Fairport Convention. I first saw them live in Germany, supporting Jethro Tull on the latter's *Crest of a Knave* tour in 1987. I then saw them in their own right in Bochum in 1991 on their *Five Seasons* tour. They were great – I loved the record and it was the first time I had the chance to meet the guys after the concert.

Wolfgang Höhl and his wife Julia

I started to collect all their records and discovered a whole universe of new music (Iain Matthews, Dave Swarbrick, Ashley Hutchings, Richard Thompson, Sandy Denny, Jerry Donahue…). In the summer of 1996, I was in the UK for a holiday and spent a weekend with a friend at Cropredy. I remember great concerts from David Hughes, the Hellcasters, King Earl Boogie Band, Dave Swarbrick and, of course, Fairport Convention, with a lot of their past members joining them on stage. After the weekend, I was sure I would return to Cropredy. Which I did in 1999, and then every year until 2017, and again in 2019.

One fantastic thing about Fairport is their relationship with their former band members. I know no other band on the planet where so many ex-members come to play with their former band. Highlights are always Jerry Donahue and Richard Thompson, especially when they play together. Another highlight was where the very first line up plus Gerry Conway played songs from the very first LP and another special occasion was when Fairport Convention played the whole of *Liege & Lief* with almost the original line-up.

Meeting the band on different occasions is always fun, eg. talking to Chris Leslie about his appearance in the TV series *Midsomer Murders*, or having breakfast with Dave Pegg on a Sunday morning in one of the tents near the field. Or meeting Ashley Hutchings and his family at the famous Talking Elephant stall or at one of his many concerts at and around the festival. Thanks for all the good conversations – and, of course, the fantastic music, Ashley!

Meeting other people at Cropredy is another highlight. And when I have told my friends about it, quite a few have come to the festival too. A personal highlight is from 2013, when my fiancée Julia came to Cropredy with me. Our marriage plans for that October were already in hand. I remember she bought a blue dress on one of the stalls at Cropredy and came smiling and dancing towards me on this special field in Oxfordshire.

A MEXICAN RESTAURANT
NOVEMBER 1987, SOMEWHERE IN THE USA

BRIAN O'MALLEY

There must have been 20 people sitting at dinner – all of Tull, all of Fairport and some radio and record company execs. Maartin Allcock and I were sitting next to each other, and Ian Anderson was sitting directly across from us. The waitress asked, 'Anyone want a shot of

GONNA SEE ALL MY FRIENDS:
A PEOPLE'S HISTORY OF FAIRPORT CONVENTION

tequila?' To which Maartin and I both replied, 'Fab.' We had our shots of tequila. 20 minutes later the same waitress said, 'Two more shots of tequila?' Ian Anderson looked directly at me and said, 'Don't you think we should settle the bill before you two get out of hand?' One shot of tequila in 1987 was probably a dollar!

CENTRUM
21 NOVEMBER 1987, WORCESTER, MASSACHUSETTS

GREG & BUBBA THOMPSON

Like many American Fairport fans, we were first exposed to Fairport Convention as the opening act for Jethro Tull in the USA on the *Crest of a Knave* tour in 1987, became instant fans and started seeing them on every American tour from then on. The Iron Horse Music Hall in Northampton, Massachusetts became our favourite local venue to see Fairport Convention play and a fun place for them over the years too. The band quickly discovered a pub they loved around the corner called Packard's (named after the old automobile) and it became tradition for us to join the band for drinks after the show. It was the first thing they would ask us about when they came to town. We have wonderful memories and

Greg and Bubba Thompson first encountered Fairport in 1987 but have crossed paths with Peggy and the boys since

stories from those tours, shows and after-parties with the guys.

Memorable events include Peggy purchasing a beautiful old Gibson Mandolin from a music store next to the venue, him sitting on Big Pete's motorcycle out front of the Iron Horse Music Hall – and the time he shat his pants walking down the street (or so he told us).

Peggy was always the most generous and giving with his time and appreciated our Tull connection. We have had the chance to socialise many times over the years and he always treated us like equals and friends whenever he saw us, making us feel warm, welcome and appreciated as fans as well as people.

We went to Cropredy in 1996 as part of our honeymoon (right before our wedding ceremony) where Dave Pegg provided us a wedding toast greeting and Ric Sanders played a special wedding song for us called 'Greg and Bubba's Wedding' after the Mill warmup gig for *Cropredy*. We recorded it and played it at our wedding ceremony, so the Fairports were a part of our wedding. We had backstage passes for *Cropredy* in 1996 too.

IN REAL TIME: LIVE '87
RELEASED 4 DECEMBER 1987

JOHN LESTER

As kids at school in the Seventies, we used to watch *Top of the Pops* but I didn't follow music. That changed around the third year of senior school, when I discovered prog rock and began listening to bands such as Deep Purple (and the spin-offs Gillan, Rainbow and Whitesnake) and Yes, Black Sabbath, etc. and started going to watch them in concert. Then came the New Wave of British Heavy Metal, with Iron Maiden. On leaving school and starting work, I stopped following music.

The third car I owned had a cassette player so I dug out my old tapes and started listening to music again. In 1987

John Lester feels part of a large family as a Fairport fan

I heard Jethro Tull's *Crest of a Knave* and became an instant fan. Getting into Tull big time, I started to buy *A New Day* magazine. Through them and Dave Pegg, I first heard about Fairport and decided to buy a live album. The first one I bought was *In Real Time* (which we now know was a studio album with live applause).

Not knowing what to expect, I put it on and after about a minute turned it off again, thinking, 'What the hell is this?' But having bought it, I played it again and the more I listened the more I liked it. With the band growing on me, I then bought *The Five Seasons* and started to buy later material as it came out. I also went back to the early days and discovered Sandy Denny, Richard Thompson, Ashley Hutchings and Dave Swarbrick – a whole type of music as a kid I never knew existed. I first saw Fairport in 1995 and have seen them every year since (except the lockdown year), and sometimes twice or three times in the same year. As the chap says in the *It All Comes 'Round Again* video, following Fairport has become a way of life. You feel part of a huge family rather than just a fan of a band.

ANDREW BELCHER

Being on the cover of *In Real Time* is a memory to last all my life. Such an amazing weekend. I even got a wave off Peggy in Banbury centre.

SHORELINE AMPHITHEATRE
1 JUNE 1988, MOUNTAIN VIEW, CALIFORNIA

DOANE PERRY, JETHRO TULL

In the late Sixties and early Seventies, I would always read *The Village Voice* to see who was going to be playing in New York City, particularly at the Fillmore East, and I believe that was the first time I saw the name, Fairport Convention. I didn't see them on any tours they did in the States at the time, although I heard some of their music. They remained more in the underground than Tull did, but they had a great reputation from the very beginning. Later, when Fairport toured with Tull (and even later when I eventually played with them), I became profoundly aware of their extraordinary body of work. They were a highly talented, eclectic home grown, cottage industry kind of folk group and they seemed to have remained that way, although I recall Peggy once calling them 'a very loud folk band'. I suppose when I performed with them that became more true than ever!

They seemed to have a very dedicated and hardcore following, like Tull and some of the other offbeat English groups who were able to carve out a distinctive direction and go their own way. I suspect they probably didn't have a lot of interference from their record company because they certainly *sounded* like they did exactly what they wanted. They were often drawing from a rich vein of traditional English folk music, which was largely unfamiliar to mainstream US audiences at the time and sounded completely original to our American ears. They had this idiosyncratic, charismatic style of 'storytelling as songwriting', whether reinterpreting other people's work or performing their own. The material was often quite involved, adhering to unpredictable and unusual song structures, which often arose out of these labyrinthian tales of love, woe, joy… and drinking.

They supported Jethro Tull many times over the years and it was always a complementary musical pairing. Our audience loved them, while they brought along their own following, who in turn seemed to really like us, so there was a wonderful overlap and cross-pollination of audience and music… and ultimately of band members. A lot of the Fairports have played in Tull over the years; Dave Pegg, Maartin Allcock, Dave Mattacks and Gerry Conway, while Simon Nicol, Ric Sanders and Chris Leslie have all notably guested with Tull.

When they opened for Tull on one big American tour, I was asked to play drums with the Fairports as Dave Mattacks (or DM, as he is more widely known in Fairport world) couldn't do it because of previous obligations. On that tour they were called 'Fairport Friends'. I guess I was 'the friend', as the line-up was Peggy, Simon, Ric and Maartin. Maartin, Dave and I were also playing in Jethro Tull, along with Ric and Simon guesting on a couple of Tull pieces, so we got this energizing warm up playing with Fairport every night.

The biggest challenge for me was learning their homegrown style of music. Of course, Peggy breezily said, 'Ahh, it's easy, you'll get it in no time.' I'd heard it already, of course, but as any musician knows, it's one thing to experience music passively as a listener and quite another when you have to be inside of it and then *play it* correctly, particularly as the drummer when confronted with music like that. You're having to negotiate a lot of new maps and unusual traffic signals.

Finally, I wrestled a board tape out of Peggy. I was unable to get anything out of them which we were going to be playing *until* we were in the car driving up to the first gig at the Shoreline Amphitheater in northern California, where we were going to be performing in front of a sold-out crowd of about 15,000 people!

I listened to it, this time properly analyzing it… and gulping. I nervously felt myself murmur a barely audible 'uh-oh'. Now that I was closely examining the music, without benefit of rehearsal or adequate preparation time, it took on a nerve-wracking dimension. Naturally, they were all utterly laissez-faire about the whole thing. 'Don't worry, it's easy, you'll pick it right up,' was repeated again to my unbelieving ears. We didn't even have a rehearsal… just a casual run through in the dressing room, a brief soundcheck… and then the gig.

Some of it was straightforward, but there was also some incredibly tricky stuff that they'd been playing for years and years, that they didn't have to think about. It's hardly as if they got all the Fairport 'charts' out and you simply sight read it. That would have been far less intimidating and nerve-wracking! There's all kinds of unusual time signatures and little twists and turns in the form. I made a hell of a lot of mental and written notes, which were taped all around my drum set and on the floor beneath me.

Some of it is non-traditional but relatively simple song form. Other songs are quite involved, often with many, many verses, and that wide range of approaches is absolutely part of the charm of the music. I don't *remember* any train wrecks — although a decent audio tape of the performance might prove otherwise. I don't know how we navigated it, but without question, I gained an entirely renewed appreciation for just how good Fairport Convention really are and what excellent musicianship exists in that band. I sometimes wonder if they fully appreciate just how challenging their music is. Their ability as musicians and entertainers to pull off such *seemingly* simple but, in actuality, quite complex music at times is a tribute to the natural way that they play together and interact with their audience.

GONNA SEE ALL MY FRIENDS:
A PEOPLE'S HISTORY OF FAIRPORT CONVENTION

The musical part of what they do so effortlessly occasionally gets eclipsed by the folklore surrounding the band. Among other probable (and improbable) tales, there are no shortage of stories about Fairport's heroic drinking prowess. But their highly developed musicianship, as individuals and as an intuitively collective music unit, can be overshadowed at times by the legendary and occasionally non-musical stories that precede them... which as it turns out, are mostly true.

There's a slightly bent sense of humour and off-the-wall free association between song banter, that they regularly and surreally bat around between all of them. It was impossible to know what they were going to say but it was always entertaining and sometimes baffling. The English audiences cotton on to the language, the slang, and the occasional odd bits of cultural nomenclature a lot easier than the Americans did, but the Americans *loved* their exotic music.

It was not out of the realm of possibility that some of them could occasionally be quite 'refreshed' when they went on stage. I was amazed at how they could play flawlessly in that state. I cannot. Drinking with the Fairports? Maybe on a day off, but it's *not* a good idea as a toe-to-toe competitive sport because you'll just never, ever win... gig or no gig.

I went to see them on one of their headlining tours in England. Going backstage at intermission and into their dressing room, I noticed there was a head-height shelf that ran around all four walls apart from the doorway. It was lined with a multitude of different mysterious looking drinks, elixirs, bottles of beer and shot glasses, containing God-knows-what and providing an atmosphere similar to colourful Christmas decorations, although it was mid-summer. At first, I very mistakenly thought they were there as a permanent backstage fixture to invoke a relaxed atmosphere of conviviality in the dressing room for the visiting artists. But they were all freshly poured and highly active... a potent rainbow of convivial drinks... and all for the band at intermission! After my dawning awareness, I just burst out laughing. It didn't seem to affect them at all and they went out, stayed vertical and played brilliantly.

But first and foremost, it must be said that they are superb musicians, songwriters, storytellers and raconteurs. Everyone who has ever been in Fairport possesses a distinctive musical voice... you *know* it's Fairport. They have a completely unique identity and history as a band, setting them in their own distinguished corner of the musical universe.

There was one song we played when I was touring with them entitled 'Reynard the Fox', which I loved singing along with (but *not* into a microphone). Early in the tour Peggy said, 'There's that a cappella thing at the beginning, and then another one in the middle,' and he talked me into getting a microphone. He said reassuringly, 'Just sing along with us.' It was a big venue, 10,000 to 15,000 people. We got to the a cappella section and everyone stopped, and then it was a five-part vocal harmony… in reality probably a four-part vocal harmony… plus *whatever* I was singing.

Ohhh, I *should* have known. Suddenly, I heard something terrible and got a queasy, uneasy feeling, 'Gaaahhhd, what is that awful sound surrounding me and coming out of the side fills and all the monitors?' But ever the professional, I kept plugging away, only to shortly realise that the awful sound surrounding me was the sound of *my* own voice. Apparently, someone in the Fairports (who, oh who could *that* have been…? Daaaaaave?) had instructed the monitor mixer, 'Now when we get to that a cappella section, mute everyone else on stage and just solo Doane's vocal mic… and set the levels to stun.' This resulted in my solo vocals blasting across the stage, in every monitor, every side fill and possibly the front of house mix too, as it broadcast my puzzlingly confident and nervy high-wire vocal solo turn to the delighted band members and probably many thousands of surprised and undoubtedly perplexed audience members as well.

I didn't fully realise the broader implications until we were at least halfway through the a cappella section. I cannot and mostly would rather not imagine what it sounded like out front, but the only thing you *could* hear on stage was me. Mortifying – yes. Hilarious – absolutely… although not experienced *exactly* this way in that precise moment in time. Of course, the band were just dying of laughter… as was everyone on the side of the stage who was in on it. I don't know *how* we finished the song. This is why I stopped being the lead singer of my band at the age of 12.

Predating that career-topping incident, I sat in with Fairport at Cropredy several years prior. Tull's tour manager picked me up from the airport after a long transatlantic flight and, I believe, took me straight to Cropredy. I remember being seriously jet-lagged, although that may have put me at about the right tempo with everybody else, as they were all pretty 'relaxed' by that point, which seemed to be just a comfortable onstage state of being for them.

A PEOPLE'S HISTORY OF FAIRPORT CONVENTION

Anyway, on this first introduction to Cropredy, I was playing jet-lagged percussion only (no drums) in the front line with them. Playing along with me was Geoffrey Hughes ('Eddie Yeats') from *Coronation Street*, who was playing the bodhran… and pretty darn well too… far better than I could *ever* handle that tricky Irish drum. Peggy, Maartin and I used to do a little acoustic trio piece at the front of the stage during the Tull set and I played the bodhran… but not half as convincingly as Geoffrey. That little instrument is actually quite hard. I'd practice it backstage every night far more conscientiously than warming up on my practice pad to play my full drum set. But Geoffrey played really well, was very gracious to me and all I had to do was follow along and pretend I knew exactly what I was doing. Wherever you are, thank you Geoffrey!

Everybody who loves Fairport knows that DM is a brilliant player. He has a very different sound and feel to me, with a wonderful 'slightly behind the beat' and relaxed way of playing that fit them perfectly, so interpreting his way of playing with Fairport was a challenge for a New Yorker like me, brought up on a slightly more aggressive urban musical diet. The same can be said of Gerry Conway and Bruce Rowland, each possessing a different and individualistic style, which always made Fairport's music work so cohesively,

Fairport did a few tours with Tull in America, an outdoor summer shed tour and some indoor arenas, and played in Europe with us as well. The Fairports are wonderful, good-humoured and down to earth people, making it great fun to tour with them. I love their music, they are hugely entertaining to be around and I think the fanbase that has exponentially grown around them over their 55 plus years together would be a fitting and loving testament to those musical and extra-musical qualities.

Fast forwarding some years later, Tull headlined an extremely soggy night at Cropredy. It was pouring buckets of rain, at times coming down at about a 45 degree angle, as I was marvelling at the sea of umbrellas which suddenly appeared without complaint or fanfare. The stage, the audience and the grounds were getting seriously soaked, but everyone appeared to be unfazed by the predictably unpredictable English weather. We had a fantastic time and it looked like the audience did too and of course, the Fabulous Fairports were phenomenal hosts! No one got electrocuted and everyone left suitably 'refreshed'.

GONNA SEE ALL MY FRIENDS:
A PEOPLE'S HISTORY OF FAIRPORT CONVENTION

Photos: Ian Burgess

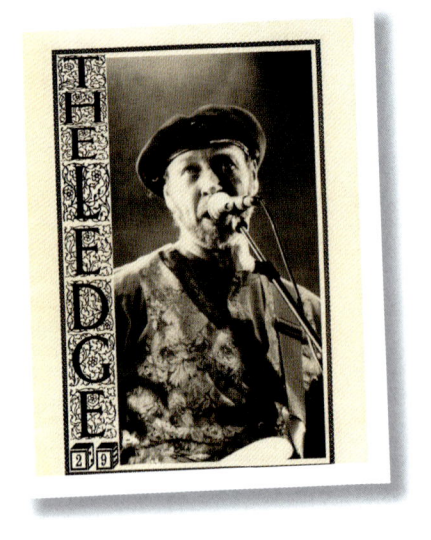

GONNA SEE ALL MY FRIENDS:
A PEOPLE'S HISTORY OF FAIRPORT CONVENTION

Photos: Ian Burgess

WEMBLEY ARENA
19 JULY 1988, LONDON, UK

NIK RANKIN

I first saw Fairport opening for Jethro Tull's *20th Anniversary* gig at Wembley Arena. Peggy played bass with Fairport and then Jethro. It was a splendid show. I was there with a friend who was a big Jethro Tull fan living in London but originated Dortmund, Germany. Thinking back, I had seen Peggy playing with Tull during the *Stormwatch* tour, replacing the recently deceased John Glascock

Fast forward to the mid-2000s and I started regularly going to Fairport gigs. The band now featured the current line-up, which has been stable for a good number of years. I recall seeing them perform in Edinburgh in 2012 at the Queen's Hall where I picked up the fabulous *By Popular Request* album celebrating 45 years with rerecorded studio versions of favourites as voted by fans. That was a fine idea and such a fine result and it's so good to have that in my collection. I recall a nice German lady in the merchandise area too.

A favourite venue was the Borderline in London (now closed) with memorable gigs in May 2013 and May 2014 (with a lovely performance of 'Mercy Bay' and 'Now Be Thankful') and May 2015 (with a lovely performance of 'Farewell, Farewell'). I enjoyed the intimacy of this small capacity venue, with everyone standing, a low stage and dim lighting. I also caught Peggy and Gerry here on a couple of occasions, performing as part of The Dylan Project. More recently I've seen them five times at the Union Chapel in London between 2015 and 2019, with the February 2017 *50th Anniversary* show seeing them joined by opening act Sally Barker for another fine and emotional rendition of 'Meet on the Ledge'.

Nik Rankin was at the 50th Anniversary show at Cropredy

I had been saying for many years, 'I'll have to go to a Cropredy Festival.' Well, I finally made it for the 50th Anniversary in 2017. I set off from Stevenage, near Knebworth, thinking of Fairport taking this line of travel from Knebworth all those years ago to play the farewell in August 1979 after performing on the same bill as Led Zeppelin, when I was an 18-year-old thinking about going to see Led Zeppelin play Knebworth.

It was worth the wait. The ambience was lovely and what a line-up. Sadly, Judy Dyble and Maartin Allcock are no longer with us but the memories live on. So many act impressed me with first class performances such as Plainsong, Petula Clark, Richard Thompson, and The Morris On Band providing so much feelgood. The crowded stage during 'Meet on the Ledge' will also be a lasting memory and a perfect ending to my first *Fairport's Cropredy Convention*. I congratulate Fairport for being such a classy act, providing so much pleasure and bonhomie – and morphing into a national treasure!

GONNA SEE ALL MY FRIENDS:
A PEOPLE'S HISTORY OF FAIRPORT CONVENTION

CROPREDY FESTIVAL
12 – 13 AUGUST 1988, CROPREDY, UK

TRISTAN BRYANT, FAIRPORT CONVENTION'S TOUR MANAGER

I remember Fairport Convention and especially *Gladys' Leap* being played in the house from when I was about seven. You know how as a kid you have a favourite band that you love and defend, no matter what anybody says at school? Well, Fairport were my band.

The first time I saw Fairport was at *Cropredy* in 1988. I remember so much of the experience. I was blown away by everything to do with it: the stage with its sound system and lights, the variety of bands performing, the scale of the festival site, the buzz of all the people, the way Fairport were in the crowd at times – and, of course, the fresh doughnuts stall.

I remember hearing Dave Mattacks doing the soundcheck and the energy of the kick drum hitting my chest. I'd never experienced that feeling of a kick drum taking a bit of air out of me before. I thought, 'I want to do this when I'm older.'

I loved how Fairport always came out after their shows to sign bits and pieces and have a chat. And because I was a young kid, which was obviously a bit of a novelty at a Fairport gig, they all remembered who I was. That sense of connection to the band, even though I was only nine or ten, made me feel part of something special. They were always so supportive and encouraging.

As I was getting near to leaving school, I wrote a letter to Peggy one day asking, 'Can I come down to do some work experience at the studio?' I got a really nice postcard back saying, 'Yes, definitely. Contact Mark Tucker.' Mark was the Woodworm studio engineer. They booked me in for a slot doing David Hughes' *Fifty Yards* album and Peggy had me doing everything. I was going from helping patch in some microphones to making cups of tea (a key part of work experience if you're in a studio), but I also ended up painting his weathervane and putting together his new gas barbecue. I think he thought, 'Hang on, this lad might be useful to us.'

I applied to the Liverpool Institute for Performing Arts (LIPA), which is the music college that Paul McCartney helped set up. At my

GONNA SEE ALL MY FRIENDS:
A PEOPLE'S HISTORY OF FAIRPORT CONVENTION

Tristan Bryant started out as a young fan and is now Fairport's tour manager

interview, the head of the course said, 'What music do you like?' and I said, 'I love Fairport Convention. That's the band that have inspired me.' And he went, 'Oh wow, Fairport. I love Fairport Convention too.' My interview was a half hour discussion of our favourite albums and gigs and then he said, 'I guess I'll see you in September.'

Paul still attends the LIPA graduation ceremony at the Philharmonic Hall in Liverpool and hands out the degrees to everybody. He calls out the names and you go and shake his hand, and he gives you your degree. My parents were in the audience, and I think they were more excited about me meeting McCartney than they were about me getting my degree.

Whilst at LIPA, I'd always pop along to a local Fairport gig and update them. As soon as I graduated, they said, 'Do you want to come and do backline for the tour?' I'd been helping out at *Cropredy* since 1997, but now I was working for Fairport directly. 2001 was my first tour with the band. Rob Braviner, the band's agent, tour manager and sound man was a wonderful mentor during that time (RIP Rob x). Fairport and their crew have been instrumental in pretty much all the work I've had since leaving university, and I am forever grateful. It's included touring with Jethro Tull, Larkin Poe, Jools Holland, *Bottom* (with Rik Mayall and Ade Edmondson), Patty Griffin and, currently, Richard Thompson and Saving Grace, featuring Robert Plant.

When somebody asked me what I wanted to do when I left school, I said, 'I'd love to do Fairport and Richard at Glastonbury.' I've done Fairport and I was due to be with Richard at Glastonbury in 2022 until Covid intervened. As agent and tour manager for Fairport and as stage manager for the festival, I really haven't got any more dreams to tick off. Should McCartney get in touch and ask if I can do his next tour, then I'd only consider it if Fairport weren't on the road at the same time.

Thanks for all the gigs chaps, especially the first one. Let's hope the last one is some way off.

JIM WALSH

My older brother's friends were in their twenties when they discovered Cropredy thanks to their (now departed) friend Steve Tong, who worked at Wood Green Library with Judy Dyble. The following year my friends and I in our late teens and early twenties, joined them. It was something else to do and involved camping and drinking – folk music was for old farts, so that's what we called the older crew, the Old Farts. They regarded us as vacuous and silly, so named us Tufties, after the squirrel. We've been going ever since, introducing friends and finding new ones. We're still defined by those names, and I've grown to enjoy Fairport a lot more. That field has become a common and much-loved thread throughout our lives.

If people hear a cry of 'tilt!' in the field, it's a warning that Fishy Mick has drunk to excess again and is about to topple over.

GONNA SEE ALL MY FRIENDS:
A PEOPLE'S HISTORY OF FAIRPORT CONVENTION

HAMMERVELD
20 AUGUST 1988, ROERMOND, THE NETHERLANDS

ROLF BOOMSMA

My wife Lynn and I saw Fairport for the first time at a festival in Roermond, Holland. The annual *Cropredy* event was mentioned on the back of a live album we bought at the festival, and we have been coming to *Cropredy* off and on ever since. We were hooked by the atmosphere created by Fairport and also by the folk-rock sound created by them.

We've been to loads of other gigs over the years. I'll never forget the concert at Fairfield Halls 30 odd years ago, when we got the fright of our lives by looking at the poster announcing the gig to see that my friend Maart Allcock had disappeared to be replaced by Chris Leslie, nobody told me. We loved Maart, and met him a few times. We always brought him Dutch speculaas (shortcrust biscuits, or 'speculations' as he called them). What a nice man and terrific musician he was. I met him backstage just before he died. His death was such a shock.

Rolf Boomsma and his wife Lynn first saw Fairport at a festival in Holland

GRAND THEATRE
22 JANUARY 1989, WOLVERHAMPTON, UK

NICK REGNAULD

I'm 71 now, but I started following Fairport from just after the first album. We'd started watching them again when they started touring again with the new line-up. We'd been to a couple of concerts and taken a couple of our sons with us. We were due to go to one in Shrewsbury at the Butter Market, and we couldn't take children because it was in licensed premises. My middle son was quite miffed about that, so he wrote a letter and asked me to give it to the band. I gave it to Simon at the gig, and he put it in his pocket and we thought no more of it.

On the next Saturday we went out into town and left the eldest on his own. We got back and he said that Simon Nicol has been on the phone. I thought he was having us on, but he said, 'No, he's read the letter and he wanted to speak to you and invite you down for a gig and whatever, he'll be in touch in the week.'

A few days letter, my son got a letter on a piece of paper the shape of a pig. It said how touched they were, and how they wanted to invite him down with a friend and parents to Wolverhampton to meet the band and have some photos taken, go on stage, etc. So that's what we did, and strangely enough the lad that we took with us is now in a band himself and it was the first gig he'd been to. We went to see them recently and mentioned this story on stage.

We'd seen them every year on the winter tour for three or four years.

Nick Regnauld's son got a special invite from Simon

GONNA SEE ALL MY FRIENDS:
A PEOPLE'S HISTORY OF FAIRPORT CONVENTION

CANAL STREET TAVERN
MARCH 1989, DAYTON, OHIO

STAN GRAHAM

I lost my job in Cincinnati but found a new one in Dayton, Ohio. I hadn't been there a week when I heard on local public radio station (WYSO) that Fairport were coming to play in Dayton. It was a Sunday night show and I had work the next day. I went there early and was third in line. A large queue quickly developed behind me. Shortly before the doors were due to open the promoter, Steve Carson, stuck his head out and saw the huge line. He said, 'Everyone's got a ticket, right? It's a sold-out show!' Panic struck me. No, no!' I shouted. 'I don't have one.' Steve looked me over and said, 'I remember you. You come to a lot of my shows. I held a few tickets back. I'll sell you one, but you'll have to sit at the bar.'

I sat at the bar and ordered a beer. The next thing I knew, Peggy was sat on the barstool next to me. He ordered a beer and asked me how I was doing. I told him what had occurred outside and about the show I had seen in Cincinnati a couple of years prior. Then I asked about Jethro Tull and again Peggy came to life. He told me they were working on *Rock Island*. We really hit it off and were having a grand time.

Someone came out of the office and spoke to Peggy. He told me he had to go do a radio interview for WYSO, but that he would be back. I thought to myself, 'He's not coming back. Why would he come back and talk to a nobody like me?' But 20 minutes later, he came and sat back down next to me and said, 'Stan, would you like another beer?' How could I say no?

We drank and talked all the way up until showtime. Peggy then excused himself, saying that he'd better get up there, but that he'd be back at the interval. Up he went and an amazing show commenced. At the interval, he brought the entire band over and introduced them to me as his new mate Stan. He asked what I did for a living, and I told him I was an accountant. Peggy smiled and said there would be a surprise for me in the second set.

After the interval (and a few more pints), the band returned to the stage and Peggy stepped up to the microphone and said, 'This song is dedicated to my new mate, Stan!' Fairport then proceeded to play the

Monty Python song, 'Accountancy Shanty'. What a hoot! I wish there was a recording of it.

After the show, Peggy bought all of my drinks. I couldn't keep up with him! I would be halfway through a pint and Peggy would say, 'Stan! You ready for another?' I have this hazy memory of DM playing a tape after the show of flatulence he had recorded on the tour van. We stayed way after closing time. When the owner kicked the fans out, Peggy insisted that the owner let me stay and we drank late into the night. I have no idea how I drove home that night. I certainly should have been arrested for drink driving. But somehow, I made it home and avoided the law.

The next day I didn't hear my alarm go off and I awoke five minutes before I was supposed to be at work. However, I quickly realised that I was still drunk! I had only been working there for a week, but I had to call off sick as I would have been fired for going to work drunk. My employer wasn't happy that I had only been there a week and took a sick day. But I had no choice.

SOMERVILLE THEATRE
17 MAY 1989, SOMERVILLE, MASSACHUSETTS

DEREK BLACKWELL

I first witnessed the lads onstage at the Somerville Theatre near Boston, a great old place with a sizeable stage and filled to the brim. I got a ticket at the last minute and they'd put an extra row of chairs in front of the front row, so amazingly I had front row centre. Spirits were high. What a bunch of goofballs they were, and a great contrast to the very seriously together music. There was lots of posing during 'Dirty Linen'. I decided Simon was the most eloquently funny person I'd ever seen on a stage, but Maart ran him a close second.

Simon, Maart and Peggy kept doing this weird thing of holding their picks aloft, repeatedly, at every chance when not playing a note. The three musketeers? Somebody clue me in. But the highlight of hilarity was DM plugging the latest disc. He had a canned *Tonight Show*-style intro track which was a scream. He apologised for us having to get the disc from a shop in Italy, and recommended going to our local store, taking the assistant manager by the lapels and demanding, 'Why haven't you got it, dickhead?'

GONNA SEE ALL MY FRIENDS:
A PEOPLE'S HISTORY OF FAIRPORT CONVENTION

BERMUDA FOLK CLUB
22 MAY 1989, HAMILTON, BERMUDA

BOB BRADBURY

Dave Pegg again stayed at my house for Fairport's second trip to Bermuda. Inconveniently, my son Jon chose to be born on the day of the concert, requiring me to be in two places at once. I arranged a stand-in compère, attended the birth and dashed back to the venue in unseemly haste, arriving just in time to hear Simon's opening words, which were to do with the number of babies born during their American tour. The whole band joined me afterwards to wet the baby's head at the Ram's Head pub.

Along with Bob Dylan, Fairport Convention have been a constant in the soundtrack of my life.

Until the late 1980s, I believed that the heart of Fairport was Swarb and Peggy and the magical chemistry

Bob Bradbury enticed Fairport to play in Bermuda

evident between them. I couldn't understand all the fuss over Richard Thompson. At a *Cropredy Festival* around 1993, I stood at the front of the area facing the stage hoping to find out. The skill of Richard's guitar playing, and the cleverness of his storytelling knocked me off my feet and I've been a fan ever since. The song was '1952 Vincent Black Lightning'.

WHATELY HALL HOTEL
JUNE 1989, BANBURY, UK

RICHARD LAURIE
Being a teenager in the 1980s, I went through a number of musical trends and fashions. From being a New Romantic listening to Ultravox and Duran Duran to a Mod dressing in purple and listening to The Jam, and, in 1984, becoming an indie boy, with a flat top haircut and listening to likes of The Smiths, New Order, The Cure, The Wonder Stuff, The Pogues and The Wedding Present. But being brought up in Byfield, Fairport is in your veins from an early age. The house Sandy

GONNA SEE ALL MY FRIENDS:
A PEOPLE'S HISTORY OF FAIRPORT CONVENTION

and Trevor lived in was just around the corner from my family farm. Sandy and family would come out and watch the cows come past on the way to milking. Byfield was also home to Swarb! Although slightly younger than me, I went to school with his children, Alex and Izzy. My main influence on getting into the band and the festival came from the Lamb family, who owned Fiveways garage. Dad (Ken) was a massive fan through the early years and this passed to his sons, and my good friends, Mike and Rob. So from August 1987, when I was 18, and for the next ten years or so, the masses of Byfield's youth migrated the short distance along the A361. We never worried who was playing, but knew we would have a great time together and finish with dancing to Fairport and singing 'Meet on the Ledge'.

Richard Laurie grew up with Fairport in his veins

By the end of the 1990s, Byfield friends had moved on or had children so the numbers camping together stopped. I still attend but with uni friends I have indoctrinated along the way. Friends tend to attend the fringe that has grown up at the pubs and other venues. One of my favourite memories is not of the festival or a tour, but of an event at the Whately Hotel in Banbury. Not sure of the date either 1988 or 1989. We bought tickets thinking it was a gig but arrived to find it was a ceilidh with Fairport providing the music. We were much younger than the average attendee and as a group of lads with only one female in our party, joining in the sets and circles provided difficult. Three friends took it on themselves to go and dance freestyle at the front. One danced so vigorously, he needed medical treatment from a St John's Ambulance member that happened to be there. Anyway, having been asked by the organisers to stop, the band had noticed our presence and at the end of the evening played a rousing reel of jigs. We had the floor to ourselves and even though they kept increasing the tempo, hoping that we would yield, we kept going. I must admit, I am glad they finally drew the evening to an end. I was knackered. It was great to be back at Cropredy in 2022. It was probably my favourite to date. Fairport Convention, thank you for the music and the memories.

CROPREDY FESTIVAL
18 & 19 AUGUST 1989, CROPREDY, UK

STEVE WATT

Strangely winding paths brought Fairport into my life. I was always into folk, folk inspired rock, prog and the like. Uni in the 1980s could be a depressing place musically for someone with my tastes. Eventually, I found like-minded people off the beaten track, and via raucous folk nights at the Cumberland Arms in Byker, *Rothbury Folk Festival*, and tiny venues all over the Northeast, it turned out good music was still out there if you knew where to look.

Steve Watt (second left) at Cropredy '89 with (left to right) Mike Tozer, Viv Scheffers, Steve Ryder, Jon Bradshaw & Jo Polwin

A mate suggested we go to see Fairport Convention – odd name for a band I thought. After 'John Barleycorn', I thought, 'How the hell have I missed this band – they're bloody brilliant.' 'Crazy Man Michael', 'Matty Groves', 'Polly on the Shore', and much assimilation of undiscovered treasure followed.

Another mate, Chris Dougal, suggested we go to see Fairport at *Cropredy* – somewhere near the equator, way down south. He crewed at the event every year but always maintained he hated the music which never made any sense to me. So, we made the trip and had a great weekend. Standing with thousands of kindred spirits in the warm dark evening, singing 'Meet on the Ledge' tied us to this place from then on, and I could see the same spell being cast all around me. We made the pilgrimage several more times in the 1990s before marriages and kids shifted priorities.

I also remember seeing Fairport at a tiny gig at the Kings Head in Allendale. It was such a small venue, Maart Allcock hid behind a curtain to try to keep the noise down. We all sang along way too loud and had a great night.

The last *Cropredy* gig we went to was August 2000, which was scorchingly hot. I remember carrying a round of Wadsworth's 6X back to our spot by the sound tower, to my best friends in the world (and future wife), with the sun shining, a million happy people singing along to songs that we all knew and thinking that it doesn't get any better than this.

JOHN DALY

I only went because Steeleye Span were headlining the Friday night. My initial thought on Fairport on the Saturday was, 'What a bunch of self-indulgent tossers.' But then I learned to love the music. My favourite song is 'Wat Tyler', and my favourite moment was Maart's heavy rock intro to 'Matty Groves' in 1992.

NIK LE SAUX

As a teenager in Hastings in the 1980s, I only had ears for heavy metal. Then one day my older brother said, 'There's a band called Fairport Convention playing at the Congress Theatre, Eastbourne. You'd like them, they're like rock – but with violins!' My friend Chris Frampton and I went along and were blown away.

Nik Le Saux (right) at Cropredy in 2022 with schoolfriend Paul Reynolds

As the months passed, albums were bought and borrowed, and a film of a Fairport concert was shown on TV which was watched, studied and re-watched. Around that time, Jerry Donahue, appearing on a documentary about the electric guitar, gave a masterclass which left my friend, a budding guitarist, speechless; we needed more of this.

Still at school, Chris and I plucked up the courage to ask our parents if we could go to a festival. At the Eastbourne gig, flyers were given out about *Cropredy*, and I had kept this. To our surprise, our parents agreed, so we saved up our paper round money and sent off for tickets. We travelled by train, had no idea where to go when we finally arrived in Banbury, and asked someone, 'Which way to Cropredy?' We then walked to the festival, over a bridge where a huge road was being built (now we know it as the M40), and with our two-man leaky tent, one guitar, a few cans of cider and much excitement, arrived a few hours later.

That night, we saw a wonderful performance by All About Eve. The following day, my friend plucked up the courage to try his luck at the bar, and after some nervous minutes, we had each a four-pint brown jug of 6X in our hands. The thrill, the first tentative sips and the sweet bitterness confused our young taste buds, but set us on a journey of real ale for life.

Fairport finally arrived on stage, and this time we knew some songs. It went on for hours with guests we'd never heard of but soon got to love. Moved by the whole experience, we pledged a return the following year, which we did; and the year after that. Other friends and partners joined us as it grew into a big summer social event. 33 years later, we're still there, enjoying the summer ritual with our sons and daughters, old friends and new, as much a part of our life as ever; a joyous constant in an ever-changing world, and long may it continue.

ALAN ARCHER

Kath and I got together in the spring of 1989, after our respective marriages broke down. Kath's musical taste was a bit lacking, and having been a fan of Fairport since '71, I suggested going to see them at Verbeer Manor (a great venue, now sadly closed. Kath loved them – yippee! Afterwards, we met Peggy at the bar and he asked if we were going to Cropredy? We took the offered flyer and went away to

GONNA SEE ALL MY FRIENDS:
A PEOPLE'S HISTORY OF FAIRPORT CONVENTION

think about it… The following day, tickets were booked.

August came and we were off to Kath's first ever festival. My brother, also a long-time fan, was driving, as he had a car and I didn't. We had borrowed a massive frame tent. On arrival we were put in what is now Field 11, which is quite steep and has massive ridges. The frame tent spanned two ridges with its four corner legs, leaving its two centre legs suspended twelve inches in the air. It was challenging, and could have been mine and Kath's first and last festival together. But it was life changing and has become something we look forward to every year.

Alan Archer with his wife Kath, 30 year veterans of Cropredy

In 2019, and 21 years married, we celebrated 30 years together, 30 years of our attending Cropredy and, of course, Fairport's 50th. My wife made waistcoats for my brother and me to mark the occasion. Over those 30 years we have pitched up with children, grandchildren, friends and hankies. We have listened to some first class bands, switched off from the outside world and recharged ourselves.

'The Hiring Fair' was played in 1989 at Cropredy and it has remained a very special song for us. In 2022, it was played again and it couldn't have been better, with the great weather and that big, beautiful moon. It was a special moment. We have enjoyed so many happy times, great bands, met some wonderful like-minded folk, laughed, loved, shed tears of joy and sadness and endured the sun, the rain and the storm of 2019. Thank you to Fairport and your brilliant crew for this unique, brilliant festival.

GONNA SEE ALL MY FRIENDS:
A PEOPLE'S HISTORY OF FAIRPORT CONVENTION

THE RAVEN FOLK CLUB, GROSVENOR ROWING CLUB
NOVEMBER 1989, CHESTER, UK

ANDY WILLIS

I don't believe I'd ever heard the name Fairport Convention, or enjoyed anything vaguely folk or trad before the 16-year-old me received a cassette tape, in a box of various tapes donated by an older friend, of *In Real Time: Live '87*. For the whole of that summer, the tape hardly left my Walkman and marked the

Andy Willis has only kept two cassettes

start of a voyage of discovery during my sixth form years that included highlights such as: more Fairport acquisitions (*Liege & Lief* being the obvious choice for my second album), branches out to other bands, some via pointers in the 'family tree' in the sleeve notes of *A History of Fairport Convention*, with *Morris On* being just one of the memorable discoveries, and a night out at Chester Folk Club to see a visiting Swarb.

Whilst I have a reasonable excuse (I was at sea for much of the following decade), to my shame I didn't get to *Cropredy* until I was in my thirties. In the intervening years, I had built up my Fairport collection and my first time at the festival almost felt like I was coming home. I've never looked back and have never had anything other than an amazing time at *Cropredy*.

Fairport Convention are a band that has stayed with me over the years and the evolution of my tastes with increasing age has never taken me away from them, but has simply meant a shift in my favourite albums and tracks. Some tracks that I might, in my youth, have paid little attention to have grown in meaning and impact over the years, whilst old favourites remain so. As for 'Meet on the Ledge' and 'Who Knows

Where the Time Goes?', these have always been well-loved, and I can't seem to listen to them now without a huge hit of nostalgic emotion.

I last saw Fairport live just before the pandemic hit and, with the current line-up, the band is as strong as it has ever been. Long live FC. I only own two tapes now. I couldn't part with *In Real Time* because it was where it all started for me, and I won't part with *Liege & Lief* because it was autographed by Swarb on that memorable night in Chester.

PEBBLE MILL STUDIOS
16 MAY 1990, BIRMINGHAM, UK

PETER CLARKE

My wife Lorna and I had wanted to move from Coventry to Shropshire for a long time. We bought a cottage near Shifnal in Shropshire and moved in at the end of 1989. We paid over our budget and there was work to be done, but as a couple in our thirties, we reckoned we had the time for that. Very sadly and very unexpectedly, Lorna died suddenly of a brain haemorrhage in February 1990.

This was pretty devastating and my sense of loss was exacerbated by having only lived in the area for just a few weeks.

Peter Clarke got an invite to see Fairport recording an acoustic set at the BBC's Pebble Mill Studios

The following three months were difficult but I was fortunate to work alongside some supportive new colleagues, one of whom was involved in the local BBC Radio folk programme. She knew I had been part of the folk music scene some years before and suggested that, instead of heading for the local pub hoping to be cheered up, I should join her and her husband at the BBC's Pebble Mill Studios in Birmingham to be part of the audience for an acoustic set from Fairport Convention that was being recorded that evening.

I said yes and the rest is, as they say, history – my history anyway. I was blown away by their musicality, skill and humour (very important) and transported by their music – and I don't mean in a Peter Bellamy way. We went for a drink in the bar afterwards, where the band were sitting in the corner dissecting the gig. I didn't realise at the time how approachable they were, otherwise I'd have said 'thank you' and bought them a round. I have done that quite a few times since mind, because after that night, the only way was up. Hundreds of gigs and around 30 Cropredys later, I still get the same buzz from seeing them and never fail to come away feeling positive and happy.

So it's, 'Thanks, chaps – what'll you have?'

CROPREDY FESTIVAL
17 & 18 AUGUST 1990, CROPREDY, UK

LES COCKBURN

It was my first year at Uni in 1969 and, while browsing through the student union record library, came across *Liege & Lief* and thought it looked interesting, but I had never heard of the band. Like so many other people, I was blown away.

At that time, I played mandolin in a wee folk group and hearing Swarb's playing made me take up the fiddle, teaching myself. I never achieved anything like his brilliance, but he was always an inspiration.

I ended up playing in the folk-rock band, Avalon and, in the company of bass player Roy Martin, went to many of Fairport's Edinburgh gigs. I even managed a drink with the band after one Usher Hall gig. This was not long after Ric had joined and I remember saying to him that I knew he could play – but didn't realise he was a

Les Cockburn's band Avalon played Cropredy in 1990

madman on stage. At that time, he was quite an 'athletic' performer.

But the crowning glory of my support for Fairport was actually getting to play *Cropredy*. In 1990 Avalon actually opened the festival on the Friday night and, although people were still gathering, we played to a welcoming crowd and I thought I'd died and gone to heaven.

I've reached the ripe old age of 70 and I'm still excited by going to a Fairport concert – even to the extent of travelling down to Morecambe all the way from Edinburgh in March 2022 and dragging my partner along, who had never seen the band in concert before. She was so amazed that she agreed to go to her first *Cropredy* in 2022.

Lang may yer lums reek guys!

MARIE AND STEVE LUCY

Prior to the pandemic, it would have been our 30th *Cropredy Festival*. On our first year, we arrived late on the Friday evening in the pouring rain, travelling down from North Manchester. We slept in the back of our Ford Escort. We fought with the wind and rain to help my brother put up his two-man tent minus some of the poles. We made our

Marie Lucy (centre) with (left to right) her brother Tom Keegan, husband Steve and Dempsi and Shannon Keegan

way to the concert field to be entertained by the Bootleg Beatles. Everyone dancing in bin liners, hands over our beer to try to stop the rain from diluting our beer down. There was only a few thousand attended then. From bringing six-month-old babies, to now bringing grandchildren and becoming pensioners there's no place like it. We are the custodians of the pink and green aliens flagpole, who over the years have guided us back to our hallowed piece of ground, especially when it gets dark and we're coming back from the bar. We raise a glass each year to our much loved and missed family and friends who look down on us from the ledge.

GONNA SEE ALL MY FRIENDS:
A PEOPLE'S HISTORY OF FAIRPORT CONVENTION

JUDE MCEWAN

My first time at *Cropredy* was in 1990, when it was just two nights (I know that makes me a festival virgin even now to some). I remember seeing the Bootleg Beatles on the Friday night when it was peeing down with rain. No one left. I've been going every year since, bringing various people along for the ride. I got the hump with the husband one year as we had to go back to the tent early before Procul Harum played as he had forgot his hat and got sunstroke. My husband's best friend Kevin shouted out, 'Giz some Paranoid' when Eddi Reader asked for requests. Our 18-year-old has been going to the festival for 19 years (first as a bump), and thanks to Gareth was reunited with his phone and bag after dropping it in that special field in Oxfordshire. We had fabulous times with our friend Kevin and his kids watching Alice Cooper, and we were so grateful a few years later to have AJ read out our message after Kevin passed away. Keep on keeping on, we love you all.

Jude McEwan's husband Kevin is also a police fan

CIVIC HALL
25 JANUARY 1991, WOLVERHAMPTON, UK

BARRY SMITH

After many years listening to classical music and prog-rock, I met Peter and was delighted to discover that he shared many of my musical tastes. I had felt I would enjoy folk music but had no idea where to start. Peter had a great knowledge of folk, and we started attending gigs together, beginning with a solo gig by Liam O'Flynn, in a village hall in Staffordshire. Kathryn Tickell and Davy Spillane followed in quick succession before, in January 1991, I went to Wolverhampton Civic Hall to see Fairport. I was blown away by the experience.

  I immediately identified with the rock element and the storytelling within the songs. They were not a million miles from my prog background. The musicianship was superb, and I can still remember Maart's solo at the end of 'Wounded Whale'.

The greatest surprise was after the concert. As I walked into the crowded foyer, I caught sight of someone who looked like Dave Pegg. My previous

Barry Smith and his friend Pete

experience of seeing famous bands had been at stadiums or arenas, and you certainly didn't see the band milling around afterwards, chatting to the punters. I assumed it was a coincidence and a Peggy lookalike. But then a Simon Nicol lookalike appeared, and a Ric Sanders one. They were not lookalikes, I realised, but the band, talking to anyone.

The CD and programme were quickly purchased and I joined the throng for autographs. Starstruck, I was unable to string together much in the way of coherent conversation but garbled what I hope was appreciation in proportion to how I was feeling to each of Peggy, Simon, Ric and Maart. I then returned to the merch desk, behind which stood DM. 'Thank you, that was brilliant,' I stuttered, proffering the items for signature. The man I later discovered to be one of the world's best drummers, and session drummer with some of the all-time greats (and who was recording in George Harrison's home studio when news came of John Lennon's death), looked me in the eye and said, 'Thank you for coming, glad you enjoyed it, really appreciate your support.'

I was completely stunned by the experience. The following few days saw me book tickets for further gigs on the tour, as well as to a benefit for Swarb, *Cropredy* warm-ups and then my first *Cropredy*. We've been to virtually every tour since, and are always warmly welcomed by the band – for many years as 'the chaps', now as Barry and Peter (sometimes joined by Allison and Sue). We have lots of wonderful memories over the last 30 years, so – thanks guys!

GONNA SEE ALL MY FRIENDS:
A PEOPLE'S HISTORY OF FAIRPORT CONVENTION

CLIFFS PAVILION
3 FEBRUARY 1991, SOUTHEND-ON-SEA, UK

Martin Driver (left) was given the hard sell by Peggy in 1990

MARTIN DRIVER

I met Peggy and Maart outside Brighton Dome where Jethro Tull were performing later that night as part of the *Brighton Music Festival*. During our conversation Peggy suggested I should go to a Fairport Convention gig. I replied along the lines of, 'I really like *The Bonny Bunch of Roses* album, but I didn't realise that Fairport were still a working band.'

Eight months later, on a bitterly cold, wet and windswept February evening in Southend, I attended *The Five Seasons* tour. Arriving outside the theatre, who should I bump into but Peggy, trying to scrounge a fag off a punter. Peggy said, 'Hello mate, what are you doing here?' 'I'm here to see Fairport', I replied.

With that, he grabbed my arm and said, 'Follow me'. We entered the theatre through the stage door, and Peggy led me directly onto the stage where the band were preparing to sound check. He introduced me in turn to Maart, DM, Simon, Ric and tour manager Rob Braviner, with words that I'll never forget. 'Hi guys, this is my mate, Martin.' That is how I first met the Fairport Convention family.

CROPREDY FESTIVAL
16 & 17 AUGUST 1991, CROPREDY, UK

CAROL LAW

I first experienced *Cropredy Festival* in 1991, after my then boyfriend Ade said, 'It's a very friendly festival.' Off we went in his old VW camper and I was hooked. By 1992, we were married, and *Cropredy* was considered part of our annual holiday. In 1993 our daughter Katie came along for her first ever *Cropredy* at twelve weeks old. It was her first holiday. *Cropredy* 1995 saw us with baby Josh at five months old and Katie 26 months, still in our old VW camper, with Ade and I sandwiched between Katie sleeping on the back parcel shelf and Josh in a carrycot over the front seats.

Carol Law's family get together twice a year, at Christmas and at Cropredy

GONNA SEE ALL MY FRIENDS:
A PEOPLE'S HISTORY OF FAIRPORT CONVENTION

For 1996, we upgraded to an old Sherpa camper. Katie and Josh enjoyed the children's entertainment on the field and the playbus. A few years later, we set up camp next to a family with children the same ages as our children and they played together. Richard was Katie's age and Aimee was Josh's age. We ended up spending the whole weekend with Steve and Marie and made arrangements to meet up for *Cropredy* the following year. They were from Cheshire, and we were from Northamptonshire. We still meet up every *Cropredy* to this day.

The children loved trying circus skills on the field, storytelling and making things from newspaper. Eventually they were allowed to wander together without the parents, girls heading for the Doodah stall for face paints or tattoos and the boys to the musical instrument stall, whilst us adults enjoyed the music.

Through sunny and rainy years, we've been at *Cropredy Festival*, spending time on campsite if raining, or maybe in the village pubs. Occasionally we've caught the bus to the Ye Olde Reine Deer Inn in Banbury for lunch. A few times we've walked along the canal into Banbury. All these wonderful memories for me and my family are because of *Cropredy*. Katie is now 28 and a teacher and she still loves *Cropredy Festival*. Josh is 27 and in the music industry as a sound engineer. The 2015 festival was a highlight, when Josh took a bow on *Cropredy* stage with Tradarrr, as their backline technician. I was a very proud mum. That year, Katie sent a message for the big screen, 'All set for my 23rd *Cropredy Festival*.'

Our children have their own lives now. We rarely all manage to get together. I say to my family, if we can be together for *Cropredy Festival* and Christmas Day each year I will be happy. So far, I've been lucky.

APOLLO THEATRE
23 FEBRUARY 1992, OXFORD, UK

ROBERT COLEMAN

In the early '90s I was a grad student at Oxford and very involved in the vibrant Oxford folk scene. At least 15 musicians and singers would play folk sessions at the Temple Bar each Sunday afternoon and evening, and a large crowd regularly turned up to listen.

One Sunday lunchtime, two young ladies we hadn't seen before turned up. They listened intently, applauding after each song or tune. After about three hours, one of them shyly approached one of our number as he bellied up to the bar for another beer and said, 'So what do you do with Fairport Convention?' They had heard a rumour that Fairport held an open rehearsal at the pub every Sunday and somehow thought we were them.

The guy they asked told them that there was a mistake and that nobody in the bar was a member of FC. They left so fast they looked like they had been shot out of a cannon. A few weeks later, Fairport played the Apollo Theatre in Oxford. A few of us went to the bar across the street before the concert and ran into some of the band. We told them the story. Their reaction was, 'We have groupies? Where?'

GROSVENOR HOUSE
10 JULY 1992, LONDON, UK

LEE SODEN

My first and oldest memory of seeing Fairport in one of the first line ups was at the University of Leicester's Queen's Hall, a student venue with the very much missed Sandy Denny mesmerising the students with the purity of her voice. Ever since I have seen the band in so many venues and am still hooked. I have also had the privilege of booking the band a number of times over the years at a number of very memorable events. One such example was a London black tie event, with an unusually suited and booted Fairport at the Guy's Nurses Ball at the Great Room in Grosvenor House. It was a fantastic performance in front of over 1,000 nurses and their partners. We all consumed the most champagne ever and it was a night to remember.

In 2022, 145 Fairport fans were on the Amadeus Queen travelling down the Rhine from Amsterdam to Basel for the ultimate Fairport experience of great music with the true Fairport family. The whole trip was great with some truly memorable performances, tinged only by Simon's absence through illness after the second performance. The rest of the band rehearsed to give great unforgettable performance with great guests.

Lee Soden remembers copious champagne consumption

CROPREDY FESTIVAL
14 & 15 AUGUST 1992, CROPREDY, UK

JENNY IDDON

I was first introduced to Fairport when we dropped into the final night of Cropredy on the way home from our holiday in Sandy Balls, a caravan park in the New Forest. I was eight years old. I'd never been to a concert before, let alone a festival, and I was mesmerised by it – by the stalls, by the children's bit at the back, by the portaloos and, most of all, by Fairport Convention. Everyone was so friendly. We had bought glow-in-the-dark wands at Sandy Balls and everyone stopped by to admire them.

A year or so later, we went to see Fairport at the Cambridge Corn Exchange. Me and my little brother were right down the front, where my mum likes to be. Fairport came on and Ric clocked us and asked security to let us sit on the other side of the crash barrier – wow. It was amazing to be able to watch from that perspective, being passed cokes by our parents while, all night, Ric smiled at us or made a passing joke. That was a lovely and it's a wonderful memory still.

Jenny Iddon remembers stopping off at Cropredy with her family on the way home from holiday

We've been back to Cropredy most years. I've always loved it, but I didn't realise until 2022 year that every corner of Cropredy has a memory for me; it's like being back in a magical land with all your friends.

The music of Fairport holds so many memories for me and my siblings Stuart and Patrick – trying desperately to get hold of a CD of *Glady's Leap*, their music being on my playlist when I was in maternity with my daughter, seeing my brother and sister-in-law have the first dance at their wedding to 'The Hiring Fair'.

I don't think a week (possibly not even a day) goes by without me playing something by Fairport Convention. Their music, especially with Simon singing, is the first thing I'll turn to if I'm happy or sad. Thank you so much for all the brilliant music, but also for all the other music you've introduced us to along the way.

PAT CLAYTON

We were having lunch in the Red Lion on the Wednesday before Cropredy. A group of Germans were at a nearby table. On another table, a Yorkshireman began to talk loudly with his friends about Swarb and Ric, making spurious comparisons about two very different fiddle players. I said something to this effect and my comments were endorsed by one of the German visitors, Wolfgang, who was there with his wife Gaby and their friend and colleague Gernot. A conversation began which led to us agreeing to meet on the field at the festival.

After the festival we remained in touch, initially by letter. In 1995, Wolfgang returned to Cropredy without Gaby, who stayed at home with their small son. Gernot returned too, with his partner (also called Gabi), and we all enjoyed each other's company. Gernot and Gabi would then come to Cropredy whenever (them being teachers) school term dates allowed. For Wolfgang, as a parent of two small children, returning was less easy.

John Clayton (front) with (left to right) Pat, Gabi and Gernot

Spending the whole week together, going to the warmups and sitting on the field has become a tradition for Gabi, Gernot, John and me. It has also resulted in holidays together in the UK, Germany and Belgium. We've stayed in each other's homes and explored new places like Berlin and Leipzig. One highlight was when we four went to the Bardentreffen in Nuremberg to see Fairport. Gabi and Gernot have also made many trips to the UK to see the band, sometimes flying in for the weekend.

Our Cropredy week has evolved into a pattern of attending the warmups and the festival, with a picnic at Broughton Castle mid-week (if it's Wednesday it *must* be Broughton Castle). We used to have mega picnics outside The Mill before the warmups, complete with Peggy coming for a strawberry, accompanied by him saying, 'Don't take the biggest one or the last one,' and promptly doing just that.

Most years have also included our *Cropredy Vision* contest, where we award marks to the artists (up to ten for both content and performance). John the Statto ensures that adjustment is made for anyone who has missed an artist/set and we then come up with a ranking. Individual scores vary but Fairport invariably win, although RT runs them very, very close when he's on the bill! But we have greatly enjoyed many other wonderful artists and bands appearing over the years.

The friendship has come to mean so much, symbolised by what happened when John and I were unable to attend the festival in 2002 because I was in hospital in Birmingham. Gabi and Gernot took time out from their busy week to come and visit me.

We four, along with Gabi and Gernot's Cairn terrier Lucky, and with Wolfgang and Gaby when they can make it, will continue to Meet on the Ledge for as long as we are able. For the friendship, love and joy that a chance encounter in the Red Lion has brought us over nearly 30 years, thank you Fairport.

KRZYSZTOF OPALSKI

In Poland in the '60s and '70s, there were no Western-pressed records in the shops. Although there was a fair amount of British music broadcast on the radio, I don't remember ever hearing Fairport Convention. There were some record fairs in the bigger towns, but compared to the west it was much more difficult to be a Fairport fan in the '70s.

My connection with Fairport began in the autumn of 1976 when I moved from my hometown of Kalisz to study at the Technical University in Wroclaw. I bought Island's sampler *Bumpers*, which, amongst other things, included the Fairport track, 'Walk Awhile'. I liked it very much and started to look for other Fairport Convention records.

Swarb and Peggy at Cropredy

Richard and Vikki Clayton at Cropredy

GONNA SEE ALL MY FRIENDS:
A PEOPLE'S HISTORY OF FAIRPORT CONVENTION

This was not easy, but a few years later I did finally buy *What We Did on Our Holidays* and *The Bonny Bunch of Roses*. While listening to the former, I learnt about Sandy Denny for the first time. I was so impressed with her voice and her musicality. She was so talented. My next purchase was *The History of the Fairport Convention*, which provided me with more information about the band's story and discography and the solo careers of its members.

Swarb at Cropredy

While in Oslo, Norway in the summer of 1987, I bought a few other Fairport Convention items: *Nine*, *Expletive Delighted*, and Sandy Denny's boxset *Who Knows Where the Time Goes*. All those records were great, but the *Expletive Delighted* LP was especially important because I found a note on its back cover saying that if I wanted to know more about the band, I could write to one of three addresses. I ended up getting a response from Paul Hartman, the editor of *Dirty Linen* magazine. He was so surprised to get a letter from Poland and kindly sent me free copies of the magazine for a few years. He also put me in touch with Cliff Furnald, with whom I exchanged records as he was interested in Polish music. Most importantly, through this I learnt about the *Cropredy Festival*, about which I started to dream of visiting.

That dream came true in 1992. It was so great to see Fairport Convention live for the first time, and with different line ups from the past, including Richard Thompson, Dave Swarbrick, Jerry Donahue, Ashley Hutchings and Bruce Rowland. It was also a surprise to see Robert Plant as a special guest. I was very lucky because it was the 25th anniversary of the band and a year later the double CD of that concert was issued.

At the beginning of the 1990s I started to work as a radio DJ, at the first private radio station in Wroclaw (Radio Serc), and later at the

GONNA SEE ALL MY FRIENDS:
A PEOPLE'S HISTORY OF FAIRPORT CONVENTION

Polish National Radio Station Branch Wroclaw. I presented a lot of Fairport Convention in both stations. I also sent letters to various record companies to support my programmes, and Woodworm Records was so kind as to provide me with some CDs.

Inspired by Fairport Convention, I became interested in Polish and Eastern European traditional music. There are loads of tunes and rhythms that would be great to give a modern arrangement to!

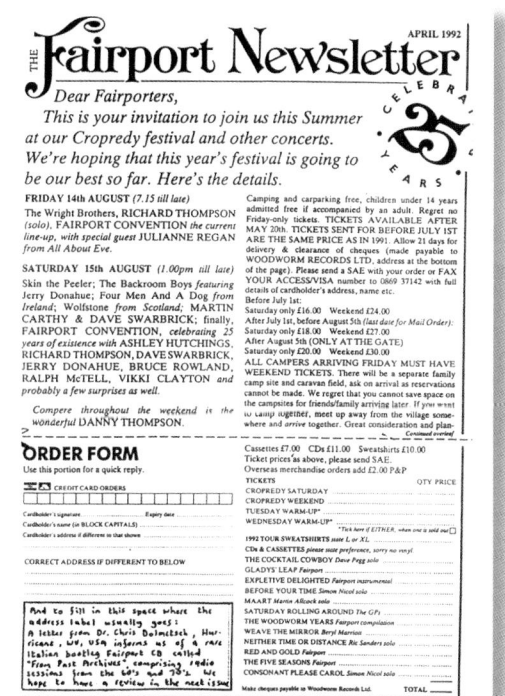

Photos: Ian Burgess

Arrangements for Cropredy 1992

GONNA SEE ALL MY FRIENDS:
A PEOPLE'S HISTORY OF FAIRPORT CONVENTION

Photo: Oliver Ilgner

CROPREDY FESTIVAL
13 & 14 AUGUST 1993, CROPREDY, UK

KEVIN HAWKINS

In 1979 Fairport Convention announced that they were disbanding. I believed them. I didn't get to see them on their farewell tour as I had just bought my first house and finances were a bit tight. I bought the *Farewell* album and thought it a fitting tribute to the end of an era and the demise of a band that had given me much pleasure over the years.

With soaring mortgage rates and children, my financial situation remained awkward for a few years so I stopped going to gigs (except that I did see the Stones in Leeds in 1982 and Lindisfarne at some point)

Kevin Hawkins thought Fairport were toast after 1979

and rarely bought any records. With no interest in the popular music of the 1980s I convinced myself that I had outgrown the music scene and consoled myself with the thought that my formative years musically had coincided with very talented musicianship, of which Fairport Convention had been a big part.

It was in a newsagent's in late 1992 when I saw the front cover of the magazine then called *Folk Roots* announcing Fairport's 25th anniversary. I had no idea the band was still going. I bought the magazine and read about the band. The following day I took the magazine to work to re-read in my lunchtime. A work colleague spotted it and said he was a Fairport fan. 'Do you go to the festival?' he asked. I said I hadn't been – I didn't like to mention that 24 hours earlier I had never even heard of *Cropredy*, and that indeed I was under the impression that Fairport had packed in 13 years earlier. He told me how great the festival was, and I booked to attend for the first time in 1993. It was as good as he had said (the weather in 1993 and indeed in 1994 was brilliant, which undoubtedly helped). I have been to *Cropredy* every year since then, and regularly seen them on tour and most recently on their Rhine cruise. I think I have finally made up for those lost years.

DAVID FLINTHAM

I first saw Fairport Convention live in January 1985, and have seen them about 30 times since. Winter wouldn't be winter without my annual trip to the Union Chapel. I have so many memories and have had so many good times. But my most unusual memory comes from 1994, when Dave Pegg asked me to write a piece about the Battle of Cropredy Bridge for that year's festival programme (1994 was the 350th anniversary of this English

David Flintham wrote an article for the 1994 Cropredy programme

GONNA SEE ALL MY FRIENDS:
A PEOPLE'S HISTORY OF FAIRPORT CONVENTION

Photos: Oliver Ilgner

Richard and Danny Thompson at Cropredy

Maart at Cropredy

Civil War battle, an event which inspired the *Red and Gold* album). I was honoured to oblige. My fee took the form of some festival tickets and a t-shirt. This kick-started my 'career' as a military historian which to date includes three books, more than 60 articles and, recently, some TV work.

Mr Pegg is a true gentleman. He recommended which mandolin I should buy, we always manage to have a natter before concerts, and we stayed in touch by e-mail during the pandemic. As well as being incredibly accomplished musicians, Fairport are without doubt the nicest people in the music business.

CROPREDY FESTIVAL
12 & 13 AUGUST 1994, CROPREDY, UK

DAVID GLASS

I first met members of Fairport in New York in 1981 and went to my first of several *Cropredys* the following year. From 1989, I became Fairport's de facto American manager, checking their contracts for their US tours, working on their contracts for their records with Rough Trade and Green Linnet, and doing their banking. I took no money for this, but, in exchange, the band gave me the great privilege of travelling with them up and down the East Coast of the US on all their tours from 1989 onwards, allowing me to see many great gigs.

There are a lot of highlights from 40 years. I cherish having my name in 'The Card Song'. I remember the first Fairport gig at New York's Bottom Line in 1989 where, in the late show, Peggy and Simon performed an amazing but very naughty version of 'The Alphabet Song' as an encore, and I recall watching from the wings as they played a great gig to a packed-out crowd at the *Newport Folk Festival*.

David Glass has had numerous Stateside and UK encounters with the Fairports

I also remember being induced, after several pints of 6X, to don a complete Santa suit at *Cropredy* in 1994, and prancing around the stage throwing Christmas candy to the crowd while Roy Wood and his Big Band blasted out 'I Wish It Could Be Christmas Everyday'. Another memory is going with the band to a very strange Green Linnet weekend party for their acts in a weird hotel, and witnessing Fairport's weekend closing gig, including the most beautiful version of 'Who Knows Where the Time Goes?' I have ever heard Simon sing.

I have felt blessed to know three versions of Fairport over 40 years and to have seen many of their shows, and to become and remain friends with them. I love all their records, so won't name one. They were, and remain, a great band. Long may they reign.

HARBOURSIDE BRASSERIE
9 APRIL 1995, SYDNEY, AUSTRALIA

IAN JONES
A friend of mine, John Gallagher, commenced putting Fairport shows on in Sydney. This concert was part of the Sydney Folk Festival at the Harbourside Brasserie, just near the Sydney Harbour Bridge. Other acts included Eliza Carthy and Kristina Olsen and it was a fantastic night. In March of the following year, Fairport performed at the Birkenhead

Tavern in Drummoyne just near the Parramatta River, supported by Dave Swarbrick and Alistair Hulett. The carpet there was so sodden with beer that your shoes stuck to it. Fairport returned to the Birkenhead Tavern a year later and were again supported by Dave Swarbrick and Alistair Hulett.

JEWEL IN THE CROWN
RELEASED 9 JANUARY 1995

KARLA ELLIOTT

My dad Michael was a Fairport superfan. Born in Ballarat, a small city near Melbourne in Australia, he led a quiet life. His loves were his three children, his bass guitar – which he played in small indie bands in Melbourne – and music, especially Fairport Convention. No one who knew him can talk about him today without mentioning Fairport. He and my mother divorced early on, and these days my dearest childhood memories are dancing and singing – usually to Fairport Convention – with my brother and sister in our dad's small log cabin living room. Dad would play along on his guitar, or perhaps his violin, which he learnt to play later in his life. CDs and records were chosen from his enormous collection and played loudly through his stereo system. I was eight years old when *Jewel in the Crown* was released.

My dad died very young, at 44. I was only 13, my brother Patrick and sister Eleanor even younger. They played 'Close to the Wind' and 'Meet on the Ledge' at his funeral. But after his death, we lost touch with his side of the family. Most of his things were sold. No one left behind knew how to grieve this sweet, quiet man, and certainly no one taught his three children how. For me, the only way to go on was to slowly push memories of my dad to the depths of my mind, until he was locked far away, and I'd forgotten his face, his voice, what it was like to be around him. His memory was lost to me for the next 20 years.

But *Jewel in the Crown* always fluttered at the edges of my consciousness. On the rare occasion that a thought of my dad did pop into my mind, so did the bright reds and blues of its cover. So did a whisper of the lyrics of the title song. And one night, not so very long ago, I pulled the album up on Spotify and pressed play.

GONNA SEE ALL MY FRIENDS:
A PEOPLE'S HISTORY OF FAIRPORT CONVENTION

I remembered every single note from this album that I hadn't listened to for 20 years. Memories of the man my dad had been began to rush back in, and it began a quest to reconnect with his memory, to bring him back into my life. I began to meet with old friends of his. One of the first things they would inevitably mention was Fairport Convention. An ex-girlfriend who was very dear to my dad right up to his death told me how much he had admired Sandy Denny. I played *Liege & Lief*, and the feeling of listening mesmerised to her voice as a child returned to me. I dug out old family video tapes. In one, I danced with my dad at my brother's 3rd birthday party to a song I instantly recognised. I searched frantically through Spotify again until I figured out what it was: 'The Rutland Reel'. Every track on *Expletive Delighted!* felt like home. I finally collected up the few bits and pieces of my dad's that people had saved, in particular his record collection. I brought all those albums home and thumbed through the masses of Fairport, Steeleye Span, and Richard and Linda Thompson, to name just a few. I bought a record player and began to play them. With the Fairport albums I was less familiar with, I liked to put them on and imagine how my dad must have felt when he first bought and listened to them.

My journey of remembering my dad continues. But now, whenever I feel lost, or disconnected from his memory, or when the world becomes too much, I can put on Fairport, and suddenly my dad is right here with me again.

Karla Elliott (left) with her dad and her brother and sister

GONNA SEE ALL MY FRIENDS:
A PEOPLE'S HISTORY OF FAIRPORT CONVENTION

CROPREDY FESTIVAL
12 & 13 AUGUST 1995, CROPREDY, UK

HUW WILLIAMS

I was in a duo called Huw & Tony Williams, and our biggest time was during the '90s when we started to play theatres and were getting quite a large audience. This was due to Fairport Convention, particularly Simon Nicol, and Ralph McTell. I started to write songs for them, because at the time they didn't have a song writer. I don't think Simon realised I was writing songs. I think he thought I was just finding him songs.

Tony and myself used to attend a local folk club. One week there would be a guest, someone from outside, and the following week would be a singers' night. On a singers' night, me and Tony would always play. On a guest night, we were only there for a night out. I remember turning up one night in the '80s, and it was quite a big night. You could tell this because there was rowed seating and no tables.

The organiser of the club came up to me and Tony and said, 'Boys, are you singing tonight?' and we said no so he went away. But then he came back, 'Give us one song.' We said we didn't have anything with us, and he said, 'Borrow my guitar.' Tony didn't have his double bass and I didn't have my guitar. Then he came back a third time, and said, 'Come on boys,' almost as though he was annoyed. 'Give us one song.' Why he wanted us to sing, we didn't know. Eventually we agreed, as long as we were on early.

I looked to Tony and said, 'What can we do with only one song?' Tony said, "The Flanders March' and 'Rosemary's Sister'.' We were on early and played them. The guests for that evening were Dave Swarbrick and Simon Nicol, who were fantastic. That's where Simon Nicol heard the song 'Rosemary's Sister'. He then contacted me and said he was thinking of doing a solo album and asked if he could record it. Well, I'd heard the name, but it was just a name that I knew. I remember telling Tony that this guy from Fairport Convention wanted to record one of my songs. He said, 'Huw, that's a big deal'.

Simon Nicol recorded this version of 'Rosemary's Sister' which then everyone else in the country who was into folk music started to do. There were people in New Zealand singing it and people in America singing it. Then I started doing other songs for them. First of all, it was Simon Nicol solo, but then the band started to record them. I did another one called 'Ginny' which they recorded. This went on for a while.

Through that we met Ralph McTell, and we toured with him. Then we toured with Fairport in '95, and this whole relationship began. It's basically how Tony and I became known. To this day, if I do an occasional solo gig, someone will turn up and they'll have a Fairport Convention shirt on, and they'll ask me to do one that Fairport did.

A whole relationship developed between us and the band, and without that relationship, and indeed the relationship with Ralph McTell, nothing would ever have happened. I sometimes think back to that evening in the folk club, and think what if we'd just continued to say, 'No, we're not playing.'

Tony and I also played *Cropredy* twice. I remember, at the first one, I was a bit distracted, and Maartin Allcock introduced me to someone, a guy with big curly hair, and I thought, 'Oh right, how are you?' We had a bit of a chat, and the next time I saw him, this guy walked across the field, and I thought I don't know his name, so embarrassing. He said, 'Hiya Huw,' so I had to bluff it with, 'Hello, how's it going?', talking about the weather. Then the third time, we were at *Cropredy* again, and this guy comes across the field towards me and my friend, and I just couldn't remember his name. Same again, and I managed to get away. The person I was with said, 'I didn't know you knew Robert Plant?', and I said, 'That was Robert Plant?'

I don't think there's another band like them. The whole Fairport family, they are quite a phenomenon.

SARAH-JANE RICH

I was at *Cropredy* with babe in arms and the TV news camera caught us. When they introduced the short piece, they said, 'And this festival appeals to the young and old,' zooming in to a close up of us both. My daughter is now a folk-dance caller in her own right.

GONNA SEE ALL MY FRIENDS:
A PEOPLE'S HISTORY OF FAIRPORT CONVENTION

THE KING'S HEAD
DECEMBER 1995, ALLENDALE, UK

ED WALLAGE

The King's Head, Allendale in 1995 was Fairport acoustic. The '90s was the era of 'unplugged' performances. Most of these were, however, just stripped-down band formats using acoustic instrumentation; but still relying on amplification. I cannot say why Fairport decided to do this particular gig acoustically, but that's what it truly was: all acoustic instruments and no PA. The upstairs room in the pub was small enough to perform to a folk club like audience. It was a four-piece line-up of Ric, Simon, Peggy, and Maart. Maart as usual was playing a variety of stringed instruments until he produced an accordion to accompany 'The Deserter' (S Nicol solo album version), a gentle song. An accordion was a relatively loud instrument compared to the rest of the line-up. Maart realised this and retreated to the rear of the small stage. Still too loud. So, he turned to face the window curtains. Still too loud. In a last-ditch effort, he drew the curtains around himself. The audience started laughing; the band saw what had caused the laughter, they stared laughing, and the performance disintegrated. The

Photos: Ed Wallage

Ed Wallage saw a truly acoustic version of Fairport

song was abandoned, and the accordion put aside.

Of the many times I have seen Fairport play over the last 52 years (over 100 plus times) this remains one of the most memorable. It was an intimate, unique event, made special by the band not playing.

After quizzing Peggy, the only other time Fairport have played truly acoustically was on a US tour when the PA failed, so this was the only planned acoustic gig.

CROPREDY FESTIVAL
9 & 10 AUGUST 1996, CROPREDY, UK

STEVE SHELDON

Summer 2022 saw the delayed 25th anniversary of the Fairport versus Cropredy Village cricket match. Cropredy Sports Club issued the original challenge to Dave Pegg in 1996 and he accepted it, knowing the interest in the game from Richard and Danny Thompson. My involvement came about because I was Dave Swarbrick's

Back row l. to r: Simon Nicol, Peter Bateman, Terry Sylvester, Pete Richards, Dave Pegg, Steve Knightley, Ian Wilkinson
Front row l. to r: James Holman, Danny Thompson, Steve Sheldon, Richard Thompson, Gerard O'Farrell

Steve Sheldon recalls the first time the Fairport XI won the annual Cropredy cricket match

Back row l.to r. - Dave Kadwell, Dave Pegg, Danny Thompson, Simon Nicol, John Shaw, Peter Bateman, Richard Thompson
Front row l. to r. - John Jagger, Steve Gibbons, Steve Sheldon, Mick Bullard, Paul Mitchell

GONNA SEE ALL MY FRIENDS:
A PEOPLE'S HISTORY OF FAIRPORT CONVENTION

website editor. He knew that I was a regular cricketer, and he arranged a meeting with Dave Pegg. I was a long-time Fairport fan and so Dave recruited me to organise and captain the side. I set out with the intention of including as many musicians as possible plus festival staff and a sprinkling of 'proper' cricketers.

The 1996 team included Steve Knightley (Show of Hands) and Terry Sylvester (ex-Hollies) as well as Peggy, Richard, Danny and Simon Nicol plus a smattering of festival staff. Before the game got underway, a somnolent camper had to be removed from the outfield. His tent, with him in it, was picked up and deposited over the boundary. Highlights during the game included a small, brown dog's entirely successful search for a toilet just behind the stumps and umpire Pete White's call of no-ball as Peggy reached the pavilion, two minutes after having his stumps splattered.

Chris at Cropredy

Swarb at Cropredy

Photos: Oliver Igner

Since then, we've played every year, weather and plague permitting, and have had terrific fun. In 1998, the Fairport XI won their first match. As a result, I've become part of a Fairport 'family' and been lucky enough to meet and become friends with my musical heroes. I had no idea, that when I turned on a small transistor radio one day in 1968, that there would be so many memories to come.

GONNA SEE ALL MY FRIENDS:
A PEOPLE'S HISTORY OF FAIRPORT CONVENTION

SPOTKANIA Z PIOSENKĄ ŻEGLARSKĄ I MUZYKĄ FOLK 'SZANTY WE WROCŁAWIU'
15 DECEMBER 1996, WROCLAW, POLAND

KRZYSZTOF OPALSKI

Playing in a band, I got to know some promoters and festivals organisers here in Poland, so decided to try and persuade them to invite Fairport Convention to play in Poland. The *Folk & Shanties Festival* agreed and in 1996 I became involved in arranging Fairport Convention's only ever Polish gig. It was also the last gig with Maartin Allcock as an official member of Fairport Convention.

The organiser could not arrange the plane tickets from Warsaw to my hometown Wroclaw for the

Krzysztof Opalski remembers the visit to Poland – and the vodka

Photos: Krzysztof Opalski

whole band, so Maart and Simon Nicol travelled by train. As the trip lasted around six hours, they bought some vodka in Warsaw to make their trip more comfortable. I picked them up from the train station in Wroclaw. Maart was in a worse condition than Simon (although they were both in a very good mood) and fell down the stairs on the train station. I caught him, saving him from serious injury. The Fairport concert was great but Maart wasn't at his best as he was still not feeling very well. When the band got home, I got a fax from Dave Pegg saying that Maart was not a member of Fairport anymore. I wrote a review of the gig for the Polish rock magazine *Tylko Rock*.

Photos: Krzysztof Opalski

MARLOWE THEATRE
24 FEBRUARY 1997, CANTERBURY, UK

FRASER NIMMO

I didn't see Fairport live for quite a while. I moved to London and was making my living in the folk scene. Then, in 1978, punk hit and I got cancellations from folk clubs. Every folkie was in the same boat, up to and including Fairport, and I had to find another source of income, so I moved into the corporate sector. I needed a lot of guitar players for functions and that's where I encountered Maartin Allcock. The line-up would be at least a fiddle, a guitar and a bass, and Maartin was the only person I ever met that could take the top line, the middle and play the bass and do them all well.

Maartin was the best musician I've ever come across. I was trying very hard to get into open guitar tunings and he, recognising my lack of understanding of the mechanics of music, very kindly and painstakingly wrote out this little book of open tunings for numpties. I still have that little red memo book in my studio, and I still use it every gig I do.

Maartin was retained by the company I worked for, for quite a long while. He became a part of the musical furniture. Then in 1985 or '86, he came to me one night looking quite crestfallen. I thought perhaps he needed money, but he said, 'I'm leaving. I'm going to join a band.' I said, 'They can't give you any more money than we do. That's ridiculous – who is this band?' And he said, 'Fairport Convention'.

I nearly fell off my chair. For a moment I just couldn't take it in. I'd seen Fairport live but these people were still in the demigod part of my imagination, while Maartin was the guy I shared a dressing room with. When his last night with us came, we were all in tears, because he had become a very good friend.

I was working all the time, but I could get people to deputise for me and so I would go and see Fairport whenever I could, and because Maartin was in the band, I got to know them. In 1996, I got invited to do the support on the *Wintour* in 1997. This was the same time as Maartin left the band, so I toured with the wonderful Chris Leslie. We did 35 gigs and most of them went pretty well apart from the pranks that they would play on me. It's traditional on the last night of a big tour that Fairport will take the mickey out of the support act. So there were five of them conspiring with their production manager – the late, great Robert Braviner – to destroy my show.

My big song, 'Any Spare Change?', is about dispossessed people on the streets. It has a nice big, moody chorus – 'Have you spare change, any spare change, any spare change today?' – which I encourage the audience to sing along to. And as I sang the chorus that night in

Canterbury, I could hear giggling. And behind me, a big, galvanised steel bucket had descended from the flies on a rope. It was lit up, and I could hear this clinking as, one-by-one, each member of the band and crew came along in full view of the audience and threw a coin in the bucket. I was giving off my soul and they were turning it into a pantomime.

My last song that night was my version of 'Loch Lomond', which is mean and moody and quite effective. The audience couldn't hear it, but I had Fairport Convention singing out of tune through the monitors whilst I was trying to entertain 1,200 people. It was five-part disharmony. I just wish I had a tape of it, because I gave as good as I got. And they knew what they were doing, and I didn't. At one point, I said, 'This is all happening because that guy up there on the desk – Rob Braviner – has got all the hair but I've got all the talent, which is why he's up there and I'm down here.' And at that point the sound went off to thunderous applause.

I lay down on the stage kicking my legs in reluctant surrender. It was a memorable night. I'm shaking remembering it.

CROPREDY FESTIVAL
8 & 9 AUGUST 1997, CROPREDY, UK

GRAHAM DAY

I had a passing interest in folk music. However, at the dawn of the 1970s, a new genre emerged marrying folk music and rock to form – 'folk rock'. I quickly discovered that the chief exponents of this format were Fairport Convention. I bought the 1969 album *Unhalfbricking*, with the elderly middle class couple on the cover, and enjoyed listening to it occasionally. In 1983 I moved jobs to Oxfordshire. It was not long before the staff at Cherwell District Council in Banbury told me about Fairport Convention's annual festival at Cropredy.

Ashley and Swarb at Cropredy

Photos: Oliver Ilgner

GONNA SEE ALL MY FRIENDS:
A PEOPLE'S HISTORY OF FAIRPORT CONVENTION

During my three years in Oxfordshire, I became aware of a new Fairport Convention album, on Woodworm Records and issued in August 1985, titled *Gladys' Leap*. Like all good folk tales, it had a grain of truth in it. This was named after a redoubtable Gloucestershire post-lady, Gladys Hillier, who had been delivering mail in her village of Cranham for many years. To save a two mile walk to reach just one property, she leapt a three-foot-wide stream. It was not long before her gymnastic abilities were mentioned and this was somehow picked up by the Ordnance Survey, who ensured that Gladys' Leap was identified on their latest map. I liked the story and bought the record, which is still a favourite. At some stage we went to an Oxfordshire church where Fairport were performing, as I can distinctly remember Simon Nicol singing.

Simon at Cropredy

The job did not work out for me and we moved 120 miles back to our home turf in Suffolk in 1986. However, all things Fairport continued to be interesting, and eventually we decided that it was about time that we went to the *Cropredy Festival*. I bought two tickets for August 1997, booked a Travelodge and set off on a hot Saturday.

On arriving at Cropredy, we bought some fish and chips and sat on the grass, watching the act on at the time, the duo of John Otway and Wild Willy Barrett. Eventually, Fairport Convention took to the stage. The line-up that day included Simon Nicol, Richard Thompson, Ashley Hutchings, Dave Swarbrick, Maartin Allcock, Dave Mattacks, Cathy LeSurf and Ric Sanders. The set list was huge and entertaining, and we had real value for money.

Highlights for me were 'Danny Boy', 'John Barleycorn', 'Three Left Feet', 'Rutland Reel', 'Sack the Juggler' and 'Fiddlesticks'. I was especially pleased to hear 'John Barleycorn' as I had always loved the Traffic version in the early 1970s. The fiddle playing of the late Dave

Swarbrick was atmospheric and superb, whilst Dave Mattacks drummed energetically and almost maniacally.

The heat of late afternoon turned to a warm evening, and then darkness came, and the stage was illuminated by a vast number of lights. The final two numbers were 'Si Tu Dois Partir' and 'Meet on the Ledge', and at midnight the festival was over. The huge ovation and warm applause Fairport and friends received at the end could probably have been heard hundreds of miles away, it was that loud.

It was one of the most entertaining and wonderful concert trips ever, cementing a lifetime musical interest in Fairport Convention, nurtured and developed by an altogether otherwise unsuccessful career move. The memories, particularly of the sounds and singing of the final numbers with the band members illuminated on stage, are still fresh today. As a result, we still love Oxfordshire and Gloucestershire. Our autumn Cotswolds trip will include on the itinerary visits to Gladys' Leap, a craft ale shop in Broadway called John Barleycorn and a search for the recordings of the 1997 festival.

STAN GRAHAM

In 1996 Fairport were again at Canal Street Tavern in Dayton, Ohio, and in 1998 I saw them at Southgate House in Newport, Kentucky. Each time, I reintroduced myself to Peggy and he remembered me. Chatting after one of the shows, I asked why they didn't sell t-shirts at the shows. He explained that it was too much to transport from England. They would love to do it, but it just wasn't practical.

In 1997 I made my first pilgrimage to Cropredy. I didn't have a lot of money, but I had a credit card and put almost everything on it. My brother was living in Cornwall at the time, so he split costs with me. I managed to get tickets to both warm-up shows. I was really excited for the second night, because both Swarb and Richard would be playing. At the time, *Angel Delight* was my current Fairport fave and I was excited to see the full *Angel Delight* line-up, and when they played 'Journeyman's Grace', I was in heaven.

This was back in the day when the Saturday night Fairport set was over four hours long. They played 46 songs that night, opening with 'Jennie's Chickens'/'The Mason's Apron' and (of course) finishing with 'Meet on the Ledge', where everyone was arm-in-arm, swaying as they sang along to 'Ledge'. It didn't matter that we were strangers. We were all bonded that night.

GONNA SEE ALL MY FRIENDS:
A PEOPLE'S HISTORY OF FAIRPORT CONVENTION

KULTURZENTRUM KREUZ
12 NOVEMBER 1997, FULDA, GERMANY

WOLFGANG TÖLCH

Hurrah, Fairport Convention in my hometown. It felt like a long-awaited dream come true at last. What great moments to recall, including helping Simon park the van (which to my great joy did contain the drum kit – so much for the 'acoustic evening' printed on the poster), getting him interested in the local Hochstift beer (just the one), my friend Ulla receiving an apparently oversized Swiss Army knife containing, said Simon, everything but an ironing board.

Finally, me and my good friends Gernot and Gaby presented Peggy and DM with a large box of Nürnberger Lebkuchen (gingerbread cake) to express our love and gratitude to the band. 'We'll eat them all tonight!' was Peggy's immediate response.

Wolfgang Tölch was pleased it wasn't an acoustic evening despite the billing

Peggy told me that he had been in Fulda before, with his band The Uglys, on the day of the 1966 World Cup Final. Peggy recounted that The Uglys had a gig that day at the local American NCO Club. As the Americans supported the German team, Peggy made a bet with the servicemen that he would have his hair cut off if the English lost. Fortunately, as we all know, Peggy got to keep his hair.

Wolfgang Tölch gave the band German gingerbread which Peggy assured him would get eaten

GONNA SEE ALL MY FRIENDS:
A PEOPLE'S HISTORY OF FAIRPORT CONVENTION

CROPREDY FESTIVAL
14 & 15 AUGUST 1998, CROPREDY, UK

JOHN T SAURUS

I have to blame Dave Trivett who dragged me along, somewhat reluctantly, to my first *Cropredy Festival* somewhere in the late Nineties. I danced in the rain to Richard Thompson and cried my eyes out to 'Meet on the Ledge', which I still do to this day, and have been back every year since. I am lucky enough to work at the festival with the awesome Bounty Crew and couldn't imagine not being in the field with the sign crew. What a privilege, thank you.

PAUL MITCHELL

The first time I was asked to play cricket for the Fairport team in '98 was when the Fairports were all still young enough to play. It was me and Richard Thompson out in the middle batting together, and we needed around 15 to 20 runs to win the game. Richard was the one who loved cricket, and the reason there was a team was so he could play when he came over from the US, but he said to me, 'Look, I'm happy for you to face and get the runs.' Between us, we won the game without about an over to spare.

That was also the year when Steve Gibbons took an amazing catch. He had been roped in at the last minute to play, and we couldn't find any shoes for him, so we painted his winkle pickers white. He hadn't played cricket since he was at school, took this unbelievable catch on the boundary – and everyone jumped on him!

BERGHPOP
6 JUNE 1999, NOORDWIJK, NETHERLANDS

KOEN HOTTENTOT

Fairport (acoustic) had a one-off gig near Noordwijk, Holland, at an annual free festival called *Berghpop*. The line-up looked strange – in the afternoon, many local heavy metal bands performed. Fairport were due to appear at 8.30pm, to be followed by a rather popular Dutch band called Trockener Kecks. Fairport looked mightily out of place on paper.

GONNA SEE ALL MY FRIENDS:
A PEOPLE'S HISTORY OF FAIRPORT CONVENTION

And I guess they were. But a very good time was had by all.

Eight of us convened at my friend Dick's place in Amsterdam. The weather was atrocious in the morning but had begun to clear up in the afternoon and we were able to enjoy the sunshine for the rest of the day. By 4pm we were on the road for Noordwijk. The venue was a complex of buildings in a park-like environment, like some kind of institution.

Koen Hottentot with Chris and Peggy

The festival took place on a grassed area. It had a village festival atmosphere, with many rather unusual characters in the audience, not generally seen at concerts. One would expect a sizeable portion of those present to suddenly burst into that old hit, 'They're Coming to Take Me Away, Ha-Haaa!' by the legendary Napoleon XIV.

Into this bizarre environment, Fairport arrived. They were to play in a tent, and after checking out the venue, came looking for drinks. They were quite early, so they had quite a few of them. They hit the stage after a bit of a delay, at 9pm. The tent was extremely noisy and not the ideal place for a Fairport gig. Indeed, the quieter songs were half lost in the audience noise, although from where I was stood on the front row the up-tempo stuff seemed to down well.

Fairport played it safe, with no surprises whatsoever, material-wise. None of the new material premiered on the winter tour was performed. Instead, it was 'Wishfulness Waltz', 'Close to You', Royal Seleccion', 'Jewel in the Crown', 'Matty Groves', etc. all over again. They played well, and Simon broke the obligatory string (during the intro to 'Jewel in the Crown'), giving Ric the chance to perform his solo fiddle piece 'PDC (Pretty Damn Cosmic)', which was cool.

Matthijs, a teenage fiddle player from Holland, who had visited *Cropredy* with his family several times and jammed offstage at Fairport gig in Vlissingen the previous year, was invited to play with the band. Chris Leslie had asked him earlier whether he fancied it and he was obviously gobsmacked at the suggestion. But it didn't show once he was on stage and he went down really well, and got a well-deserved applause. They played 'Dirty Linen' together and something else, and later Matthijs was dragged back on stage to play fiddle on 'Meet on the Ledge'.

WILBERT'S
4 NOVEMBER 1999, CLEVELAND, OHIO

STAN GRAHAM

In 1999 approached, I had changed jobs and was in charge of finance and merchandise for a minor indoor soccer team in Dayton. I wrote to Peggy at Woodworm proposing to have tour t-shirts made locally, if he would send me the artwork. I would drop-ship them to the first venue and sell them at the Ohio shows. We would split the profits from the Ohio shows and then I would sell the remainder at cost for the band to take with them for the rest of the tour.

I remember coming home from work one day with a message on my answering machine: 'Stan… Dave Pegg here, calling from England. I got your letter and we want to do it. Here's my personal number. Call me tomorrow to work out the details.' Peggy had the artwork sent to me. The 1999 tour shirts weren't the greatest as far as artwork goes. It was a digital photo of the band. But people would have a souvenir from the tour. I think we charged $15 for the shirts. What didn't sell, we sold online from Fairport's website.

In 2000, Fairport (acoustic) again came to the US and, again, Peggy and I worked on having tour shirts made in the USA. The artwork was much better on this shirt. It was the *Wood and the Wire* tour and the artwork was quite nice. It wasn't a large tour, and only eight venues got to enjoy this show, but it was very good.

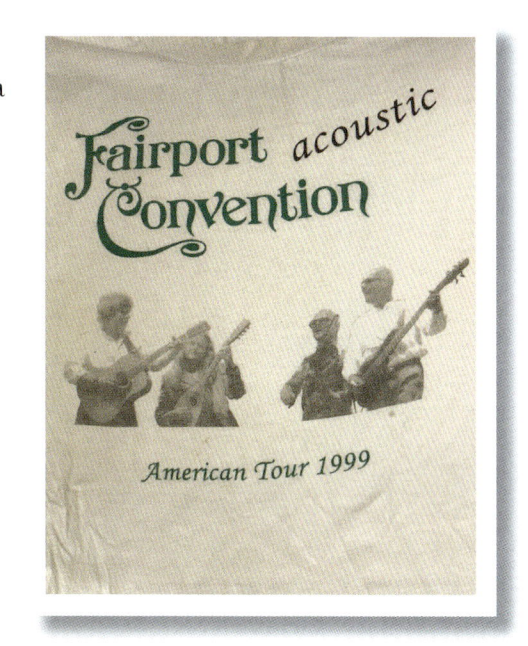

Stan Graham made tour t-shirts for Fairport to sell in the USA

GONNA SEE ALL MY FRIENDS:
A PEOPLE'S HISTORY OF FAIRPORT CONVENTION

PICTURE PLAYHOUSE
31 DECEMBER 1999, BEVERLEY, UK

MIKE BURSELL

My first Fairport gig was at the Caird Hall during my second month at Dundee University, in November 1973. I had already been lucky to catch Sandy Denny solo at Dundee Uni a couple of weeks earlier. My next Fairport gig was again at Dundee Caird Hall, a year later. This was the only time I ever saw Sandy with the band, the rest of the line-up (Swarb, Peggy, DM, Jerry D and Trevor) being unchanged from the year before. Those two Fairport gigs are the only times I have ever seen Fairport *sans* Simon. Two lasting impressions of those gigs are of Sandy's voice and Peggy – with the long hair and the distinctive shuffle in those enormous boots as he played.

Mike Bursell saw Fairport in Dundee and at the end of the Millenium

A question which seldom crops up these days is, 'Where were you on the Millennium Eve?' Well, I know exactly where I was – at the Beverley Picture Playhouse with my wife, daughters, and Fairport. One daughter was (and still is) very much into Fairport whilst the other was more of a Beyoncé fan at the time and only went under sufferance. That said, photos taken that evening show a grin from ear-to-ear. Come midnight we entered a new century, wondering where the time had gone. After 'Meet on the Ledge' something wonderful happened, Fairport started jamming. My memory is hazy, but Fairport kicked off the new millennium with an extended encore of rock 'n' roll classics – The Beatles, probably Elvis and a tinge of Led Zep. It was wonderful. Oh, for a tape.

GONNA SEE ALL MY FRIENDS:
A PEOPLE'S HISTORY OF FAIRPORT CONVENTION

KOEN HOTTENTOT

My friends and I arrived at the Picture Playhouse way too early. There was no one else there, so we took another stroll through town. We would have liked to get into a pub for half an hour, but they all seemed to be charging big bucks for the pleasure of spending New Year's Eve in their premises, so once we were back on the market square in front of the theatre, we decided to simply wait the remaining three quarters of an hour. At least we would have the advantage of going for the best seats, as we were the first. The doors opened at 7.30pm, by which time the queue had become rather long. Once inside, we went for second row seats in the middle, and were very happy with our spot. And, this being a Fairport gig, we then went to get some drinks.

The theatre was lovely – I can see why Fairport

Koen Hottentot saw the Millenium gig

had earlier been rather taken with this place and had embraced the idea of staging the concert there. And the organisers had done a grand job. It didn't feel like 'just a gig'. It already looked like a true party before the show started, with tables full of plates with food - sandwiches, toast, salad, crisps. And boxes with bottles of champagne, to be distributed later that evening.

A little after 8.30pm, Fairport (Electric!) Convention hit the stage, greeted by loud cheers. Simon promised a bit of a party, 'But, please, don't mention the M-word.' Indeed, especially on the television or the little I had seen of it that day, every second word mentioned was 'the Millennium'.

'Royal Seleccion No 13' has become the traditional opener for a Fairport gig, just like 'Meet on the Ledge' is its finale, and it was grand to hear this kick ass once again with a drummer, the wonderful Gerry Conway. The third or fourth number Fairport played was a great new instrumental with a leading role for Chris Leslie who, however, did not play an instrument on it: instead, he put bells on his legs and went into Morris dance mode (but where were the handkerchiefs?). The tune – featuring Simon on electric guitar – which Chris danced around to (and sounded great), was introduced by him as 'Come Haste to the Millennium' (agh! - the M-word!). Another high point in this set was the return of 'Rosemary's Sister', performed by just Simon and Ric, and it was very moving. You could hear a pin drop.

The second set was mainly filled with material from the new album, *The Wood and the Wire*. I was glad when they dug deep into the past and came up with an unexpected classic gem, the beautiful 'Now Be Thankful', previously only associated with the *Full House* line-up and to my knowledge, not played at all between 1970 and the 1997 *Cropredy Festival*. It's one of my own all-time favourite Fairport songs, and Chris Leslie sang lead, and very well he did it too.

The break after the second hour's set was used to distribute the bottles of champagne (which were included in the ticket price). We saved our champagne for midnight, so there was still room for another beer at the start of the third and last set. A pleasant tension was gradually building up by now. Back home in Holland, they had already entered 2000. Now that it was coming very close, 2000 didn't seem a very big deal. Just another New Year's Eve out there – but I felt really grateful to spend it at this particular concert, with some of my best friends and my favourite all time band.

With about ten minutes left until the turn of the year, it was time to once again go into reflective mode and wonder where indeed all that time goes to. Simon remembered the unforgettable Sandy Denny and how she first played him the song they were now going to play, back in 1968 and again everyone in the theatre was very silent. Simon then sang a heartfelt version of 'Who Knows Where the Time Goes' with the band in great form. And, was it just me or was Gerry Conway fighting tears behind the drum kit during the song? It was a great moment, with Ric and Chris on the fiddles extending and improvised the song a bit when the singing was over, until the clock next to the stage nearly hit midnight. The band stopped, Chris Leslie stepped to the mic and we counted down the last seconds to 2000. Happy new year!

Champagne bottles were opened, and an immense number of balloons descended upon us from the ceiling. There was a lot of hugging and kissing and noise everywhere, and in his attempt to open his champagne bottle, my friend Chris Bates poured its contents mostly on two other friends. Party poppers were popped, porty pappers were pepped - it was that kind of moment.

Amidst this mayhem, Simon, Peggy, Ric, Chris and Gerry once again took the stage, wishing everyone a happy new year and launching straight into 'Walk Awhile', which had the Picture Playhouse shaking on its foundations as we all sang along to it at the top of our voices – and we never did sit down again. Balloons were flying around all over the place, and it was a nice sport to try and throw them on stage, where Simon was ready to kick the balloons back into the audience again with the neck of his guitar – most of the balloons didn't survive the guitar, so there were loud bangs. Meanwhile, Peggy was looking like Elvis Presley, with a big Elvis wig and huge Elvis sunglasses.

My champagne bottle was emptied very quickly, but I had brought another one with me from Holland so we emptied that one too as the band launched into 'Matty Groves'. This was once again sung with such enthusiasm by the audience that Simon didn't actually have to sing it and could concentrate on damaging balloons, and mostly lip synching the lyrics. 'Matty' then turned into 'Dirty Linen' and, 30 minutes into the year 2000, Jacqui McShee from Pentangle – looking a bit tipsy, but then again weren't we all? – got up on stage and it was time for 'Meet on the Ledge', sung by everyone on stage and in the audience. This, folks, was probably even better than *Cropredy*.

GONNA SEE ALL MY FRIENDS:
A PEOPLE'S HISTORY OF FAIRPORT CONVENTION

ARTS CENTRE
20 MAY 2000, KING'S LYNN, UK

ANNA RYDER

I did a lot of support for Fairport in 2000, including for their acoustic tour. In May we played at the arts centre in King's Lynn. We arrived and were doing the soundchecks when I noticed that there was a proper Steinway grand piano backstage. The stage manager or technician, John, said that I could use it, and then he went away.

Anna Ryder (left) recalls a disastrous soundcheck

I thought this would be really great, and I'd just push it onto the stage with the Fairports' help. I was urging them on – 'Come on, get your backs into it' – and they all got behind the keyboard part of the piano and began to push. As it went onto the stage there was this terrible, horrible shearing sound of cracking wood and we realised that the stage had a little slope and that the pedals were now sticking down. The pedals just geared forwards and were just dangling there.

I looked at the piano, horrified, and then turned around and all the Fairports had disappeared. I was left on my own, when John came back. I think Peggy and Simon had run into the dressing room. I could see Ric's feet sticking out from behind the back curtain keeping very still. Chris was nowhere to be seen. I had to explain to John what had happened. 'Oh no,' was his initial response. He told me that the piano ought to have been lifted onto the stage by a special hoist. I just didn't know what to say.

He then crumpled onto the ground and did that thing that John Cleese did, putting his hands over the top of his head, and, 'Aarrrggghhh.' I said, 'I'm really sorry, what can we do? I'm sure it will work.' He said, 'No, it's Saturday. It's Sunday tomorrow. There's a concert pianist coming tomorrow night to play a concert here.'

When we started the gig, we looked at the piano and it did work if you put two weights by the pedals to keep them straight. I thought, given we had actually pushed it onto the stage, I'd use it for my set, which is usually half an hour or so. We got to the gig, and I went out and played and the pedals were sort of working, although John still had his head in his hands. I finished my set and then Chris appeared from the wings, and gave me the signal to carry on, so I carried on for another song. Another thing about that gig is that there was a story the next day in *Lynn News* about that gig – apparently there's a review called, 'Who Knows Where the Time Goes, eh Simon!'. So I had finished my song, and was looking up, and Chris came again and mouthed 'more'. I carried on and must have done 45 to 60 minutes. But after this I decided to stop, because I wasn't who people had come to see.

This caused a slight problem because then Chris and Ric had to do impromptu fiddle tunes and Morris dancing because Simon wasn't there – the reason I had had to play on. Apparently, Simon had fallen asleep in the bath in the hotel opposite the gig, and one of the stagehands had to go and fetch him. Chris was suggesting all of these fiddle tunes to a slightly confused Ric. He would offer to play them and sing the beginning. Ric said, 'You can sing it, but I still don't know it.'

I knew the Fairports quite well, but I'd only known them for a couple of years. They had a sixth sense for when things go wrong, that was why they all disappeared and just left me to face the music. They were hiding, and they said absolutely nothing in my defence, nothing at all and feigned complete ignorance. But obviously John knew that they would have had to have helped me

CROPREDY FESTIVAL
10 - 12 AUGUST 2000, CROPREDY, UK

RICHARD GASCOYNE
Cropredy 2000 had an amazing line up; there wasn't a band I didn't want to see or hear. On the Friday I was particularly looking forward to seeing the Incredible String Band, who I had only ever heard on vinyl

GONNA SEE ALL MY FRIENDS:
A PEOPLE'S HISTORY OF FAIRPORT CONVENTION

and who I hoped would live up to their former glory, as well as my own memory. We and a couple of friends stood near the sound tent and watched them perform. After a few minutes, I realised that they weren't going to be as I remembered them from their initial albums, but I gave them the benefit of the doubt and watched and listened closely. After a couple of numbers, a certain Mr Dave Pegg walked onto the field, accompanied by none other than Robert Plant. Peggy exchanged a couple of words, asking us all how we were enjoying the festival so far, and we then all stood together watching ISB.

Halfway through the set, Robert turned to me and simply suggested that the band were either brilliant or rather dreadful and, in his view, it was the latter. As I have tried to convey, I was trying very hard to understand the ISB set and was sort of enjoying it, but the moment Robert expressed his very forthright view, I heard myself answering him by totally agreeing that they were indeed dreadful. There

Photos: Krzysztof Opalski

Krzysztof Opalski was at Cropredy in 2000

was no way I was going to disagree with Mr Plant; after all, he really was – and still is – a musical hero. Equally, I must apologise to Robin, Mike and Clive for not sticking up for them. I can only hope they will forgive me.

Just before the end of the set, Peggy and Robert started to head backstage. They said their goodbyes and set off across the field. Someone ran after Peggy and Robert and asked them if he could have a photo. Both agreed and stood, side by side, waiting for the shot to be taken. The fan gave his camera to Planty and went and stood with Peggy. When he was asked by Robert why he was suggesting the photo be taken this way, the fan simply said that no one else in the world would have a photo of himself, taken by one of his musical heroes whilst he stood next to another of his musical heroes. After the photo was taken, Robert was heard to say to Peggy, 'This could only bloody well happen at Cropredy.'

CROPREDY FESTIVAL
9 – 11 AUGUST 2001, CROPREDY, UK

STEVE TILSTON

I was booked on a tour of Scandinavia with Fairport Convention and Mott the Hoople in 1972, the singer-songwriter sandwiched in between. They were strange times, because Peggy and Swarb were the only original Fairport members left, and they had picked up a couple of Birmingham musicians along the way, a drummer called Tom Farnell and Roger Hill on guitar. I think they were old friends of Peggy's from various bands. A four piece, they were a bit ragged. They were good players but they weren't really *au fait* with the material and so it was learning as you go. Meanwhile, Mott the Hoople were on the verge of disbanding and a bit despondent. Ian Hunter told me that they had just recorded a song with David Bowie called 'All the Young Dudes' and that it was their last throw of the dice. Obviously, it became a big worldwide hit and they didn't disband.

It was a strange situation but springtime – May – in Scandinavia was great. We toured around and I really enjoyed Peggy and Swarb's company. I have fond memories of sitting in a sauna somewhere in Finland and chatting away to Swarbrick. And we played somewhere in the north of Sweden, and although it was springtime, there might have been ice in the hotel swimming pool. There was definitely a wager going on that Swarbrick wouldn't jump into the swimming pool fully clothed. Which of course he did – and won a lot of money. He had a perpetual cigarette hanging out of his mouth, and I swear to God he jumped in the pool and the fag was still burning when he got out.

In Helsinki, there was a press reception in a fancy club one afternoon. I remember getting up with various members of Fairport and Mott the Hoople, and me fronting this line up that played Elvis Presley numbers. It was great because it was so off the wall.

I bumped into them a few times and the line ups changed but Peggy was a constant. And out of the blue I got a call from Simon or Peggy saying that they wanted to record two of my songs for the album, *Jewel in the Crown* – 'Slipjigs and Reels' and 'The Naked Highwayman'. I was flattered that they wanted to do that, and they did great versions of them. I was still a touring musician when Fairport Convention first wanted to record some of my songs. It was a jolt in the arm. It certainly didn't hurt having somebody like Fairport do them. 'Slipjigs and Reels' all of a sudden got a life of its own. A lot of people picked up on it and there are now over 80 cover versions of the song.

Ultimately, Fairport went on to record six of my songs. It was great to get to know Peggy again. I did a tour in 2001 and supported them. Because they'd done a few of my numbers, it was a nice vantage point to do it, although there were a few comments from audiences along the lines of, 'Why do you do Fairport songs?' and I had to say, 'Well, actually I wrote them.' I wrote 'Over the Next Hill' specifically for them.

They're one of the great constants on the British music scene. The whole *Cropredy Festival* is such a great gathering of the Fairport clan from all corners of the world and quite a special get together and quite different from lots of other festivals. It has got its own flavour to it. I've not seen them for a couple of years because of the pandemic but hopefully our paths will cross again sooner rather than late, perhaps over a curry in Bradford at the Kashmir. It's one of their favourite haunts when in Yorkshire.

ROYAL SPA CENTRE
1 FEBRUARY 2002, LEAMINGTON SPA, UK

PAUL GOODE

My introduction to Fairport Convention was because of a chance meeting with someone I got chatting to one evening, about 23 years ago now, after work in the local pub. The 'someone' introduced himself to me as Michael Chalmers, and we got chatting about stuff, including music. Michael's passion in music was Fairport, and I had to admit to not knowing much about the band.

A few days later, I wandered into the pub again, and Michael was there at his favourite end of the bar, set up with a pint. As I walked towards him, he held up a supermarket carrier bag filled with CDs, insisting that I take them home to listen to. He hardly knew me, and this was only the second time we had met, but I soon discovered that Michael's generosity

GONNA SEE ALL MY FRIENDS:
A PEOPLE'S HISTORY OF FAIRPORT CONVENTION

and trust were very much part of the way he was made. I took the CDs home and played them, became hooked straight away, and became a close friend of Michael's.

Not long after, Michael asked me if I would like to go to see Fairport in nearby Leamington Spa. He had a pair of tickets, but no transport after his car had expired, so I would have to be the chauffeur. And there was a second catch; we had to be there at 5pm because Michael was to meet with Fairport to discuss photographs that he had taken which were potentially going into a CD or DVD booklet. Off we went and, armed with a letter from the band, we were shown into the green room.

I was given a drink while Michael discussed the photographs with Fairport and/or their management – I'm not sure now, more than 20 years have gone by. But my first Fairport gig and I was in the green room! It was a brilliant gig and a fantastic evening; I even bought the t-shirt and a CD (the 35th anniversary *Wintour* t-shirt and *The Wood and the Wire* CD).

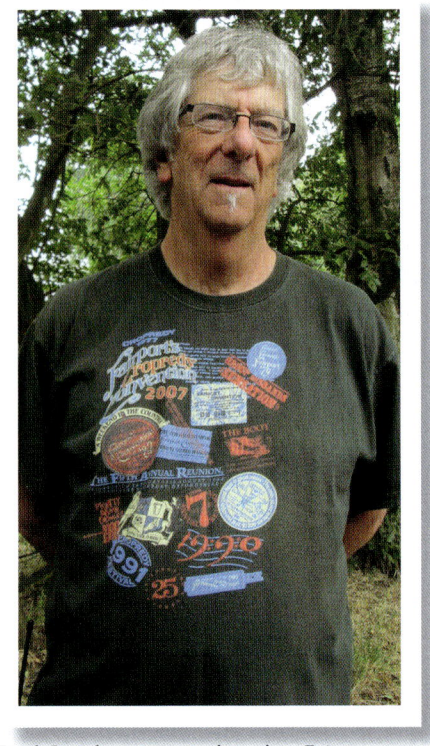

Paul Goode was introduced to Fairport Convention by a man called Michael

Michael and I stayed friends but saw less of each other as time went by, until Michael finally persuaded me to attend *Cropredy* one year. I wasn't much of a camper in those days, but off I went. It was the year the usual camping fields were all flooded, and I camped somewhere beyond Field 8. I had heard that Michael was less well than he had been and discovered that he was really quite poorly in fact, and, sadly, he took a turn for the worse at *Cropredy* and had to return home. I had no real idea how ill Michael was. And he sadly passed away not long afterwards.

Michael had started a relationship with Annie in the intervening time since our chance meeting in the pub, and they became man and wife a few days before his passing. Annie made formal arrangements to scatter Michael's ashes in the Concert Field at *Cropredy*, and Simon, Ric and Peggy all came to say goodbye to him in the field that day (Hallowe'en, of all days). We went back to The Red Lion in the village and managed a tear-stained rendition of 'Meet on the Ledge' over a few pints.

I became a huge Fairport fan in my own right, thanks to Michael's generosity and that initial loan of his precious Fairport CDs. I have loads of Fairport albums and books of my own now, and I've been to loads of gigs and to *Cropredy* about 15 times in all. Only once with Michael in body, but always with Michael in spirit.

Michael Chalmers – the most kind-hearted man I ever met, always a Fairporter, forever at *Cropredy*.

XXXV
RELEASED 12 FEBRUARY 2002

THE GEORGE
12 FEBRUARY 2002, BARFORD ST MICHAEL, UK

MIKE BURSELL

I was invited to join Fairport and friends at The George in Barford St Michael for the launch party for the *XXXV* album, marking Fairport's first 35 years. There was a presentation to Fairports by Nigel Schofield and Neil Wayne of Free Reed (a framed map of the 'Folk-Rock Golden Triangle' around the Banbury area). It was all very emotional and there was a pregnant pause...

Mike Bursell was 'just an ordinary fan' at the launch event for XXXV

I was on the point of jumping in to fill it, but I hesitated (well, it wasn't my place) and then the moment was gone. I've often thought about it since, about what I should have said – about how circumstances had brought me there as a representative of the ordinary Fairport fan, how we'd followed the band for 35 years and about what made them so special. Through the triumphs, the tragedies and the might-have-beens, Fairport always had that special bond with their audience. I should have said something about the way they'd be available after the gig to chat, sign LPs and have a drink. That wouldn't happen with The Beatles, the Stones, Pink Floyd – but it was what always happened with Fairport. It made them very approachable and made the relationship very special. That was why Fairport were holding this celebration with their friends in a pub, and not on the 35th floor of a record company skyscraper. Fairport have always been close to their fans – thank you. We love you for it.

THE BASEMENT
6 MARCH 2002, SYDNEY, AUSTRALIA

IAN JONES

Fairport's last appearance in Sydney was at the famous Basement in March 2002. They were supported by Mick Thomas, who had previously fronted folk rock group Weddings Parties Anything.

In March 2021, I was lucky to see Fairport streaming a concert from the Brasenose Arms in Cropredy. I feel very fortunate to have followed Fairport for so many years. My love of them led me to the Fairport family tree which includes Steeleye Span, Matthews Southern Comfort, Iain Matthews, Richard Thompson, The Albion Band and Martin Carthy. My life has been enriched by all this wonderful music. Hopefully we will meet on the ledge, or is it just 'farewell, farewell' to Fairport playing live in Sydney?

GONNA SEE ALL MY FRIENDS:
A PEOPLE'S HISTORY OF FAIRPORT CONVENTION

THE MILL
5 & 6 AUGUST 2002, BANBURY, UK

STAN GRAHAM

In 2002 I made my second trip to Cropredy. I wasn't able to get tickets for the second warm-up show, which always sells out quickly because Richard Thompson plays that one. After the first warm-up show at The Mill in Banbury, Peggy and Simon came out to have drinks and chat with the fans, as they often do. I walked up to Peggy and said, 'You probably don't remember me, but I did the US tour shirts in '99 and 2000…' Peggy immediately grabbed my hand and said, 'Stan! Yes, I remember!' after which he immediately said, 'Are you coming tomorrow night? Richard's playing with us, you know.' I explained that I couldn't get a ticket. Peggy responded, 'Come tomorrow about an hour before the show. Go around back to the side entrance and I'll put you on the guest list.'

The next night, I waited around the back of The Mill. I could hear the soundcheck going on. When it ended, Peggy stuck his head out the door and looked around. I gave a wave and he beckoned me in. He explained that because the show was sold out, I couldn't have a seat, but I could just stand next to the stage during the show. That was fine by me!

I watched Jerry Donahue finish his soundcheck and, after he walked off the stage, I yelled out, 'A round of drinks for the sound crew, on me!' Rob Braviner jumped up from the sound board and said, 'Don't you just love a Yank with money?' We sat outside The Mill, drinking pints and getting to know each other and had a jolly time. The show was amazing and there I was next to the stage.

CROPREDY FESTIVAL
8 – 10 AUGUST 2002, CROPREDY, UK

ULI TWELKER

'Does it always rain when I play?' Richard Thompson asked. He'd happened upon a murky weather front. In spite of a bad forecast, the record attendance of the *30th Anniversary* was surpassed at Cropredy in 2002 with over 20,000 fans attending. After Thompson's emotional roller-coaster between sad ballads and solid rock 'n' folk – with Danny Thompson on double bass on 'Victoria' – the weather cleared for the first gig by our hosts: 'The Early Years' were on the agenda with the Fairport Convention chaps from the beginning. Iain Matthews, Ashley Hutchings, fiddler Dave Swarbrick (in a wheelchair) and Richard Thompson sang the hymns of their early era, *Liege & Lief*, enforced by original singer Judy Dyble as well as Vikki Clayton – the latter a recognised interpreter of the repertoire of the unforgettable Sandy Denny.

The following evening, Fairport presented another mega-set and Saturday was dedicated to the current band. Simon Nicol, Chris Leslie and Ric Sanders performed brilliantly in front of the inspired drums and bass foundations courtesy of Gerry Conway and Dave Pegg. Eddi Reader assisted with the Byrds/Dylan classic 'You Ain't Goin' Nowhere', while 'The Naked Highwayman' belonged to their best chuckle-friendly songs. 'Red and Gold' was rendered by its composer, Ralph McTell, and for the finale, 'Meet on the Ledge' was sung movingly by everybody at midnight, as if it was a one-off.

DEREK VAN RYNE

The Dubliners had Top 10 hits in 1967 with 'Seven Drunken Nights' and 'Black Velvet Band' and so folk music became my favourite type of music. But like every other teenager, I was also a fan of rock music, and my love affair with Fairport began with the release of *Liege & Lief*. Here was a band that combined my two favourite types of music.

I returned from a day trip to Boulogne, where

Derek Van Ryne was on a boozy trip back from Boulogne when he bumped into Simon and Swarb

the beer and wine flowed freely, and arrived back at London Victoria with a bagful of duty-free wines, spirits and tobacco. Catching the

GONNA SEE ALL MY FRIENDS:
A PEOPLE'S HISTORY OF FAIRPORT CONVENTION

10.06pm train home to Horsham, West Sussex I fell asleep, and woke up in Bognor Regis sidings at 3am.

Having sobered up a lot, I gathered up my things before realising I had nowhere to go, so I moved to a more comfortable first class compartment and went back to sleep. I was woken by the train moving and wondered where it was heading. Luckily, it was only going into Bognor Regis station to form the first train up to Victoria that Sunday morning. So I moved myself back to second class and the train duly dropped me off at Littlehaven station, which was the nearest one to my flat.

As I arrived at the entrance to my block of flats, the door opened and Swarb and Simon came out. I thought I was seeing things and slapped my face to wake myself up. However, sure enough, it was the pair of them and I was so gobsmacked that I didn't say anything to them. At

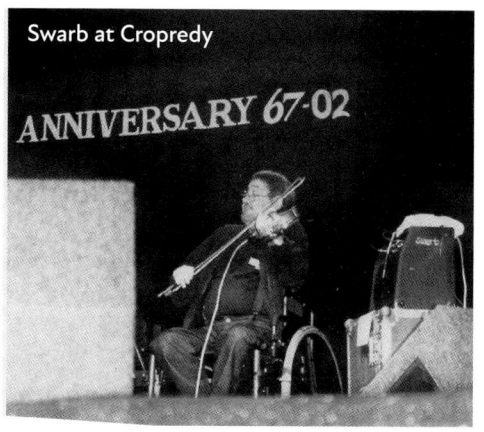

Photos : Oliver Ilgner

Swarb at Cropredy

257

the time, Fairport had disbanded and Swarb and Simon were touring various folk clubs as a duo. It was six months before I discovered that one of my neighbours, a bloke called Doug Lake who lived on the floor below me, was a big friend of the band and that Swarb and Simon had been staying at his flat following a gig in (I think) Arundel before heading up country that Sunday morning for another one.

Of all the Fairport concerts I've seen, the one that really stands out is *Cropredy* 2002. The Dubliners, on their *40th Anniversary* tour, topped the bill on the Friday night and blew the crowd away. I bumped into Peggy on the field the next day and said how much I had enjoyed them. He agreed they were awesome and said he was pleased Fairport didn't have to follow them.

BOTTOM LINE
13 JUNE 2003, NEW YORK, NEW YORK

REBECCA MAXFIELD

My dad went through a stretch of listening to Fairport a lot when I was a kid, so I'd hear their albums in the car and around the house (without much distinction of era – I really only grasped the band's history later). I was an early reader and a total bookworm, and I loved fantasy and historical fiction. I wonder if the idea of a ballad or a song that told a story was cool and novel to me in terms of being a thing I could actually buy a CD of and listen to, rather than being something that just happened in *The Lord of the Rings* or *Redwall*. I remember being in the car with my dad with 'Matty Groves' on, at a point where I'd grasped the general plot, but still had trouble following it line by line or verse by verse, and asking, 'Is Matty dead yet?'

Fairport were certainly an odd band to have as my favourite when I was in school (in the age of, among other things, Evanescence and Maroon 5), but I managed to get one or two friends to listen to them too.

Actually being able to go to a Fairport concert, when they toured in the US, was amazing for me as someone who'd only heard their albums, and also a great bonding activity to do with my dad. The first one was at the Bottom Line in New York City, and we later went to a few at the Towne

Crier in Pawling where I got the band to autograph my CD booklet and some photo collages I'd made. I screwed up my courage to ask Chris if he'd ever considered writing a song about the Flying Dutchman legend, which I'd recently read a book or two about. Luckily, he took this young teenage kid seriously and ended up incorporating that idea into 'Edge of the World', on *Sense of Occasion*.

My early love of Fairport and their music has had a lifelong impact on my writing and performing interests.

THE THIRSTY EAR
21 JUNE 2003, COLUMBUS OHIO

STAN GRAHAM

This was the last time that I saw Fairport. Early in the show, Simon was doing 'The Hiring Fair' with Ric. But for some reason, people in the bar were not listening and were rudely talking. With the quietness of 'The Hiring Fair', the talking was quite annoying and was clearly affecting Simon. When he finished the song, he took off his guitar and threw it down, saying, 'I can't do this!' and stormed out the front door. The rest of the band stood frozen on the stage with looks on their faces like, 'What just happened?' Peggy ran after him in the parking lot.

I was standing at the back of the bar with Steve Carson. Suddenly, Simon came storming back in and came right back to Steve and I and cried, 'I just wanted them to be quiet!' and smashed in the top of the coffee machine with his fist. He then turned to the bar where a couple were watching, wide-eyed. They both had a shot glass of whiskey on the bar. Simon grabbed the shots and threw them back quickly and stormed back out the front door. Steve and I looked at each other and didn't know what to think.

A few moments later, Peggy came back in and announced that the show was over and that he would refund any money for people that wanted it. Then they packed up and left. Fortunately, Little Johnny England had opened for them, and they set back up and played a long electric set that was awesome. But… I still have no words for what I witnessed.

Fairport never came back to the Midwest where I lived, so I haven't seen them since. Their last trip to the United States was in 2007. Afterwards, there were stories that Rob Braviner was messing with the sound in Simon's ear, but I don't believe that's true. Based on what I witnessed, it was the rude American crowd that was talking loudly during 'The Hiring Fair'. Why would people buy a ticket to a show and then talk through the whole thing? But it was a sad night.

As I write this, I'm getting ready to travel to Cropredy for the 2022 show. I can't believe that it's been 19 years since I've seen them, and I can't wait. I feel lucky that I've been able to see them and meet them and have great experiences with them. This year is 40 years of Fairport being my favourite band. They've been an important part of my life just for the music. The rest is just icing on the cake. Thanks chaps!

CAMBRIDGE FOLK FESTIVAL CHERRY HINTON HALL GROUNDS
3 AUGUST 2003, CAMBRIDGE, UK

DAVE KEY

Back in the mists of time, when mastodons roamed the Earth, a cheeky young whippersnapper with a visual impairment named Edmund used to come to *Cambridge Folk Festival* and blow his horn (like Little Boy Blue) from the disability enclosure. Not that he sought to annoy anyone; Edmund simply suffered from an excess of enthusiasm and, as a talented musician, a feeling of having been left out... Until one day a fellow punter threatened to 'Ram that thing down your throat if you don't shurrup!'

One fortuitous day at *Cambridge Folk Festival*, a main stage artist cancelled at the last moment and Fairport Convention stepped in to fill the breach. The crosswinds must have been blowing in the right direction that afternoon, for the plaintive tones of Edmund's trumpet trying to blend in with what they were playing were picked up by the keen-eared Fairport crew. Far from being annoyed, Fairport invited him backstage after the gig where they told Ed he had 'a good tone'

GONNA SEE ALL MY FRIENDS:
A PEOPLE'S HISTORY OF FAIRPORT CONVENTION

and that his brass instrument made their wood and strings 'Sound like *Sgt Pepper's Lonely Hearts Club Band*'. They invited him to play with them at *Cropredy* the following weekend. As his guide dog and fly-on-the-wall sidekick, I was invited too.

One of the crew (possibly roadie Martin Driver) said he could furnish us with a small tent and away we wide-eyed innocents went, never suspecting that this chance encounter would lead to a 20-year (and counting) relationship with Fairport. Edmund has been invited back year after year to sport his oak (or rather, brass) on the vital Saturday night climax of 'Meet on the Ledge', with occasional turns on 'Wat Tyler' or 'Red and Gold'.

Edmund and Richard Thompson

Aside from Fairport themselves, Edmund has made many friends and fans over those 20 years at *Croppers*, as well as chance encounters with the great and good of the folk world, including Richard Thompson and Ralph McTell.

Through thick and thin, drenching rain and/or blistering heat, angry wasps at one's beer or bhajis, mossies and midges biting one to buggery, camping on sloping rough-hewn and bumpy, cow-patted ground when landed with the short straw of pitches upon arriving too late to compete for a half-decent one—which was pretty much every year.

Yes, through all adversities, Edmund and I, courtesy of Fairport, have come back every year, camping out in our increasingly dilapidated little tent, until COVID brought the curtain down. And it has been worth every minute.

One year in particular stands out, when Dave Swarbrick, the demon fiddler of legendary renown (RIP), returned from a spell of ill health to play what proved to be his farewell gig with his former bandmates. Due to a lifetime of smoking, drinking and (perhaps other) artificial aids to a sense of well-being, Swarb had developed emphysema. He could only be brought on stage (in his wheelchair) for ten-minute bursts before being wheeled off again for a blast on the old oxygen tank. But the Paganini of folk did not disappoint.

It was a heatwave weekend and the habitual after-hours party for traders and crew was held out in the open, in a large circle, with Swarb holding court at the twelve o'clock position, leading many of the tunes and reels. Albeit the craic was never so boozy as to spoil the skilful playing and singing, what the Irish would call a hooley ensued, with Swarb staying up way past his bedtime (and doctor's advice) until three in the morning.

'Was that the same year we came across Dave Pegg semi-comatose on the browned grass at 5am, Ed?' 'Dunno, mate. Lost in the mists of time, when mastodons roamed the earth.'

'Meet on the Ledge' indeed, Swarb! Edmund salutes you, and hopes to see you there one day, when 'it all comes round again…'.

CROPREDY FESTIVAL
7 - 9 AUGUST 2003, CROPREDY, UK

PAUL MITCHELL

At 2003 *Cropredy*, four months before Jonah (Johnny Jones – Fairport's old road manager) died, I had the first stock of CDs for his audiobook, *A Fist Full of Festivals*. I asked the guys running the record and CD sales tent if they would display and sell it, and Fairport put a free ad for it in the programme. We waited to see what sales would be like.

On Sunday morning when everyone was packing up and getting ready to leave, I went to the tent to collect what hadn't been sold and the cash for sales. To my delight, 150 units had been sold and they handed over £1,500 along with the remaining stock. I hurriedly took the cash over to Jonah, who was absolutely delighted, especially when he found out that he had sold more CDs that weekend than Richard Thompson.

About an hour later, Peggy's son Matt ran towards me saying the guys at the CD tent needed me to go back and see them as there was some kind of problem. It turned out they had only sold 15 copies of Jonah's CD and therefore they had overpaid us by over £1,000. They asked me for the money back. I said I'd given it to Jonah now and wasn't happy about asking for it back, but that they were welcome to try. Not knowing Jonah, they said that they would. But on approaching him and seeing his build, his face and his demeanour towards those he didn't know, they decided against it as they felt they might get hurt.

Jonah went to his grave in December of that year thinking he had outsold Richard Thompson, a fact of which he was both delighted and amazed.

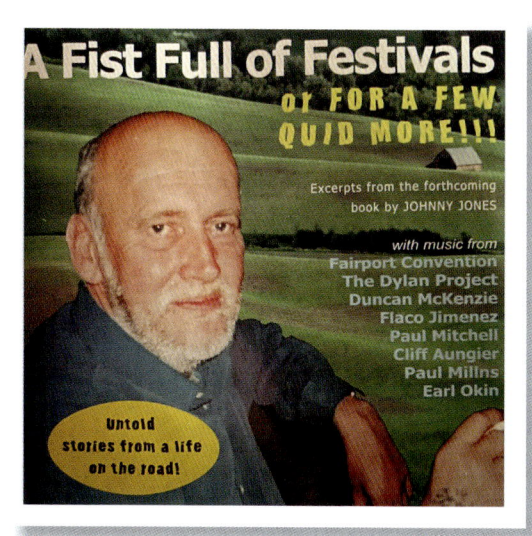

Jonah's 'best selling' CD

IAN RALPH HUCKIN

Despite living all of my life in Oxfordshire, and most of that in Banbury, I didn't go to *Cropredy* until 2003. Someone sold me a cheap ticket and, as Procul Harum, Lindisfarne and Dennis LeCorriere were all playing,

Ian Ralph Huckin with Marion Fleetwood (Trad Arr, Colvin Quarmby, Jigantics, Feast of Fiddles) being photobombed by Anna Ryder and Sally Barker (IOTA), at the bar at Cropredy

it was a chance too good to miss. I 'discovered' several other acts whilst there, including Colvin Quarmby. Folk music then became an important part of my life, and I've not missed a festival since. 15 years later, I was down the front for the Gerry Colvin Band. It suddenly dawned on me that every person playing on the stage with him (including his guests) was a friend of mine. I now help run Banbury Folk Club, with Gerry Colvin and Marion Fleetwood as patrons, and I get to book some astonishingly great performers, including members of Fairport themselves. As life-changing moments go, 2003 is up there with the best. To this day, I still get a little tingle when I walk onto that field on the opening Thursday.

KULTURBRUKET PÅ DAL
18 NOVEMBER 2003, MELLERUD, SWEDEN

LARS NILSSON

In November 2003 there was a very a small piece in *Göteborgs-Posten*, the main newspaper in the west of Sweden. 'Most unexpected. Fairport Convention to play Mellerud.' Mellerud, about 130 kilometres north of Gothenburg, is a small town of about 5,000 people, and usually we travel to the big city for concerts. On this occasion, a number of people made the reverse journey.

I had heard of Fairport but had not taken much notice until the Island record-sampler *El Pea* was released. The opening track was 'Lord Marlborough'. One listen and I was hooked. I immediately bought *Angel Delight*, and have built a collection of records, books and music books since.

When we planned a folk music festival in Mellerud, Fairport were the obvious choice for a headliner. They could not make it, but we were offered a gig on the North European tour in 2003 instead. The gig was advertised months in advance and preparations started. First there was the question of the backline. Fairport travelled light so we had to provide both amplifiers and a drum kit. The latter caused a lot of work. The request was for a Yamaha Recording Custom set. We searched far and wide for someone to lend us one, but it seems West Sweden is a recording custom-free zone. Likewise, we had problems finding the right amplifiers. Then there was the question of food, drinks and refreshment. A quite extensive list, but we managed most of it.

The big day came. We had sold most of the 240 available tickets. Half of them were sold locally, to people who had never heard the band, but trusted my assurances that they were great. The other half were people from other places. There were quite a few cars from Gothenburg driving north that day. But the record was the guy who travelled 500 kilometres from Gävle.

In the afternoon the band turned up, one by one, for their line checks. I'd had nightmares about it for more than a week. Would they accept the back line we had put together? Gerry seemed pleased with the Yamaha Stage Custom set we had found in our music school. And neither Simon nor DP complained about their amps. Then Ric sent my heart jumping with his remark. 'A Peavey, I have never played through one of those before.' My voice trembled when I asked if this was a problem. 'No, it will be exciting.'

Then it was time for the soundcheck with everyone on stage, and after that the hot meal. Chris put on his coat and asked where the restaurant was. I told him we were using the staff room in the adjoining school where my wife Kickie had prepared a meal. When Ric and Chris saw the salad bar Kickie had prepared, they probably thought that this was all they would get. But they lit up when she said the main course was lasagne, one meaty and one vegetarian. As Simon would say four years later when they played here again, and I told him Kickie would cook for them. 'Great, I still dream of Swedish lasagne.'

It was unallocated seating, so when the doors opened all the fans from far away immediately filled the front rows. I was standing by the stage door with the band, waiting to introduce them. I turned to Simon and said they had better be good, because half of the audience were there on my recommendation, and if it was not up to scratch, I would probably have to move. He looked at me and said the immortal words, 'You really have stuck your neck out, haven't you Lars?'

I should not have worried. From the opening chords, the fan club in the front rows gave them a marvellous reception and the not-yet fans joined in. And the band responded. I have seen them numerous times and this one of their best performances ever.

The reaction afterwards was phenomenal. I received email after email thanking me for bringing them to Mellerud and the concert was reviewed in four papers. One wrote that it was the best concert in this part of

Sweden in 2003. And *Göteborgs-Posten* devoted three whole pages in their culture section to the gig, with a picture of Chris Leslie on the front.

Kickie summed it up when she said, 'It was the food that did it.' Maybe she's right. She still gets hugs from band members when we turn up at gigs.

BLUE MOON
2004, BANBURY, UK

IAN NORTHCOTT

I have several very fond stories of Fairport, but the one that stands out is when a colleague of mine called Vanessa, who is a singer, was doing a charity single for Care of Police Survivors (COPS). She was let down by a guitarist and a producer and was distraught. I was going to see Fairport that night at Huntingdon Hall, Worcester and took Vanessa along. We chatted to Peggy and Simon and Simon agreed to help.

A date was arranged for a recording session at Blue Moon recording studio in Banbury and we went down there with Vanessa, recording 'Who Know Where the Time Goes?' and 'The Rose'. Simon was on guitar and I watched my guitar hero playing the most beautiful chords I have ever heard, with harmonics I could only dream of. Simon then said, 'We need some violin', and called up Chris who then immediately came down and recorded his part which made it so special.

It was an amazing day for us, which just going to show what a fantastic bunch of lads the guys are. Vanessa raised plenty of money for COPS and I can't thank the guys enough.

DOLWYDDELAN VILLAGE
MAY 2004, DOLWYDDELAN, UK

MIKE SKERRETT

I live in the village of Dolwyddelan in North Wales. When long-time Cropredy site manager Mick Peters got married, Fairport came to a mini-festival that Mick organised in the village. Mick wore his best armour and it was a wonderful event. The whole village had a great day

GONNA SEE ALL MY FRIENDS:
A PEOPLE'S HISTORY OF FAIRPORT CONVENTION

and when my late friend John Glynn enjoyed himself so much that he was overcome and had to rest, Simon helped him for reasons only known to himself.

I ran the local Spar shop in the village and knew Mick and Moggie, the girl he was marrying, quite well. Mick organised the wedding like a mini *Cropredy*. He also made sure it was local. And he made sure not to upset anyone in the village – he invited everyone.

He ordered most of his catering sundries through me, the local hotel provided the onsite bar and there was a large marquee with stage light show and PA. A variety

Mike Skerrett was at Mick Peters' wedding cum mini Cropredy

of acts played on the night, including the Circus of Horrors who I supplied fluorescent tubes to – to be swallowed. We had a few other local acts, but the highlight of the evening was Fairport Convention.

The band stayed in our local hotel and wandered around the village mingling with all and sundry. Ric and Chris sat outside the village pub chatting to anyone and everyone. Most of the village had no idea who Fairport were, not being folk fans, but everyone had a great time.

As far as I know, the band played for free for Mick's wedding, but Mick organised and paid for everything else. I am sure his contacts helped him out, but it was a great free day out.

GONNA SEE ALL MY FRIENDS:
A PEOPLE'S HISTORY OF FAIRPORT CONVENTION

HOSRSTED KEYNES STATION
12 JUNE 2004, HORSTED, UK

STEPHEN ROYSTON

Fairport played an acoustic gig in a marquee on the Bluebell Railway in Sussex. My wife Frances met Ric and Chris at Sheffield Park station, just down the line.

Above: Stephen Royston's wife Frances with Ric Sanders and Chris Leslie

Left: Fairport at full steam on the Bluebell Railway

CROPREDY FESTIVAL
12 – 14 AUGUST 2004, CROPREDY, UK

RUTH EYRE

My father knew Dave Pegg's father-in-law, Percy, and owned Dennis Eyre Butchers as well as a sausage, meat and pie factory. I think Percy may have lived close to the factory and my father was so fond of him. When I was a young child, we were taken to Dave Pegg's home and I could not keep my eyes off Chris's diamond in her tooth. Woodworm Recording Studios was wonderful, and Dave was ever so warm and welcoming. *Cropredy* in 2004 through the eyes of a young girl was just wonderful in every way: the naked painted people, the food, the sunshine, the smell of beer and cider and, of course, the music, with Ian Anderson leaping about the stage, puffing his breath into the flute, with its magical notes transforming him into the pied piper. Sadly Percy died, but I shall always remember him fondly. My dad also died aged 46, from cruel cancer. I was 19.

MILESTONES
28 SEPTEMBER 2004, ROCHESTER, NEW YORK

FREDERIC NOYES

I grew up mostly in Syracuse in upstate New York, a musical wasteland in the 1980s. There were no radio stations playing new, progressive or even vaguely cutting-edge music. Not too many popular bands played in the area because of the lack of radio support, so I began catching Fairport shows in far flung places like Long Island, Manhattan, Northampton, Massachusetts and Rochester, New York. I eventually resettled in southern Vermont, close to Northampton, where I got to keep up with one of my favourite bands until they ceased scheduling tours in the USA.

Frederic Noyes (right) with Peggy

Fairport started to enter my consciousness around 1982 from reading about Led Zeppelin, Roy Harper, Bert Jansch and many others. I found the first albums around 1985 and '86, and began actively collecting about a year later. A year and a half after that, I came to London for the first time.

Maart was the first member of the band I had the chance to speak with before a show, in Putney. 'I've waited quite a while to see you guys,' I said enthusiastically, which was met with a big smile from Maart.

At one memorable show in Rochester, New York, Fairport were joined by a troupe of Morris dancers who had some acquaintance with Ric. It was good fun and it felt like they had turned the 'Trad English' knob up to eleven.

The Fairports came pretty routinely to the north-eastern US in the 1990s and early 2000s, and there were many fun and memorable moments seeing them perform in New York and New England. The band members were pretty approachable and I have several great memories of conversations with Peggy, Simon and Maart, as well as tour manager Rob.

Unfortunately, after the terror attacks of September 11, 2001, the hassles for the band to travel to the States increased and probably made it more challenging to be a profitable scenario. They came a few times as a trio without Peggy and Gerry and performed sets with more swing jazz in the mix, enjoyable to a degree, but not really what attracted me to Fairport. The death of Rob Braviner may have also been a factor.

LIDINGÖ CITY HALL
17 NOVEMBER 2004, STOCKHOLM, SWEDEN

BOSSE EHNSIÖ

I've been a Fairport Convention fan since 1970 when I heard 'Walk Awhile' for the first time on the radio. Over the years, I've seen them play so many times that I've lost count. Two of the more memorable occasions occurred in the autumn of 2004. On Fairport's website, I read that the band were giving a concert in Lyngby, a suburb of Copenhagen.

Bosse Ehnsiö accidentally gatecrashed a private party

Tickets could be booked through a Danish website. When I went to the Danish site, I also saw that, a few days after the concert in Lyngby, there was a listing for a concert at 'Lidingö City Hall'. No more details were provided.

GONNA SEE ALL MY FRIENDS:
A PEOPLE'S HISTORY OF FAIRPORT CONVENTION

Lidingö is a suburb of Stockholm, and since I live in Uppsala, 70 kilometres from Stockholm, I was curious. I sent an email to the Danish booking company asking for more details. When I didn't get a response, I visited the site and submitted a new request. I did this a few times until one day a name suddenly appeared under the text 'Lidingö City Hall'. I checked the phone book and there was a man with that name who lived in Lidingö so I called him up, introduced myself and asked, 'Do you know anything about a gig with Fairport Convention in Lidingö City Hall?'

The line went quiet for a long time and then he said, 'How on earth have you found out about that?' When I told him that his name was on the Danish site, he explained that it was a mistake and that his name was not supposed to be there. He had engaged Fairport for a private birthday party and Fairport's appearance was meant to be a surprise. I then asked a little timidly if a friend and I could come and listen. After some hesitation, he said yes. 'But you must promise not to tell anyone what to expect. It is, as I said, meant to be a surprise.' I promised we wouldn't say a word to anyone.

When the date of the concert arrived, three of my friends and I took a flight down to Copenhagen and continued by train. We found the concert hall, went to a nearby restaurant to get some food and then returned for the concert.

We were the first to arrive. Up on the stage, some men were busy getting the gear ready for the concert when four men with backpacks walked into the room. One of the men on stage stepped down and came up to us, mumbled something inaudible, and signalled to us to come along. We looked questioningly, both at him and at each other, but followed him as he started to walk towards a door further into the room. He showed us backstage and continued down a flight of stairs. We were still confused but kept on following him. Halfway down the stairs, one of my friends grabbed me by the arm and whispered, 'He thinks we're the band.'

I looked back in disbelief, but when we got down the stairs, it turned out he was right. The man showed us into a dressing room, where food and drink were provided. He pointed to a door and said in broken English, 'There are the showers.'

My friends and I didn't know what to say at first, but in the end one of us pulled himself together and explained to the man that we were not

URBAN GÖRANSSON

In the late Sixties, I saw Fairport Convention on Swedish television performing one or two songs from an outdoor concert in the UK. I have no idea what songs they performed then, but I remember thinking it sounded okay.

In 1972 I found the album *The History of Fairport Convention* in a little Swedish record store. Wasn't it a little early for that title? Anyway, I bought it and listening to that album was the first time that I really came into contact with the band's music. The song selection and the information on the album cover was a really good introduction to both the music and the band. I really liked it.

In 1975 I visited London and spent a lot of time in many of the city's record stores. I wanted to buy some records to take home and had decided that one would be a Fairport Convention record. I chose the brand-new *Rising for the Moon*. After playing it, I realised I would soon have a much larger collection of Fairport Convention albums. I was hooked.

My 50th birthday was coming up in November 2004, and I was asked what kind of birthday party I wanted. 'I'm not going to have a party at all,' I replied. I wasn't interested in having any special celebration. But

Urban Göransson organised the Town Hall show

Photos (this page and opposite): Thomas Svensson

when I was asked if there wasn't something that I would really enjoy doing, I started thinking about an idea that I first thought was impossible to realise, which was to arrange a concert with Fairport Convention for family and friends.

I sent an email to the band asking them if they would do it, and I couldn't believe it when their booking agent replied, 'Yes'. Three months later, I invited relatives, friends, colleagues and neighbours to a concert, but I didn't tell them what kind of concert or who would play. When I entered the stage and greeted everyone, I surprised them by telling them that they soon would be listening to the amazing Fairport Convention. Need I say it was a success?

Thank you, Fairport, for that evening and for the way you made us feel like you wanted to do your very best for us. I'm still very grateful.

THE STABLES
16 FEBRUARY 2005, MILTON KEYNES, UK

DAN WALTON
I was first taken to see Fairport Convention in 2005 when I was ten years old. My mum (to whom I am eternally grateful) was educating me in folk music and I was just beginning to get a grip on what it sounded like. That was until she played me *Over the Next Hill*, which was the then

GONNA SEE ALL MY FRIENDS:
A PEOPLE'S HISTORY OF FAIRPORT CONVENTION

current Fairport album, and I heard electric guitar and drums. On a folk album. I was so excited to go and see them.

So, there I was, at the fabulous Stables in Milton Keynes, having my life changed by this unbelievable band. I loved the songs. Even at a young age I could sense the musicianship. I loved their personalities on stage. It made a lifelong fan out of me and completely changed my musical pallet for the good. They pointed me in the direction of some of my other favourite bands like Steeleye Span, Levellers and Jethro Tull. And where would I be without my musical hero, Richard Thompson?

Dan Walton was introduced to Fairport by his mum

17 years later, and between winter tours, acoustic tours and various sets at *Cropredy*, I have seen the band a total of 58 times. I have had the pleasure of meeting members of the band more times than I can count, and it's always a pleasure. Chris Leslie and his cool and calming nature. Ric Sanders and his endless generosity. Dave Pegg, who sees everyone as his friend whether he's known you his whole life or if he's meeting you for the first time. Simon Nicol, who always seems genuinely touched by the love we show as fans. And Gerry Conway, who is so genuine and so kind.

I cannot imagine my life without Fairport Convention. And so, I thank you, band members past and present, for all the joy and memories you have brought me.

GONNA SEE ALL MY FRIENDS:
A PEOPLE'S HISTORY OF FAIRPORT CONVENTION

MILESTONES MUSIC ROOM
2 JUNE 2005, ROCHESTER, NEW YORK

DORIE JENNINGS

I saw a surprise warmup act for the Fairport Acoustic Trio in June 2005. Chris Leslie's Morris dance group from Adderbury were touring America at the same time as Fairport and turned up at the venue shortly before the start of the show. Chris may have been the only one who knew they were coming. In fact, I'm not even certain that he knew. The audience were seated and waiting for the show to start, and suddenly it was 'Everybody outside', where the Adderbury team (including Chris) performed. Morris dancing is unfamiliar to most Americans. The venue was on a busy street, and the looks on the faces of passers-by were priceless.

Dorie Jennings witnessed a spot of impromptu Morris dancing

FAIRPORT'S CROPREDY CONVENTION
11 – 13 AUGUST 2005, CROPREDY, UK

KAS PITT-SIMKUS

My son Dan and I went to *Cropredy* for the first time in 2005. A few days later, we went to see Richard Digance at our local folk festival. We spotted a man in a fez and wondered if he was a member of the Fairport

GONNA SEE ALL MY FRIENDS:
A PEOPLE'S HISTORY OF FAIRPORT CONVENTION

fan forum, *Talkawhile*, but were scared to go and ask. When we got home, I posted on *Talkawhile* to ask if it was any of them but no one replied. Nine months later, Stan looked at a random post on *Talkawhile* and it happened to be mine. He answered and actually scolded him for taking so long to answer. We got chatting on the forum, eventually decided to meet up and we've been together since. We got married on 11 August 2010 so we could have our honeymoon at *Cropredy*.

Kas Pitt-Simkus with (left to right) son Dan, Talkawhilers Matt and Mara and (right) husband Stan

MARLOWE THEATRE
19 FEBRUARY 2006, CANTERBURY, UK

TIM BENNETT

Simon Nicol proposed to my girlfriend, Judy, at this gig. In fairness, I had asked him to, and he was doing it on my behalf. I've been a Fairport nut since my brother brought *Gladys' Leap* home one day in the '80s after seeing Fairport on tour. Since I never miss a *Wintour* or *Cropredy*, when I was looking for a novel way to propose to my long-Fairport-suffering girlfriend, I thought getting one of the band to do it from the stage would be a fab idea. I hadn't really prepared other than getting tickets to the gig and bringing the ring with me, so at the interval I dashed to the foyer, desperately hoping to bump into one of the chaps.

   Luckily, Chris Leslie was there, and after I explained the situation, he said he'd be happy to make the proposal, but that it was more of a 'Simon-sort-of-thing' to do, and said he'd pass my request on. I returned to my seat in anticipation.

The moment came. Simon asked if Judy would marry me, I whipped out the ring, she exclaimed, 'Oh my God, what have you done?' but then remembered to say yes. Simon then dedicated the next song, 'Western Wind', to us. In the excitement, the news of the positive response did not reach the stage.

Tim proposed to Judy at the Marlowe with a little help from Simon

After the show, we went to the foyer for the usual signing of merch and caught up with Simon. We introduced ourselves as the newly-betrothed couple. At this, Simon got the attention of the still fairly sizeable crowd making their way home, and loudly announced, 'She said yes!' The foyer erupted into a mighty cheer. Mission accomplished.

We are still together, and in 2011 we took our twin girls to their first *Cropredy*, aged one. So, I can only apologise to my wife for the surprising proxy proposal and thank Chris and Simon for their part in making it happen, and to all of Fairport for all the great gigs, but especially that one.

FAIRPORT'S CROPREDY CONVENTION
10 AUGUST 2006, CROPREDY, UK

JOHN BRIGHOUSE

For us, *Fairport's Cropredy Convention* is not just a celebration of Fairport Convention, but also an annual celebration of our Fairport wedding. We married at Whately Hall in Banbury accompanied by some of our favourite Fairport music: 'Portmeirion', 'Some Special Place', 'The Rose Hip', 'White Dress', 'The Golden Glove', 'Like an Old Fashioned Waltz', 'The Bowman's Retreat', and 'Wishfulness Waltz'. Straight after the ceremony, limousines took us in full

GONNA SEE ALL MY FRIENDS:
A PEOPLE'S HISTORY OF FAIRPORT CONVENTION

John and Jane Brighouse had their wedding reception at the festival

wedding attire plus guests to *Cropredy* for the first day of the festival. Wadworth's featured our photograph in their magazine celebrating the festival and Fairport themselves autographed our Order of Service.

I attended my first *Cropredy Convention* with my children Christine, Simon and Peter in 1995 and took Jane for the first time in 2001. Over the years we have been joined by more and more friends: Fiona Urquhart, Diane Vaight, Mike and Lorna Harrison, Phil and Ann Pugh, before we decided that our wedding would be Fairport-themed and celebrated at *Cropredy*.

We have returned every year since, always looking forward to celebrating our wedding anniversary with Fairport and our friends. How we have missed the festival in the two lockdown years.

GONNA SEE ALL MY FRIENDS:
A PEOPLE'S HISTORY OF FAIRPORT CONVENTION

ALBAN ARENA
7 MARCH 2007, ST ALBANS, UK

DAVID CULLEN

I've been involved with the Fairports and Cropredy at various times through my work in event tech and stage management. My most treasured moment has to be when it rained on them – indoors…

I was working with the Alban Arena for one of their tours. We'd had a cracking first half, my stagehand had dropped the fire curtain as the audience left for the bar and I joined the boys briefly in the Green Room for a cuppa. Just before the second half was about to start, I went back into the control room, donned my headset for stage comms – and was surprised to hear rain. Realising it wasn't raining

David Cullen remembers a rain-affected performance

outside, I made my way hastily to the stage. The 'drencher' – the large water reservoir high above the stage designed to soak the fire curtain in the case of the unthinkable – had sprung a leak (something I'd never known in all my years in the industry) and was gently drizzling down onto the stage, right along the line where Ric, Simon, Peggy and Chris should be standing.

Not wanting to create a bit of theatre for the millstream moment in 'Matty Groves', I secured the drencher and went down to tell the boys they had an extended tea break while the crew moved the stage monitors and other electrics forwards a bit to keep them safe, before starting to dry the stage. Unfortunately, the front of house manager hadn't got the message, so we ended up performing a Morecambe and Wise-esque stage show with mops and buckets as the audience returned, accompanied by appropriate backing music.

It only took a few minutes of frenzied activity before we were ready to start again. I went down to invite the boys back up and completed the farce by handing them each an umbrella as they came on for the second act.

WOODFORD HALSE SOCIAL CLUB
7 AUGUST 2007, WOODFORD HALSE, UK

DAVID DE STEFANO

I am one of those USA fans who was 'reeled in' by the 1987 release of *In Real Time*. As a major Jethro Tull aficionado, my first exposure to Fairport was their opening for Tull on the '87 tour. Impressed, I quickly picked up the LP and was immediately drawn to the jigs and rockier songs, appreciation for the ballads came later. Soon enough, I was attending Fairport shows all along the East Coast Philly/NY area. I became aware of Festival Tours and attended *Cropredy Festivals* in '89, '90, '92 and '07 making some great friends and wonderful memories along the way. I have come a long way since the early years, when I was chastised by veteran Fairporters for professing a dislike of Sandy Denny's voice. I have long since been reformed. Unlike many, I have a great love of Fairport's more recent output – songs such as 'The Fossil Hunter', 'Reunion Hill' and 'Man in the Water' joining 'John Gaudie', 'Polly on the Shore' and 'Rising for the Moon' as personal favourites, alongside the classics. A favourite Fairport memory is the 2007 warm up show. In between songs, the band was ready to go, but Swarb was taking his time puttering about. Simon gave a look, then said, 'Well, if the Grim Reaper has to wait, so can we.'

On a trip visiting National Parks in 2016, I ventured into a bar in Jackson Hole, Wyoming. I wound up seated next to a gentleman with a British accent. In conversation, I inquired as to what area he was from, and he replied 'Oxfordshire'. I then asked if he was familiar with the *Cropredy Festival*. Immediately, a strange look came over his face. He then

David De Stefano won the Aunt Sally competition

took out his ID which showed he was a resident of Cropredy. He was stunned to find out that I had been to four festivals, knew about and had seen the Festival Bell and was up to date on the gossip concerning the Red Lion Pub. What were the chances of that kind of encounter?

FAIRPORT'S CROPREDY CONVENTION
9-11 AUGUST 2007, CROPREDY, UK

JOSS MULLINGER

I first met Simon Nicol in 1969 when he visited a friend of mine called Chris (a band drummer) at our school. We were already great fans of Fairport, enjoying both the first Polydor album and *What We Did on Our Holidays*. But, following the tragic death of Martin Lamble, Chris had applied to join the band. Simon brought a white label copy of *Unhalfbricking* for us to listen to whilst he spent time with Chris. Chris subsequently auditioned for the band while they were spending time at the Farley Chamberlayne village rectory. Sadly, he didn't get the job.

Years later, after enjoying Fairport at many gigs, I started attending their *Cropredy Festival* in 1994. I was already a keen amateur photographer and from then on, at every festival I took many photographs of the colourful audience and performers. I often showed the previous year's results to the many *Cropredy* friends I was making who suggested I should publish them in a book.

Joss Mullinger had a book of Cropredy photos published

Joss Mullinger presenting charity cheque to Richard Shaw (Teenage Cancer Trust) with Danny Thompson at Fairport's Cropredy Convention 2007

This culminated, with enthusiasm, a steep learning curve and Simon Nicol's encouragement and contribution of a foreword, in the publication of *Festival Folk – A Celebration of the Unique Style of Fairport Convention's Cropredy Festival* in 2005, in time for the band's *Wintour*. The band were surprised and pleased with the result and went on to sell many copies during their tour.

A launch party was organised by Patrick Neale and Polly Jaffé at the Chipping Norton Bookshop, where the assembled throng was entertained by a wonderful half hour instrumental set performed by Simon Nicol, Ric Sanders and Vo Fletcher.

Excellent reviews were received in the press and the book sold out 1,500 copies via the festival that summer and other outlets. The profits (including £500 contributed by my employer) amounted to some £2,829 which were donated to the Teenage Cancer Trust on stage at *Cropredy* 2007. I still love going to every *Cropredy Festival* with my friends and 28 years on, I haven't missed one yet.

MICK FISHER

I first became aware of folk music and Fairport in particular in my early teens via my brother, Dave, who was a big fan. In later years we used to attend the *Cropredy Festival* together, even though we lived far away from each other. It was a highlight of most years. The first one we both went to was the *Fifth Annual Reunion* in 1984. Both of us were married with young kids by then, but we went to the festival with our respective families.

In 2006, Dave was diagnosed with a brain tumour. By the time 2007 came round, it was obvious that his time was running out. One of his wishes was to attend *Cropredy* one more time, so that August

Mick Fisher's brother Dave was determined to be at Cropredy in 2007

I accompanied him and his family – wife Nadine, sons James and Tom, daughter Hannah and daughter-in-law Kelly. He couldn't stop for the Saturday night due to his deteriorating condition, so Nadine, Hannah and Kelly took him home early. Tom, James and I stayed on and sang along with 'Meet on the Ledge' with great gusto, silently dedicating it to Dave. Sadly, less than two months later, he passed away.

Fast forward to 2022 when I went to the festival with my two sons Matthew and Paul. We saw for the first time a plaque dedicated to Dave on Jonah's Oak

THE SAGE
22 FEBRUARY 2008, GATESHEAD, UK

PETER SMITH

Almost 30 years after I'd last seen Fairport, my friend Will and I decided it was about time we checked them out. I'd been to see Fairport Acoustic at Alnwick Playhouse that Christmas, and I had really enjoyed it so decided that it was time to see the full band again. We arrived in time to watch the support act, Anthony John Clarke, who treated us to a lovely set of acoustic folk. Fairport then took to the stage to a very warm welcome. They played two sets with an interval between. At the time, I was a little out of touch with the band, and not so familiar with much of their material. Despite this, it was great to reconnect with them after so many years and to hear 'Who Knows Where the Time Goes' and 'Meet on the Ledge' again. I bought a signed poster and a programme. It had been a very pleasant evening and a great chance for me to reacquaint myself with a very important band. I decided there and then that I would check them out more often.

AN ALL-STAR FAIRPORT CONVENTION CONCERT, BARBICAN THEATRE
22 JULY 2009, LONDON, UK

JOE BOYD

Since I stepped back from the band, I have just watched from a friendly distance. I've been to *Cropredy* regularly. In 2009 I held a reunion event at the Barbican. The Friday night was the Fairport reunion. Of course, it was sad not having Sandy, but it was just so great to hear them again.

Especially in the rehearsal room, spending a day at close range listening to them play.

Either that summer, or the following year, I went to *Cropredy* and heard the first three albums as a Saturday night closer set. They had a really great PA system, and I sat out there in the audience and heard them do 'Time Will Show the Wiser', 'Sloth' and one tune after another. And you feel this was some pretty great music.

FAIRPORT'S CROPREDY CONVENTION
13 - 15 AUGUST 2009, CROPREDY, UK

KEN JACKSON

I got into Fairport convention about 20 years ago when I married a big fan of the band. We went to a few Fairport Convention concerts and my wife said how much she had previously enjoyed going to the *Cropredy* festival with her brother. To be fair to my wife, she didn't put pressure on me to go to *Cropredy*, knowing that I'd never slept under canvas and that I'm not overly fond of big crowds. However, after one concert, in which Simon and Peggy enthused about *Cropredy*, I whispered into my wife's ear that I would give it a go, just for once, thinking I'd hate it but not wanting to deny her the chance to go again.

Ken Jackson (left) with his waistcoat made from dyed underpants

The rest, as they say, is history. We first went in 2009 and have been to pretty much all of the *Fairport Cropredy Conventions* since then. We enjoyed it so much that two friends now go with us, and we have the best of times, creating memories that will last a lifetime. It's become a tradition that I wear a Christmas gift from my rather eccentric brother-in-law, a waistcoat made from my father-in-law's dyed underpants. I can't say that I am overly fond of camping but we're not in the tent much as there is too much to see and do around Cropredy and, of course, on the hallowed field listening to the best live music ever.

MICHAEL THORNTON

In February 2009 I turned 40. I was asked by my wife Linnet, 'How would you like to celebrate your fortieth year?' After thinking I said, 'A trip to Cropredy would be nice.' Tickets were bought and then the six month wait for August began. The day before, the car was packed with tent, clothes, sleeping bags, camping stove, food, camping chairs and raincoats and we made the long drive from Halifax, West Yorkshire to Banbury for an overnight stay at the Travelodge at Cherwell Valley Services on the M40.

On Thursday morning it was time for the 'wacky races' to get to the campsites. Once there, and once our tent was erected, it was time to explore the village and stalls. We got our wristbands on and then it was time to set up on the field. Everything was going well, with the music and food excellent, until the Buzzcocks came on. My wife was at one end of the row, with our three children in the middle and then me at the other end. The message came down the line, 'Mum's crying.' So that was it. 'We'll pack up, get back to the tent and go home in the morning.'

But she wasn't crying because she was not enjoying the festival. Once she had calmed down and could get the words out, she said, 'Why haven't you made us do this before?'

Michael Thornton's wish for a trip to Cropredy reduced his wife to tears

GONNA SEE ALL MY FRIENDS:
A PEOPLE'S HISTORY OF FAIRPORT CONVENTION

ANDREW DAVIES

I saw Fairport at Aberystwyth Kings Hall in 1968 with Ian, Sandy and Richard. I was mesmerised but didn't get to Cropredy until 2009 and then the two years following that. I camped solo with my motorbike, a Honda ST1100 and then a Kawasaki 1400 GTR. My Igloo tent is now sold sadly. My wife (who I met in Aber) will now only glamp.

DES COLLINS

In 2009 I was able to get tickets for *Cropredy* when visiting England. Fairport announced that they wanted attendees to play along with a new song, 'Ukulele Central'. So off I went to Shaftsbury Avenue to get one. I could now boast that I had played with Fairport at *Cropredy*. Other Fairport songs sound good on the uke too…

Des Collins bought himself a ukulele

ALLAN PICKETT

In 2009 I decided to go to a music festival for the first time since the early '70s. I'd always wanted to see Jethro Tull, who were headlining. I was all geared up for it when it was controversially cancelled at the last moment. I was telling my friend, Brian Green, about it and he suggested *Cropredy* as an alternative. I'd not heard of it, but I

Allan Pickett had a gap of 38 years between Fairport shows

enjoyed Fairport at Crystal Palace Bowl in 1971, so decided to give

GONNA SEE ALL MY FRIENDS:
A PEOPLE'S HISTORY OF FAIRPORT CONVENTION

it a try. I had to buy tickets at the gate, so I got there early and sailed straight through. I was on my own, but the weather was kind and I was able to explore the whole area. I never met anyone I knew until Saturday night, when I bumped into Tim Paine, a fellow guitarist, at the bar. He'd been supporting Richard Digance earlier that day. He introduced me, and I had my photo taken with him, just before Cat Stevens came on. It was a great end to the festival, and I really enjoyed the whole experience. I told my friend all about it, and he hinted that he should really go again, as he'd not been since the '80s. I said I'd definitely go again the following year, and that he could come with me. He jumped at the chance, and we've been every year since. My wife Paula bought me a 'Lord of the Strings' t-shirt which I've worn at every festival, and it's been signed by all the members of FC, although it's now fading a bit.

GONNA SEE ALL MY FRIENDS:
A PEOPLE'S HISTORY OF FAIRPORT CONVENTION

BREW HOUSE
1 OCTOBER 2009, GOTHENBURG, SWEDEN

NIKLAS NILSSON

I saw at the Fairport Convention in Gothernburg in 2009 and took these photos.

Niklas Nilsson had his camera with him in Gothenburg

Photos: Niklas Nilsson

GONNA SEE ALL MY FRIENDS:
A PEOPLE'S HISTORY OF FAIRPORT CONVENTION

FAIRPORT'S CROPREDY CONVENTION
12 – 14 AUGUST 2010, CROPREDY, UK

STEVE GAYTON

My introduction to Fairport Convention came through my school drama teacher who insisted that I should listen to them. This was in the middle of the punk era, so I wasn't sure about them at all. But I bought a copy of *Nine*, and thought it was alright in a 'meh' teenager way. I listened to them often over the next few decades, but in the early 2000s I became a single dad of my two children, aged eleven and 15, and had no idea what to do. I remembered that the *Cropredy* festival was a thing and that it wasn't too far away, so I got us tickets for 2010.

Steve Gayton's first Cropredy was 2010

We were woefully under-equipped; it rained almost constantly and at one point the thunder and lightning was so bad proceedings had to halt to wait for it to subside. We had the best of times. My son and daughter loved it. We discovered the awesome nature of the folk who went to the festival. A lady near us saw what a hash I was making of trying to plait my daughter's hair and took over. When the rain came in, we were adopted by a large family group who wrapped us all in their tarpaulin and shared cakes with us.

We have been going back to the festival every year and now my grandchildren come too. Fairport Convention have become a big part of our lives. My son's partner cleans the house to 'Matty Groves', and my daughter often asks how 'the lads' are. The members of Fairport Convention have become friendly, slightly eccentric uncles. We don't see them often but when we do they fill us with great joy and happiness.

Standing arm-in-arm with family, friends and complete strangers singing 'Meet on the Ledge' is a moment when all seems possible because, if you really mean it, it really does all come round again.

GONNA SEE ALL MY FRIENDS: A PEOPLE'S HISTORY OF FAIRPORT CONVENTION

BUDDY WOODWARD, FOUNDER/LEADER, THE DIXIE BEE-LINERS

We – The Dixie Bee-Liners, a 'progressive bluegrass' band from America – were seconds away from kicking off our opening number at *Cropredy* 2010, in front of 25,000 impatient people on the Friday evening. I'm a huge Fairport fan from way back and had been fantasising about playing *Cropredy* for decades. So, no pressure. Immediately before, downbeat Simon Nicol walked over and hugged me. I forget what he said, unfortunately, but it was likely a British version of that familiar old Show Biz trope, 'Knock 'em dead, baby,' and suddenly all the anxiety dropped away, and we did indeed knock 'em dead. We are forever grateful for the kindness and hospitality shown us by Fairport and their staff, and I'll always cherish that moment of solidarity Simon gifted me with.

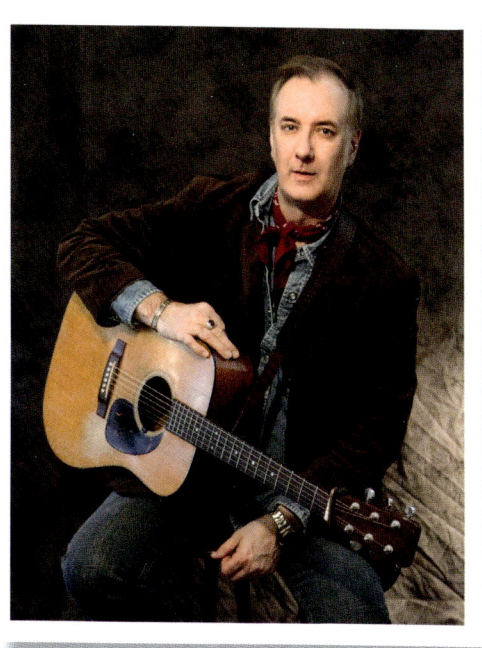

Buddy Woodward got a pre-gig hug from Simon

Photo: Deone Jahnke

HELMUT ÖLSCHLEGEL

The first time I came to *Cropredy* was 2010, when I was accompanying the great Excalibur show, together with the crew of the promoter Robert Wagner from Bavaria.

It was a great adventure to see all the guest stars

Helmut Ölschlegel has photographed three Cropredy Festivals

on stage with Fairport Convention, especially Johnny Logan, John Helliwell (Supertramp), Martin Barre (Jethro Tull), Alan Simon and others. Later, I came to the *Cropredy Festival* again in 2014 and 2017, and I became a friend of the band, especially of Simon and Peggy.

HELEN GAMMAGE

I went to *Cropredy Festival* every single year from the age of two (in 1986) until I was 26 and loved every single one of them. The most memorable festival, other than being a kid and playing on the inflatables and the big dice, was my last – when I nearly died. I was stung by a wasp on arrival and went into anaphylactic shock. I was ambulanced to hospital, but made it back in time for the evening to see Fairport play.

PICTUREDROME
8 MAY 2011, HOLMFIRTH, UK

ELIZABETH ASKEW

My dad, Martin Robinson, became an avid fan in the 1960s after borrowing *Liege & Lief* from a record library found at the end of the Redfearn Bar in Leicester as he earnt money collecting glasses. I wasn't a fan as such – I just listened, nodded along and then went back to my own tapes and CDs. Mum (Ruth) and dad would head off to the occasional gig and Dad would return full of tales from the setlist.

Elizabeth Askew has seen Fairport all over the north of England with her dad

Cut to 2010. I was really struggling to buy Dad a gift. He has what he needs and I had two children under two years old so I needed help. Mum

Elizabeth Askew has seen Fairport all over the north of England, including at the Devil's Arse in Castleton

suggested I buy a ticket to 'a gig'. I found that Fairport had a gig booked at Holmfirth Picturedrome so I booked two tickets. My thinking was, 'He'll love it, I'll cope and I imagine it will be an interesting venue.' Little did I know…

We arrived at the gig and while Dad found us somewhere to sit, I went to the bar. The *Festival Bell* album was being launched that year and what really captured me was the storytelling combined with the flawless musicality and precision of the band. I had never experienced anything like it. I was hooked from the start to the encore and so began the Fairport journey for me and Dad. Our memories began to be made. The journey home was filled with his tales of gigs gone by, of festivals and treasured albums and memories he connected to them. A new bond between father and daughter was established.

We decided to see Fairport in as many different venues in the north as we could and particularly wanted to support 'old' theatres or independent venues – it's how we both were able as teens, decades apart, to see live music and fall in love with it. We have been all over, from Lytham to Leek, from Southport to Salford and from Bury and Burnley too – not forgetting the very unique experience of the Devil's Arse cave! We have just booked Oswaldtwistle and plan to add Leeds to the list. We have attended over 20 gigs in the past eleven years and have made some wonderful memories together.

We've invited others in along the way; my mum, my sister, my husband

and my brother-in-law. A stand out memory is when my dad and I took my two children, Sam and Ruth, to their first ever gig – Fairport at the Royal Northern College of Music in Manchester in February 2020. It was a highlight for us to have three generations on the front row together, and it was made extra special when Chris Leslie kindly dedicated 'Moon Dust and Solitude' to the children.

'The bus goes on…' and we are sure to ride it, hopefully for many more journeys to come.

BIRNAM ARTS CENTRE
11 MAY 2011, DUNKELD, UK

FRASER NIMMO

I opened for Fairport for the 50th time and we all played my tune, 'Retreat from Santa Ponsa', as the handover song. They blew the overfull house apart, despite having travelled a very long way to make the gig and with all the attendant road weariness that goes with that territory. It was a great success for all concerned.

About a month later, I was in my local about six miles from the venue. I was approached by 'Sandy', a local builder and enthusiastic, mature Fairport fan who went on at some length about how much he had enjoyed the night. I was nodding along in beery agreement. There was a pause in the conversation. This became increasingly inflated as the seconds ticked by. Eventually he spoke up, 'They fairly made us wait for it, though.' 'Sorry, Sandy,' I said, 'I don't know what you mean.' 'That wan… 'Meet on the Ledge' – that's ma favourite wan o' theirs. I couldnae believe how long I had to wait tae hear it.' I bit my glass.

That song, at the end of every Fairport gig, and particularly Cropredy, is as sociologically relevant and spiritually uplifting as 'Bread of Heaven' at Cardiff Arms Park or 'Abide with Me' at Wembley. Inventing a musical genre (as they did) does not necessarily engender a feeling of timeless optimism. Writing and adopting as a farewell anthem a song which has become a contemporary psalm of eternal togetherness elevates the Fairport family to cloudland. Long may they float there.

GONNA SEE ALL MY FRIENDS:
A PEOPLE'S HISTORY OF FAIRPORT CONVENTION

PACIFIC ROAD ARTS CENTRE
18 MAY 2011, BIRKENHEAD, UK

TOM PLUMPTON

Tired after a day's work in the Eighties, I had fallen asleep while watching TV to be awoken in the early hours by the rather pleasant sound of song I did not recognise, being performed by a band that I also did not recognise. The song was 'Red and Gold', and by the time it ended, I was wide awake and eager to discover the name of the band. When the televised concert ended, I found that the band was Fairport (I had heard of them). The concert, which included Maartin in the line-up, was, I believe, filmed at Birmingham. I went out the following weekend, and after a short search through the local record stores, I returned home the proud possessor of the *Red and Gold* album on cassette.

Tom Plumpton and wife Dee feel part of the Fairport family

It was sometime later that I eventually got to see Fairport live, at a small venue called Alexander's Wine Bar in Chester. There was only room there for 100, so my wife Dee and I were very fortunate to get tickets. Maart had recently left the band to be replaced by Chris. We met Simon, Dave, Ric and Chris (no Gerry, as it was the acoustic set up) and had very friendly conversations with each of them (even though Ric had just lost one of his parents). This friendliness surprised us, as our only reasonably lengthy conversations with music stars had previously been with David Essex (who always had time for people), Peter Noone and Jan Akkerman (of Focus). But the lads from Fairport were in an entirely different league when it came to the way they treated fans – like family!

It was another few years before we got to see Fairport again, this time at Pacific Road, in our home town of Birkenhead. Even though so much time had passed, the lads recognised my wife and I straight away – even to the extent that they remembered our names. One of my workmates (who was, in all honesty, not a great fan of the genre) went with us to this concert, and by the end he had been won over by the warmth of the band's connection to the fans. The fact that the lads mixed with the fans both during the interval and at the end left my friend surprised, to say the least.

I don't believe there has ever been a band that, even with changes in personnel over a long period, has maintained a type of extended family relationship with its fanbase. Fairport Convention is a truly great band, producing truly great music consistently over its lifetime, while remaining firmly grounded, respecting fans of all ages, shapes and sizes, and going out of their way to make each and every one of those fans feel part of the Fairport family.

FAIRPORT'S CROPREDY CONVENTION
11 – 13 AUGUST 2011, CROPREDY, UK

JANE L BUTCHER
Cropredy really does cater for everyone. One of my highlights was The Blockheads in 2011. I danced through the whole set and made an idiot of myself, but I don't care.

24 DECEMBER 2011, ADDERBURY, UK

STEVE CARSON
Back in 2011 my wife died. She was a close friend of all of them. After my wife died, my two daughters and I decided that we couldn't spend Christmas at our house. We had to do something other than sit here and be sad. Simon and Sylvia Nicol invited us over, and so did Chris Leslie and his wife. They said, 'Why don't you spend Christmas over with us?' We took them up on it and it was one of the most special Christmas Eves I've ever had. We did an old-fashioned walk around Adderbury with Chris. It was such a wonderful experience. We went all around the village and ended up at the pub. Rosie (my daughter who became a fiddler and toured with Fairport and played at *Cropredy*) had her fiddle and Chris had his mandolin, and there were a few other musicians there. It was such a wonderful thing for them to include us.

The next day was Christmas, and we spent that with Simon and Sylvia.

Simon made Christmas dinner, just another wonderful day. I ended up living in Chipping Norton for about 13 months, just a five-minute walk from Simon. And they helped me get the apartment.

I almost died of throat cancer in 1999. I was pretty out of it for almost a year. And as I was just beginning to get back, and think I might live a little bit longer, it was my birthday, and the phone was ringing. Simon was singing happy birthday to me. Actually, so did everyone in Fairport Convention. They were rehearsing, and said, 'Let's call Steve.' They did this separately; they didn't sing as a group. Each guy in the band took a turn, and it warmed my heart beyond belief. Simon sang, then Chris sang, then Peggy and then Ric. I still remember saying to Simon at the end, 'Now I know why you don't let Ric sing.' I've been with them in bad moments, and with them when they've been angry, and when they're in wonderful form.

I'd like to give a huge thank you to Fairport and all their family members. They have always been super. Not only have I made great friends with them, but something that becomes very apparent is all the friends people make through Fairport and *Cropredy*. I have dear friends through them. Because of people like Simon Nicol, Swarbrick and Peggy. They're amazing. I also want to emphasise that I've never met anyone better than Chris Leslie. He's the best human being I've ever known. He's just a grand human being.

PLAYHOUSE THEATRE
21 JANUARY 2012, OXFORD, UK

KIERAN GOSS

I'd started building a bit of a fanbase in the UK from 20-odd years ago, but I'd let it slip. My wife Annie and I live in Sligo, on the west coast of Ireland. Over the previous ten years we had really focused on Germany and Switzerland and had gone to live in Nashville for a while. I'd been a long time out of the UK, and if you're long enough out of any market you have to start again. I came up with this mad idea of contacting Peggy and saying that I was thinking of going back to the UK, and it might be a good idea to go out and do a support tour for them.

GONNA SEE ALL MY FRIENDS:
A PEOPLE'S HISTORY OF FAIRPORT CONVENTION

Thankfully it worked out.

They were doing their winter tour, and in 2012 that meant 39 shows through most of February and into March. It was a ball-breaking amount of work for a band to be doing, and I remember thinking, 'God, these guys are still working hard, where the rubber meets the road. They're doing the miles and putting in the gigs.'

I'd been a fan way back in the day, but as well as admiring them musically, what I loved about them is that they were such decent human beings on so many levels.

Annie was travelling with me at the time and our experience as the support act, particularly in the States, is that it's often 'them and us'. But on the very first gig on that tour in Oxford, there was a dressing room for us when we arrived. We were pleasantly surprised that such thought had been given to that. But we were also struck by how each of the band individually came and knocked on the door before the show and said, 'We're delighted to have you on the tour. Feel free to come to any one of the band or to go to the tour manager if there's anything we can do to make the whole thing more pleasant and easy for you.' And I remember thinking, 'Wow, that's a breath of fresh air in this business.' That lack of ego. That decency. That warmth and inclusiveness.

That was the consistent theme right throughout the tour, to the extent that every night Ric introduced me to the audience. They had a set up at that stage where they would join me for my last song. Then I would leave the stage and they would continue. It was a lovely kind of endorsement; you get to play a song with the band and then you leave, and they carry on with their show.

Annie remembers that the band, and particularly Simon and Peggy, had been up and down the motorways of the UK so often that it didn't matter where you were going, they had this encyclopaedic knowledge of the good places to eat. It's amazing how those things become important when you're doing 39 shows in seven weeks. We'd invariably get a call from Peggy saying, 'Where are you?' We'd tell him and he'd say, 'Well, you're not far. We're stopping here for lunch. If it suits you and you're not already past, come in and have lunch.'

You can't take that sort of inclusiveness for granted. It really speaks volumes about them as people, but it also explains why they've lasted so long. They have that lovely human quality of including everyone, whether it's the support act or the roadie or the lowest level of whatever you are in the venue. That goes a long way in life and a long way in the music business. The successes they've had don't happen by accident. It's a just reward for the way they comport themselves in life, and that's before you even get into the music and how groundbreaking it was.

I'm not really a traditional folkie, but I'm Irish and I'm on the edges of that acoustic world. I'm a songwriter. I'm probably as much influenced by The Beatles as I am by Fairport Convention. Growing up, Irish folk music was for your parents. When you got your first electric guitar, you considered folk music to be for family parties where an old uncle would sing some old song while your dad would play the accordion.

But I've been a big fan of an Irish band called Planxty, and what Planxty did in Ireland is reclaim traditional Irish music for the youth. They had long hair and ripped jeans and were a bit mad and a bit wild. That allowed a whole new generation of young people to reclaim traditional Irish music. It seems to me that Fairport did the same in the UK. They made traditional music cool, and that's quite a trick to pull off.

Because I live in Ireland and I'm Irish, I'm not sure Fairport get the credit culturally for what they've done, because everyone benefits from a band kicking open the doors for everyone else to walk through later. I don't think it was ever a marketing strategy. They were what they were, and they were passionate about the music. That combination opened up a whole new world.

People talk about building a 'community' now, not an audience. It was really obvious to me from about the first or second gig on that tour that that's what they had. To go out and play 39 shows and have them sell out many, many years after having your first hit is quite a staggering achievement. I was immediately struck by the loyalty of their audience and how some of the audience had an encyclopaedic knowledge of the band. They'd be having conversations about whether Simon had sung the third verse before the second verse that night. On one level you might consider it quite nerdy, but if you're in a band and audiences are that engaged, that really is quite a remarkable thing. There aren't many bands that can say they have that.

THE SAGE
26 FEBRUARY 2012, GATESHEAD, UK

PETER SMITH

Four years after last seeing Fairport at the Sage in Gateshead, Marie and I spent a very pleasant evening back there again. This time the band had chosen to visit the smaller Hall 2, which had been sold out for some weeks. We bought a programme on the way in, which Dave Pegg and Ric Sanders, who were sitting at the merchandise table, kindly signed. Support came from Irish singer songwriter Kieran Goss, who delivered a short but enjoyable set, before being joined by Fairport for a nice version of 'Reach Out (I'll Be There)', the old Motown classic. This was Fairport's 45th anniversary tour, and for the occasion they had invited fans to nominate songs, via email, that they would like to hear from their massive back catalogue. This resulted in a set list with old favourites and a few surprises. For me, the highlight of the night was a beautiful rendition of Sandy Denny's 'Fotheringay' from the 1969 LP, *What We Did on Our Holidays*. The sound was crisp and clear; the Sage has wonderful acoustics. A superb set from a seminal band.

FAIRPORT'S CROPREDY CONVENTION
9 – 11 AUGUST 2012, CROPREDY, UK

MICHAEL MOYSE

I did a support slot with Linda Watkins for Dave Pegg and PJ Wright (PJ also played on an album Linda and I recorded) at Banbury Folk Club. Peggy signed the poster, 'To Mike – a proper bassist.' He said he did this because, along with my electric bass, I played upright bass with and without a bow, something which he doesn't do. A really nice guy.

In 2017, my friend Colin Henney decided he wanted to make an album of piano tunes, improvised around people's instinctive playing on a piano in Woodworm Studios. The project was to be recorded in one day. I took my daughter to the studio and she played a few random bits and we left. Later, I found out that only one other guest had submitted a piece remotely and that was Maartin Allcock. The album was released in

2019, and so was one of the last that Maart played on.

Maart and I had several email conversations as fellow bass players, and he sent me a few signed books of his Fairport transcriptions. We were due to meet in the real world but sadly I couldn't get to *Cropredy*, and he passed away before we could meet at his home. I've also played support for Chris and Ric when they've done solo gigs. Always nice friendly and supportive guys.

My favourite Fairport song, apart from 'Meet on the Ledge' (which always brings a tear to my eye, having heard that at a concert with close friends right after I nearly died from gall bladder surgery) has got to be 'My Love is in America', which I first heard at *Cropredy* in 2012. A beautiful song with a great story. It's one of those songs which has its own video that plays in my head as I listen.

THE DUCHESS
3 NOVEMBER 2012, YORK, UK

UIRASSU & GEORGIA

I am Brazilian and living in Brazil, so not an expat in the UK, which would make my Fairport Convention addiction easier. I came across Fairport's music in the '80s, along with that of Steeleye Span, the Strawbs, The Albion Band and other British folk bands. I used to exchange tapes and CDs with friends in Europe and would ask them to send me stuff related to folk and rock in return. After that, I myself began purchasing Fairport CDs and vinyl from abroad and adding them to my collection.

Uirassu & Georgia flew from Brazil to see the boys

From the very first time I listened to tunes like 'Matty Groves', 'Who Knows Where the Time Goes?', 'Crazy Man Michael', and 'Doctor of Physick', and heard Sandy's voice, Swarb and Ric's violins, Dave Mattacks's unique playing and Peggy and Simon with their special chemistry, I knew there was something very special about Fairport. And from these classic songs I went on digging further and in no time was completely immersed into the Fairport world. With the arrival of Chris and Gerry, each with their own style, musical perspective and personality, I was sky high that so many nuances could be reached by one band.

By the 2000s my wife Georgia, then still my girlfriend, joined me in this Fairport craziness. In 2012 we took the plunge and flew from Brazil to the UK to see them live, as they were playing in York. We took a flight from São Paulo to Manchester, via Lisbon, throughout the night across the Atlantic Ocean, a distance of over 5,000 miles. It was a dream come true.

In Manchester, the immigration officer asked us what we planned to do while we were in Britain and we told him we were going to attend this very special event, a Fairport Convention concert. He politely asked us, 'Are they new or old?' What a tricky question. I replied, 'They never get old!' He giggled at us and stamped our passports. We rushed to the airport exit to take the bus (the train service had been interrupted that particular day) to York, with practically no sleep and jet lagged, and in the early evening that day we arrived at The Duchess, where the concert would take place.

There was Peggy by the merchandise table. We introduced ourselves to him, got our hands on their latest CD at the time, *By Popular Request*, and had it signed by Peggy and Simon, Chris and Ric, who we also chatted with. Peggy told us about his gigs playing bass with Jethro Tull in Brazil. We had started off on the right foot.

As the show progressed, the music stopped and Peggy announced that there was a couple from São Paulo, Brazil in the audience that night. Everyone stared at us, we looked over our shoulders, and then there was a big cheer. What an unforgettable moment.

The band resumed playing some of their anthems, like 'Fotheringay', 'Matty Groves' and 'Meet on the Ledge' (the latter being Georgia's favourite), and it was total bliss. After the gig we spoke to Chris, and he was really nice. It was indeed a memorable night with Fairport Convention.

Unfortunately, not too long after we returned to Brazil, I discovered a serious and life-threatening health problem which needed to be dealt with immediately, and in my early forties I was facing a really hard situation. It was a few years before things were back to normal, but listening to Fairport Convention and all the memories of that wonderful day helped me a lot and provided me with comfort and solid support as I went through all that pain and distress.

We look forward to the day that we'll meet Fairport again, and for sure it will be as wonderful as ever! Oh, and of course we'll bring our *By Popular Request* CD with us to collect that signature that we're missing from Ric.

THE ROSES THEATRE
31 JANUARY 2013, TEWKESBURY, UK

CHRIS NEWTON

I'll never forget the moment Simon Nicol did something that changed my approach to music. I had just bought a CD, at the Roses Theatre start-of-tour gig, seven or eight years ago, and I was trying to get the cellophane wrapper off so he could sign it. He just took it from me, ran his fingernail down the groove over the hinge, and the cellophane was off. Now that's talent.

Another memory is of a gig at Deer Park School in Cirencester when I found Simon with a beer outside the front of the building just a few minutes before the show was due to start. The fellow folkie I was with insisted on chatting to him, although I was afraid that we would make him (and ourselves) late. Simon appeared to have all the time in the world and we chatted for about five minutes before he sauntered in to start the show. (There was no support.)

At that same gig Simon brought the house down by changing a line in 'Matty Groves': 'How do you like my feather bed and how do you like my sheets. And how do you like my curtains (gestures to stage curtains) that I got in IKEA last week.' I've never heard him do it again.

In Birmingham in about 1971, where I was working as a trainee newspaper reporter, I was involved in running a folk club (Coleshill Folk) and one night a couple of us went down to the Jug O' Punch in Digbeth for their weekly folk event. We were standing next to two blokes with pints who were enjoying the music, and my friend whispered, 'Do you know who that is? It's Dave Swarbrick and Dave Pegg from Fairport Convention'. We got chatting to them about nothing in particular. I was doing a spot and went on and did a couple of songs. I was a very poor singer and a useless guitarist, but that didn't stop Peggy congratulating me when I came off. I reminded him of this after a gig at Gloucester Cathedral a couple of years ago, and he was delighted at the story and my memories of his very long hair.

FAIRPORT'S CROPREDY CONVENTION
8 – 10 AUGUST 2013, CROPREDY, UK

ELSIE SELF

I discovered Fairport when I was a bump. My favourite album is *50:50@50* and my favourite songs include 'My Love is in America', 'Travelling by Steam', 'Meet on the Ledge' and 'Love at First Sight'. My favourite *Cropredy* memories are when I got an ice cream with nine or ten flakes in it and when got a half a pizza for free in 2018. My favourite bands I have seen at the festival are Alice Cooper, Madness and The Bar-Steward Sons of Val Doonican.

ULLA HILGER

Alice Cooper had played on the Thursday night, and what a great show. He was electrocuted and beheaded, and the snake was on stage as well.

The next morning, we had met at Peggy's caravan for a glass of something sparkling when he showed me his leg, telling me that he had two ticks on it and asking me to remove them. He laid his leg on my lap and I took a look at the ticks. One was easy to spot, and I pulled it out. The other one looked suspicious, not like a common tick and deeper in the vein, so I told him that I didn't dare touch it and that he should show it to the paramedics on the top field.

In the evening we met again at the caravan, a little over-refreshed after a great day of excellent music and beer. Peggy laid his leg on my lap again and said, 'Take another look and get it out.' I checked the tick, and it looked like it was full of blood, so I took it out.

GONNA SEE ALL MY FRIENDS:
A PEOPLE'S HISTORY OF FAIRPORT CONVENTION

A fountain of blood sprayed out and I was covered in blood, and everybody was screaming. Ellen got a roll of kitchen towel and I tried to stop the bleeding with my hands. I pressed hard on the wound, but every time I let go, the fountain started again. Somebody showed up with a bottle of whisky for disinfectant, but Peggy promptly asked for a glass so he could drink it!

For more than 20 minutes, I pressed my hand on the wound trying to stop the bleeding, while Peggy complained that Steve Winwood was waiting for him at the bar. Finally, we decided to call the paramedics. Two nice guys showed up and Peggy greeted them with, 'Alice Cooper is a wimp, we do it all with real blood!' They tried to stop the bleeding for another 20 minutes but failed. So, they called an ambulance and Peggy was driven in an ambulance, with blue lights flashing and sirens wailing, through the crowd to the hospital in Banbury. And there it took the doctors more than three hours to stop the bleeding.

I went to the toilet to clean up and two ladies I met in there screamed, 'Do you need help?' I took a look in mirror and realised I was covered in blood. I said to the lovely ladies, 'Oh no, don't worry. This is not my blood. It's Peggy's.' Back in the field people kept their distance from me.

The next morning Ellen told me that the second 'tick' I pulled out of Peggy's leg was in fact a varicose vein!

Ulla Hilger nearly killed Peggy

GONNA SEE ALL MY FRIENDS:
A PEOPLE'S HISTORY OF FAIRPORT CONVENTION

ROSES THEATRE
31 JANUARY 2014, TEWKESBURY, UK

EDWINA HAYES

I supported Fairport on their 2014 *Wintour* and was the 26th artist to do so, not counting Bob Fox, who'd done it twice. Peggy called me before Christmas to let me know this, and said I'd be playing six songs to open the show for the 31 nights of the tour. He said that they would come out and join me onstage for the last one, and asked me to choose a song for us to do together. He suggested choosing a song from one of my albums as there'd be no payment, but I could sell my CDs. He also said I'd be joining the band for their 'Meet on the Ledge' encore every night, and that I'd be singing the Sandy verse. As if that wasn't all exciting enough, he added that the *Wintour* support always gets to play a set at *Cropredy*, so I'd be doing that too.

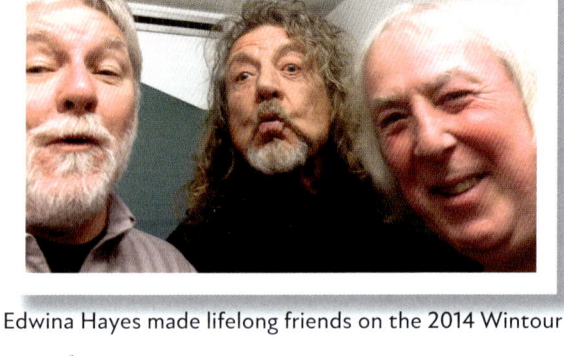

Edwina Hayes made lifelong friends on the 2014 Wintour

Photo: Kevin Smith

And so, at the end of January the tour began in Tewkesbury. And what an incredible five weeks it was, I loved every minute. The band and crew were so welcoming and lovely and I followed the band tour bus, driven by tour manager Mick Peters, and the big blue van, driven by crew manager Andy Salmon and soundman Owain Richards, around all the shows in my little car. I had an absolute blast.

My initial thoughts about the band were how hard they worked to put on a great tour. They had rehearsed a new set list for 2014, which I discovered they did every year, and even though, at their level, they could have got away with playing a selection of 'greatest hits', the opposite was the case as they performed a mix of songs old and new, all rehearsed and arranged prior to the tour. I also loved how they came out to meet and chat with the audience every night after the show, signing autographs and posing for photos until everyone had gone. They were, quite simply, brilliant; hard working and at the same time always funny and easy going.

Just before the tour, Peggy had sadly cut the tendon in his hand on a glass while unloading a dishwasher, so his son Matt stepped in at the last minute and was a lovely addition to the band; relaxed, smiley, and easy going like his dad. Peggy meanwhile manned the merch desk with Ellen, wandering on and offstage during the show to sing a little bit here and there, with a glass of red wine in his good hand. Every night I'd meet him backstage before going on for the encore which was always a riot, as by then he was usually quite tiddly and always very, very funny.

I was asked to write a blog of the tour, as John Watterson had written one the year before when he was the support, so on my day off each week, I set to and wrote a memoir of the tour, which is up online for posterity and remains the first and only blog I've ever done.

Since the tour we've all kept in touch, crossing paths on the road at various gigs and festivals. I started the tour not knowing them at all, and ended with up a group of lifelong friends and having had the experience of a lifetime. I also sold 903 CDs – which Peggy declared a *Wintour* support record.

CONNAUGHT THEATRE
26 FEBRUARY 2014, WORTHING, UK

SALLY ROSE

If you had asked me who Fairport were 25 years ago, I wouldn't have had a clue. But then my late husband walked into my life. His car was littered with Fairport CDs that I heard incessantly. When we moved to Worthing in 2010, he was so excited to see they were in concert.

But due to certain circumstances and my own ill health, we didn't book to see them until 2014.

By this time Tony had an operation to remove a grade 4 brain tumour, but he was insistent he wanted to go. He met Dave Pegg in the interval who autographed his ticket, and he so enjoyed the concert.

Sally Rose with her late husband Tony

And to my surprise so did I. Waking up in the morning all I could here was him singing 'Meet on the Ledge' and 'Farewell, Farewell,' accompanied, of course, by Fairport.

Tony sadly passed away in 2015, but in memory of him my friend Polly and I go to the Fairport concert in Worthing, usually every February. Each year I am pleased that Tony showed me this great music.

I must admit the memories when I hear 'Farewell, Farewell' and 'Meet on the Ledge' are bittersweet. However, they also give me such wonderful memories of my lovely husband of ten years, taken away from me too soon.

FAIRPORT'S CROPREDY CONVENTION
7 - 9 AUGUST 2014, CROPREDY, UK

REG MEUROSS

After I'd played to several thousand folks at *Cropredy Festival* in 2014, Simon Nicol set up the PA and did the sound for me at a tiny pub in Kent, with a capacity 50-ish.

The house of show folk has many mansions.

GONNA SEE ALL MY FRIENDS:
A PEOPLE'S HISTORY OF FAIRPORT CONVENTION

MARK TAYLOR

In 2014 I was asked by a friend of Peggy to make Lego minifigure versions of the members of Fairport. I did this and we sent photographs of the figures to Peggy. When I bought the festival programme that year, I was absolutely made up to see that the photographs had been included in the pages.

Since then, I have added to the collection by making the characters

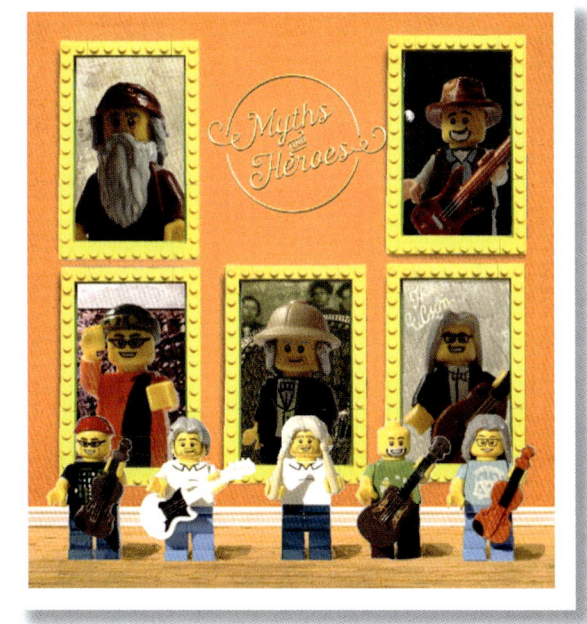

Mark Taylor created a Lego version of Fairport

from the *Myths and Heroes* album cover and each year I make some of the past members of the band too. I even had a little Lego festival in the back garden during the 2020 lockdown.

All of the figures happily reside on my *Cropredy Festival* hat – I think there's still room to squeeze a few more on it.

STUART GALE

I have memories of Fairport dotted throughout my life. I was born and brought up on the Isle of Man. Radio Caroline was moored in Ramsey Bay and I have a very clear memory of hearing about the motorway accident that claimed Martin and Jeannie on the transistor radio in my bedroom, aged 13. The music came slightly later.

I read about *"Babbacombe" Lee* in an *NME* that was left in our school library. The story fascinated me and I asked my mum to get the album for me for my birthday. The local record store had a limited assortment of records – Jim Reeves' *Greatest Hits* was a hot seller – and my Mum, bless her heart, came home with Traffic's *John Barleycorn Must Die*. I never had the heart to tell her it was the wrong record, and, in any event, I liked it. But thereafter I got everything that had gone before and everything that came after. Having discovered that a Simon Nicol was in the band, I wanted to claim him as my long-lost cousin as my mum's maiden name was Nicol, my grandfather was one of 16 children from Scotland (on that basis I thought I was related to everyone called Nicol in Britain) and one of my great uncles was an operatic tenor, so there seemed at least a chance. But apparently not.

Stuart Gale took his wife Sara to Cropredy on their first date

Throughout my university days, Fairport and all offshoots – Iain, Sandy, Tyger and Richard – were essential parts of my life. In the 1980s, I started going to Cropredy. By this time, I had become a lawyer, and in 1990 I was doing a case which lasted for over a year about a blow-out on a North Sea oil rig – not Piper Alpha – and I got into the habit each day of listening to *The Five Seasons* on the tape in my car on the way to court. In the song 'The Wounded Whale', two lines – 'And we have circulation' and 'See how she sinks with her chimney on fire' – rang with that case. One of the main issues was whether those in charge of the rig had achieved circulation of gas from the bottom of the well, and she sank with her chimney on fire. Every time I hear that track, I'm back to Aberdeen in 1990 awaiting with utter stomach-churning fear to cross examine 'Red' Adair. In the many times I've seen FC, I don't think I've ever seen them play that song. Hint.

For many years *Cropredy* was a highlight of the year. One year, I was sitting in the field reading the programme and having my first Wadworth's when from the programme out sprang a mention of the 'Greek plane spotters' who had been arrested on the ridiculous charges of spying. One of those men – I will identify him only as the Yorkshireman – I shared a flat with at university, when we also shared our love of FC.

In 2014, I took someone on what was really our first date to *Cropredy*. The next year Sara became my wife.

GONNA SEE ALL MY FRIENDS:
A PEOPLE'S HISTORY OF FAIRPORT CONVENTION

BALTOPPEN
23 MARCH 2015, BALLERUP, DENMARK

NIKLAS NILSSON

I had my camera with me when I went to see Fairport in 2015 in Denmark.

Niklas Nilsson was in Denmark in 2015 and photographed the band

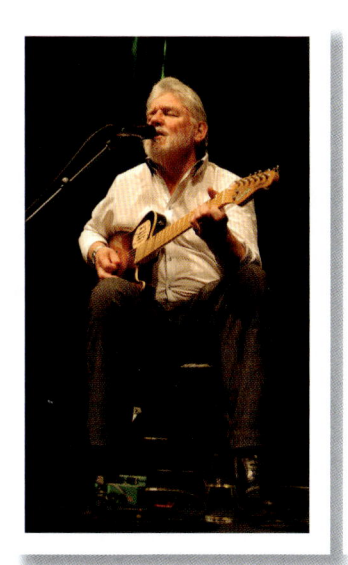

GONNA SEE ALL MY FRIENDS:
A PEOPLE'S HISTORY OF FAIRPORT CONVENTION

FAIRPORT'S CROPREDY CONVENTION
13 – 15 AUGUST 2015, CROPREDY, UK

HELENE ROBINSON

I had escorted Edmund Whitcombe, who always accompanies FC on 'Meet on the Ledge', onto the main stage to the mic he shared with Ric before I retreated to the wings. After 'Meet on the Ledge', Swarb, Edmund and myself were standing together and having a good catch up and laugh backstage. Mid-conversation, Swarb placed his fiddle and a very large glass of red wine on one of the speakers and went off to the other end of the stage. Suddenly, the technician guys arrived and started rapidly pushing the speaker, which was on wheels, away.

Helene Robinson drank Swarb's red wine

I rushed to retrieve Swarb's fiddle and glass of wine from the fast-rolling trundling speaker, and held onto them while I continued talking to Edmund. After what seemed like a really long time, Edmund and I began to think Swarb had become engrossed in something, or had completely forgotten about his wine, so we stood there and between us merrily started drinking Swarb's wine – until we had completely polished off the entire glass!

Suddenly, Swarb appeared and looked panic-stricken when he saw that the speaker had gone, along with his fiddle. But a look of huge relief spread across his face as he saw that I was clutching his fiddle. He said it was his most precious one and was from around 1888. He didn't ask about the wine, so Edmund and I told him we'd drunk it for him. All three of us couldn't stop laughing. Sadly, *Cropredy 2015* was to be Swarb's last Cropredy.

Swarb, a legend, always engaging and entertaining! And his spirit lives on...

GONNA SEE ALL MY FRIENDS:
A PEOPLE'S HISTORY OF FAIRPORT CONVENTION

DRILL HALL
14 FEBRUARY 2016, LINCOLN, UK

KIM CROFT

It's hard to begin really, telling the story of how I came to love Fairport. My husband's brother lives in the village of Cropredy and in the late '90s we began our Fairport journey at the *Cropredy Festival*. We would go most years as a couple and then, after our two girls were born, continued the pilgrimage, falling in love with both the festival and the band. The record collection became extensive and treasured. Various gigs were attended every year. Rarely a day goes by without spinning the vinyl and dancing around the kitchen as a family.

Kim Croft's daughter recreated Cropredy in a painting

Little did I know that my career path would take me to a career in theatre, where at the Drill Hall, Lincoln, I was fortunate to welcome the band every year in my ten-year history as Front of House manager. It's hard not to love each and every one of them, from the band to the crew; perfect gentlemen who are always a joy to work alongside.

Sadly, the Drill Hall closed due to funding and the Covid pandemic in March 2020.

Fortunately, my relationship with Fairport remains valued and strong and I catch up with the band where and when I can and treasure the memories I have, most recently when they performed again in Lincoln in March 2022 where I got to talk to them briefly, Covid permitting. My most landmark moment was when they dedicated a song for me as a tribute to the days when they would come to the Drill Hall. It's hard to pick a favourite song but 'Cider Rain' has a special place in my heart, as it was the song dedicated to me.

I look at Fairport as friends. How lucky am I? My niece painted a picture for me depicting the festival with our family in the foreground, and it reflects the value we place in the memories we have – luckily signed when the boys were in the Drill Hall. I will treasure it always.

FAIRPORT'S CROPREDY CONVENTION
10 - 13 AUGUST 2017, CROPREDY, UK

DOMINIC WALSH

With Fairport's half century came the set of the century. FC members past and present formed a three hour-plus set from the finest in folk rock: essentially the blueprint for folk rock.

The current line-up started the show with 'Ye Mariners All' from *Tipplers Tales* and a cut from the band's latest *50:50@50* album, 'Summer by the Cherwell' (the river that runs through Cropredy). It was from here that Fairport Convention showed just exactly how influential and important they are. Forming a 1967 line-up, with Richard Thompson, Ashley Hutchings and Judy Dyble amongst its ranks, the opening slew of songs was completely mind-blowing. Songs that made up their self-titled album were brought to life in such an exact and refreshing way. Covers of Leonard Cohen's 'Suzanne' and Joni Mitchell's 'I Don't Know Where I Stand' were impeccable. However, it was the bombast of Fairport's track 1 side 1, 'Time Will Show the Wiser', which stole the (early part of the) show. Iain Matthews, Richard Thompson and Judy Dyble provided impassioned vocals for the short and sweet number that was the signal point for what was to come in this great band's future.

It was during this period of the set, and at the mention of Martin Lamble, that I found it really remarkable to realise that FC are celebrating their 50th birthday. After Lamble's tragic death in a road accident and Dave Mattacks was drafted in, the band went on to record arguably the most revered folk rock record in history, *Liege & Lief*. Again, the songs showcased as part of this set were given incredible fire; 'Come All Ye', 'Tam Lin' and 'Lark in the Morning' medley sounded completely vital all these years on.

As the concert rolled into the *Full House* era, where the band was a five piece, the Thompson/Mattacks/Pegg combo was again out of this world. The epic 'Sloth' once more showed Thompson's incredible talent on the six-string. Another great cut from *Full House* is the largely ever-present 'Walk Awhile'. In this particular set, the band's vocal, like 'Time Will Show the Wiser', was delivered with great vigour.

Other acknowledgments in the set came from PJ Wright taking the place of Trevor Lucas, and it's hard not to talk about Fairport without mentioned Lucas' wife, Sandy Denny. 'Who Knows Where the Time Goes?' is a song for the ages. As has been the case on many a night at *Cropredy*, Chris While delivered a superlative version to pay tribute to one of the greatest English singers ever. In the same vein of paying tribute, Ralph McTell offered his assistance on 'White Dress' from 1975's *Rising for the Moon*. McTell's skills as a songwriter were also on show during one of Fairport's finest songs, 'The Hiring Fair'.

A brief interlude from the band's *Wintour* support artist slowed the pace and momentum of the set after two of the most exhilarating hours of music the *Cropredy* has witnessed for many a year. Another revolving door of members saw out the rest of the set including 'Dirty Linen', 'The Hexhamshire Lass' and the newer and superbly autobiographical 'Our Bus Rolls On'.

The rousing conclusion came from perennial *Cropredy* closer, 'Meet on the Ledge'. The stage was awash with white light and filled with many of the artists who contributed to the weekend, and in particular Fairport's set.

Cropredy really is a great festival. The vibe around the festival and the village is second to none; it's no surprise that *Fairport's Cropredy Convention* has previously won awards for being Britain's friendliest festival.

GONNA SEE ALL MY FRIENDS:
A PEOPLE'S HISTORY OF FAIRPORT CONVENTION

JAY WILKINSON

I am a Fairport fan who grew up in rural Mississippi in the United States in the '60s and '70s. This was quite a feat, as you were more likely at that time to run into a blues great like Willie Dixon or Hubert Sumlin in person than you were to find a Fairport record. And from what I understand, radio back then was

Jay Wilkinson was at Cropredy in 2017 and survived the rain with wife Angela Yeung

different in the UK to America. In Mississippi, despite being somewhat of a cultural backwater, we were lucky to have one of the first FM radio stations that focused on more eclectic album-oriented tastes. That made it possible to hear fellow travellers like Pink Floyd or even the Soft Machine, but not Fairport. It wasn't until a publicly funded classical music station (WRKF) was founded in 1980 that I heard Fairport for the first time.

WRKF must have been struggling for programming because they let a young disc jockey by the name of Mark Time take over the airwaves late at night on Saturdays. His real name was Allen Broussard, and he was a great fan of Fairport. On occasion, he would devote entire shows to British folk rock. WRKF was located an hour and a half drive away from where I lived, so the signal was sometimes hard to pick up and always subject to fading in and out. But there were places you could drive to where the signal was stronger, like a favourite hill above a creek in the piney woods southwest of my house. It was a great summer to roll down the windows of your car and listen to 'Tam Lin' and 'Sloth'.

It took years to track down all the records and it wasn't until the ascension of the internet that it was possible to keep up with coming and goings (many goings) of the always evolving Fairport line-up. Despite moving around quite a bit, I never lived where I could see Fairport in

GONNA SEE ALL MY FRIENDS:
A PEOPLE'S HISTORY OF FAIRPORT CONVENTION

any of their incarnations and I never thought I would see them live until I read about the plans for the 2017 *Cropredy Festival* and the celebration of 50 years of the band.

All things nostalgic become more suspect the older I get. I expected the current Fairporters to be professional and tight, being the longest tenured line-up, and I hoped the entire *Cropredy* experience would be enjoyable and memorable. And it was, and they were – and more. There were many highlights over the three days, and just enough rain to say that we survived Banbury in August. But that final closing performance of Fairport that year featuring all incarnations (with a little help from some friends) was a thing of great beauty. Everyone's appreciation of music is influenced by their experience hearing it. When a band (or more properly, a convention) perseveres for 50 years, they and their listeners have accumulated so many layers of experience that there is risk that a performance may capsize from the freight of warring expectations. But that night, every song and every line-up was a revelation and inspired great joy. It truly felt like you were glimpsing a 50 year chronicle of shared experience – old, new, borrowed, blue.

GONNA SEE ALL MY FRIENDS:
A PEOPLE'S HISTORY OF FAIRPORT CONVENTION

LEEK ARTS FESTIVAL
17 MAY 2018, LEEK, UK

DAVID FARRAR OBE

A key Fairport memory comes from the mid '70s and the opportunity to see Fairport play at the De Montfort Hall, Leicester during the Sandy Denny/Dave Swarbrick era. Life's challenges and parenthood, including a spell living in Salt Lake City, Utah, still had me focused on priorities other than going to gigs. But listening to recorded music continued to be an important part of my life, along with the occasional live gig along with supporting my offspring in their various musical and other endeavours.

David Farrar OBE is a regular at Cropredy and at Leek Arts Festival

In 2014, tragedy struck when my wife, Yvonne, passed away following a courageous ten-year battle against breast cancer. I was lost. Knowing of my love of listening to music, especially that of Fairport, my youngest daughter, Rebecca, now in the music business herself, encouraged me to embrace live music as a mechanism to cope with my grief. I was aware of the *Cropredy Conventions* but, as a consequence of my family and work commitments, I had never been to one before. However, Rebecca encouraged me to make attendance at the upcoming convention a target. So, the 2014 weekend was my first attendance at *Cropredy* or any music festival, for that matter.

What an eye and ear opener – not only Fairport, but Steve Hackett and Marillion as well, along with all the other acts. At that time, I also became aware of the annual Fairport appearances at the *Leek Arts Festival*, not too far from my hometown of Congleton. I have not looked back since. *Cropredy* has become an annual diary date for the Farrar family, as have the gigs at the *Leek Arts Festival*. I also have been to the most local Fairport gig during their various tours, the last one being Northwich in 2022. In recent years, I have made myself known to the various members of the band and have found them all to be a friendly bunch and have appreciated their welcoming attitude.

Live music has become an integral and important part of my life since that fateful day, until COVID struck that is. My interest extends into the solo careers of the Fairport family – Sandy, Judy, Richard, Iain, Simon. I have amassed a near complete LP/CD discography of Fairport Convention and a pretty comprehensive collection of the solo recordings.

I was once called for a CT scan and decided to take a copy of the Simon/Dave CD *When We Were Very Young* along for entertainment. As usual, I was asked to keep very still during the scan. What I had forgotten was that track three is 'The Dogs They Had a Party'. Try keeping still when you are listening to those lyrics.

I have difficulty in nominating a favourite Fairport song. 'Who Knows Where the Time Goes?' is high up on the list because of the poignancy of the lyrics. I would choose 'Reno, Nevada', 'Chelsea Morning', 'Sloth', 'Come All Ye', 'Fotheringay', 'Dirty Linen', 'Knights of the Road', 'Mercy Bay', 'Portmeirion' and 'Don't Reveal My Name' as fine examples of the contributions and influences of the various members of the band over time. Listening to the *What We Did on Our Saturday* set, both live on a Saturday in August 2017 and on the resulting CD, reminds me of why I am a fan of Fairport's music. Their interpretation of the then current West coast sounds in the early days, subsequently developing into their unique folk-rock style hooked me in. You might be forgiven for thinking that the band that released *Shuffle and Go* in 2020 is not the same band that released *Unhalfbricking* in 1969, but you would be wrong. Go along to one of their gigs and hear how their legacy lives on – sing 'Meet on the Ledge' with your friends and loved ones.

In memory and celebration of Yvonne's life, I funded a bench at the local Astbury Mere Country Park. The inscription that I chose in her memory was 'Who Knows Where the Time Goes'. I forgot to include the '?' on the inscription, but I have not forgotten Yvonne. The song brings a tear to my eye every time I hear it.

GONNA SEE ALL MY FRIENDS:
A PEOPLE'S HISTORY OF FAIRPORT CONVENTION

FAIRPORT'S CROPREDY CONVENTION
9 – 11 AUGUST 2018, CROPREDY, UK

FRASER NIMMO

I go to *Cropredy* every year. It's the most important event in the year and the first thing that goes in my diary. 2018 was Maartin's last *Cropredy*. His performance on 'Matty Groves', then 'Meet on the Ledge', is the most moving thing I've ever witnessed. Thank God for the rain that night – it disguised the sight and sound of 20,000 Fairporters sobbing.

   I spoke to him backstage for about an hour on that Saturday, which was his last performance. We sat in the crew tent. Maartin was sanguine. He said, 'My situation is sorted and I'm going onto somewhere else.' There were no tears. There was no, 'Oh – why me?' and I just wondered how we would all be in that situation. It was summed up best by Simon Nicol at Maartin's funeral when he said of Maartin, 'He taught me more about music than I can ever even remember, but his lasting gift to me will be how, after all the best efforts of the NHS and the medics, he showed us all how to face that music at the end. He saved the best for last.'

   Maartin was getting ready to do his bit on stage with the Bar-Steward Sons of Val Doonican and I walked up to the backstage part of the main stage with him. He was very frail and weak but determined. We got up this quite steep slope to the stage area and he wasn't required for a few minutes. He looked as if the wind would blow him away and I said to him, 'Maartin, shall I get you a chair?' And he turned to me and said, in a very emphatic way, 'Fraser, I'm dying. I'm not ill!' He was brilliant and indomitable to his last breath.

   Maartin was always putting things over on me, kidding me on about this and that. It was harmless and funny, but I didn't have time for jokes because I was far too busy running shows. At one point, Maartin and his wife Gill were getting their stuff together to get their first flat. He didn't have a lot of money, and he understood nothing about motorcars. My brother and I were sitting having a beer after the gig when Maartin came back with the gearstick from his car in his hand. He said, 'My car is not working.' He didn't have breakdown cover. I thought, 'I'll get you now,' so I gave him my AA relay breakdown cover card.

   My full name is Duncan Cameron Fraser MacMaster McKay Nimmo. On the AA card it read 'D C F M M Nimmo'. Maartin looked at it and said, 'What's all this about?' I said, 'That's my full name. You are going to have to say that when the AA man comes. He'll say the number and the response you've got to give him is, 'My name is Duncan Cameron Fraser MacMaster McKay Nimmo,' and if you don't say that, Maartin, there will be no relay service for you. You will have to push your car back to Ealing.'

So at about half past midnight, I left Maartin walking up and down the pavement outside this gig in Blackfriars, waiting for the AA man and walking up and down the pavement outside the gig in Blackfriars repeating my name, 'Duncan Cameron Fraser MacMaster McKay Nimmo, Duncan Cameron Fraser McMaster McKay Nimmo…' When the AA man turned up he said, 'Oh hello, Mr Nimmo. We don't need all that guff. We've got all your details on file.' Whenever I met Maartin after that, he would call out my full name. And the more refreshed he got, the more difficult it was to do. If we saw each other across the bar at *Cropredy*, he would shout it out across the bar. It's a point of real human contact I will never have, with anyone, again.

Maartin was the guy that really introduced me to the family of Fairport. If you meet another Fairport fan, who you might recognise through the memorabilia they are wearing, you are instantly a part of that Fairport fraternity, that Fairport brotherhood. Fairport are held in such reverential esteem because, from the early days they were groundbreaking. They invented a genre. Not many bands can say that. It is a great achievement, and it will last. The Fairport family will outlive the band. It can't not do. It's too big and it's truly international.

SCOTT DOONICAN, THE BAR-STEWARD SONS OF VAL DOONICAN

I'm the lead singer of the comedy folk band The Bar-Steward Sons of Val Doonican, who played *Cropredy* in 2018 and in 2022. I was really late to the party. I always am. In late 2012, I was sent a late-night friend request on Facebook from Maartin Allcock, who introduced himself as Maart and told me that we had one thing in common – our adoration of comedy-folkie Mike Harding. Mike was very much – like Richard Digance, Jasper Carrott, Max Boyce, Tony Capstick and Billy Connolly – the folk-musician who turned comedian. Having seen Mike tread the boards at Belfast Opera House in 1984, when I was a mere five-year-old, I knew right then that I wanted 'to be one of those'.

GONNA SEE ALL MY FRIENDS:
A PEOPLE'S HISTORY OF FAIRPORT CONVENTION

Photo: Clive Lane (Maart's brother-in-law)

Maartin Allcock waiting to take the stage at Cropredy in 2018

It didn't take long for Maart to tell me that he had started out getting his first 'paid gig' as the bass player in Harding's infamous 'Brown Ale Cowboys', their *Captain Paralytic* album that I had played to death (containing a young Maart on four-string duties), cementing our friendship instantly. Over time, I realised that my new virtual friend had more strings to his bow, and the names Fairport Convention, Jethro Tull, the Mission and the Bad Shepherds all were familiar to me. I had actually seen Maart in the Shepherds' first incarnation, before we knew each other, when they hit nearby Sheffield.

Later in the year, I decided to try and release The Bar-Steward Sons of Val Doonican's first *Bestest Bits* album, the irony being that we had nothing in the way of chart-bothering success, and certainly nothing of note to warrant recording a second volume the following year. On announcing this, Maart messaged me and said that he would love to

322

work with us. Knowing now of his credentials in two of the biggest exports of English folk/rock music, I didn't hesitate to say yes. The product of our efforts was a Barnsley-inflected version of the hip-hop outfit House of Pain's biggest hit, 'Jump Ararnd', featuring myself and my (former) bandmates, Maart on bass, Hugh Whitaker from The Housemartins on drums, Eliza Carthy on fiddle, Mike Harding on tenor banjo and harmonica and Graham Oliver from heavy metal titans Saxon on electric guitar. The backing track that we recorded still gets used every night on stage to this day. We all worked remotely, with everyone sending their parts via email. On finishing it, it wasn't long before we got the gang back together for a second track.

Our second outing saw the Doonicans join forces again to rework the Charlie Daniels Band's 'The Devil Went Darn to Barnsley', with Maart taking on bass, baritone electric guitar, synths and all production duties alongside Mr Harding as a Lancastrian Devil, Eliza on fiddle and backing vocals and Graham back on guitar duties. The result was us sounding better than we ever had previously (well, let's be honest, with a band like that you can see who was doing the heavy lifting).

This became the genesis of a 'thing' in which every October, Maart would call me and say, 'So what are we doing for this year's charity Christmas single, Scott?' And every year, I tried to come up with something funny and imaginative, because Maart was not only brilliant to work with, but he had funny bones and was a great soul to know. The more time I spent working with Maart, the more he introduced me to new music, culture and educated me in ways only he could.

Three Christmas singles followed over the next three years, and my partner Amanda and her mum and dad and I attended Sheffield City Hall to see Maart along with Beth Nielsen Chapman to finally meet up properly after all the years of working together over the medium of the internet. It was during a conversation at the bar that Maart suggested that I apply to *Fairport's Cropredy Convention*, but knowing of our small burgeoning status on the UK's festival circuit, I really didn't think we were ready for something of that colossal size. Maart had other ideas. What I didn't know was that he had been tipping Simon and Peggy off about this comedy parody outfit from Barnsley and had been singing our praises for quite a while.

GONNA SEE ALL MY FRIENDS:
A PEOPLE'S HISTORY OF FAIRPORT CONVENTION

By pure luck, we were booked to headline the second stage at the *Acoustic Festival of Britain* in Uttoxeter, whilst Fairport were booked to headline the main stage. As chance would have it, we went on stage about ten minutes before FC finished their set, and the bar-tent happened to be where we were playing. Maart always joked that, 'Fairport Convention aren't a folk band, they are a British drinking team.' This meant that in order to get a pint after playing their set, Simon, Peggy and the gang would be subjected to having to watch some of these scruffy-arsed beatniks from Barnsley whilst they waited for their festival ales to settle. It was only as I was crowd-surfing over a narrow line of people to the bar that I spotted that we were being watched. Simon's better half was at the side of the stage filming our antics.

Maart messaged about a month later to tell me that we had made an impression on some of his friends. I didn't put two and two together and he was fairly cryptic about it all. It was only when in the January of 2018 that I got a phone call from Peggy, who was in Brittany recovering from his hip-operation, asking if we were free to play *Cropredy* that the penny dropped – along with my jaw.

This was when I finally became a Fairport fan. Having never previously heard much more than 'Meet on the Ledge', 'Tam Lin' and 'Matty Groves', I didn't want to walk into Fairport's own festival unprepared. However, it didn't take long to catch up. Alan, our accordion player, has been a massive fan of Fairport for years and years and was quick to point me in the direction of *Liege & Lief* and *Full House*, and after devouring those in quick succession, I went to HMV and bought the first ten FC albums (who needs Spotify when physical albums are still king!). Their exceptional musicianship and folk-rock credentials made me realise that I had been missing out for years. And to make matters stranger, Bjorn, our young multi-instrumentalist then introduced me to Tull. I then binged on all of Tull's late Sixties to late Seventies output too. It was a treasure-trove of undiscovered music that I, as a metalhead at heart, had completely missed.

Fast forward to August 2018. I was aware that my friend Maartin was pretty poorly, but that he was determined, even if the doctor's orders were not in his favour, that he was making his final farewell at *Cropredy*. He also very graciously chose to join The Bar-Steward Sons of Val

GONNA SEE ALL MY FRIENDS:
A PEOPLE'S HISTORY OF FAIRPORT CONVENTION

Doonican on stage for 'The Devil' and 'Jump Ararnd', the two tracks that we had first worked on together. Seeing Maart walk out on to that stage in my day-glo 'EY UP! LET'S GO!' tank top in front of 20,000 plus fans was a sight to behold. Just before we took to the stage to the largest crowd we had ever played to, he saw how nervous I was and said, 'Now remember lads, that's *my* stage, and I am letting you borrow it for an hour. Go out and make 'em smile, and don't forget to have fun!' It was magical. And it *was* Maart's stage.

Maart passed away the following month. It felt like I had lost an older, wiser brother. At his funeral he had requested that I sing 'Do-Re-Mi' from *The Sound of Music*, because with his Catholic upbringing he 'hated nuns' despite loving the musical. Everyone at the congregation was expected to wear something colourful, and absolutely no black was to be seen. I wore my *Cropredy* stage tank-top, and Maart's wife, Jan, wore the 'EY UP! LET'S GO' tank top that he had worn on stage just the month before. It was an incredibly uplifting day, despite its sadness.

That October, Maart didn't call to ask about the Christmas single. He couldn't. But he had left us with a final offering, a folk/prog (Maart called it 'frog') rendition of Greg Lake's 'I Believe in Father Christmas', which we had recorded the year before. I made it my personal mission to try and 'Get Maart to Chart', and so we started a month-long social media campaign to try and get Maartin Allcock into the Christmas Day chart. We didn't do badly; at its highest point in the midweek chart, we got to number 33 in the UK iTunes charts, dropping down to number 80 on the UK's Official Chart on Christmas Day. It wasn't a huge achievement, but a top-100 single for Maart and ourselves made me incredibly proud and I know he would have found that level of Spinal Tap silliness incredibly funny. Something worthy of a *Bestest Bits* album, for sure.

When it came time for The Bar-Steward Sons to start work on our eleventh studio album, during the lockdowns of 2020 and '21, I had the idea of creating a parody of *Liege & Lief* and emailed Peggy to see if there would be any copyright issues. I was utterly gobsmacked when all of the remaining members of the *Liege & Lief* line-up emailed back to give us their blessing. Richard Thompson had even said that it was nice to have been asked. Peggy and DM even joined us as the powerhouse rhythm section on 'The Broadside Ballad of Maggie Gove', our homage to Matty, which featured Maart's 'Surfeit of Lampreys' as the outro tune. We even recorded our own version of 'Meet on the Ledge' for the CD's hidden track.

Since being introduced to the world of Fairport Convention, through my friendship with Maart and my bandmates, my life has been richer. Long may they continue to weave the magic that they do. I just wish I had known sooner, but I am grateful that there is one helluva legacy to continue discovering. Thank you, you wonderful human beings.

STEVE PHILLIPS

I've been a fan of Fairport since I was an undergraduate at Cardiff in the early 1970s. I first saw them in 1978, aged 27, and the last time was a few weeks ago, aged 71. I've probably seen them 60 or 70 times, including many times at *Cropredy*, and am lucky enough to have got to know the band quite well. They even recorded a special 'Happy Birthday' video for my 70th, which is much treasured.

I had my photo taken with Ric in 1989 at a Gordon Giltrap gig at the Dylan Thomas Theatre in Swansea.

Steve Phillips has met Ric twice, 29 years apart

I was in plaster, having recently come off my Lambretta scooter. I also managed to get a photo on the field at *Cropredy 2018*. We were waving to my wife Jacqui, who was unable to attend that year because of illness. When I sent her the photo, with the caption 'Ric says hello', she replied with, 'Arghhhh, why aren't I there?'

Just after this, I had the pleasure of bumping into Judy Dyble further up the field, and had a brief but interesting chat. A lovely lady.

GONNA SEE ALL MY FRIENDS:
A PEOPLE'S HISTORY OF FAIRPORT CONVENTION

NICK HELFRICH

My brother and I were in the queue behind a lady at the mobile shop that used to come around the camping fields at *Cropredy*. We seemed to have been waiting a long time when we noticed the owner had been rummaging for a while, looking for whatever the lady had asked for. He finally came to the front, very happy with himself and put a pack of sanitary towels down in front of her. She said, 'I asked for tent pegs!'

ROSES THEATRE
30 JANUARY 2019, TEWKESBURY, UK

BRENDAN MURPHY, THE 4 OF US

Fairport Convention are one of those names that you know are important, like Jethro Tull, but I didn't know more than that. I knew that they were established, and a bit establishment. But I didn't know any of their songs. However, when we were told that we could open for Fairport, it was exciting because of the history. It was a thrill just for the idea that we would be entering their world, which, with two acoustic guitars, was a world that we also sort of belonged to without realising it.

   The 4 of Us had been in existence since 1989, so it wasn't like we were kids, and we'd done a lot of touring. Fairport was unlike any act we toured with, and it happened immediately. The first thing we were told was our last song was going to be their first song. They wanted us to pick one of our songs, and then we would introduce them, and they would play along with us, which would be the first song of their set. We couldn't believe this because it was an immediate endorsement of us by them, and it just seemed very generous to us in a way that we hadn't experienced before. Then I got a phone call from Peggy who was trying to work out the song that we had picked. We had done it in lots of different keys, and he was going, 'What key is it? The record's one key, you play it differently here?' This was my first conversation with him, and he was so warm on the phone. There was none of the distance that sometimes you experience when you're touring with a bigger act. There was immediately a sense of camaraderie, and the fact that our last song was their first set the scene for us.

GONNA SEE ALL MY FRIENDS:
A PEOPLE'S HISTORY OF FAIRPORT CONVENTION

When we arrived at the show on the first night, we could see that the band would come out after the end of the show into the foyer where the audience were. You expect that to happen at folk clubs, but these were big rooms. We realised at that point that what we were dealing with was a tribe of people. I think Peggy had said to me that, 'We are like the Grateful Dead with real ale'. I had not experienced that level of connection between the audience and the band in 30 years of touring.

That was the very first show, and again when they came out and did the first song and Simon let me know that as the tour progressed, his performance of our song would get better. He was just so relaxed, they were so relaxed, there was just a tribal element to the whole experience.

I remember thinking after about the third or fourth show that we could learn a thing or two from the connection Fairport had with their audience. It changed our approach to our audience. We realised that we could get a much closer connection than we had previously had. People talk about the music and songs, but the heart of Fairport to me is their heart

We ended up on the *Cropredy* stage, and they also came over to Ireland. They'd been interested in this, and we had a decent-sized audience in Ireland, so we were happy to introduce them, and of course we still went on before Fairport because they have a big audience in Ireland. There's sort of a warmth with Fairport and a warmth with their audience. If you enter their world you benefit from that warmth.

It was us having been around the block that made us understand that this wasn't a normal experience. Then I became curious about the music. So suddenly, from a guy who didn't know too much about them, I was looking them up. Once you start delving into the Fairport history, it's a bit of a wormhole, it's like going into the Tudor dynasty. You're moving back through generations, it's like a family tree of Richard Thompson and all these names of people who have made Fairport the band they are today. As I got more and more curious, I would speak to Peggy and ask him a question about some period, and he is the funniest. He has so many stories, it's just incredible. Everyone in the band are very different characters, yet together they are one big genial collective. They are very different really. Everybody in the band is a very distinct personality.

I didn't think I could be taught too much at this point. The longer you do this, the less surprised you get by things that go on, but the

GONNA SEE ALL MY FRIENDS: A PEOPLE'S HISTORY OF FAIRPORT CONVENTION

Fairport experience was totally surprising for me and Declan. And it was transformative for us. They're not that much older than us, but I turned around to Declan and said, 'I want to be them when I grow up.'

NEUADD OGDEN
28 MAY 2019, BETHESDA, UK

JEFF PRINCE

After a long life of following the Fairports, it was time to introduce my son, Steff, to the joys of seeing the band live. He was at university in Bangor, North Wales, and the boys had a gig nearby, albeit 200 miles by road from me. So, tickets were bought and arrangements made. On the day of the concert, I drove up and took Steff into Bangor to do a bit of shopping, wearing one of my trusted *Cropredy* t-shirts, as one does. In a charity shop, a Brummie accent behind us said, 'Nice shirt'. I turned around and there stood one Mr Pegg, bass player extraordinaire. We chatted, had a celebratory picture taken, and I explained that I'd driven up to give the lad his rite of passage into Fairports live. Peggy was great, and said he'd see us later.

Jeff Prince and his son Steff bumped into Peggy in a charity shop

At the gig, Dave was at the foyer, selling and signing. He recognised us and made my lad welcome. During the gig, he dedicated a song to Steff and explained that I'd driven 400 miles in all to bring him here, and that he owed me a pint or two. This left a stunned and very happy father and son, who is himself now an impressed and devoted fan. This all goes to show that the Fairports aren't just great musicians, but are also great people who appreciate us fans.

GONNA SEE ALL MY FRIENDS:
A PEOPLE'S HISTORY OF FAIRPORT CONVENTION

FLEUR DE LYS
9 JUNE 2019, EAST HAGBOURNE, DIDCOT, UK

JOHN SMALLWOOD

In the '90s I owned a hotel in Santa Fe, New Mexico, where I still live. I was friends with Ian Wallace (an English drummer of some repute) and he called to say that Dave Mattacks and his wife Caron were visiting Santa Fe and were about to check in at a hotel just a block away from mine. I drove over there and convinced them to stay with me. This was a start of a nice friendship, with Dave and Caron visiting several times over the years. A few years later, Dave called to let me know that he was playing in Albuquerque with Roseanne Cash, and I enjoyed catching up with him then too.

John Smallwood first crossed paths with one of the Fairport family in Sante Fe

Ian Wallace was playing with Procol Harum, who were opening for Jethro Tull in a nationwide tour. I joined them on the tour, and the night before the show at the Greek Theatre in Los Angeles, I met Dave Pegg at Barney's Beanery, where I heard him tell funny, ribald tales of life on the road with Jethro Tull. Don't worry Dave – my lips are sealed!

In the early 2000s, Fairport were touring the US east coast, and Peggy and Ellen stayed with us in Santa Fe for a week or so. We had a nice time, and they enjoyed some nice meals with our family. I finally had a chance to see Fairport live in 2019, with Simon and Peggy kindly providing my sons and myself tickets to a show in Didcot.

GONNA SEE ALL MY FRIENDS:
A PEOPLE'S HISTORY OF FAIRPORT CONVENTION

FAIRPORT'S CROPREDY CONVENTION
8 – 10 AUGUST 2019, CROPREDY, UK

CHERYL HARDISTY

In 2019 we went to Cropredy with our friend Richard, who we had met for the first time in the 50th year. Recently, he'd had various illnesses and he asked Amanda and myself to look out for him in case he became ill. Over the weekend, he had seemed all right, so I wasn't too concerned. On Saturday, he was in good spirits throughout the day but around 6pm, he disappeared.

Cheryl Hardisty was asked to keep an eye on her friend Richard (in the hat), who promptly disappeared

Amanda and our other friend, Paul, thought he would turn up before Fairport's set. When he didn't, I started to panic. Paul and I had gone down the front of the crowd but my gut told me something wasn't right. Amanda had stayed back with the chairs to keep an eye out for Richard, and I went back to sit and wait with her. An hour later we still hadn't seen him so I said, 'I'll do a lap of the arena field.' There was no sign of him. I went to first aid. No one had been in all day. I went to 'lost children', who I thought might also cater for lost adults, and they told me to go and check his tent. I left the arena field at the cow shed end and saw the Thames Valley Police. I explained what Richard was ill with and gave them his description. They gave me a lift down to Field 4 and we checked his tent. Still no sign.

The police took me back to the top of the field where I told lost children (and adults) Richard wasn't in his tent. They notified security. There was very little else I could do. I made my way down to where Amanda was.

Maart's wife was on stage so I started crying, and even more so when 'Meet on the Ledge' was playing. At the end, the camera panned across the crowd and, to my surprise, there was Rich down the front, smiling and having the time of his life. My tears instantly turned to rage, with me telling Manda, 'I'm gonna fucking kill him!'

Same time next year?

RICHARD ILLIG

In 2019 my mate Andreas kindly gave me a lift to Cropredy in his motorhome. He'd been a festival regular for a few years. My partner Uschi had been to Cropredy with me twice before, but this year decided to visit her sister and family in North Carolina, so we agreed to spend our holidays separately. We'd have lots to tell each other afterwards, so we said goodbye in a good mood.

Unfortunately, after a few beautiful days in the States, Uschi had a serious accident while swimming in the Atlantic. With the sea in quite a normal state, she was suddenly hit in the neck by a violent wave and thrown into the sea. As she struggled to get up, she was hit again by a second – worse – wave. Doctors who saw the MRI scans said the second wave could easily have killed her. It led to a severe craniocerebral trauma, with the result that her holiday in America turned from a good-mood holiday into a nightmare. She had to stay in bed, could hardly lie down because of the pain and had to be taken from one hospital to the next.

And me? I was at Cropredy enjoying myself and had no idea about what had happened to her. After a few days of not hearing from her, Uschi finally got in touch on the Saturday afternoon. Barely able to speak, she told me the whole story of her accident. Of course, I was pretty shocked. I had been so looking forward to the festival and especially to the Fairport performance, and now this. I was thinking all sorts of pointless thoughts about whether I should leave the festival immediately, cut short my stay in England and somehow head for Heathrow and fly to America to be with her. But there are situations in life where you just have to accept that you can't do anything to help the other person and you cannot change it.

GONNA SEE ALL MY FRIENDS: A PEOPLE'S HISTORY OF FAIRPORT CONVENTION

Saturday afternoon passed in this mood for me and then Fairport came on stage. I could hardly concentrate on the music, thinking instead about what had happened and how I was in England without my partner and how I had to get through it somehow. And then, after the fourth song, Simon (or possibly Chris or Ric, I can't remember), announced, 'And now, for all of you on the field who are separated from their loved ones, we play our song, 'My Love is in America'. I was thunderstruck. Once again, the guys from Fairport had managed to touch me so emotionally that tears ran down my face.

Andreas and I stayed in the Banbury area for another couple of days. He went on to the north of England while I took a plane home from Birmingham. Uschi came back from the USA two weeks later by plane, after she was fit enough to travel again. Her accident affected her for quite a long time; she was really unwell for months and it took almost a year before she was able to work again. Now, fortunately, she is doing well again. But whenever she talks about her accident in America, I tell the story of that incredible Fairport moment.

Richard Illig's Cropredy memories are of 'My Love is in America' and his partner Uschi

SHARON LLEWELLYN

l was eating my Leon's curry (a famous festival stallholder) and sitting on the grass near the bar. A long-haired guy stepped back and put his foot into it. 'Never mind', l said, 'My fault for eating here.' It was Robert Plant. He walked off and came back with a replacement for me. What a good guy.

Anther year my husband David and I were packing up our tents on Field 2. We were with some friends from Australia, and their three-year-old boy was getting bored, so I took him for a walk around the field. At the edge was a little stream. 'Let's have look for tadpoles', I said. Being Australian, he asked, 'Are there any crocodiles in there?'

Sharon Llewellyn and family at Cropredy

PERRANPORTH VILLAGE HALL
11 OCTOBER 2019, PERRANPORTH, UK

CHRIS DENNIS

I first saw Fairport Convention in 1978 when I was a student at Loughborough University. In those days I was mostly into prog rock, so I didn't become an instant fan. It was 20 years before I saw them again, this time in my home city of Truro. Having decided to go along, I acquired a copy of *The Woodworm Years* and found that I really liked their music. That gig was enough to make me want to hear and see more, and on their next visit to Cornwall, a chat with Dave Pegg in the bar during the interval was enough to persuade me and my wife Mary to make our first trip to *Cropredy* the following summer. We've returned there most years since. As well as becoming loyal *Cropredy* devotees, we've travelled far and wide to catch tours which didn't include Cornwall, plus a few local appearances at *Mylor Sessions*, *St Ives Festival* and other touring stops over the years.

After finding that none of the tours in 2019 were coming to Cornwall, I decided to take matters into my own hands. Having no experience of music promotion, I investigated how to get Fairport to come to the

GONNA SEE ALL MY FRIENDS:
A PEOPLE'S HISTORY OF FAIRPORT CONVENTION

Chris Dennis took matters into his own hands and promoted a Fairport gig in 2019

county. I knew the promoters of their previous Cornwall gig at St Petroc's Church in Bodmin in 2018 and they put me in touch with tour manager Tristan Bryant, who said there was a possible date on 11 October on the autumn *Acoustic* tour, between gigs in Devon and Dorset.

So we had a date and the next thing was to find a venue. I made enquiries of the Perranporth Memorial Hall, where

GONNA SEE ALL MY FRIENDS:
A PEOPLE'S HISTORY OF FAIRPORT CONVENTION

Photos: Oliver Ilgner

DM on the drums

Gerald the caretaker couldn't believe it was actually the real Fairport Convention I was looking to book. The only 'famous' act he could ever remember being in the hall before was The Boys of the Lough, many years before. He said I could hire the hall for £150 so long as the pantomime rehearsal that was due to take place that day could be moved.

The Perranporth Memorial Hall holds 190 people, so to make it financially viable for the tour, I needed to provide the PA system and lights and get an events licence to include the bar. I decided to make it a charity benefit gig, hoping there might be a surplus from the night. Planning started in earnest in February, when I was able to meet Tristan at Exeter Corn Exchange on the Fairport *Wintour*. I set up my own online ticket sales site and started the promotion of the gig everywhere I could think of, including the local Facebook page for Perranzabuloe (Perranporth) parish. The organisers of *Cornwall Folk Festival*, which is held at Wadebridge on the August Bank Holiday, were very helpful in promoting the gig, allowing me to hand out flyers and give on-stage plugs for the gig at their evening concerts. It was touch-and-go whether the sums would add up right until the week before, by when the gig was sold out, and we were good to go.

The great day finally arrived, and I could hardly believe that I had

GONNA SEE ALL MY FRIENDS:
A PEOPLE'S HISTORY OF FAIRPORT CONVENTION

somehow become a music promoter and that Fairport were actually playing at the Perranporth Memorial Hall. Setting up and sound checks had gone well, as it turned out that the acoustics in the hall were good, and my volunteer 'roadies' had an easy job with it being an acoustic tour. There was much to-ing and fro-ing

Peggy with some new hair

during the day, collecting a cask of ale from the Driftwood Spars brewery in nearby St Agnes, setting up the bar and tea area, and putting out all the seats. By the time the tour bus arrived at the hall, everything was in place, including the excellent PA person, Brendan of Cornish Underground. I was in charge of lighting and was grateful to the lighting technician from the Perranporth Players, who had shown me the ropes and the on/off switches for the princely fee of £20.

The front of house and bar volunteers I'd recruited from my choir and other clubs turned up, and we were ready on time for the audience, who started to arrive at least an hour early. My wife Mary's green room catering was well-received by the band pre-show, as was the inclusion of a Barolo in the wine on offer (especially by Peggy). Mary's sister and our neighbour manned the refreshments hatch where the non-alcoholic beverages and cakes were served. Knowing how much beer, wine and cider to provide for the punters at the bar was a challenge, and I over-ordered on the cask ale (never a bad thing) but under-ordered on the white wine which necessitated a high speed dash to the local Co-op to restock.

There was a brilliant buzz of excitement in the hall. I checked that all were ready to go, turned the lights down as instructed, and ventured into the bright stage lights to announce the band, who came on to rapturous applause. The show was underway and for me as an aspiring promoter, this was probably the best moment, as everything had come together after many months of planning. I was able to retire to the bar area and enjoy one of my friend Fluffy Pete's excellent cask ales in the relative calm that ensued once the gig had started.

Fairport were as good as ever and made many new fans that night. The audience included friends and neighbours who did not know Fairport and who came along simply because I'd persuaded them to. Comments from friends who had heard of Fairport were the typical, 'They're not still going, are they?' or, 'How many of the original line-up are there?' I've never understood why people are perfectly happy to see their favourite football teams go through countless changes of personnel since they first saw them but if a band makes any changes in their history, then it's just not the same. With this line-up being the longest continuous one by far in the band's history, and approaching 340 years of age between them, I assured people that it was the most authentic Fairport they could possibly see.

The first set finished, it was all hands to the bar to dispense as much as possible of the large quantity of cask ale as we could, and to continue to serve the surprisingly sought-after white wine. The band's traditional mingling with the audience in those pre-pandemic days was well-received and the interval charity auction boosted the £500 raised for White Gold Cornwall, who provide support and mentoring for young people facing major life challenges.

The second set started, and the band got another great reception which carried on throughout, and especially when they returned for the traditional 'Meet on the Ledge' encore. After much clearing up and chair stacking, I was able to see a few of them back in the hotel bar on the sea front in Perranporth, just a short walk from the venue.

For my first attempt at promoting a gig it had gone as well as I could possibly have hoped. This was helped enormously by the band's helpful and professional approach and by all the volunteers I'd recruited to help. The success of this gig inspired me to organise more of them but then along came Covid, bringing a temporary halt to my short career as a music promoter. But two and a half years later I'm back, promoting a whole series of gigs which are bringing many of my favourite musicians to perform at Falmouth's Princess Pavilions, including Fairport in October 2022.

THE SAGE
2 FEBRUARY 2020, GATESHEAD, UK

PETER SMITH

I went to see Fairport Convention along with my carer Lisa at the Sage Gateshead. Since sustaining a spinal injury, I use taxis to get around which makes going to concerts significantly more expensive and a lot more complicated. However, I couldn't miss seeing Fairport, who have become a firm favourite and a must-see band for me.

Our first stop was to buy a programme which was kindly signed by bass player Dave Pegg. I picked up one copy for me and another for my friend, John, who now lives in America. Peggy reminded us that he is the oldest member of the band and that this was his 50th year as a Fairporter. Once in the packed hall, it was nice to bump into my old friend Mike and his wife Maureen who, like me, were very much looking forward to the evening's show. Our seats were in the usual wheelchair spot, very close to the stage.

I must admit I lost faith in Fairport Convention during the mid-Seventies, finding that they had become too 'traditional' for my tastes. However, in recent times I have returned to the fold and really enjoy seeing the band again. The format was similar to that of recent years. The concert began with support act Smith and Brewer, a close harmony Americano duo who played a very pleasant 30-minute set, warming the crowd up well. At the end of their set, they were joined by the members of Fairport Convention for a song or two. Fairport then continued their set including a short interval; the first set containing several numbers from their new album and the second set comprising several songs from *Full House*, which was celebrating its 50th anniversary later that year.

It was great to see them perform 'Who Knows Where the Time Goes?' in a version which did justice to the original. Closing songs were, as always, 'Matty Groves' followed by the encore 'Meet on the Ledge', for which they were joined by support act Smith and Brewer. Then it was back in the taxi and on my way home, picking up second carer Chris who had kindly agreed to help get me back to bed. All in all, it was great to see Fairport Convention again, and I looked forward to further encounters in the future.

GONNA SEE ALL MY FRIENDS:
A PEOPLE'S HISTORY OF FAIRPORT CONVENTION

THE ARTRIX
16 FEBRUARY 2020, BROMSGROVE, UK

MAX PARKIN

I've been a fan of Fairport Convention since I was 10 years old. Attending the Cropredy Festival is a family tradition; I've been going since I was 18 months old. At school, conversations would arise in which we discussed favourite bands and music. When I would say that my favourite band was Fairport Convention, people would look at me confused and say, 'Who?' or, 'I've never heard of them.' I first met Fairport at the Huntingdon Hall in Worcester, on the *Acoustic* tour back in 2015, where they signed my Cropredy poster.

Max Parkin got selfies with the band at The Artrix

Watching Fairport at Cropredy has become the most important moment of my year, and I'm always counting down the days. Afterwards, I would memorise the set and be able to remember the setlist – in order! At the last few Cropredys, I have been making videos. I've met Fairport at the signing tent and a few of them have kindly agreed to do five second pieces to camera for me, saying a line or phrase. Having that as a memory makes me feel positive whenever I'm feeling down.

Another great memory is meeting Fairport at The Artrix in Bromsgrove on the *Wintour* of 2020. I had selfies taken with each of the band and got a warm feeling of positivity from this and from talking to them. I'll treasure these memories forever.

GONNA SEE ALL MY FRIENDS:
A PEOPLE'S HISTORY OF FAIRPORT CONVENTION

LOCKDOWN
23 MARCH 2020

CHRISTIAN DOUBBLE

Far too late to the party I know, but lockdown steered me towards Fairport Convention. The opportunity to drift while waylaid at home drew me into a world of folklore and landscape that has started to haunt my imagination in recent years. Visits to the music of The Velvet Underground via streaming triggered an algorithm into which materialised *Liege & Lief*. The subconscious paralleling of the two bands resonates in many ways, one stalking the pavements of New York's underbelly and the other ploughing the cultural fields of Britain. Both honing in on poignant tales of drama, emotion and tragedy. The Velvets finding sustenance in the sleaze and decadence of urban Americana that take on an urban 'folkloric' quality and Fairport mirroring this with transposing pre-industrial story ballads onto a contemporary soundscape. Each pushing to the fore virtuoso guitar work, be it Sterling Morrison or Richard Thompson. The use of violin and fiddle pre-eminent in their respective make-ups and enigmatic 'front persons' in the guises of Sandy Denny or Nico.

Living in South West London, layers of synchronicity started to interweave. I listened further and became absorbed in reading about how Fairport Convention had flourished and evolved over time. My wandering territory during lockdown absorbed the environs of Wimbledon Common. A kind of ley line started to emerge in my hiking pattern. A trajectory landmarked by the Marc Bolan shrine up towards Barnes, the site of a 'sacred well' nestled on the common, and the traces

Christian Doubble remembers lockdown

of an Iron Age hill fort now embedded in a golf course fairway. Keeping with the music waymarkers, a paddock still stands that was used in a photo shoot of post-Syd Pink Floyd nonchalantly gathered by it.

Then I learnt that Sandy Denny had lived and grown up in Raynes Park, minutes from our home. Crowning this was the realisation that the cover for *Unhalfbricking* was photographed in the grounds of her parents' house along Arthur Road in Wimbledon Village – the spire of St Mary's Church visible in the background. Before reading this, the strange coincidence was that my chosen daily escape route had taken me past it for several weeks already. These pleasing moments of coincidence and happenstance have prompted me to spend time discovering more about this remarkable band.

THE BRASENOSE ARMS
5 AUGUST 2021, CROPREDY, UK

TERRY HARROP

I've been in a band for a long time. I was for a long time removed from anything so-called 'Fairporty'. When I was growing up my main band was Joy Division, and then New Order. A long time ago, just through my own prejudice, I just decided that Fairport Convention were not going to be a band that I would

Terry Harrop knew he'd hate Fairport

like, because the idea of folk and rock combining was not something I thought could work. Despite seeing *Liege & Lief* come up a lot, I just thought it wouldn't work.

I've been trying to avoid Fairport Convention most of my life, but in the last 18 months they've become the most important band in my life. It's made a massive difference to my musical outlook. Through Fairport I've branched out to other bands, and my life feels so much more enriched because I've finally accepted that Fairport Convention are a very important band and hold a very important place in British music history.

I used to buy *Uncut* and *Mojo*, and you always got the free CD. Around about 2000, there was an *Uncut* free CD with a host of different artists on it. One of the artists on it was Sandy Denny, and the song was called 'Listen, Listen'. And I just thought, 'My God, this might be the greatest song I've ever heard in my life.' I had never heard of Sandy Denny in my life. Then through that I bought *Listen, Listen: An Introduction to Sandy Denny*. It was only when I read the notes on the CD that I realised that she died in '78. I listened to it every summer, but never made the connection to Fairport. Around the same time, there was a song on another *Uncut* album by Nick Drake. Again, I thought, 'I really like this guy.'

I was playing Nick Drake and Sandy Denny a lot every summer. Eventually I bought Richard and Linda Thompson's *I Want to See the Bright Lights Tonight* album. I bought that because it was in *Uncut's* Top 100. I couldn't stand Richard Thompson's voice, but I loved it when Linda sang. I thought, 'I don't want to go near Fairport if Richard is singing half of the songs, not knowing that he wrote them, but didn't sing.' This went on for a few years.

Then, around about 18 months ago, I watched a documentary about Sandy Denny. It went into her Fairport period, and it played 'Who Knows Where the Time Goes?', and I just thought, 'How have I missed this song? This is one of the greatest songs I've ever heard in my life.' So, I asked Alexa to play songs by Fairport Convention, and it went through mostly the second, third and fourth albums featuring Sandy Denny. I thought 'Wow, I've missed out so much because of my prejudice.'

I started to buy Fairport vinyl, and I got the vinyl of *Brighter Later* – and it showed the musicians on that album were Fairport members. Unbeknownst to me, I'd essentially been listening to Fairport play on Sandy Denny's and Nick Drake's solo stuff for 20 years, and not realised it. Then I listened through their back catalogue. I started buying all the old vinyl, *The Bonny Bunch of Roses*, *Full House*, *Nine* – how did I miss out on this?

As a result, I wrote to Dave Pegg during lockdown. He wrote back and said that my letter had cheered him up. He said I should go to *Cropredy*, so I got tickets with my wife. Of course, *Cropredy* last year was cancelled, but then there was an announcement that they'd be doing a gig at the Brasenose (and I realised that that was on the album *Nine*). My wife and I got tickets and came down from Scotland to see Fairport for the very first time.

Just to finally be in front of Fairport, doing these songs that finally felt like mine, was a momentous moment for me. I brought down the album *Nine* and got my wife to take a photo of me holding up the photo of Fairport on the Brasenose wall.

After that I went to see them in Carlisle, I'm going to go and see them in Glasgow, I'm going to *Cropredy* in 2022. I went to see Richard Thompson at the Royal Concert Hall a few months ago, and realised he wasn't a bad singer.

It's funny how Fairport have gone from being nobody to me, to my most important band. If I could speak to my 20-year-old self, I'd say, 'You need to go and listen to *What We Did on Our Holidays*, because it will change your life. You need to go back and listen to it.' One of my biggest regrets now, is that I'll never see Swarbrick, or Donahue, or Lucas play with Fairport. I'm so glad that there's so much footage of Fairport playing, particularly at *Cropredy*, so I can at least try and capture what I should have had. I was just too young, I just wish that I had had someone to guide me, to tell me that I would really like Fairport Convention. I'll be at Cropredy in 2022 to see the *Full House* line-up.

WELLS CATHEDRAL
16 OCTOBER 2021, WELLS, UK

JENNIE SUMNER
In the mid-Seventies I was into traditional style folk music and followed The Spinners and the like. Then I met this great guy at work and joined him and his mates to see Fairport Convention. I had never heard of them but after that first evening I was hooked. Sadly, the guy and I split, but I still went to the concerts locally, either alone or dragging my

younger brother along. I don't think I ever truly converted him to the sound.

When I met my husband, our musical tastes could not have been further apart and I still went to concerts alone, but he was always outside the venue at the end to collect me and drive me home.

Jennie Sumner is a fan even if her husband isn't

I can't remember how or why, but I stopped going to concerts until one day, when shopping in Weston-super-Mare, I saw a poster… Fairport Convention were playing a concert at the Playhouse. I went and got a ticket straight away. I enjoyed the evening and was back in the fold, bringing home *The Jewel in the Crown* CD.

From then on, I went to all the concerts I could at Weston with my husband waiting patiently outside for me at the end. I bought all the CDs to annoy the neighbours with (given how loud I liked to play them). Concerts stopped in Weston – I'm not sure why as they were always well attended – so we started touring locally during every *Wintour*: Tewkesbury, Frome, Bromsgrove, Wimborne. My husband now waits in the foyer and knows by the music how much longer I'll be. I'll get him to attend one day.

Choosing a favourite concert is difficult, but the one in Wells Cathedral in late 2021 must rate up there. It was part of the 'Museum of the Moon' celebration so the location, sound and moon were amazing. Plus, we were all so happy to be there after so long in lockdown.

Over the years there have been so many great songs and tunes that will always go round in one's head from many wonderful song writers. Thank you to those friends back in the Seventies for introducing me to Fairport, and to Fairport for still bringing us all pleasure to this day and the future. Let's hope 'it all comes round again' until we can 'Meet on the Ledge'.

GONNA SEE ALL MY FRIENDS:
A PEOPLE'S HISTORY OF FAIRPORT CONVENTION

PLAYHOUSE
2 MARCH 2022, WHITLEY BAY, UK

PETER SMITH

As for many bands, the Covid lockdown restricted Fairport's ability to get out on tour. So it was a joy for the band to play, and for fans like me to witness their return to, the north-east, this time to Whitley Bay Playhouse, which is a lovely medium-sized venue. My wheelchair space was perched right at the back of the hall, looking down on the crowd and the band below, but with a great view of the stage and the concert.

The crowd was warmed up by the support act, Luke Jackson. We arrived during his performance, which was great. He was soon joined by Fairport Convention who started their first set with the normal opening song, 'Walk Awhile', which dates back to 1970 and the *Full House* album. A great opener to a great night.

After a few more songs, Fairport had a break giving time for a short interval, during which I bought a programme. The band explained that, because of Covid restrictions, they would not be meeting fans and signing programmes during the interval as normal. However, to make up for it, the programmes were all already signed by the whole band, with an honesty box into which I placed my £10 for two programmes: one for me and one for my friend John in America.

After a quick pint of Guinness, I was off back up in the lift to my seat. The rest of the set was a mixture of old songs, and quite a few new ones from the new album. Fairport were showcasing tracks from the *Full House* album, which celebrated its 50th anniversary in 2020.

I always get the feeling that being in the presence of Fairport Convention is like joining a family get together. They are obviously all good friends and always make the audience feel very much 'at home'. Original member Simon Nicol and long-time member Dave Pegg lead the rest of the band, who have now all been part of the family for many years themselves, through a series of songs which are the usual blend of traditional folk and rock music. The closing song was, as usual, the lengthy traditional folk ballad 'Matty Groves'. For the encore, as always, they were joined again by the support act Luke Jackson, for a joyful singalong 'Meet on the Ledge', taking us back to 1969 and the *What We*

Did on Our Holidays album. A great evening spent with some peaceful, joyful songs performed by a band who really do make everyone feel at home with them.

MILTON ROOMS
20 MAY 2022, MALTON, UK

MARTIN SUNLEY

I met Dave Pegg recently at a Fairport gig in Malton and reminded him of the time he bought a motorbike from Kawasaki. He was with Jethro Tull at the time. Ian Anderson had a trail bike, so Dave wanted one too. I worked for Kawasaki's PR company at the time and picked up the phone to Dave, who explained he was looking for a trail bike, but more importantly he loved the lime green and red team jackets and assured us he would wear it on stage if he could have one, which he duly did. As a thank you, he gave us four tickets to *Cropredy*, and we had a fantastic time.

FAIRPORT'S CROPREDY CONVENTION
11 – 13 AUGUST 2022, CROPREDY, UK

JOHN HARRISON

My favourite memory will forever be the time I proposed to my fiancée Lauren during Fairport's set at *Cropredy* on Saturday in 2022.

I had fortuitously bumped into Ric Sanders the previous afternoon and mentioned my plan. He asked if I'd sent a message

John Harrison proposed to fiancée Lauren at Cropredy in 2022

to the team. I wasn't sure where to send it, and he said he didn't know either, but I wrote it down and he said he'd see what he could do. So, I legged it to the merchandise tent to borrow a pen and paper, met him at the bar, and we came up with a plan. During their Saturday performance, Ric announced my intention as part of his introduction to 'Steampunkery'. I knew all the band members were an extremely friendly bunch from my previous encounters, but this act of kindness was the icing on my *Fairport Cropredy Convention* cake. To top it off, Fairport played my favourite album (the first one I ever heard), *Full House*, in its entirety, for our engagement party with over 20,000 guests!

PAUL LEITCH

Cropredy 2022 was one of the hottest I've been to, and I've been coming since 1992. In 1997, it was hot. I had brought my three-year-old son and me wouldn't sit under the shade of the umbrella we bought because 'it isn't raining'. You can't argue with the logic of a three-year-old.

My other highlights over the years are The Leningrad Cowboys and Alice Cooper. There are so many bands that I have been introduced to by *Cropredy*, like Four Men and a Dog and (since 2022) Turin Brakes. The variety of music is always exceptional, and it is the one festival I buy tickets for without checking the line-up.

Paul Leitch's Fairport memories reach back over the years

And there is the always welcome performance by Fairport, who I've been listening to and watching live since my teenage years. Plus the spin off personnel such as Richard Thompson; I've seen Richard live more times than I can count. You've got to love his banter. I once arrived late to a gig in Edinburgh and had to sneak in to seats close to the front, to be heckled by him from the stage, 'The Innuit Shakespeare Society gig is next door.'

GONNA SEE ALL MY FRIENDS:
A PEOPLE'S HISTORY OF FAIRPORT CONVENTION

For many years I was manager of The Sun Hotel in Hitchin, who hosted Hitchin Folk Club on Sunday night. It was always great for meeting luminaries of the folk world. I have met all of Fairport there except Ric in their varied 'other band' guises – PJ and Peggy, WAZ! with Maart, The Albion Band Christmas Show and St Agnes Fountain, and Swarb with a number of collaborators including Martin Carthy. I remember Simon turning up with a pair of Christmas reindeer antlers on his head and saying to me, 'Mr Nicol checking in', like I didn't know who he was. I also recall sitting with Maart until daybreak listening to his stories, and chatting to PJ and Peggy after their gig.

Around the early '90s, I managed a hotel in Scotland. Fairport were playing Edinburgh and then Aberdeen. I sent an email to Fairport Towers offering an overnight stay at my hotel, which was about halfway between the two venues. I then forgot about it until the receptionist called through to say that there was a Mr Pegg on the phone asking for the manager. Thinking it was a business call, I was blown away to find Dave Pegg on the other end of the phone. Unfortunately, they couldn't stay. However, whenever you meet Peggy in the field or at a venue bar, he is always welcoming, and it feels like he recognises you. My Peggy highlight was getting a pink spot face paint on the end of my nose from him at a Cropredy bar.

A few years ago, I took my son to see Fairport in Birnam, Perthshire. He got to meet the band after the gig and they all very kindly chatted to us at length whilst dismantling the equipment. Thoroughly nice chaps all, and Ric offered me his bottle of beer. A few years later my son was at Cropredy with me 20 years after he visited as a three-year-old. It all comes round again!

ELSIE SELF

2022 was my sixteenth *Fairport Cropredy Convention*. I first started going to the festival in 2006, when I was just six months old, but technically I first went in August 2005 when my mum was pregnant with me. My favourite memories are from 2013, when Alice Cooper played (when he played 'Poison', my mum was on call with my auntie and she cried so much she nearly peed her pants) and 2016, when Madness played – Suggs was in sunglasses the whole time.

GONNA SEE ALL MY FRIENDS:
A PEOPLE'S HISTORY OF FAIRPORT CONVENTION

Every time Fairport play 'Red and Gold', I remember the Battle of Cropredy Bridge in 1644. I enjoy Thursday afternoon because the main field opens at three in the afternoon, and an hour later Fairport do a 20 minute set. I also love Saturday at lunchtime because Richard Digance does the world's largest morris dance and everything he says is funny. The atmosphere is amazing and wherever you go people are nice. When you are in the main field with friendly people and you are in a friendly crowd, everyone wants to speak to you. The best thing about the festival is that it is child friendly and dog friendly, all the food is nice and all the staff are nice. And if you don't like a band, you can go to the Brasenose Arms or the Red Lion!

EMILY WOOD

I was eight years old when I first went to the Cropredy Festival, with my mum, late father and two sisters. We have been coming ever since. Sadly, we missed 2005 as my dad passed away in the early August. 'Meet on the Ledge' was played at his funeral. In August 2015, I brought my husband. We married that February and I walked down the aisle to 'White Dress', sung by Sandy Denny. In 2017, I brought my eight-month-old son. And in 2022 I came with my family – my mum, her partner, my husband, our son and our two dogs. We look forward to many more summers by the Cherwell.

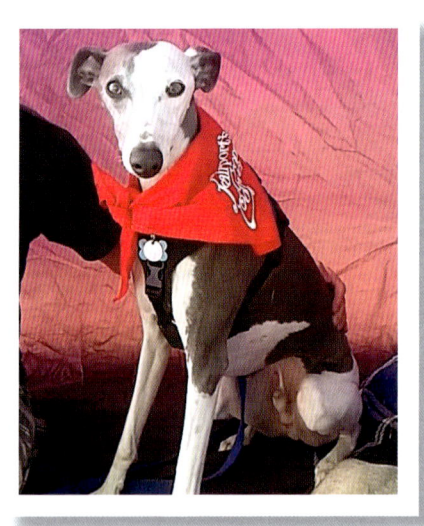

Emily Wood's dog Jake was amongst the revellers in 2022 at Cropredy

MARK WARD

It's 1980, I'm 17, I'm living in a small, backwater Midlands town and I'm bored of the heavy metal which dominates the music scene there. I'm looking for something else. I'm very keen on Jethro Tull (still am) and quite like their folky direction, and reading that new boy Dave

GONNA SEE ALL MY FRIENDS:
A PEOPLE'S HISTORY OF FAIRPORT CONVENTION

Pegg was from a respected folk-rock band, I decide to check out Fairport Convention.

Luckily for me, whoever is in charge of the town's record section of the public library has extremely eclectic taste, as it has an absolutely ripsnorting record section and is particularly well-stocked with folk and folk rock. Perhaps not such a backwater, then, and thanks, Library Person, whoever you are.

Fabbo de fab – there's loads of Fairport here! Which to choose, though? *Tipplers Tales* sounds fun, so I borrow that. And as the opening notes of 'Ye Mariners All' romp out of my stereo I think, 'This is it - this is what I've been looking for!' Over the next few months, I borrow all the other Fairport LPs; the library's got the lot. I'm very keen on this new discovery – very, very keen (still am). How to see them live, though? I check out an *Encyclopaedia of Rock*, also from the library. What? They've just split up? Curses, curses, curses. (Incidentally, the Encyclopaedia also describes the band as extremely unlucky.)

Mark Ward discovered Fairport via Jethro Tull

I go to uni. There's an older student there who lives in a Fairport Conversion t-shirt. I'm green with envy. After uni, I do a stint of volunteer work at a museum in my home town. There's only a small poster from the 1970s advertising a old Fairport gig in the town in the storeroom, isn't there? Sigh. Are the band haunting me?

Then my girlfriend at the time moves to London, and when I plan a visit, I look to see what bands I might catch whilst I'm there. Holy guacamole – Fairport are playing the Putney Half Moon! I'm so there! It's a great gig, I love the venue (still do) and, miracle of miracles, Fairport seem to have gigged ever since. Their - and my - luck seems to have turned out alright in the end.

GONNA SEE ALL MY FRIENDS:
A PEOPLE'S HISTORY OF FAIRPORT CONVENTION

TIM HAYES

I have been a fan of Fairport for over 50 years. The first time I saw them live was at the LA Troubadour for the *Full House* gig. What an amazing show! In September of 2002, I attended a gig at the Pasadena Institute of Technology and was sitting outside before the gig when Peggy sat down next to me and we started a conversation. He told me about the Cropredy Festival and said that I should attend. What great advice! I attended the following year and have not missed a festival since. Starting in 2006, I started working at the festival in the press area and continue helping out there every year. It is the highlight of my year and the friends I have made there are so cherished. It truly is 'England's friendliest Festival'!

Photos: Tim Hayes

GONNA SEE ALL MY FRIENDS:
A PEOPLE'S HISTORY OF FAIRPORT CONVENTION

ULI TWELKER

I'm frequently asked, 'Why do you still bother with Cropredy at almost 70?' I could rattle off a thousand answers as to why I still love to take the trip from Bielefeld to Banbury. Well, where else but on the shuttle bus from Banbury to Cropredy could I explain to a young lady that I hailed, 'All the way from Bielefeld, Germany,' only for her to joyfully reply that her residence was in Manassas, Virginia?

Uli Twelker has a whole list of reasons as to why he still visits Cropredy with his wife Senta

Where else but at a rain-affected Cropredy could my wife Senta and I buy a small triangle tent, carry the pack onto the field, study the instructions and go about putting the tent up, thinking the surrounding spectators were absorbed in enjoying an afternoon gig by the majestic Richard Thompson, only for them to break into hearty applause when we finally finished our complicated camping prep procedure? (I'm sure Mr Thompson took the applause as acknowledgement of the magnificent solo that he had that second finished.)

Where else but at Cropredy do you not only feel amongst friends but realise that you are, because people call out your name? Where else but at Cropredy do you order a pint of prime brew, only to find yourself standing next to Robert Plant or Roy Wood doing exactly the same? Where else but at Cropredy could you find a band that can brilliantly imitate Led Zeppelin, Jethro Tull and Procol Harum – on top of being the inimitable Fairport Convention?

Where else but at Cropredy would the courageous but ailing Dave Swarbrick be wheeled on stage to perform brilliantly and movingly with the help of artificial respiration, returning to Cropredy later after a successful transplant?

The ultimate Cropredy experience each year is around midnight on the final night, wandering round the whole field and listening to 'Who Knows Where the Time Goes?' and 'Meet on the Ledge'. Every time, tears of happiness flow without fail.

GONNA SEE ALL MY FRIENDS:
A PEOPLE'S HISTORY OF FAIRPORT CONVENTION

NIGEL SCHOFIELD

In 2021, with Covid still at crisis level and rules eased, a small and largely invited audience had gathered behind the Brasenose Arms in Cropredy to see and hear Fairport play again for the first time since early 2020. It rained torrentially, but no spirit was dampened.

In 2022, we reconvened for the first time in three years. 2022 brought the hottest Cropredy on record and a line up scarcely altered from the intended 2020 running order. Dust rose from the roadways. The moon rose over the field. A Fairport phoenix rose on the flame-filled t-shirts. 4pm rolled around on Thursday afternoon. The Fairport Festival bell chimed with its heavy metal companions across the Cropredy fields. Fairport, with a bonus Dave Mattacks, kicked off proceedings.

Gradually over the next two days, the field got fuller, the music filled the air, the air got hotter and Fairport's MC, Anthony John Clarke, regularly warned us to drink plenty of water. Backstage, an American film crew interviewed Fairport and other players for a documentary due for release in 2024.

52 hours later, after Richard Thompson and friends had delivered an impressive set, Fairport returned. We were invited to share in a jug of this. Songs from their latest (January 2020) album *Shuffle and Go* were interspersed with classics – 'Fotheringay', 'Lalla Rookh', 'Hexamshire Lass', 'Honour and Praise' – and memories of Sandy, Maart, Swarb and Trevor all came round again.

Eventually, Richard returned with DM and, delayed two years from its planned 50th anniversary outing, *Full House*, in sequence and in its entirety, was played for the first time, introduced from the big screen by Steph Pegg, the little girl running across the original gatefold picture. After the last track on side two, 'Flowers of the Forest', a breakneck bonus of 'Jenny's Chickens'/'The Mason's Apron' led us into another screen appearance, with Georgia Rose Lucas, all the way from Australia, introducing the current Fairport's version of her mum's most famous song, 'Who Knows Where The Time Goes?'.

Backstage, worried eyes checked watches: the show was over-running, something which simply never happened. So, in another unique moment, 'Child Ballad Number 81', was dropped from the running order. 'Matty's got another year off,' announced Dave Pegg as, led by Richard, I joined the lucky few to come on stage and be part of Fairport's anthem.

'Meet on the Ledge' is always an emotional Fairport moment, this year even more so. 'Your turn,' said Simon Nicol, and the crowd spread before us responded… no mere singalong but a communal, choral confirmation. Then band members, old and current, along with guests, friends and fans came together as one. Tears flowed. Hands were clasped. Hugs were exchanged. 'If you really mean it…'

Nine minutes into Sunday and no one wanted it to end… but for now it must. Peggy pre-empted Simon's last line of nearly a quarter century. 'Same time next year?' And yes, oh yes, we really were going to see all our friends.

COLIN FOSTER

My wife Gill and I became Fairport fans only about 12 years ago. In my quite large record collection, I only had one Fairport album, *The Bonny Bunch of Roses*, compared with probably about a dozen Steeleye Span ones. We were out for a walk one weekend and stopped at a picnic bench for the necessary coffee and cake at the café from our local country park. We talked about the Steeleye Span concert we were going to see that evening. Another couple

Colin Foster and wife Gill are recent converts

sat at the other end of the bench and were talking to each other about going to *Cropredy* and Fairport Convention. Our conversations eventually merged as we started earwigging their conversation and they ours. They said we should go to *Cropredy*. I said that if they could get tickets for the Span gig that evening and would meet us in the bar for a drink, we would go to *Cropredy*. They duly turned up, we enjoyed the Span concert and I bought the drinks. So we bought *Cropredy* tickets and a tent, and we have been going ever since and have met them every year at the bar.

We have met and made so many friends over the years, and found friends on the field that we didn't even know were Fairport fans. A part of our social life now involves our local folk club (I do the lighting) and 2022 (our retirement year, finally) revolves around the six festivals and the many concerts we are going to, with the highlight being *Cropredy* and all due to a chance conversation on a picnic bench.

JOHN TREVOR-ALLEN

I can't tell you when I first discovered Fairport, but they were there when I was small. Dad would sing 'General Taylor' to me to help me sleep. My earliest musical memory is of listening to the Albion Band's *Rise Up Like the Sun* on his car cassette player and pressing my ear to the car's speaker and turning the volume up to max on 'Time to Ring Some Changes' probably damaged my hearing. Apart from that cassette player, most of my Fairport exposure came from Dad's record collection. I became pretty skilled at dropping the needle on the record to catch the start of 'Sailor's Alphabet'.

I showed enough enthusiasm for Fairport to encourage Dad to take me to my first ever *Cropredy* in 1997; I remember

John Trevor-Allen was at Cropredy in 1997 and in 2022, with son John and daughter Annabel

clinging to his waist as we rode down the M40 on his bike. I also remember the vibrancy of that first ever festival – the enthusiasm, the happiness, the noise… and the incredible, devastatingly powerful silence when Simon Nicol introduced Sandy singing 'Who Knows Where the

GONNA SEE ALL MY FRIENDS:
A PEOPLE'S HISTORY OF FAIRPORT CONVENTION

Time Goes?' with, 'Just listen as she sings for us one last time.' Even at the age of twelve, with a youthful obliviousness to what loss and grief really meant, it was an amazing thing to hear; so many people listening in pure, blissfully appreciative silence in a field that had been buzzing with noise only a few moments before.

Two months later, I stood in our local crematorium, listening as the same song played while the curtains jerked closed around my dad's coffin, and I understood – at least a little bit better – what could make so many people fall so quiet at once.

As I edged into my teens, Fairport was a way for me to stay connected to my dad. I missed most of the 'typical' connections – getting taught to shave, or to pick myself up after a break up, or to apologise for sneaking a beer – but he and I had Fairport in common, even if he didn't know how long my enthusiasm would persist. It could be bit awkward, in the wake of the Britpop era, to answer the dreaded question, 'Hey, Oasis or Blur?' with an, 'Uh… Fairport Convention?', because it felt like nobody my age had ever heard of them, but I was too hooked for peer pressure to make any difference, earnestly explaining the lyricism of 'John Barleycorn' over the odd underage pint and eventually graduating from Dad's LPs to my own CDs, which I took off to university.

At university, to my surprise, I finally discovered it wasn't just me who liked Fairport. Quite early in my first year at uni, a girl from my halls happened to call round to my room just as my CD player cycled round to 'Jewel in the Crown' with its instantly recognisable opening guitar line. She broke off, mid-sentence, paused for just a second to hear Simon's voice cut in and then said, 'Is… is that Fairport Convention?' in a tone of such confusion that it was instantly obvious that she'd never met anyone else our age who knew about them either.

I don't say that was the only reason we got together, but that early proof of mutual interests definitely helped. Ruth and I went to our first – and my second – *Cropredy* in 2007, and in 2010 the last song at our wedding was, perfectly, 'Meet on the Ledge'. (Our first dance was to Richard Thompson's 'Old Thames Side'.) We've managed a couple of *Cropredys* since then, and in 2022 were joined by our daughter Annabel and son John, who is one of few five-year-olds who could tell you, with infectious enthusiasm, just who John 'Babbacombe' Lee was.

GONNA SEE ALL MY FRIENDS:
A PEOPLE'S HISTORY OF FAIRPORT CONVENTION

I can't tell you when I first discovered Fairport, because they've always been there, a brilliant and inspiring part of my life and providing a musical backdrop to everything from peeling potatoes and chopping firewood to studying for exams, attending job interviews and getting married.

But 25 years after my first visit to *Cropredy*, watching my son dance along with a ridiculously wide smile on his face at being part of something so vibrant, enthusiastic and happy, I can tell you this: if you really mean it, it does come round again. And for that, I'll always be grateful.

TJ MCGRATH

I first heard Fairport Convention on college radio while I was attending Muhlenberg College in Pennsylvania in 1971. Back in the day, student DJs would spin records and not always announce the artists or the titles, so I had no idea who did 'Tam Lin', but it was love at first listen. By the summer of 1975, on my first trip to London, I managed to track down that Fairport Convention recorded 'Tam Lin', and I bought the two-record set *The History of Fairport Convention*, and I was hooked.

TJ McGrath founded the Fairport fanzine *Dirty Linen*

Fairport with Sandy Denny had actually come to Allentown to play in October 1974, but I missed them because I didn't know who they were. Tragedy of the highest order.

David Fricke, who was a few years older than me at my college, was most likely the DJ playing Fairport's music, since he was music director at the station at the time. Fricke today is considered one of the premier music journalists of all time.

By the autumn of '75, I was buying as much Fairport Convention vinyl as my bank account would allow. Soon it became quite evident that I had a problem. I needed to reach out to others in my pursuit of everything Fairport. I put together *Fairport Fanatics* while living in Connecticut in 1983. The scrappy fanzine was a plea for fans to share their love, their Fairport collections, and what cassette tapes they had or wanted, and by 1985 I had over 500 subscribers.

Realising I couldn't pursue my doctorate, edit a magazine, and teach full-time, I willingly handed over the fanzine in 1987 to a good friend, Paul Hartman, who transformed the 'zine' into an international magazine sensation: *Dirty Linen*. Paul broadened the scope of the magazine to include world music, roots music, folk music, country music, rock, etc. With the help of Sue Hartman (Paul's wife) and Lahri Bond (illustrator and art genius), *Dirty Linen* was available with great distribution in most book shops around the world.

I continued to write music reviews and do interviews from 1987 until 2010. I was fortunate to meet the members of Fairport many, many times when they played shows in New York City and the Northeast of the USA, and every show was memorable, in my mind. One of my uppermost highlights was going to Cropredy and interviewing various members and guests backstage for *Dirty Linen*. And the Fairports on stage were a joy to listen to.

All good things come to an end, alas. *Dirty Linen* went out of business in 2010 for various business reasons. Yale University in New Haven, Connecticut contacted me in 2011 and asked if I was interested in donating *Fairport Fanatics/Dirty Linen* to their Music Library. You can't turn down Yale, so I handed over all 145 issues of our magazine for safe keeping and for music scholars to do research on Fairport Convention and music.

I still play Fairport Convention and 'Tam Lin' and 'Matty Groves' still give me chills every time. I don't have to go into details about the talents of the various past and present band members. All have played a part in one of the most talented and inspirational bands of the era. Fairport forever.

GONNA SEE ALL MY FRIENDS: A PEOPLE'S HISTORY OF FAIRPORT CONVENTION

OLIVER ILGNER

I was born in Germany into a family of Austrian and Silesian descent before *What We Did on Our Holidays* was eventually released in Europe; in fact, my mother was in labour when The Beatles performed their legendary rooftop concert. My father was a semi-professional lead guitarist in a dance band, so my earliest musical memories include Baden Powell, Herb Alpert's Tijuana Brass, James Last and The Shadows. During my kindergarten days my father's band used to accompany many a local star, so I remember being exposed during rehearsals to the original sounds of Peter Maffey, Iren Sheer, Bata Illic and lots of others. But my mother's younger brother was an avid record collector who bought many fine albums on their release and played them to the family on Sunday afternoons. It was through him that I first listened to an English outfit called Jethro Tull, and in the early 1980s found out that most Tull members were also playing fantastic music outside the band. The music that appealed most to me was, of course, the music of Fairport Convention; there was everything and more!

Being a theologian and also a musician playing with many local bands, my day job is working as a teacher for music and religious education at a comprehensive school in Germany. Reflecting my enthusiasm for all things Fairport, I try to use Fairport's songs and tunes during lessons where appropriate. This resulted in the whole of *"Babbacombe" Lee* being used in a school project in 2010, performing the album but also transforming the narrative content into small theatrical scenes, thus enabling a complete stage play to be performed.

If there hadn't been the Fairport connection, I might never have met Fritz Rau or Peter Bursch, Rob Braviner would have never chosen microphones in the rehearsal room in our house for an annA rydeR gig, and Simon wouldn't have introduced my then three-year-old daughter to Ralph McTell in the Cropredy field in 2012 the way he did. 'Emma, this is Ralph! Ralph, this is Emma!', and them both then shaking hands. A year earlier, Chris Leslie had tried to introduce himself to Emma, but she reacted by crying instantly (which is strange, as Chris is such a lovely person).

Aged four, I went to a music school that had the usual programme for kids – recorder and glockenspiel. I then attended piano lessons given by a Romanian pianist of Hungarian descent, Vera Reminyi, but the instrument never appealed, before I started to play the double bass and the drums. I never seriously considered becoming a guitar player. But in 1986, aged 17, the Fairport thing really took off and I bought my first mandolin, got my first mandola from a left-wing cultural association I was working for at the time, acquired a bouzouki and then a tenor banjo and then had a dulcimer made for me by a friend. Then I plunged deep into folklore. It's fair to say that Fairport had changed my life. For most jobs outside of school business these, days I am asked to play bass or mandolin, so the Fairport influence is responsible for some of our regular family income. My favourite choice of bass is a Rickenbacker, since listening to 'Magical Mystery Tour' and *Wings Over America* all those years ago. My Maple-Glo Rickenbacker 4001 will be 59 years old this year, nearly six years older than me. When relating how I got interested in Rickenbackers to Peggy, he just said, 'Oliver, it's not the bass, it's the player…!'

JOHN WILLIS

Simon and David Swarbrick were playing the Rockingham Arms in Wentworth village for Rob Shaw, who ran 'The Rock' (The Rockingham Arms Music Club) for nearly 40 years. At some point, I took our two artistes for a curry at The Slamma (Islamabad) in Attercliffe, Sheffield. The following day Swarb called Rob to say he'd enjoyed the gig, and the curry. He did, however, mention he'd burned his fingers wiping his arse.

KATHLEEN KING

The first time I saw this gang of artists was before I heard them play as a band, not knowing the music at all until a trip in 1989. I felt like I discovered part of my long-lost family at the Falkland Arms, Great Tew. That night I heard them play in the Half Moon, Putney, I fell in love and pretty much stayed in love all these years. Thankfully, I've met loads of new friends that got me up to speed with their entire discography.

MICHAEL J C TAYLOR

Fairport's music has provided the soundtrack of my life for nearly five decades, since I took a chance on a $1 purchase at a thrift shop on the first album because I thought the cover was interesting at 13 years old.

GONNA SEE ALL MY FRIENDS:
A PEOPLE'S HISTORY OF FAIRPORT CONVENTION

Alas, I have never had the pleasure and privilege of seeing the band in action (although I did attend a gig with Swarb at McCabe's Guitar Shop). They always seemed to be where I wasn't, but I'm most grateful for the music Fairport has recorded, for it all holds a special place in my affections.

JON LEATHERWOOD

Simon and Swarb played a pub gig in my local – Maggie Mae's in Austin, Texas – in the early 1980s. The night was magical, but my prevailing memory is of Simon introducing a song by recounting his long-time interest in church music. He proceeds to convulse us all with a ditty about all the dogs in the world having a party, to the tune of 'The Churches' One Foundation', containing the immortal line, 'And each one took his asshole and hung it on the hook.' I'd dearly love to have a recording of that.

NIGEL OLIVER

I discovered Fairport at a Jethro Tull convention in Worcester, with the tag line 'where ferrets eat lard', after buying the *Cropredy* 25th anniversary double CD. I later worked for a Bob Pegg on the Isle of Wight, who claimed to be Peggy's brother. He was about six foot eight tall and had six sugars in his tea. I never had the balls to ask Peggy if this was true, even while discussing the condition of the Guinness at Ryde Theatre.

MICHAEL J ROWBOTTOM

The first time I saw Fairport was at Potters Bar, with RT failing to make it back from France for the gig. A certain Mr Simon Nicol apologised for the absence and mentioned a homicidal intention before continuing to give us a wonderful night with Swarb, Peggy and DM. It ended with the guitarist from the support band joining them for a rock 'n' roll jam. I believe RT and Simon have made up since.

NIGEL CANTER

Fairport were playing in Yeovil. I worked with Swarb's brother Peter and persuaded him to come along, as he had never seen Dave play with Fairport. Pete brought his eleven-year-old son, Simon. Simon said to Swarb, 'Will you teach me to play the violin please, Uncle Dave?' He did.

GONNA SEE ALL MY FRIENDS:
A PEOPLE'S HISTORY OF FAIRPORT CONVENTION

STEPHEN WIGGINS

The first time I heard Fairport was on a pal's Walkman going to an exam in Nottingham. The track was 'Now Be Thankful'. I thought I like them. So, when later in the year they were going to play Burton Town Hall, me and another mate went to see them. One of the worst gigs I have ever attended. The sound system was crap. This was the case until about halfway through the gig when I went for a pee. The sound from the band in the toilet was amazing. I listened to rest of gig in the gents. I've seen them many times since. Thank god for the acoustics in Burton Town Hall's bogs.

PETER O'CONNELL

They played a 23-minute version of 'Sloth'. Afterwards, Simon said, 'I got carried away, and when I get carried away the rest of the band go to Mars.'

NAOMI KING

My now-husband was a massive fan and took me along on one of our first dates. He was at the bar. Simon and Peggy were sat at a table near the front, just having a drink and there were several spare seats on their table. I unknowingly went up and politely asked if they were staying there all night or if I could sit there. Next thing I knew they were up on stage. My husband was mortified when I told him what I'd done.

ANTHONY JOHN CLARKE

My bedroom was a barren, poster-less, single-bedded cell in early-seventies Ulster. I was a teenager: angst-ridden, long-haired, and pathetic with no girlfriend. When my parents were out, my mates and I would congregate and play cheap guitars and smoke even cheaper cigarettes: my mum's best saucers were the ashtrays. Our talk was of bands and girls. The only papers we read were *Sounds*, *NME*, and *Melody Maker*. We studied the UK's album and concert reviews and envied our musical comrades in England, Scotland and Wales. We would never see Bowie or the Velvet Underground. Was Keith Emerson as good as Rick Wakeman? Was Mick Ronson the genius we thought he was?

Some of us could play a little traditional music but it wasn't exactly cool. We did know some girls who owned violins, but we only ever saw the cases as they dawdled to their music lessons. My older brother owned a mandolin, but he never played it.

Radio 1 was playing. The room was quiet as I was trying to record John Peel's show onto my Marconi reel-to-reel

AJ Clarke taped Fairport off John Peel's radio show

tape recorder. We had all heard of Fairport Convention, but because a guy we didn't like who lived around the corner raved about them all the time, we dismissed the band out of hand as folkies. John Peel played 'Flatback Caper' from *Full House*. That bedroom which my father referred to as a 'sticky little warren' was the birthplace of our affection for Fairport's music and influence.

A week later we were carrying Fairport Convention LPs under our arms to school. Four decades later, I was lucky enough to play 'Flatback Caper' with Dave Pegg on our *Mirth and Mischief* November tours. My old cell mates are sadly all gone but not forgotten.

MIKE BILLINGTON, BROADCASTER

I first saw Fairport at Liverpool University in the early 1970s when I was there studying law. From 1984 to 1989, I produced and presented the folk programme on BBC Radio Manchester and caught up with the band many times on tour and especially at *Cropredy*. Peggy and I would link up on the phone every year and he'd donate a couple of tickets for the festival to the first caller who answered a question correctly. One year, I had a Fairport track playing on the turntable and rang through to Peggy at a pre-arranged time, but it was a strange voice that answered the phone. It transpired that our favourite bassist was on the loo.

I could see the needle getting ever closer to the end of the track. I

GONNA SEE ALL MY FRIENDS: A PEOPLE'S HISTORY OF FAIRPORT CONVENTION

asked who the mystery voice was and it turned out to be Ralph McTell, who was visiting Peggy's house. 'Okay', I said, 'Can I interview you until Dave is off the loo?' So that's how I managed to interview Ralph McTell live on the air by accident.

When Simon and Swarb played the folk clubs as a duo, I booked them three times for my club in Manchester. Dave would always sleep in the following day until midday. On one visit, I was dancing with Gorton Morris Men in the centre of Manchester the following day and Simon was keen to come along. He has a great interest in the folk customs and heritage of the land and so I wasn't surprised when he invited himself along. Ah, those halcyon days.

Mike Billington caught Peggy on the loo

Photo: BBC Radio Times

I was good friends with Maart; both of us Mancunians. I was speaking on the phone with him one day when I said I'd love to record an album. 'Why don't you?,' he said, to which I replied that I didn't think I was good enough, to which he replied, 'Look Mike, we were all on the same page once. I just got lucky. Go ahead and record an album and I'll be on it if you want.'

So I have recorded two solo albums and Maart played on both. He did much to give me the confidence to do so. A sadly missed friend.

GONNA SEE ALL MY FRIENDS: A PEOPLE'S HISTORY OF FAIRPORT CONVENTION

FREDERIC NOYES

1989 was my first *Cropredy*. It was a terrific weekend with Ian Anderson and Julianne Regan joining in, along with Swarb and several alumni. I returned in 1994 and since that time I have come every other year, prioritising the big anniversary shows and bringing my four and eight-year-old children in 2017.

1994 was a favourite *Cropredy* weekend because the bill included both Lindisfarne and Roy Harper, two other performers that I loved and admired. 1997 was also a great year with so many of Fairport's greatest songs in the setlist, where Ashley narrated as they worked their way through the decades.

There are so many reasons to love *Cropredy*: the friendly and inclusive vibe of the festival; the friends and families that return over and over again to take part in the rituals; wandering around the village; stopping in the churchyard to read some headstones; helping to open and close the lock gates on the canal; and checking out the talent and the ales at The Red Lion and The Brasenose. The food and drink, the people watching, the shirts from every tour and every festival are also fun, as is spotting fellow fans like Robert Plant, Jimmy Page, Geoffrey Hughes and dozens of other musicians and actors in the crowd who are hardly being noticed by many in the audience.

I was apparently extremely lucky to have attended the mostly dry and usually warm and pleasant years. I had heard all of the jokes about RT being the Friday night rain god, but it hadn't been my experience until fairly recently. Having camped in my younger years, I was glad to find accommodations in Banbury as we got into the 2010s. This meant a dry night and a warm shower before returning to the festival grounds. However, it also meant there was nowhere to go when the rains finally caught up with me.

I had a couple of opportunities to find myself backstage after the echoes of the Saturday night Fairport set had faded. On one memorable night/morning I found myself in an open sided tent with eight or ten other people singing Beatles numbers and whatever else anyone suggested, with Peggy playing guitar and still happily singing even as the sun came up on Sunday morning.

In recent years there have been fewer chances to speak with Peggy or

GONNA SEE ALL MY FRIENDS:
A PEOPLE'S HISTORY OF FAIRPORT CONVENTION

Simon, but I have been glad to have several conversations with Ric about Bernie Sanders, progressive politics and lamenting the setbacks and disappointments in developments toward a better future.

I have attended 15 *Cropredys*, included 2022 which I attended with my now 13-year-old son. If he experiences even a fraction of the joy I have found in that cow pasture in Oxfordshire he will be having an amazing time.

ALFREDO MARZIANO

I didn't discover Fairport's music until I was in my early 20s. It happened in the summer of 1979 in a small village in Northern Italy where, before the Flying Burrito Brothers went on stage, the PA system blasted out the version of 'Sloth' that appears on 1974's *Fairport Live Convention*. I was hooked for life, and so began my trek backwards in time in order to know what had happened before then.

Years later, coming to *Cropredy* as both a fan and a journalist became a sort of pilgrimage for me, and nothing sums up the experience

Alfredo Marziano heard 'Sloth' and was hooked for life

in the same way as hearing Simon singing 'The Hiring Fair' or 'Red and Gold' at the site of the Civil War battle. Over the years, I've been to *Cropredy* with numerous friends and made many more, including meeting the Dutch guys I've since encountered at countless Richard Thompson gigs, saying hello to Judy and her greyhounds, a ritual that began one year after I interviewed her at her home, chatting with John Penhallow or Danny Thompson, and tasting Leon's delicious zuccotto prior to hosting him at my home near the Alps. Although I've been a frequent visitor to *Cropredy*, I didn't have the nerve to attend Maart's last show on earth. Words like, 'I'm gonna see all my friends,' and, 'If you really mean it, it all comes round again,' have acquired a genuinely deep meaning for me, and Fairport Convention have become a part of who I am. And yet in many ways I continue to regard its members as creatures from another world: I still wonder how Peggy could play such a mean bass after eating a huge plate of polenta and ossobuco, washed down with vast quantities of red wine one very hot day near Milan in the mid-1990s, while Gerry bravely handled his drums as his open mouth gradually filled with mosquitoes.

JOHN ALDERDICE

I was listening to a Fairport bootleg in the car a few weeks ago and 'Meet on the Ledge' came on. I've been to Cropredy quite a few times and understand the poignancy the song has been infused with, but I've recorded my own version with new lyrics. It's on Bandcamp as 'Porky's Song' by Johnny Glencoe.

JACK WESTWOOD

Every year, Swarb and I had a £1 bet on the outcome of the Scotland vs England Calcutta Cup rugby matches. No actual money ever changed hands (surprisingly) but we used to text each other during the matches as they were being played. During one match at Twickenham, Scotland flanker Kelly Brown was injured and was being stretchered off the field of play. Swarb took great delight in telling me this, texting, 'Ha ha! One of your players is being stretchered off!' I texted

Jack Westwood has some Fairport memories

him back and stated, 'Now, now, Swarb. Be fair, you yourself have been stretchered off before, haven't you?' He responded, 'No, I won't have it. I have however been stretchered ON once or twice.' Some months later, Simon confirmed to me that this had indeed been the case…

Once, my wife Justine and I were in the tour bus with the boys as they headed into Middlesborough for a gig at a new venue. It was in the days prior to the internet or mobile phones. As the venue was proving elusive, Peggy said to Rob Braviner to stop the van and said he would ask a local for directions. Brummie Peggy jumped out, all six foot two of him, in cowboy boots, bootlace shirt and electric blue jacket. He stopped a local Smoggie, who was wearing a flat cap and brown coat to his ankles. There ensued a very animated discussion with much pointing, nodding, smiling, laughing, further pointing, patting on shoulders and more laughter before a final handshake and a wave as these two new friends parted. Peggy got back into the van. 'Well?' said Rob. Peggy replied, 'I haven't got a clue what he said…'

Fairport had been booked to play at the famous *Celtic Connections* festival in Glasgow. As they had landed in town on the morning of the gig, I met up with Simon and Rob for a spot of lunch at the Rogano in the city centre and then directly to the sound check which was early, about 4pm. Once completed, Rob asked the local production manager if he could whistle up the courtesy bus to take the band back to the hotel for a while. After much radio activity, the young lad stated to Rob that the courtesy bus was unavailable as it was just taking the big-name acts back and forward. Hackles rose. Rob's complexion became reddened as the veins began to stand out on his neck and his fists tightened. He grabbed hold of the young lad and lifted him off the ground by his lapels. Just as we were preparing to grab Rob, he said to the young lad, 'Listen son, I don't think you realise how famous we used to be…!'

BRIDGET GIBSON

My brother, Rob Woodward, was a lifelong Fairport fan and had all of their albums and CDs. Sadly, he passed away aged 67 in 2020 with prostate cancer, having caught Covid. He was a very talented guitarist and musician and played in local bands in the Cotswolds and surrounding areas for the majority of his life. 'Meet on the Ledge' was one of his favourite songs. He saw Fairport live many times, attended the Cropredy Festival and took us to see Fairport at the theatre at Chipping Norton.

Bridget Gibson remembers her brother Rob Woodward, a lifelong Fairport fan

GONNA SEE ALL MY FRIENDS:
A PEOPLE'S HISTORY OF FAIRPORT CONVENTION

MARTIN SHORT

I have often commented to my wife that I feel like the Forrest Gump of Fairport as, without planning it, I have made contact with various members of the band...

Many years ago, a good friend of mine from the folk club I frequented, Cathy Lesurf, called me to say she had a friend coming down from London and that I might like to have a drink with them in Canterbury. I spent a very pleasant evening in the company of Cathy and DM.

Martin Short with his wife, Huw Williams and Maart

We were in the process of sadly closing the pub we had been running for many years, and it was our last ever Sunday music night. I was about to stand up for the first time to sing (nervously) a thank you to all that had supported us, when a good friend of ours, Debs Earl, walked through the door accompanied by Maart Allcock and Huw Williams. Obviously this added to my nerves, but Maart was a charming guest and the evening concluded with my wife and I behind the bar blubbering whilst he serenaded us with 'Meet on the Ledge'.

Knowing Debs Earl for quite a few years through our music nights, it has happened that we have got to know Simon Nicol very well, and I would say regard him as a friend. It's quite surreal when I think back to sitting in a mate's bedroom 50 plus years ago being introduced to this man and his mate Richard Thompson's music.

At the end of a recent Cropredy Festival, we went to watch a good friend of ours who used to run our open mic nights, CJ, take part in the cricket match. He was playing cricket for the performers team. By chance, she introduced me to Richard and we discussed the previous night's music. I cut the conversation short, not wanting to intrude on his cricket.

In August 1979, I found myself, along with most of the Oyster Band of that time, plus some Oyster Morris mates, on a narrow boat holiday coming down the Oxford Canal. We moored at Cropredy for the night and I had agreed with the landlady of the Red Lion that the guys could have a music session that evening. Swarb and Peggy came through the door and stood at the bar, having a pint or two. I got into conversation with the two of them. The atmosphere between them was very sombre, which I later realised was because they had just had their farewell concert at Cropredy. This was a hugely poignant moment for Fairport Convention. The mood suddenly changed when Swarbrick asked if the assembled musicians knew a Morris tune, which I identified as 'Lads A'Bunchum'. I was at that time Squire of Oyster Morris and this is a dance we did often. I said to him we would not only play, but if the landlord would allow it, we would dance this in the pub.

Swarb not only joined the session and sang a few songs, but we were all invited back to his house with Peggy until the early hours. Many things I can vividly recall from that evening: a cask of Theakston's Old Peculier that we were invited to partake of, the filthy version of 'Sailor's Alphabet' and one of the most moving moments of the evening, when I suggested to John Jones from The Oyster Band that he sing to Swarb 'The Last Waltz', a Swarb song from *The Bonny Bunch of Roses* album that John had started singing at the end of Oyster Band ceilidhs. There were tears in Swarb's eyes and he expressed how moved he was. The poignancy of this hit me much later!

MAURO REGIS

Liege & Lief was my first encounter with Fairport Convention, in 1977. I was 19 and I'd been listening to music for a couple of years. The beat was a faraway sunset, progressive was at its peak and punk was growing. What did an old band playing electro-acoustic traditional music have to offer me? Well,

Mauro Regis has seen Fairport seven times over the years, including in Italy

it was a perfect recreation and incarnation of ancient and modern, drums and fiddle, ballads and instrumentals.

Living in Italy, I've seen the band in concert seven times since 1994. The shows have always been full of power and, at the same time, joyful and thoughtful, moving from jigs and reels to 'Matty Groves' and on to 'Who Knows Where the Time Goes?' and 'Meet on the Ledge', which moves our feet and our hearts.

Fairport has become a tree with roots expanding everywhere, with each root one of the artists who has left to go their own way, facing the future but never forgetting its Fairport past. I've been lucky enough to see, meet and talk with almost every past band member in various incarnations: Swarb with

Photos: Mauro Regis

GONNA SEE ALL MY FRIENDS:
A PEOPLE'S HISTORY OF FAIRPORT CONVENTION

Whippernapper and Lazarus; Ashley Hutchings with The Albion Band and Rainbow Chasers; Richard Thompson solo and with Danny and with his electric band; Iain Matthews; Maart; Dan Ar Braz; even Jerry Donahue. I just missed Sandy Denny, whose voice and sad life made me fall in love with the band.

Just naming these guys brings back memories that send shivers down my spine. 45 years since I bought *Liege & Lief*, Fairport have been with me, like faithful friends.

David & Sharon Llewellyn's daughter Carly gives Richard Digance a helping hand

David Llewellyn captured Peggy at the bar being served by Geoffrey Hughes

GONNA SEE ALL MY FRIENDS:
A PEOPLE'S HISTORY OF FAIRPORT CONVENTION

ROY COOK

I first became aware of Fairport Convention around 1970, through the Island sampler album *Nice Enough to Eat*, followed by the *History of Fairport Convention* compilation and the *Fotheringay* album. After doing our O levels in 1973, a group of us planned a summer trip to Cornwall, staying in youth hostels. 12 of us went, including my then girlfriend, now my wife of 45 years. We arrived in Plymouth by train, and saw posters advertising Fairport at the Winter Gardens in about 10 days time. We had no idea where the Winter Gardens were, the posters didn't say, so we assumed it was in Plymouth and thought no more about it, as we would be further west by then.

When we made it to Penzance nine days later, we found out where the Winter Gardens were. Most of our group wanted to go to the gig, and so we negotiated with the hostel warden for a late pass. There was nothing doing on that front. We made the decision to go anyway. We bought tickets, arrived early and found one of the doors unlocked, so we went in and watched the band rehearsing. As they were finishing, someone noticed us and we were told to leave, but we were straight back in when the doors opened soon after.

None of us had been to more than two or three gigs before that, so we didn't have a lot to compare it with, but it seemed great to us; Mattacks dead steady, amazing guitar from Donahue, Peggy very hairy, Lucas with his great voice and Swarb just mesmerising. I think it was the first time we heard 'Rosie', a song that my wife has always loved.

Sure enough, the concert finished too late to go back to the hostel. Did we think about leaving before the end? Not really. So, out onto the seafront. We found a van where we bought a drink and a burger, and then settled down to wait until morning. It might have been August, but it got really cold. We tried to sleep under my worn out parka, I suppose we dozed a bit, I can't really remember, but anyway we were up early and back to the hostel for breakfast.

Since then, we have seen the band many times, with many different line-ups. We saw Sandy solo and a couple of times when she rejoined Fairport. I (this being one area where my wife and I differ) have seen RT many, many times, but never as part of the band. In 1986 we saw Fairport at the Orchard in Dartford, with a line-up of Simon Nicol,

GONNA SEE ALL MY FRIENDS:
A PEOPLE'S HISTORY OF FAIRPORT CONVENTION

Dave Mattacks, Ric Sanders, Maartin Allcock and of course Peggy, the only ever present in our experience; thanks Dave. My wife was seven months pregnant at the time, and the baby did not stop somersaulting for the entire time they were playing.

DEBS EARL
I was very late to the party, although the name of the band was deep in my subconscious, probably from sick days off school watching *Pebble Mill at One*, or maybe I had 'that' copy of *Jackie* magazine. My friend Lynette said 'you really ought to see Fairport' and dragged me along to the Marlowe Theatre in 2004. I thought it was all right, I liked the twin fiddles, but I thought it too loud and totally failed to 'get it'. I'd just started to promote a few bands that I did like very much – Show of Hands, Colvin Quarmby and then Mundy Turner as a result of seeing them open for Fairport.

Once that operation became established, some regulars (Joe Passey and Paul Reynolds among them) suggested I book Fairport, but I considered them (a) way out of my league, and (b) I didn't really love the music

It took a while but Debs Earl is now firmly a fan

enough, so decided against.

A few years passed. I was dragged along to see them a few more times, to the Marlowe by Lynette, and to Margate by Joe. I wanted to like them because people I valued did, so I thought I should keep trying. I liked that they came out to the foyer and were chatty. Mr Nicol, two years in succession, commented that he liked my (long purple suede) coat. He seemed friendly, they all did, I warmed to them. More requests to 'book them please' followed so I gave their then-agent Nigel a call.

Then in 2010, six years after first seeing them, they came to play for me at Folk in the Barn, on their spring Acoustic Tour at Canterbury Cathedral Lodge, a beautiful venue in the precincts of the cathedral. I still hadn't really 'got it' and had decided I didn't really like Simon much because he started out friendly and then became a bit drunk and snarky. But I loved Ric's jokes and the audience were very happy. I made a bit of money too which was a bonus, so did it again a year later.

I don't know what happened, but I sat in the front row that year and really watched and listened and – 'ping!' – something clicked and the goosebumps did their thing. I think it was a combination of 'Portmeirion', 'Who Knows…' and 'The Hiring Fair'. I also remember being completely astonished by a Peggy bass solo. My friend Joe saw and said, 'You get it now, don't you? You took your time.'

Eleven years later I adore the music, they're my favourite band and I'm packing for Greece – where Simon and I are about to get hitched!

GONNA SEE ALL MY FRIENDS:
A PEOPLE'S HISTORY OF FAIRPORT CONVENTION

GOLDERS GREEN BOWLING ALLEY
MARCH 1967, LONDON, UK

RICHARD LEWIS

Before they became Fairport Convention, the group was called Tim Turner's Narration. I'd seen them before that – Ashley and Simon in the Ethnic Shuffle Orchestra. They were in the process of changing, so they changed the name. Tim Turner was the narrator of a short documentary series, *Look at Life*, an episode of which was screened before the main feature at cinemas, and Simon was a projectionist at the local Odeon. That's how the first name came about.

As Tim Turner's Narration, they got their first gig at Golders Green Bowling Alley in March 1967. It was more of a rehearsal but with a private audience.

It was during the Easter holidays that we were sitting around at Fairport – the house – and they said they really didn't like the name Tim Turner's Narration. They were quite keen on some of the American groups, who all had double-barrelled names like Jefferson Airplane, Grateful Dead, Moby Grape and Buffalo Springfield. We were tossing around ideas for names. I said, 'We all get together here at Fairport… convene there. Why not call it Fairport Convention?' They must have thought it was a good idea.

In April, my mum and dad went on holiday to Rome, so I decided to have a party and asked them if they'd like to play. It was Richard, Simon, Ashley and Shaun Frater and it was good. Everybody enjoyed their music. They decided to play a bit more.

They played their first gig as Fairport Convention at St Mary's Church Hall in Golders Green on 27 May 1967. On 1 May, Simon had sent me a telegram, telling me to look out for the ads for their first gig.

Richard Lewis was there at the start, as was the Fairports' taste for beer

AFTERWORD

I took up the guitar for my own pleasure at the age of 15. I just loved the Shadows, and especially Hank. Joe Brown was another hero and then, of course, The Beatles. I wanted to be like them. I knew I would never have their talent, but I swore to myself that if ever I was to pursue my dream of making a living playing music, however successful I became, I would be as nice to fans as they were to me.

Hank, Joe, Paul, James Taylor, Janis – I could name drop for ages! I thank you. Fans are the people who make bands happen and are also responsible for their longevity, or their demise! Luckily, I got the chance to play with some great musicians and join an amazing band – Fairport Convention.

You lovely peeps who have contributed to this book have given me the best present that I could hope for on my upcoming 75th birthday. The joy and pleasure that you have expressed in these pages about our little band has filled me with such happiness and, indeed, at times made me shed a tear for lost friends and comrades.

A heartfelt thank you to you all for making this possible, and for allowing me to play for 52 years in this great band.

Long may it continue. Love, peace and frock.

Peggy
Morbihan, France
September 2022

GONNA SEE ALL MY FRIENDS:
A PEOPLE'S HISTORY OF FAIRPORT CONVENTION

SPECIAL THANKS

Julie Parkin, Ian Crutchley, Andrew Deards, Peter Robinson, Frank Vlaskamp, Jop Vlaskamp; Nik Rankin, William Majer; Ian Northcott, Simon Northcott, Patrick McGuirk, Paul Bond, David George, Oliver Gray, Wendy Kenney, Nicky Mansfield, Sue Topham, Brian Perry, Elsie Self, Catherine Lowden, Jan-Egil Bjarkø, Steve Lucy, Massimo Francini, Bridget Gibson, Lawrence Stewart, Marco Danesi, Chris Newton, Adam Palmer.

Derrell Wilkinson, David Monk, Rolf Boomsma, Tim Goosey, Charles Moody, Edwin Wallage, Peter Smith, Ann Sands, Emily Wood, Stephen Phillips, June Hawkins, Linnet & Michael Thornton, Dorie Jennings, Mike Bursell, John & Jane Brighouse, David Pollard, David Allaway, Michael Hunter, Nick Regnauld, Robert Jeffries, Terry Peck, Trish Coulson, Keith Styles, John Rayner, Ian Broom, David Spittle.

Roger Haydock, Darren Allen, Carolyn Carson, Bill Windsor, Urban Göransson, Chris Griffin, Maartin Butcher, Gillian Bonner, Arie Jan den Boer, Deborah Roberts, Colin Down, Alan Pavey, Andrew Morton, Peter Checksfield, Ian McLeish, Niall Clarke, Dominic Walsh, Nigel Tant, Robert Mulford, Richard Buxton, Sally & Jim Farmer, John Schwetje, Tim Bennett, David Lieberman, Paolo Galloni, Andrea Pintelli.

Paul Harrison, Laurence Wilensky, Mark Johnson, Paul Goode, Peter Lewis, Des Collins, James DeGaetano, Christopher Taberham, Graham Spencer, David Tares, Nick Smithers, David Russell, Raffaele Galli, Judith McEwan; John Newton; Martyn Grove, Tim Howlett, John Lester, Mike Ainscoe, Stephen Blair, Roy Turner, Karla Elliott, Richard Kinder, Jon Matthews, Max Bradley, David Williams.

GONNA SEE ALL MY FRIENDS:
A PEOPLE'S HISTORY OF FAIRPORT CONVENTION

Howard Johnson, Mark Salt, Anthony Walker, Paul Siddons, Jacqueline Taylor, Richard Austin, Thomas Brandt, Penny Davies, Pat Thomas, Angharad Owen, Robert Bayman, Lars Nilsson, Samantha Briggs, James Franey, Michael Fisher, Jennifer Iddon, Marshall Blankenship, Mark O'Donnell, John Robottom, Mike Wright, Derri-Anne Thomas, Keith & Eva Dhan-Weller, Paul Woodhouse, Christian Globisch.

Jens Andersen, John Penhallow, Joanne Judge, Jennifer Wilson, Dominic Walsh, Graham Hawkins, Martin Abernethy, Stanley Graham, Paul Turner, Martin Perry, Ken Hughes, R N Banks, Gordon Tennant, John Whiting, Chris Gleave, R W Fielder, David Markwell, John Barlass, Jo Tansley Thomas, Denise Sargeant, Jennie Sumner, Gernot Buehl, Peter Roe, Jackie Thomson, Carolynne Pinder.

Sweetpea Smart, David Richardson, John Farrar, Alan Hamilton, Richard Savory, Anne Collins, Norman Wade, Peter Croft, A K Tyler, Tim Edmonds, Michael Byrne, Trevor Broadbent, Lisa Lazarus, Terence Barker, Steve Menke, Edward Haber, Trish McCourt, Frits Wielens, Gabriel Sonnino, Ian Mackintosh, Joseph Sipocz, Frederic Noyes, Joss Mullinger, Neil Parison, Anji Baker, Nicola & Ken Jackson, Keith Kelly.

David George, David De Stefano, Chris White, Staffan Wennerlund, J R Bickhart, Colin Foster, Mike Skerrett, Ian Walker, Peter Knothe, Dave Preston, Carl Hufton-Straw, Allan Pickett, Wolfgang Hoehl, Peter van Dorst, Richard Hamilton, Pat & John Clayton, Aaron Taylor, Martin Short, Andrew Loake, Raynah Thomas, Mike Donovan, Lynne Edwards, Will Sawers, Barry Smith, Martin Smith, April Phillips.

Felicity Rushmer, Phil Hall, Jack Westwood, Ian Townsend, Derek Van Ryne, John Trevor-Allen, D Kellett, Tristan Bryant, Lee Soden, Ton Schuringa, Adam Denning, John McGettigan, Katherine Milton, Kenneth Maliphant, Stephen Carter, Philip Lort, Bastiaan van der Plas, Wolfgang Tölch, Jane Mannion, Martin Lane, Stephen Skey, Michael James Crawford, Sharon Llewellyn, Bob Slatter, Neil Wells, David Flintham.

GONNA SEE ALL MY FRIENDS:
A PEOPLE'S HISTORY OF FAIRPORT CONVENTION

Lyn Jeffries, Yvonne Owens, James Nolton, Dimitri Labis, Steve Sheldon, Simon Hardisty, Gareth Roberts, Terry Harrop, Keith Jordan, Iain W Muir, Carne Burke, Frank Parry, Marcus Banks, Martin Fioretti, William Sandalls, Jeremy Ford, John Twigger, Thomas Noble, Robert Bradbury, Ian Huckin, Carol Law, Mark Ward, David Key, Edmund Whitcombe, Des & Chris & Kathy Ainsworth, David Glass, Ian Jones.

Scott Doonican, Martin Satterthwaite, John Smallwood, Graham Day, Jeff Prince, John Harrison, David Cullen, Peter Clarke, Chris Dennis, Brenda Rawlings, Uli Twelker, Martin Driver, Uwe Broemer, Nick Helfrich, Steve Gayton, Richard Pearl, Bo Ehnsio, Buddy Woodward, Stephen Royston, Tim Hayes, Mark Taylor, Dr Oliver Ilgner, Andrew Leonard, Elizabeth Askew, Chris Bates, Malcolm Garrett.

Judy Stocker, Graham Ley, Dave & Annie Kenyon, Tom Casey, Michael Pietsch, Trudy Alford, Brian Green, Tron Eivin Ovrebo, John Collinson, Christine Kibler, Kurt Thulin, Kevin Ward, Peter Brown, Alan Delaney, Helmut Oelschlegel, Michael Billington, Steve Whitefield, David Beckett, Dr Robert Starr, Richard Illig, Brendan Murphy, David Farrar OBE, Alistair Mutch, Gregory Sturdy, Christian Doubble.

Stephen Skey, Alan Archer, Christopher Saunders, David Pearce, David Tweedie, Edward McCabe, Gareth Parsons, Brian O'Malley, Jonathan Bradshaw, Nik Le Saux, Jelle de Jong, Jong, Helene Robinson, Sally Rose.

GONNA SEE ALL MY FRIENDS:
A PEOPLE'S HISTORY OF FAIRPORT CONVENTION

GONNA SEE ALL MY FRIENDS:
A PEOPLE'S HISTORY OF FAIRPORT CONVENTION

ABOUT THE AUTHOR

Richard Houghton lives in Manchester with his wife Kate and his pomapoo Sid. As well as writing books about music, he manages Spenwood Books (who specialise in fan histories of bands) and supports Manchester City FC and Northampton Town FC (not necessarily in that order).

If you'd like to share your memories of Fairport Convention (or any other band) with Richard, please contact him at iwasatthatgig@gmail.com.